MW00769530

EVERY PROMISE OF YOUR WORD

The Gospel According to Joshua

EVERY PROMISE OF YOUR WORD

The Gospel According to Joshua

Rhett P. Dodson

Rhett P. Dodson
Gal. 2:20

THE BANNER OF TRUTH TRUST

THE BANNER OF TRUTH TRUST

The Grey House, 3 Murrayfield Road, Edinburgh, EH12 6EL, U.K.
P.O. Box 621, Carlisle, PA 17013, U.S.A.

*

© Rhett P. Dodson 2016

*

ISBN
Print: 978-1-84871-669-8
EPUB: 978-1-84871-670-4
Kindle: 978-1-84871-671-1

*

Typeset in Adobe Garamond Pro 11 / 13pt at
The Banner of Truth Trust, Edinburgh

Printed in the U.S.A. by
Versa Press, Inc.,
East Peoria, IL

To my brother-in-law and sister,
Ron and Carolyn McNeely,
a token of love and gratitude

Contents

Preface

P rior to the conquest of Canaan, Israel spent forty years in the
wilderness. That is about how long I have been acquainted with
the book of Joshua. My first encounter with this marvellous
record of Israel's ancient history occurred in Sunday School where I,
like most of my fellow young scholars, was fascinated by the story of
Jericho and its tumbling walls. In my teenage years, I read the book
for the first time on my own and learned more about Jericho and the
conquest as a whole.

It was not until seminary, however, that I studied the book in
earnest. Assigned to write a paper on the theology of Joshua, I read
and analysed the text. The overall theme of the book was obvious:
God was faithful to give Israel the land he had promised to Abraham.
From that big idea, five subthemes emerged: (1) the covenant was
the foundation, (2) the presence of God was the key, (3) warfare was
the means, (4) sin was the impediment, and (5) inheritance was the
fulfilment.

Later, as a doctoral student, I spent a considerable amount of time
looking at the text of Joshua in detail as I analysed the Septuagint's
translation[1] of each of the book's Hebrew verbs. Having gone from
the 'forest' of Joshua's theology to the trees (and even the leaves on
the trees) of its Hebrew text, I emerged from the timberland in
my first pastoral ministry to teach an extended series of lessons on

---

[1] The Septuagint is a translation of the Hebrew Bible and some related texts into
Koine Greek, and is sometimes referred to as the Greek Old Testament. The literal
Greek title, 'The Translation of the Seventy', and its Roman numeral acronym LXX
refer to seventy Jewish scholars who are said to have solely translated the Five Books
of Moses as early as the 3rd century B.C.

the book's theology, expanding on the five subthemes listed above. I then preached through the book, hopefully providing a guided tour of the forest, to my patient and loving congregation, Grace Presbyterian Church in Hudson, Ohio. From those expositions this book was born. Each excursion through the book of Joshua has both deepened and broadened my grasp of Scripture, but I am keenly aware that I have only scratched the surface. To change the metaphor, I have waded into the shallow end of the pool, but there are waters here in which to swim.

Along the way, many people have read chapters and offered comments that have, no doubt, improved the work in many ways. The first person to read some of the early chapters was my friend Dennis Peterson. An author and editor, Dennis encouraged me to keep at the task. Another friend, Jim Holmes of Great Writing, took an early interest in the book, believed in its viability, and provided enormous help to find a publisher. Fellow pastor-authors Stan Gale, Doug O'Donnell, and Mark Johnston read sample chapters and offered encouraging endorsements of the work in its embryonic form. My sister, Carolyn McNeely, my nephew, Brent McNeely, and my friend Eric Anest also read several of the earlier chapters and made a number of helpful suggestions. Friend, parishioner, and author Travis Dougherty took a great deal of time and effort to read each chapter. His skill with a felicitous turn of phrase has greatly improved many sentences. To each I offer my sincere thanks.

I also want to thank the elders of Grace Presbyterian Church, the congregation I am privileged to serve. They share an enthusiasm for Bible exposition and a vision for a kingdom footprint through the printed word. My administrative assistant, Bonnie Gorzelle, has provided tremendous help in proofreading the text. Her heart for God's word and her eye for detail are greatly appreciated.

I have owned Banner of Truth books since I was a teenager. They have been the backbone of my library. I consider it a great honour and privilege to be a Banner author and to work with Jonathan Watson and all the good folks at Banner who take Christian publishing seriously.

Most of all I want to thank my wife, Theresa. She not only encourages me to write but also sacrifices for me to write, and she does so willingly.

One final word of thanks goes to Israeli guide David Tal who first showed me the valley of Aijalon (see Joshua 10:12-13).

These expositions are offered to the Lord Jesus Christ and his Church as a labour of love and devotion and with the prayer that they may be used to glorify his name and help his people.

Rhett P. Dodson
Hudson, Ohio
January 2016

I

Every Promise of Your Word!
Joshua 1:1-2

After the death of Moses the servant of the LORD, the LORD said to Joshua the son of Nun, Moses' assistant, 'Moses my servant is dead. Now therefore arise, go over this Jordan, you and all this people, into the land that I am giving to them, to the people of Israel.' (Josh. 1:1-2)

Promises! If you say the word once, it carries a note of excitement and expectancy. If you say it twice, however, it suddenly begins to produce overtones of pessimism. 'Yeah, yeah. Promises, promises', says the cynic, 'we have heard it all before.'

Promises mean very little these days, or so it seems. Politicians build their platforms and campaigns on promises that no one really expects them to keep. Every four years in America a candidate will promise to bring about the change the country needs, yet the voting public takes it all *cum magno grano salis* (with a big grain of salt) as the cynicism of the nation grows by leaps and bounds.

Employers make commitments to employees and fail to follow through. Parents do the same with children. Couples take wedding vows and make promises that they break all too easily and frequently as infidelity and divorce continue to become more commonplace and seemingly normal. Many broken lives are the result of broken promises. People scoff at Christianity because of its promises. They mock Jesus and ask, 'Where is the promise of his coming' (2 Pet. 3:4)?

Yet even though promises do not fare well in the attitude of many people, they still fulfil an important role in our lives. Making a promise has the power to change a person forever. No one can remain the same after pledging 'till death us do part'. No soldier can raise his or her hand and vow to uphold and defend the constitution of the nation and walk away unchanged. These promises are pacts; they are covenants that we make, and in turn these promises make us. In the sixth book of the Bible, the book of Joshua, promises take centre stage.

Generations earlier, God had promised Abraham that he would give him the land of Canaan as a possession for his offspring (Gen. 15:17-21). Abraham, however, had no descendants, and, as an old man past his progenitorial prime, he had no real prospects of having children. Yet a son was born (Gen. 21:1-5) and to that son, Isaac, two sons were born, Esau and Jacob (Gen. 25:19-26). Jacob fathered twelve sons, and, through a chain of events recorded in the later chapters of Genesis, he and all of his extended family found themselves living not in the land of promise but rather in Egypt. There they remained for four hundred years, and while God was clearly keeping his covenant promise to enlarge Abraham's family and make them as numerous as the sand on the seashore (Gen. 22:17), where was the land? What had become of that promise?

The Israelites became exiles and slaves in Egypt, yet God in his faithfulness delivered them from bondage to bring them to the land for which they longed. They experienced his great power as they witnessed the plagues, saw the parting of the Red Sea, and ate the daily manna, yet fear and unbelief still kept them from taking possession of their promised land. Moses intended to lead the people to triumph, but when his cadre of spies returned from their reconnaissance mission into Canaan only two of them, Joshua and Caleb, were willing to trust God to do as he had said (see Num. 13). Israel's lack of faith destined the nation to wander for forty years in the wilderness until that entire generation, with the exception of Joshua and Caleb, had died (see Num. 14:20-25). Israel found themselves delayed from entering the land year after year. Promises, promises.

Israel's wanderings in the desert brought them from the Sinai peninsula to the plains of Moab. With the people of God camped east of the Jordan, Moses delivered a series of sermons (preserved for us in the book of Deuteronomy) to prepare the nation spiritually for what was about to happen. For four centuries Israel had possessed the promises to Abraham regarding the land, but decade after decade the promise had gone unrealized. Now as they were poised on the eastern shores of the Jordan River, the conquest of Canaan still looked impossible. How could a wandering group of shepherds ever overthrow a country of fortified cities? The answer to that dilemma unfolds in the book of Joshua.

Joshua—the man

The opening words of the book focus on Joshua and his place in Israel's history. They indicate a major shift in the leadership of God's people: 'After the death of Moses the servant of the LORD, the LORD said to Joshua the son of Nun, Moses' assistant, "Moses my servant is dead"' (Josh. 1:1-2a).

Contextually, these words form a continuation from Deuteronomy 34, which records the death of Moses, an event that occurred about 1400 B.C. Moses had led the Israelites for forty years through their wanderings in the wilderness; but due to a rash act at Meribah, where he struck the rock for water contrary to God's instructions, the Lord did not allow him to enter the promised land (Num. 20:10-13; cf. Deut. 32:48-52). Who, then, would stand at the head of the armies of Israel to lead them to victory in the conquest? When we read the sequence of events from the days just after the exodus through the record of Israel's wanderings found in Numbers, it becomes obvious that Joshua was a natural choice.

The choice of a successor commonly determines the future of an enterprise or organization. In June 1937, Dr Martyn Lloyd-Jones was preaching in Philadelphia and discovered that G. Campbell Morgan, the eminent British minister of London's Westminster Chapel, planned to be in the congregation that evening. Lloyd-Jones and Morgan knew each other, but this night was to prove a turning point in their relationship. After the sermon Morgan briefly spoke to Lloyd-Jones and then turned to leave. On his way out of the church, however, he stopped several times, turning to look back at Lloyd-Jones, who had a sense of what was about to happen.

Campbell Morgan had decided to invite him to join the ministry at Westminster Chapel. Morgan and Lloyd-Jones worked together as associates from 1938, with Lloyd-Jones succeeding Morgan as the senior minister of the Chapel in 1943. Though the transition had its difficulties, Morgan's choice of an associate and Lloyd-Jones' subsequent role as his successor proved to be one of the significant turning points in twentieth century evangelicalism.[1] The choice of Moses' successor was much more momentous still as one of the great turning points in redemptive history.

The text identifies Joshua as 'Moses' assistant' (verse 1). During the entire wilderness journey, Joshua had served a key role as the right-hand man to Israel's great prophet. The first mention of Joshua in the Bible is in Exodus 17:9 where Israel encountered Amalek. Though the victory that day was entirely attributable to God's intervention (17:11, 14, 16), the Lord recognized Joshua as the man who had defeated Israel's enemies (17:13). From the beginning, Joshua was a man of war.

From his first battle with Amalek God had been preparing this choice man for a unique task. Now, forty years later, his skills as a warrior came back to the fore as God told him to 'arise, go over this Jordan, you and all this people, into the land that I am giving to them' (Josh. 1:2). From that point on, Joshua led Israel against impossible odds to achieve some of the greatest military victories recorded in Scripture.

In addition to his military prowess, Joshua was also a man of God. The Lord spoke to Joshua after the death of Moses (verse 1), but this was not his first encounter with God. He accompanied Moses on Mount Sinai (Exod. 24:13). And on his frequent trips to the tent of meeting Joshua would not depart from the tent after Moses met with God, a clear indication that he wanted to be where God was, and thus a sign of his devotion to the Lord and the depth of his spirituality (see Exod. 33:7-11). Numbers 27:18 identifies Joshua as 'a man in whom is the Spirit'. As a result of his willingness to fight in

[1] See the accounts in Warren Wiersbe, *Walking with the Giants: A Minister's Guide to Good Reading and Great Preaching* (Grand Rapids: Baker, 1976), 180-81 and Iain H. Murray, *D. Martyn Lloyd-Jones: The First Forty Years 1899–1939* (Edinburgh: Banner of Truth Trust, 1982), 329-30.

Canaan after Moses conducted the first reconnaissance, he became known as a man, like Caleb his counterpart, who wholly followed the Lord (Num. 32:12).

Of all the people written about in the Bible, men and women whom the Scripture authors paint 'warts and all', we never read anything overtly negative about Joshua. He had rebuked Eldad and Medad for prophesying, and Moses corrected him, but Joshua's reaction to Eldad and Medad seemed to have sprung more from his personal love for and loyalty to Moses than any personal grudge against the prophets (see Num. 11:26-30).

It seemed only natural that this close companion of the great Moses should succeed him as leader of the nation, but it was much more than simply a reasonable and pragmatic choice, for God had directly appointed him to the task. Even prior to the opening verses of the book, the Lord had already made it clear that this man was to take command of Israel and lead the nation to victory. With the people camped on the plains of Moab and the time of Moses' passing drawing near, the Lord said to Moses, 'Take Joshua the son of Nun, a man in whom is the Spirit, and lay your hand on him. Make him stand before Eleazar the priest and all the congregation, and you shall commission him in their sight. You shall invest him with some of your authority, that all the congregation of the people of Israel may obey. And he shall stand before Eleazar the priest, who shall inquire for him by the judgment of the Urim before the LORD. At his word they shall go out, and at his word they shall come in, both he and all the people of Israel with him, the whole congregation' (Num. 27:18-21).

Later, in Deuteronomy 31, Moses revealed to the nation that Joshua was to be his successor. The Lord then commissioned him at the tent of meeting. This natural choice proved to be nothing less than supernatural as 'Moses and Joshua went and presented themselves in the tent of meeting. And the LORD appeared in the tent in a pillar of cloud. And the pillar of cloud stood over the entrance of the tent' (Deut. 31:14b-15).

Here were two men, equal in honour in the annals of covenant history. Both were heroes of the people of God. Yet each was unique in his calling. Moses was not Joshua, and Joshua was not Moses.

Each had his own gifts to use and jobs to perform. God does not intend for all of his people to be identical in their abilities and tasks. God has called each believer to perform the undertaking which God himself has uniquely equipped them to do. In the case of Israel, Moses led the people out of Egypt, and Joshua led the people into Canaan. Both men played an important but different role in the redemption of God's people. Likewise, we must each take inventory of the gifts God has given to us in order to perform the tasks which he has called us to do.

Joshua—the book

The book to which this great leader lends his name opens with his reception of a word from God. 'After the death of Moses the servant of the LORD, the LORD said to Joshua …' (verse 1). This is the first of many times that God revealed himself to Israel's new leader. The subsequent revelations were of various instructions as he prepared and led the people to battle (4:1; 5:2; 6:2; 10:8; 11:6), divided up the land according to the allotments of the twelve tribes (13:1, 6; 20:1), and gave his final instructions, calling on the people of Israel to obey the Lord, to love him, and cling to him with all their hearts (24:2ff.).

The book of Joshua can easily be divided into several major sections. The first five chapters are all about preparation. Such an extensive military campaign as Israel was about to launch could not be approached haphazardly. Plans had to be made. Nevertheless, the emphasis in the opening chapters of the book lies not on military tactics and strategies but, rather, on spiritual preparation. The next seven chapters (6-12) describe the actual conquest of Canaan. After the first major battles of Jericho and Ai, Joshua then led his troops on both southern (10:29-43) and northern (11:1-23) campaigns.

Following the conquest, it fell to Joshua to see to it that the tribes of Israel settled in the land that God intended for them. Chapters 13-19, therefore, are taken up with the detailed description of Canaan's geographical features and particularly those features which would serve as the borders of the various clans. In close connection with these records of allotment are instructions regarding the cities of refuge, their purpose and location (20:1-9), as well as the cities and pasture lands for the Levites (21:1-42).

The history of conquest contained in the book of Joshua concludes with the tribes of Reuben, Gad, and half of the tribe of Manasseh returning to their lands on the eastern shore of the Jordan (22:1-34), Joshua's charge to Israel's leaders (23:1-16), and the renewal of the covenant at Shechem (24:1-28). The closing verses recount Joshua's death, the burial of Joseph's bones (see Gen. 50:25 and Exod. 13:19), and the death of Eleazar, the high priest (24:29-33).

Joshua—the message

More than a mere recounting of the major events of the Israelite conquest, Joshua is a book of Scripture and therefore an inspired, inerrant, and enduring revelation from the Lord. Joshua penned these words not only to keep an accurate record of Israel's history but to convey a spiritual message. Other uninspired accounts of these battles were recorded in the book of Jashar (see 10:13), which was lost long ago, but Joshua is a word from God as well as a word about God and the importance of his actions for his people.

Several themes emerge as we read through the book. Far from merely being rote lists of historical facts or abstract theological concepts, these themes work together like musical notes to form a melody. The first theme to emerge, one that overarches the entire book, is God's gift of Canaan to Israel in accordance with his covenant promises. Not only does the book begin with the command to go into the land and take possession of God's gift (1:1-9), but it also ends with the assurance that the various military campaigns have served the Lord's good purpose: 'Thus the LORD gave to Israel all the land that he swore to give to their fathers. And they took possession of it, and they settled there. And the LORD gave them rest on every side just as he had sworn to their fathers. Not one of all their enemies had withstood them, for the LORD had given all their enemies into their hands. Not one word of all the good promises that the LORD had made to the house of Israel had failed; all came to pass' (21:43-45).

If this were not clear enough, in some of his last words to the nation Joshua says, 'And now I am about to go the way of all the earth, and you know in your hearts and souls, all of you, that not one word has failed of all the good things that the LORD your God promised concerning you. All have come to pass for you; not one of them has failed' (23:14).

The 'promises, promises' of the cynic became promises fulfilled by the faithful covenant-keeping God of glory! We see this theme throughout the book in the repeated emphasis on the land as God's gift (cf. 1:13; 8:7; 10:30) and the allotment of the land as the inheritance of the various tribes (13:8ff.). The famous missionary David Livingstone rightly said, 'God is a gentleman. He always keeps his word.'

How does God accomplish all of this? In the exercise of his divine sovereignty, he calls his people to exercise their responsibility. For God's part, he promised to be with Joshua and the nation. The book's opening paragraph contains two statements of the Lord's avowed presence with the new leader (1:5, 9). It would quickly become evident to the people that just as the Lord had been with Moses, so now he will be with Joshua (cf. 1:17; 3:7; 4:14; 6:27).

God manifested his presence with Israel primarily through the ark of the covenant. It not only led the Israelites into the promised land (3:3ff.), but it also led them in their first major battle at Jericho (see the repeated references to the ark in chapter 6). This covenant chest, carried by the priests and containing the ten commandments (a summary of God's covenant with his people) became the quintessential symbol of the Lord's presence in the midst of the nation. Where the ark was, there was God.

The Lord did not travel with his people merely to stand idly by and observe events as they unfolded. He would exercise his omnipotence and fight for them. Whether it was doing wonders among them (3:5) like dividing the Jordan River (3:15-17), collapsing the walls of Jericho (6:20), or throwing down great and deadly hailstones from heaven (10:11), the Lord God fought for Israel and wanted that to be evident to all. The clearest statement of this truth appears in 23:3, 'And you have seen all that the LORD your God has done to all these nations for your sake, for it is the LORD your God who has fought for you.'

God was faithful to Israel, and, in turn, Israel was to be faithful to God and to obey his instructions. Joshua was to teach the people what God had said, and this book of the law was not to depart from his mouth (1:8). Only by obedience to the Lord would Israel have success in battle. They were to follow God's law to the letter, even if his directions seemed as ludicrous as simply marching around a city wall day after day (6:1-7). Neither Israel nor her leaders were to fear because they were to trust in God's faithfulness (1:9; 8:1; 10:8, 25; 11:6; 23:6). God would be with them and, therefore, they had nothing to fear; it was the Canaanites who would be afraid (2:9, 24; 14:8).

Why was God doing all of this? Why was he remaining faithful to his covenant with Abraham? We could pose many answers to that question, including the Lord's impeccable character and his sovereign plan for redemptive history. In the immediate context of Joshua, however, God is being faithful to his promises as a means of calling his people to a faithful response to him in return. This truth becomes evident in several ways. First, the book contains repeated calls to obedience. Second, perhaps the most well-known verses from Joshua and at least *a* key verse—if not *the* key verse—in the book is a direct appeal for God's people to choose a path of loyalty to him. 'Now therefore fear the LORD and serve him in sincerity and in faithfulness. Put away the gods that your fathers served beyond the River and in Egypt, and serve the LORD. And if it is evil in your eyes to serve the LORD, choose this day whom you will serve, whether the gods your fathers served in the region beyond the River, or the gods of the Amorites in whose land you dwell. But as for me and my house, we will serve the LORD' (24:14-15).

If this call to decision were not enough to highlight this significant theme, the book of Joshua demonstrates a remarkable literary balance in stressing the themes of faithfulness and unfaithfulness in the stories of two particular individuals and in two stories about the nation.

First, the book of Joshua recounts the stories of Achan and Caleb. Achan is the supreme example in the book of disobedience to God. Though God had forbidden it, Achan stole some of the spoils of Jericho (7:10ff.). For Caleb, on the other hand, the text claims repeatedly that he wholly followed the Lord (14:6-15). The contrast between these two men exemplified the two paths that lay before

9

the nation. Would Israel disobey the Lord or wholly follow him? Would they end up like Achan beneath a pile of stones and rubble or would they end up like Caleb, living to a ripe old age in the land of promise?

Second, the book records two stories of the nation that also demonstrate the two possible responses to God's word. When the Gibeonites came to Joshua and the leaders of Israel, they claimed to be a people far removed from the land of promise, a people who feared the God of Israel and with whom Israel could safely enter into covenant (see 9:1ff.). Joshua and the men of Israel acted unwisely because they did not ask the Lord about what they should do and they entered into a pact with the Gibeonites who, in actuality, lived in close proximity (9:14).

In contrast to this event, when Reuben, Gad, and half the tribe of Manasseh returned to their land east of the Jordan River, a distance removed from the remainder of Israel, they erected an altar of witness. Though many Israelites had grave suspicions at first that this was an attempt to set up a rival religious system, when Phinehas, the son of Aaron, investigated what these eastern tribes were doing, he discovered a people committed to the Lord. The transjordanian tribes had built the altar as a means to proclaim their unity with the covenant people. Through this witness, in days to come, their children would know that they belonged to the Lord (22:10-34). These incidents serve to underscore the book's emphasis on faithfulness, the blessings of obedience, and the disastrous effects of departing from God's truth.

The collocation of these themes combines to display a typical three-fold narrative framework of crisis, resolution, and outcome. The crisis is the land to be conquered and the conflict that ensued. The resolution is the presence of God to fight for Israel and give them the land. The outcome is obedience and covenant loyalty. When all of these notes are played in their theological sequence, the melody of Joshua sounds like this—God will remain faithful to his covenant. He will fulfil his promises by being with, fighting for, and allotting the land to his people. They, in turn, are called on to be courageous, obey his word and remain faithful to him.

The sad tale that follows the book of Joshua, however, reveals Israel's eventual faithlessness, a heart bent towards idols that will open up the entire period of Judges, lead to the failed monarchy of Saul and, in spite of the dramatic shafts of divine light in the ministries of David and Solomon, wind up in a divided and subsequently exiled nation. The cyclical pattern of obedience, victory, disobedience, and failure continued to plague the people. God was *with* Joshua, but it is only when God comes *as* Joshua (we call him *Jesus*) that an Israelite achieves complete faithfulness to the Lord.

Joshua—and Jesus

Preachers often discover that they can easily slip into predictable modes when teaching from the Old Testament. For a Christian sermon, after explaining the text, all you need to do is tack on the bit about Jesus. Australian Bible scholar Graeme Goldsworthy tells the amusing story of a Sunday school teacher who attempted to extract herself from a teaching rut with her class of five-year-olds. She opened the class by asking the boys and girls, 'Who can tell me what is gray and furry and lives in a Gum tree?' Perplexed by this new approach, they stared at her. She asked again, 'Come on, someone must know. What is gray, furry lives in a Gum tree—has a black leathery nose and beady eyes?' Still puzzled by this approach, the children sat and stared in silence. 'It lives in a Gum tree; eats Gum leaves; it has big beady eyes and furry ears.' No response. Discouraged by this completely unsuccessful new tactic, the teacher was ready to change the subject when a little girl tentatively raised her hand. Finally an answer! 'Yes, Suzie?' The little girl replied, 'Miss, I know it's Jesus, but it sounds like a koala!'[1]

It would be easy to slip into this rather predictable pattern when reading Joshua. Joshua is, after all, the Hebrew name for Jesus. Yet we must avoid merely tacking on the Jesus bit. The Bible itself draws clear lines between these two characters. In Hebrews 4:8, the author writes about the Old Testament Joshua: 'For if Joshua had given them rest, God would not have spoken of another day later on.'

[1] Graeme Goldsworthy, *Preaching the Whole Bible as Christian Scripture* (Grand Rapids: Eerdmans, 2000), xi.

From the context of Hebrews 4 it becomes evident that the biblical writer is drawing an analogy of similarity and dissimilarity between what Joshua did by leading Israel into Canaan and what Jesus does by leading his people into the rest of God (see Heb. 4:8-16). This analogy between biblical characters, events, and institutions we call *types*.

The typological relationship that Hebrews 4 highlights allows us to see in Joshua a man who prefigures Christ or stands as a pictorial prophecy of what Jesus will come to do. That, in fact, is what Hebrews 4:8 is all about. The land of Canaan itself was a type, a picture of the everlasting rest that God's people were to inherit, not in this life but in the life to come. The land was as real for Joshua as it was for Abraham, but just like the old patriarch every believing Israelite was looking for more than just Canaan. He or she 'was looking forward to the city that has foundations, whose designer and builder is God' (Heb. 11:10). This city, this new Jerusalem, this land of everlasting promise is the possession of every believer because one greater than Joshua has defeated every sin and demonic power that stands in the way of our eternal inheritance! This anointed king, Christ Jesus, has asked for and received from his Father the nations as his inheritance and the ends of the earth as his possession (Psa. 2:7-9)!

When we place the message of Joshua in its historical and redemptive context, then the relevance of this book for the twenty-first-century church becomes clear. Beyond just being an interesting relic of ancient Jewish history, what we find in this old covenant book is a profoundly Christian message. God not only kept and fulfilled his land promises through Joshua; he also keeps and fulfils his promises of salvation and of a new heavens and new earth, through our Lord Jesus (see Rev. 21 and 22). And God intends for his faithfulness to Christ to elicit faithfulness from his people as well (see Rev. 22:7). Choose whom you will serve. Like Israel assembled at Shechem to renew the covenant, a choice lies before you (see 24:1-15). Will you be faithful to Jesus, the one who has been faithful for you?

2

Never Alone
Joshua 1:1-9

'Have I not commanded you? Be strong and courageous. Do not be frightened, and do not be dismayed, for the LORD your God is with you wherever you go.' (Josh. 1:9)

Alexander Selkirk, the inspiration for Daniel Defoe's *Robinson Crusoe*, served as sailing master aboard the galley ship *Cinque Ports* during a 1703 expedition led by William Dampier. After a dispute between Dampier and Thomas Stradling, the ship's commander, the *Cinque Ports* dropped anchor at an uninhabited island some 400 miles off the coast of Chile for supplies and fresh water. Concerned with the seaworthiness of the vessel, Selkirk asked to be left on the island because he believed another ship would soon arrive. Marooned on the island, Selkirk immediately regretted his decision. He ran along the shore shouting for the ship to return, but to no avail. The other ship he expected to arrive soon would not appear on the horizon for four years!

Can you imagine the emotion that surged through Selkirk as he watched the *Cinque Ports* disappear in the distance? Alone! What a frightening word! To be isolated or abandoned evokes feelings of desolation, fear, and despair. Selkirk had a Bible with him on the island and read it often. I wonder how many times he might have read these words from the opening chapter of Joshua: 'I will not leave you or forsake you' (verse 5).

These comforting words of assurance set the theme for the first major section of Joshua 1—God's address to his great general. Twice in this opening paragraph God promised Joshua that he would never be alone. First, in verse 5, the Lord says, 'Just as I was with Moses, so I will be with you. I will not leave you or forsake you.' Then, to conclude his discourse, he reiterates his point in verse 9: 'Do not be frightened, and do not be dismayed, for the LORD your God is with you wherever you go.'

It was important for Joshua to know this truth because God was about to call him to lead Israel into a series of battles as the nation fought to take possession of the land of Canaan. The Lord had promised this land to Abraham and his descendants (see Gen. 15:16-21; cf. Exod. 3:16-17), but in God's providence four centuries were to pass before Israel could take possession of their inheritance. Joshua now stood poised on the brink of Canaan's conquest. Moses, the leader he had served for so many years, was gone; but God was still with him. For the difficult and frightening tasks that lay ahead, God reassured him that he would not have to march into battle alone.

As you look at this opening paragraph of the book, verses 5 and 9 colour and control everything God says as he commissioned Joshua to lead Israel into the land. God's presence underlies and enables the actions and attitudes necessary for the conquest of Canaan; or to state it more concisely, God's presence is the key to the fulfilment of his promises.

Gone

It was important for Joshua, and indeed all of Israel, to know that the Lord was still with them even though Moses was now dead. The passage begins by recapping the transition that had been taking place since the closing pages of Deuteronomy. The words *After the death of Moses* (literally, 'And it happened after ...' verse 1) link this passage to the final words of Deuteronomy with the closest possible linguistic connection.[1] And they introduce us to the fact that God reassured Joshua that he would fulfil his purposes even though Moses was gone.

---

[1] The first word in the Hebrew text, *wayehi*, 'and it was' or 'and it happened' signals an unbroken narrative. Other Old Testament books that open this way include Judges, Ruth, 1 and 2 Samuel, and Esther.

The death of Moses marked a break with the past, the end of the wilderness generation, a generation that perished because of its unbelief. When Moses first led the Israelites to Kadesh-barnea, the spies who ran a reconnaissance mission into Canaan reported that there were giants in the land. With that news, fear gripped the people's hearts, and they refused to invade the land and take possession of their inheritance. Numbers 13 and 14 tell the whole sad tale.

Moses' death in the wilderness was not due to his complicity with the fear and murmuring of that generation. He died for another sin, an incident that also took place at Kadesh. Earlier in their wilderness journey, the Israelites found themselves at Rephidim and complained about their lack of water. In response to their need, the Lord told Moses to go and stand upon the rock at Horeb and strike it. When he did that, water gushed out (Exod. 17:1-7). Later, when the Israelites complained yet again about their lack of water, Moses disobeyed the Lord; and rather than speaking to the rock this time, as God had instructed, he struck it twice (Num. 20:10-13). His failure to believe the Lord and 'to uphold [him] as holy in the eyes of the people of Israel' kept him from entering the land of promise (Num. 20:12; cf. Deut. 32:48-52).

Both the rebellion at Kadesh-barnea and Moses' disregard of God's explicit command should serve as stark reminders that sin has consequences. Sin has ramifications—ripples and shock-waves that affect not only us but those around us as well. The sin of one person can alter the course of a nation, as Achan's transgression will so clearly demonstrate (Josh. 7:10-26).

With the death of Moses, the last of those destined to die east of the Jordan had perished without experiencing the blessings of the land of promise. The transition from Moses to Joshua, in essence, forced Israel to make a definite break with that past, a break with the fear and unbelief that kept their fathers from possessing the land thirty-eight years earlier.

Moses was gone. I doubt that we can fully appreciate the profound sense of loss that Israel must have felt with the passing of their great leader. Moses had served the Lord and had been the stabilizing spiritual influence in the nation. But into the silence of Israel's loss God spoke. Hearing the voice of God, Joshua was reminded that Moses was not the key to the promised land—God was.

Arise and go over

As Moses neared the end of his days, both he and Joshua presented themselves before the Lord at the tent of meeting (Deut. 31). The Lord then instructed Moses to write the great song of the rock (Deut. 32:1-43), and he commissioned Joshua to be Moses' successor. God said to Joshua, 'Be strong and courageous, for you shall bring the people of Israel into the land that I swore to give them. I will be with you' (Deut. 31:23). Joshua was to take the lead as God's man in Israel, a truth evidenced even by his name. Joshua means *the Lord saves*. His name is the first name in the Bible to incorporate God's name as well.[1]

The stage was now set for God to repeat his charge for Joshua to go forward with the conquest. The time had come. The wilderness would be but a memory. Israel's future lay west of the Jordan. To experience the hope that the future held, the nation had to make its move to conquer and occupy the land. So God called Joshua—and through him, Israel—to arise and cross over the Jordan River.

The twin imperatives—'arise, go over' (verse 2)—initiate the first part of the Lord's commission. The words are simple enough. The concepts are not difficult to follow. But their simplicity belies just how formidable the task was, especially at that particular time of year when the Jordan overflowed it banks (see 3:15). But what God called Joshua to do, he would also enable him to accomplish.

Accompanying this call to enter the land, the Lord gave Joshua certain assurances to bolster his faith for the coming days. The first pledge focused on the land itself. 'Go over this Jordan, you and all this people, into the land that I am giving to them, to the people of Israel' (verse 2b). Joshua is to go with 'all this people'. Renamed 'the people of Israel' at the end of the verse, these are God's covenant people. Although their parents had perished in the wilderness, the

---

[1] David M. Howard, Jr. *Joshua. The New American Commentary* (Nashville: Broadman and Holman Publishers, 1998), 73. *Joshua* is the Old Testament equivalent of *Jesus*.

Lord had not abandoned his plan to see this remnant settled in Canaan.[1] Although thousands had fallen in the wilderness, God's grace marched on.

Joshua was to lead them to 'the land that I [the LORD] am giving to them'. Both here in the immediate context (verses 3, 6), and throughout the book, the verb *give* occurs repeatedly to emphasize that Israel did not deserve this land flowing with milk and honey, and the only reason the nation would possess it was because God had chosen to grant it to them.[2] There is no explanation as to why God promised Abraham and his descendants this land, but rather it is the gift and good pleasure of a gracious, promising God.

Further definitions of the land follow in verses 3 and 4. First, Joshua and Israel were to inherit 'every place that the sole of your foot will tread upon' (verse 3). This was the same promise the Lord had given to Moses: 'Every place on which the sole of your foot treads shall be yours' (Deut. 11:24a). A second description, found in verse 4, marks out the geographical boundaries of the territory. The Lord points Joshua first to the south ('the wilderness') and then to the north ('this Lebanon'). Next, turning his attention eastward, he marked Israel's border as 'the great river, the river Euphrates'. In the opposite direction, the 'great sea', or the Mediterranean, formed the westernmost boundary of the land (cf. Deut. 11:24b). This was 'all the land of the Hittites', a general description of Canaan used by other nations.[3]

This is the very same land God had promised to the patriarchs. Although expressed in slightly different terms, the boundaries delineated in verse 4 roughly coincide with the promise to Abram (Gen. 15:18-21) and repeated throughout the patriarchal narrative (Gen. 26:1-5; 35:9-15). The land Israel was about to possess was God's

[1] Marten H. Woudstra, *The Book of Joshua. The New International Commentary on the Old Testament* (Grand Rapids: Eerdmans, 1981), 59.

[2] The verb 'give,' *nathan*, occurs 89 times in the book and refers primarily to the land or rest as God's direct gift or the gift he mediated through Moses or Joshua.

[3] Pitkänen describes the land of the Hittites as 'somewhat further south than Anatolia proper.' Pekka M.A. Pitkänen, *Joshua. Apollos Old Testament Commentary* (Downers Grove, IL: InterVarsity Press, 2010), 116. See also Woudstra, *Book of Joshua*, 60.

gracious provision for an undeserving people allocated according to his covenant promises. Everything about this land, from the first promise to Abram to the commissioning of Joshua and the subsequent conquest of Canaan, combines to underscore the grace of God to his chosen people.

The lesson God taught Israel here is the same lesson every believer needs to learn again and again. Like Israel, everything we possess comes to us from the gracious and generous hand of God. We deserve anything but his goodness. But God so loves that he gives, and his greatest gift was not land but his Son (John 3:16).

In addition to his grace, God also assures Joshua of his power. 'No man shall be able to stand before you all the days of your life' (verse 5a). The Lord made this promise specifically to Joshua. The pronouns *you* and *your* are singular. But as Israel's leader, his success would mean the success of the nation. The armies of Canaan would not possess the military might to be able to withstand Israel's invading forces. This was no small comfort. Years earlier, Israel feared the inhabitants of Canaan and saw themselves as grasshoppers before giants (Num. 13:33). 'We cannot go into the land!' they cried. But now those voices lie silent in the grave, and only God is heard to speak.[1] With a promise reiterated from Deuteronomy 7:24 and 11:25, God assured Joshua of victory. Joshua and his troops could march into the land with confidence because the Lord had promised the success of consistent military triumph.

The Lord concluded the first part of this commissioning speech with the promise of his presence: 'Just as I was with Moses, so I will be with you. I will not leave you or forsake you' (verse 5b). That God had been with Moses from the very beginning of his call had been evident for everyone to see. The Lord had met him at the burning bush (Exod. 3:12), had given him miraculous powers in Egypt (see Exod. 7:1ff.), and had revealed to him his law (Exod. 19:1ff.). Moses had communed with the Lord face to face (Exod. 33:11; Deut. 5:4; 34:10), and as a result, his countenance shone with the reflection of divine glory (Exod. 34:29-35; cf. 2 Cor. 3:7-18). And just as God had been with Moses to challenge, comfort, deliver, and

---

[1] Robert L. Hubbard, Jr. *Joshua. The NIV Application Commentary* (Grand Rapids: Zondervan, 2009), 78-79.

overcome impossible odds, so the Lord would be with Joshua. This last provision, however, is more than one promise among many. It is the basis for all that God will do through and for Joshua. The two negative statements 'I will not leave you; I will not forsake you' only strengthen God's guarantee.

Our Joshua

God's first words of commission to Joshua remind us that this key figure in salvation history points us to a greater leader, a greater conqueror, the captain of our salvation (cf. Heb. 2:10 KJV). Jesus saw his own ministry as a commission from the Father, who sent him into the world with the assurance of his presence. Jesus said to the crowds around him, 'When you have lifted up the Son of Man, then you will know that I am he, and that I do nothing on my own authority, but speak just as the Father taught me. And he who sent me is with me. He has not left me alone, for I always do the things that are pleasing to him' (John 8:28-29).

As Jesus approached his crucifixion, he said to his disciples, 'Behold, the hour is coming, indeed it has come, when you will be scattered, each to his own home, and will leave me alone. Yet I am not alone, for the Father is with me' (John 16:32). Although Jesus was about to face the most difficult challenge of his life, he was certain that he would not face it alone.

The Lord Jesus also knew that he would be victorious. He endured the shame and agony of the cross for the joy that was set before him (Heb. 12:2). Earlier we saw that God's promise of victory to Joshua included Israel as well (verse 5), and that provides us with a glimpse into the relationship between the success of Christ, our Joshua, and the triumph of the church. The victory of God's people lies secure in the victory of the Lord Jesus. When Christ predicted his coming death and resurrection, he said to his disciples, 'Yet a little while and the world will see me no more, but you will see me. Because I live, you also will live' (John 14:19). On the cross Christ defeated all the spiritual forces arrayed against him, and in triumph God raised him from the dead (see Col. 2:13-15). His victory, however, was not his alone. Because he lives, we also live. He triumphed over sin and the grave, and so too will we!

God's chain of command extends from the Father to the Son and through the Son to you and me. Jesus said, 'As the Father has sent me, even so I am sending you' (John 20:21), and 'I am with you always, to the end of the age' (Matt. 28:20). God never calls anyone to a task and then leaves that person on his or her own to accomplish it. It is true that, like Joshua, God calls us to do hard things. The Christian life is full of difficulty and suffering. But we find comfort in knowing that even in our darkest hours God never abandons us to our own resources. To more fully understand this truth, we need to ask not for easier tasks or lighter burdens but for a greater awareness and appreciation of the Lord's presence.

The promise of God's presence also comforts us in our loneliness. We can feel isolated and alone for a number of reasons. Loneliness can come from illness, depression, the loss of a job, or a broken relationship. We can end up feeling not only cut off from other people but from God as well. When that happens, any sense of hope seems to melt away. In Psalm 31, David poured out his grief to God because of the way his enemies treated him.[1] You can hear his sorrowful solitude in verse 12: 'I have been forgotten like one who is dead.' In a moment of panic, he even thought that God had forgotten him. He said to the Lord, 'I am cut off from your sight' (verse 22a). But David's emotions didn't tell the true story any more than do ours. We might feel alone, but, as with David, God stands by our side, ready to hear our prayers. 'But you heard the voice of my pleas for mercy when I cried to you for help' (verse 22b). When we pray, faith often has to fight our feelings. By faith, however, God's faithfulness triumphs over our fears.

Be strong and courageous
In the Lord's commission to Joshua, the first set of imperatives covered his actions ('arise, go over', verse 2). Parallel to this the second set of commands, and thus the second major part of Joshua's assignment, addressed his attitude: 'Be strong and courageous' (verse 6). Godly actions must be backed by a godly attitude.

---

[1] Saul's expedition to the city of Keilah to capture David may provide the background for this psalm. See 1 Samuel 23:1-14.

The command 'be strong and courageous' is an exhortation to bravery, to display manly ability and stability in the face of danger. Why would Joshua need such courage? Because God had called him to 'cause this people to inherit the land' (verse 6).[1] Again, the simplicity of the statement masks the difficulty of the job. To cause Israel to inherit the land involved battle after battle against imposing armies and fortified cities (see Josh. 6-12). No soldier, least of all the general, can afford to be a coward. Without strength and courage, Joshua would cower into a corner and desert the cause.

Joshua would also need resolute courage to obey God's word. 'Only be strong and very courageous to do according to all the law that Moses my servant commanded you' (verse 7a). Here the addition of the words *only* and *very* strengthen the repetition of the command. This intensification highlights these imperatives, showing them to be central to the second half of the paragraph. Yes, Joshua will need strength and bravery to lead in the conquest and allotment of the land, but it will take even greater strength and courage to obey the law that God had commanded and delivered through Moses.

Does that strike you as somewhat odd? If you were asked what do you need to obey Scripture, would you have said *bravery*? Or would you have used other words like *faith* and *love*? The Lord said *courage* because obedience requires bravery. Scripture often calls us to step into situations that require sacrifice and result in our being mocked and ridiculed. Following God makes no sense to the world, it strikes them as foolishness (1 Cor. 2:14); that's why we need the courage to stick to our convictions regarding what God has said in the Bible.

The Lord does not give Joshua an option as to what he should or should not obey. He must be careful to obey 'all the law'. At this point in redemptive history, 'all the law' refers to the five books of Moses, commonly called the *Pentateuch*. These books not only contain the early history of Israel and the laws by which the nation

---

[1] The Hebrew verb *nhl*, 'to inherit' occurs here in the *hiphil* theme which is primarily the theme of causation. A. E. Cowley, ed. *Gesenius' Hebrew Grammar*. Edited and enlarged by E. Kautzsch (New York: Oxford University Press, 1910), 144 (§53c). See also Bruce K. Waltke and M. O'Connor, *An Introduction to Biblical Hebrew Syntax* (Winona Lake, IN: Eisenbrauns, 1990), 441 (§27.3b).

was to live and worship, but they also contain the promises upon which the conquest of Canaan was based. Joshua was to be diligent in his obedience to all that God had revealed through his prophet Moses. The Lord compares this kind of obedience to walking a road. 'Do not turn from it to the right hand or to the left' (verse 7b). The law is like a path that Joshua travels. God's command is not to deviate to the right by adding to Scripture or to the left by taking from it. The word that God had commanded was true and sufficient.

To change the imagery, the Bible is not like a dinner buffet from which we can pick and choose our favourite foods. We are not free to select which parts we will believe or obey and which we will reject. The Puritans understood this well. J. I. Packer highlights this aspect of their faith by telling the story of one particular pastor. Packer writes,

> Richard Rogers, the Puritan pastor of Wethersfield, Essex, at the turn of the sixteenth century, was riding one day with the local lord of the manor, who, after twitting him for some time about his 'precisian' way, asked him what it was that made him so precise. 'O sir,' replied Rogers, 'I serve a precise God.'

Packer goes on to explain:

> If there were such a thing as a Puritan crest, this would be its proper motto. A precise God—a God, that is, who has made a precise disclosure of his mind and will in Scripture, and who expects from his servants a corresponding preciseness of belief and behaviour—it was this view of God that created and controlled the historic Puritan outlook. The Bible itself led them to it. And we who share the Puritan estimate of Holy Scripture cannot excuse ourselves if we fail to show a diligence and conscientiousness equal to theirs in ordering our lives according to God's written word.[1]

A constant rehearsal of God's words proves essential for this kind of comprehensive obedience. The Lord made clear to Joshua that 'this Book of the Law shall not depart from your mouth, but you shall meditate on it day and night, so that you may be careful to do according to all that is written in it' (verse 8a). The 'Book of

[1] J. I. Packer, *A Quest for Godliness: The Puritan Vision of the Christian Life* (Wheaton: Crossway, 1990), 114.

the Law' is a reference to Deuteronomy and most likely a specific reference to the laws and stipulations found in chapters 12-26, which cover such topics as worship (12:1-32), idolatry (13:1-18), and dietary regulations (14:1-21). We can understand why God would tell Joshua not to let this word depart from his mind or heart, but why this specific reference to his mouth? For two reasons. First, the following command is that he 'meditate on it day and night'. The word translated *meditate* means to mutter. Perhaps you have seen someone engaged in intense study of a document. As he reads over the words and ponders their meaning, he actually mumbles what is before him. That is meditation, a mental and even verbal rehearsal of God's truth. The second reason this law should always be in his mouth is that Joshua must teach the people to obey. It must ever be in his mouth as he recites, explains, and reiterates its stipulations for Israel.

The Book of the Law was to occupy Joshua's thoughts day and night. He was to meditate on it ceaselessly as he focused his mind on its precepts and thought deeply about their implications. By this continuous meditation, God's word would shape Joshua's patterns of thinking and be ready at hand to inform any decision he had to make. As James Montgomery Boice wrote, 'Meditation has application as a goal.'[1]

Every believer should fill his or her heart with the Bible for this very purpose. Whether you use the 'old-fashioned' method of writing out verses on 3 x 5 cards or open an app on your smart phone, make it your goal to memorize and meditate on God's word. As you ponder the Bible's words, stories, and instructions over and over again, Scripture begins to shape and mould the way you think about life. It begins to play a role in how you decide to spend your time and money. Scripture meditation paves the way for spiritual success.

Like the blessed man of Psalm 1, who also meditates on the law day and night, Joshua will be like a flourishing tree free of withering leaves. Everything he does will prosper (cf. Psa. 1:3). Walking the path designated by the word was the key to comprehensive success

[1] James Montgomery Boice, *Joshua: An Expositional Commentary* (Grand Rapids: Baker, 1989), 17.

throughout the land. 'For then you will make your way prosperous, and then you will have good success' (verse 8b). We should not read these words as an Old Testament version of the prosperity gospel. Scripture meditation is not the pathway to health and wealth; it is the pathway to obedience, and obedience is the pathway to success. Good success in this context translates into victory in battle. Joshua is to go over the Jordan for the express purpose of defeating all of the inhabitants of the land so that Israel might possess the promised territory. If he follows God's law, then the Lord will bless him and make him achieve his purposes and aims.[1]

Finally, for a third time, the Lord repeats his command, 'Have I not commanded you? Be strong and courageous' (verse 9a). Then, to reinforce his message, he states it a fourth time using two negative statements: 'Do not be frightened, and do not be dismayed' (verse 9b). How will Joshua muster all this courage? Should he look within himself for some deep, hitherto untapped reserves of power? The hope God gave him for success is the very hope he gives for having the fortitude to lead and obey: 'for the LORD your God is with you wherever you go' (verse 9c).

Into the wilderness and into the world

Joshua needed strength and courage to obey the law because of the strong temptation to turn from it. Wasn't this Satan's temptation of Christ? When Jesus entered his public ministry and God commissioned him, he was baptized at the Jordan River (Matt. 3:13-17). What follows (in Matt. 4) is a kind of anti-conquest. Instead of leaving the Jordan and heading straight for Jerusalem or some other key locale in Israel, Jesus retreated into the wilderness. There, in a battle against the forces of evil, the devil tempted him to deviate from God's word. The subtle trick that Satan attempted was not to get Christ to abandon the word altogether but to step slightly to

[1] 'The two words we find here in our passage in Joshua (1:7-8) speaking of prosperity and success are almost never used in the Old Testament to speak of financial success. Rather, they speak of succeeding in life's proper endeavors. This happens when people's lives are focused entirely on God and obedience to him. The focus of people's endeavors is *not* to be prosperity and success but rather holiness and obedience.' Howard, *Joshua*, 88.

one side or the other. Didn't the devil quote Scripture to Jesus in
his temptations?[1] But a move to the right or left, a step outside the
bounds of Scripture, would have destroyed any success Christ came
to achieve.

How did Jesus deal with these temptations? To the devil's
allurements and misapplication of the Bible, Jesus responded each
time with quotations from the book of Deuteronomy.[2] The Book of
the Law did not depart from his mouth!

Because of his work to overcome temptation and gain victory
over Satan, not only in the wilderness but also on the cross, Jesus
commissions the church to take the news of his success into all the
world. Let's take a moment to compare the commission we find here
in Joshua 1 with the one Christ gave in Matthew 28.

God's commission of Joshua was comprehensive. Notice the
repetition of the word *all*. It occurs eight times in the first nine verses
of the book. It covers all the people, all the land, all the law, and all
the days of Joshua's life. Now compare this to the comprehensiveness
of the Great Commission. Christ calls us to go into all the world,
to make disciples of all nations, and to teach all of the words he
has commanded. How can this be done? Jesus has all authority and
promises to be with us always, literally 'all the days' (Matt. 28:18-
20). God's commission of Joshua ultimately results, through the
outworking of his plan for Israel, in Christ's commission to us.
Undergirded by the presence of God, we can carry the gospel across
the street or around the world with confidence!

Alexander Selkirk was not really alone on his island. God was
with him, whether he realized it or not. The *Cinque Ports*, the ship
Selkirk feared was unseaworthy, sailed north from the island but
sank shortly thereafter. Most of the crew perished. The few who
survived were taken prisoner and became slaves. God was with
Alexander Selkirk and saved him from those tragedies. And God
is with you! One of the names of Jesus is Immanuel, 'God with
us' (Isa. 7:14; Matt. 1:23). God has come to us in Christ. And with
every command and every promise he says, 'I will be with you.' In

[1] Satan quoted from Psa. 91:11, 12.
[2] The texts the Lord used were Deut. 8:3; 6:16; and 6:13.

every heartache and tear Jesus says, 'I am with you.' Is your task too difficult? Is your burden too heavy? Jesus says, 'I will never leave you or forsake you.' Christian, you are never alone!

3

Authority and Obedience
Joshua 1:10-18

And they answered Joshua, 'All that you have commanded us we will do, and wherever you send us we will go. Just as we obeyed Moses in all things, so we will obey you. Only may the LORD our God be with you, as he was with Moses!' (Josh. 1:16-17)

When Saul of Tarsus saddled his donkey for a trip to Damascus, he could not have imagined the dramatic change he was about to experience. For some time the persecution of Christians had been his chief aim in life. In his eyes, the sect of the Nazarene blighted the landscape of pure Judaism, and it was for his version of pure, pharisaical Judaism that he burned with a white-hot zeal. With arrest warrants in his hand and hatred in his heart, Saul headed to Damascus to rid the synagogues of any who followed 'the Way' (Acts 9:1-2).

As his caravan reached the outskirts of the city, Saul suddenly found himself surrounded by a light that flashed from heaven. He fell to the ground and heard someone say, 'Saul, Saul, why are you persecuting me?' (Acts 9:4). He asked, 'Who are you, Lord?' And the reply came, 'I am Jesus, whom you are persecuting. But rise and enter the city, and you will be told what you are to do' (Acts 9:5-6). Saul immediately got up, and although he was blinded by the light and had to be led by the hand, he obeyed the Lord, entered Damascus, and waited for further instructions (Acts 9:8-9).

That day, on the road to Damascus, Christ revealed himself to Saul, and the words of Jesus brought the persecuting Pharisee to his knees in humble submission. When he stood to his feet, he was a Christian who was ready to obey the instructions of his new Lord.

God reveals himself to make his thoughts and purposes known to us and to call for our submission and response. This response begins at conversion when we obey the gospel commands to repent and believe, but it should continue as the principal characteristic of the believer's life. Saul's conversion and subsequent obedience illustrate the spiritual dynamic we see in Joshua 1:10-18, a dynamic unfolded for us in three speeches.

Speech One: Get ready!

Having received his commission from the Lord to lead Israel to victory in Canaan (1:1-9), Joshua acted upon it. He turned his attention to the officers of the people and issued God's word to them as commands to obey. 'And Joshua commanded the officers of the people, "Pass through the midst of the camp ..."' (verses 10-11a).

Early in Israel's wilderness wanderings, Jethro, Moses' father-in-law, had advised him to establish a system of elder oversight in the nation. The task of governing the people was far too great for Moses alone (Exod. 18:13-23; cf. Num. 11:16-30). The 'officers of the people' were subordinates to these elders. They were men who helped the elders carry out various administrative tasks, whether political (Deut. 31:28) or military (Deut. 20:5).[1] Here these Spirit-filled men (Num. 11:16-17; Deut. 1:15-16) helped prepare the nation to invade Canaan.

Joshua's charge to these officers was to go throughout the Israelite camp and ensure that the people were prepared for the coming military campaign across the Jordan. Notice the chain of command: it ran from the Lord to Joshua, from Joshua to the officers, and from the officers to the people. Structures of authority are inherent in the way God works to carry out his purposes in the home, in the church, and in society. The specific charge was 'Command the

---

[1] R. Laird Harris, ed. *The Theological Wordbook of the Old Testament* (Chicago: Moody, 1980), electronic version, entry *shoter*.

people, "Prepare your provisions."' The term *provisions* is relatively rare in the Old Testament, occurring only eighteen times. It refers primarily to food that you would prepare before a trip so you would have enough to eat along the way. 'Prepare ... for within three days you are to pass over this Jordan to go in to take possession of the land that the LORD your God is giving you to possess' (verse 11). The message of these officers was 'Get ready!' The people had three days to bake, cook, and otherwise collect and store their food for the journey because soon they were going to cross the Jordan. They would not wait until the harvest season was over and the waters had subsided (cf. 3:1), but would break camp to cross the flooding river very soon.

Interpreters debate exactly what the phrase *within three days* means and how it relates to other time indicators in the early chapters of the book. For example, the spies Joshua sent to assess Jericho hid in the hills for three days before returning to the camp (2:22). Were those days simultaneous to the three referred to here, or did the Jericho reconnaissance mission occur between verses 9 and 10 of chapter 1? In 3:2 we find a reference to three days having passed. Are these the three days the spies were away or the same three days referred to in verse 11? Donald Madvig believes that 'It is difficult, if not impossible, to correlate all the references to "three days" in chapters 1-3.'¹ Robert Hubbard, on the other hand, sees the references to 'three days' as symbolic.² David Howard's solution is to interpret the reference in 1:11 as the time period that will elapse before Israel breaks camp. During this time, the spies hide in the hills near Jericho. To this period he then adds the 'three days' of 3:2, arriving at a total of at least six days.³

This chronological difficulty is not easy to solve. It seems best, however, to see the events of chapter 2 as taking place some time

¹ Donald Madvig, *Joshua*, in *The Expositor's Bible Commentary*, ed. Frank E. Gaebelein (Grand Rapids: Zondervan, 1992), 257.

² 'It denotes the stylized biblical time period to mark momentous events (Exod. 10:22, 23) or important transitions (Gen. 30:36; Josh 2:16, 22; 9:16; 1 Kings 12:5//2 Chron. 10:5). It also marks important journeys (Exod. 2:18; 5:3), especially into the wilderness (8:27, 15:22; Num. 10:33; 33:8).' Hubbard, *Joshua*, 84.

³ Howard, *Joshua*, 91.

before 1:10. Therefore, after the spies return from their three days in the hills (2:22), Joshua commanded the officers to prepare the people to cross the Jordan within three days. The next occurrence of 'three days" in 3:2 would then refer back to 1:11. This arrangement raises the question of why an historical narrative would not present us with a linear sequence of events. The answer is that biblical narrative does not always flow chronologically. The author attaches the three speeches of 1:10-18 to 1:1-9 to link thematically Joshua's commission with his assumption of command.

The bottom line to all of this is that it was time for the people to get ready to enter Canaan. In just a few short days they had to be prepared to cross the river.

Furthermore, Israel was to cross with a firm purpose in mind. They were going over to enter the land and possess it. But lest they think this will happen as the result of their own skill, Joshua reminds them that they will seize the land because God is giving it to them. Grace again comes to the fore (cf. verses 3, 6). As we find so often in the Bible, the scales of Scripture balance the divine and human spheres of activity. In an act of divine sovereignty, God gives Israel the land. The Israelites, for their part, are to make provisions and take possession of the land, both of which are clearly acts of human responsibility. 'The command itself shows a mix of prudence and faith: they will be prepared for the march, but also go in faith that the struggle is in principle won, because God gives them the land to possess.'[1]

What role do we see Joshua fulfil in this passage? He is Israel's new mediator. He receives the message from the Lord and then proclaims it to the people. This is the same task that Moses performed for Israel. When the Israelites feared the voice of God at Mount Sinai, the people begged Moses to stand between them and God, lest the Lord's word consume them (Exod. 20:18-19). In their roles of mediators, both Moses and Joshua pointed forward to the ministry of Jesus.

Jesus Christ came to be *the* mediator between God and men (1 Tim. 2:5; cf. Heb. 9:15; 12:24). In him not only do we receive

[1] J. Gordon McConville and Stephen N. Williams, *Joshua. The Two Horizons Old Testament Commentary* (Grand Rapids: Eerdmans, 2010), 15.

words from God but also the very Word of God comes to us in flesh (John 1:1, 14). In the past, God spoke through men such as Moses and Joshua, but now, in sending his Son, he has given the final word (Heb. 1:1). Jesus reveals to us the clearest representation of the Father (John 14:9). All of this amounts to a very simple lesson—if you want to know God, then you must know Jesus Christ.

Once, when speaking to the Pharisees, Jesus said, 'I am the light of the world' (John 8:12). What is that light? Jesus went on to explain to those same Pharisees that his message was the very word of God that he had received from his Father. 'He who sent me is true, and I declare to the world what I have heard from him' (John 8:26). Paul summarized it this way: 'For God, who said, "Let light shine out of darkness," has shone in our hearts to give the light of the knowledge of the glory of God in the face of Jesus Christ' (2 Cor. 4:6). Christ came to bring God to us and to bring us to God. That is the role of a mediator.

If we look closer at the text, we see that Joshua is not only the mediator of God's word but also a believer who receives God's message and acts upon it. Verse 11, the command to prepare provisions for crossing the Jordan River, is the application of verse 2, the command to arise and enter Canaan. Not content to be just a hearer of the word, Joshua went into action as a doer of the word, making preparations for the Jordan crossing. He exhibited a vibrant, word-centred spirituality. Do you have that kind of walk with God? Do you have a lively, word-centred spiritual life?

Spirituality has become a buzzword in our day. It is not unusual to hear people say, 'I'm spiritual but not religious.' Spirituality has come to mean something like a vague feeling of otherness or a connection with something more than the material world. In the Bible, however, the spiritual person is the man or woman who has the Holy Spirit (Rom. 8:9). Through the ministry of the Spirit, the Christian is united to Christ and grows into a deepening awareness of that union through the word of God, the sacraments, and prayer.

Are you listening to God's word? Do you take time to read it and hear it preached? If you are listening to Scripture, are you doing anything more than listening? Is the Bible changing your life?

31

On one occasion, after I had spoken at a church as the guest preacher, a man came up to me and complimented me on the sermon. He said that I had good content and did a good job with the delivery. He concluded, 'I give you an "A".' I'm sure that he meant to encourage me. Although he was probably mistaken as to the quality of the sermon, he was kind. Yet his words actually discouraged me because I wasn't preaching for his grade. I had no interest in what he thought about 'my sermon' *per se*. My goal was to see God's word change his life, to see him embrace the truth and to live out what the text taught. The Bible is a book for action. God expects you to put its precepts into play. If you listen to the Scriptures but never practice what they teach, then you're deceiving yourself that you actually believe them (James 1:22).

Speech Two: Remember and go!

Having sent the officers on their way, Joshua turned in verse 12 to address Reuben, Gad, and half the tribe of Manasseh. These are the tribes that took possession of their land east of the Jordan. Why does Joshua specifically address these transjordanian tribes? Having already received their inheritance, they needed to be reminded of their sacred obligations to fight with their brothers until the land of Canaan was secured.

First, a little background information will be helpful. The people of Reuben and Gad were great cattlemen and sheep herders. They had large numbers of livestock, and when they saw the land of Jazer and the land of Gilead, they knew that these were ideal places for grazing (Num. 32:1-5). So they asked Moses to give them that land rather than a possession west of the Jordan.

The request of these tribes troubled Moses. If they did not participate in the conquest, it would discourage the other tribes from fighting. Israel would find themselves in a situation very similar to Kadesh-barnea thirty-eight years earlier (Num. 32:6-15). But Reuben and Gad had a plan. They would provide for their families and livestock on their side of the river, but they would also fight with their brothers on the other side (Num. 32:16-19). Moses agreed to this proposal but reminded them that if they failed to fight on the west side of the Jordan, they could not live on the east side. The possession of their land depended upon their willingness to fulfil their obligations to their fellow countrymen (Num. 32:20ff.). The Lord included this provision not only for Reuben and Gad but also for half of the tribe of Manasseh (Num. 32:33).

Now to these tribes, Joshua says, 'Remember.' What were they to remember? The word God gave them through Moses. Again we find clear evidence that the Book of the Law had not departed from Joshua's mouth (Josh. 1:8) as Joshua paraphrases Deuteronomy 3:18-20 for these tribes: 'The LORD your God is providing you a place of rest and will give you this land' (verse 13b; cf. Deut. 3:18). These words of promise reminded them of their commitment and sustained their faith that they would return to their families and herds just as God had said. God's word gave them not only direction but also encouragement and hope.

Scripture will function this way in our lives, too, if we take care to remember it. We remember Scripture when we turn its precepts and promises over and over in our thoughts and ask for the faith to believe and act upon them. To remember the word of the Lord requires both study and a resolve to obey. It is an exercise of faith. In essence, God's instructions to us are no different than his instructions to Joshua to meditate on the Book of the Law day and night (1:8).

In verses 14-15a, Joshua reiterated the stipulations originally given by Moses. 'Your wives, your little ones, and your livestock shall remain in the land that Moses gave you beyond the Jordan' (verse 14a; cf. Deut. 3:19). These were the conditions Reuben, Gad, and half-Manasseh had originally agreed to, and, now that the time had come, Joshua reissued these words as a command. They were permitted to leave their families and livestock behind to occupy the land and to keep them safe from the ensuing battles, but the men of war had to join the fight.

'But all the men of valour among you shall pass over armed before your brothers and shall help them' (verse 14b; cf. Deut. 3:18). These 'men of valour' (or 'heroes of ability') were well-equipped, well-able, well-trained men who would prove to be an asset to the nation. We later learn in Joshua 4:12-13 that this group of mighty men numbered 40,000.

The eastern tribes were not to relinquish their duty 'until the
LORD gives rest to your brothers as he has to you' (v. 15; cf. Deut.
3:20). Reuben, Gad, and eastern Manasseh had already taken part
of the land. Numbers 32:4 refers to the places 'that the LORD struck
down before the congregation of Israel'. They had already defeated
Sihon and Og and taken their territory. Those victories were a
foretaste of complete conquest to come (Num. 21:21-35). The Lord
would continue to strike down Israel's enemies, just in a different
location. All of the congregation of Israel fought east of the Jordan.
Now all of the congregation must fight on the west as well until the
conquest was complete. After they had fulfilled their obligations,
then—and only then—would the eastern tribes return home. They
could then possess the land God had given them. As the narrative of
Joshua progresses, we see in these tribes a remarkable group of men
who obeyed the Lord. They were faithful to the end. Only after the
victory was won and the land allotted to the various clans would
they turn east and head toward home (cf. Josh. 22:4ff.).

The transjordanian tribes possessed a remarkable sense of unity
and commitment. Although the Jordan River functioned as a
natural barrier between them and the majority of Israel, they refused
to let it be an obstruction to the work of God. The unity of the
Lord's old covenant people should serve as a valuable lesson to us,
his new covenant people. In the providence of God, cultural and
denominational differences exist throughout the visible church. The
invisible or universal church, however, exists as one body in Christ
Jesus. Jesus himself stressed this truth in his high priestly prayer in
John 17:20-26. He asked the Father to make his church one just as
he and his Father are one (v. 21).

The *Westminster Confession of Faith* expresses this truth so well:

> All saints, that are united to Jesus Christ their Head, by His Spirit,
> and by faith, have fellowship with Him in His graces, sufferings,
> death, resurrection, and glory: and, being united to one another in
> love, they have communion in each other's gifts and graces, and are
> obliged to the performance of such duties, public and private, as do
> conduce to their mutual good, both in the inward and outward man.
>
> Saints by profession are bound to maintain an holy fellowship
> and communion in the worship of God, and in performing such

34

other spiritual services as tend to their mutual edification; as also in relieving each other in outward things, according to their several abilities and necessities. Which communion, as God offereth opportunity, is to be extended unto all those who, in every place, call upon the name of the Lord Jesus.[1]

Are you a Christian? Do you think of yourself as 'in Christ', or one with the Saviour? If you can answer *yes* to those questions, then how do you look at your brothers and sisters in Christ? Do you see yourself united to them in love? Do you feel the responsibility to do as much as you can to promote their faith and encouragement in the gospel? If God has called you by his word to salvation in his Son, then he has called you to live in the community of the covenant, the church, and to exercise your gifts for its well-being (1 Cor. 12:7-12).

Speech Three: Yes, sir!

In the third speech (verses 16-18), we no longer hear the words of Joshua; instead, we hear the response of the tribes. This raises the question, however, 'Which tribes?' Who are the 'they' in verse 16 who answer Joshua? Some commentators argue that the plural verb represents all Israel.[2] Given the immediate context, though, it seems best to read this as the response of Reuben, Gad, and half-Manasseh. That does not mean, of course, that all of the tribes should not or did not respond in the same way. If the eastern tribes promised such comprehensive obedience as we find in verse 16, how much more should those entering Canaan pledge the same?[3]

What these tribes pledged was an unqualified willingness to obey everything Joshua commanded. 'All that you have commanded us we will do, and wherever you send us we will go' (verse 16). No questions asked. No balking at the orders. 'Sir, you tell us what to do, where to go, command us as you wish, and we promise that there will be no insubordination.' They recognize Joshua's God-ordained leadership. No task was too much to ask; no place was too far to go. They will do whatever Joshua requires.

[1] *Westminster Confession of Faith*, 26.1-2.
[2] See Howard, *Joshua*, 92-93, 94 and Madvig, *Joshua*, 258.
[3] Hubbard, *Joshua*, 86-87.

This kind of unquestioning obedience is the response every
Christian should have to the Lord Jesus. When I was a child, I
was afraid to say to the Lord, 'I'll go wherever you want me to go'
because I was sure that God would send me as a missionary to some
snake-infested jungle. For the record, I hate, loathe, detest, despise,
abhor, and generally dislike even the thought of a snake! So I ended
up praying things like, 'Lord, Europe would be nice. I could serve
there. England or Scotland sound like great places. Or better yet,
Ireland! I've heard there are no snakes in Ireland. I surrender to go
anywhere in Ireland!'

My childish anxiety resulted in some foolish praying, but we all
fear basically the same kind of thing, don't we? We're afraid that
God is going to call us to do something that will be too hard, too
unpleasant, or too unsuited to our personality. We're afraid that
he will ask too much. The transjordanian tribes agreed to do what
Joshua said because he spoke the word of God to them. They agreed
to go wherever he directed because the Lord had promised to be
with them. With the Bible to guide you and God to be with you,
you never need to fear saying, 'Whatever, wherever, whenever, Lord.
Just say the word.'

Have you ever surrendered your life to Christ like that? How can
you know if your submission is real or an empty profession? Ask
yourself this question, 'Do I submit to the other authorities God
has placed in my life?'

After promising obedience, the tribes reiterated their pledge and
prayed for God's blessing. 'Just as we obeyed Moses in all things, so
we will obey you. Only may the LORD your God be with you, as
he was with Moses' (verse 17)! They undertake to be just as faithful
to their new leader as they were to the old one. They assure Joshua
that they will be the least of his troubles. He should have no worries
about their allegiances. They will remain loyal to him.[1]

---

[1] Howard sees this promise as less than encouraging since the tribes did not
follow through completely with their obligations and 'fully obey' either Moses or
Joshua. Howard, *Joshua*, 94-95. Calvin, however, has a different interpretation. 'If
it is objected that there is little modesty in their boast of having been obedient
to Moses whom they had often contradicted, I answer, that though they did not
always follow with becoming ardour, yet they were so much disposed to obey, that

The tribes also expressed their desire for God to remain with Joshua.[1] The first thing we should note about this wish is that it reflects God's pledge in verse 5. The Lord had already said, 'Just as I was with Moses, so I will be with you.' Second, they had recognized God's presence with Moses. They had no doubts about the power of God in his ministry. Third, the well-meaning promises made by the people were not Joshua's guarantee of success; God's presence was his hope. He hopes that the people will follow through on their commitment, but whether through their obedience or in spite of their disobedience, the Lord will ensure Joshua's triumph.[2]

What a great thing this was to say to Joshua! These people were not stuck in the past, longing for the good old days of Moses. They recognized God's providence and forward movement in redemptive history. They were ready to get in line with what God was doing to settle his people in the land of promise, fulfil his covenant, and move them a step closer to the coming of their Messiah.

But what if someone wouldn't obey? What would happen to him? Rebellion and disobedience would not be tolerated. 'Whoever rebels against your commandment and disobeys your words, whatever you command him, shall be put to death' (verse 18a). When the

---

their moderation was not only tolerable, but worthy of the highest praise, when it is considered how proudly their fathers rebelled, and how perversely they endeavoured to shake off a yoke divinely imposed upon them. For the persons who speak here were not those rebellious spirits of whom God complains (Psalm 95:8-11) that he was provoked by them, but persons who, subdued by the examples of punishment, had learned quietly to submit.' John Calvin, *Commentaries on the Book of Joshua*, trans. by Henry Beveridge (1855; repr. Grand Rapids: Baker, 1979), 38.

[1] There is some question at this point about the form and translation of the verb *yihyeh*. Is it a jussive (*may he be*) or an indicative (*he will be*)? In other words, do the tribes express a wish/prayer or a statement of fact? David Howard believes it is an indicative and hence a future of certainty. Howard, *Joshua*, 96. All the major English versions (ESV, KJV, NASB, NIV, NLT, NET, RSV, NRSV), however, take it as a jussive and translate it with the word *may* or its equivalent. The LXX uses the imperative *esto* to express the idea of a wish. The Vulgate, on the other hand, translates the verb as present, *sit* (*is*) rather than future, *erit* (*will be*). I believe the best conclusion to this question is to take the verb as a jussive and have thus followed the translation of the ESV.

[2] According to Pitkänen, 'The qualifier *raq* (cf. v. 7) in verse 17 calls for Yahweh's help.' Pitkänen, *Joshua*, 117.

earlier generation of Israelites rejected God's promise and failed to invade the land, they all died in the wilderness (see Deut. 2:14-18). Disobedience would bring a death sentence now just as it had then. What lies beneath this pledge is the principle that the Lord will not hold anyone guiltless who breaks his law. Within a few short weeks Israel would see this truth played out in the death penalty enacted against Achan (7:10-26).

The text describes those who disobey as rebellious. A rebel is an obstinate person who is unwilling to listen and actively rejects what he does hear. God intends for us to obey his word. His demands for obedience are not those of a tyrant who must have his own way but those of a loving Father who knows what is best for his children. To turn a deaf ear to God's word is to reject his love.

Do you obey God? Have you heeded his call to come to Christ for salvation (Matt. 11:28)? If the rejection of Joshua's commands brought death, how much more serious is it if we reject the word of Christ and the offer of grace? The author of Hebrews writes, 'Therefore we must pay much closer attention to what we have heard, lest we drift away from it. For since the message declared by angels proved to be reliable, and every transgression or disobedience received a just retribution, how shall we escape if we neglect such a great salvation' (Heb. 2:1-3)?

Finally, reflecting God's three-fold call to courage in the first half of the chapter, the eastern tribes called on Joshua to be strong, resolute, and brave. 'Only be strong and courageous' (verse 18b). Here the word *only* intensifies the force of the command. 'This is essential, Joshua. Above all else, be valiant!'

I want you to notice two important lessons in the final sentence of verse 18. First, the people used God's word to encourage their leader (repeated here from verses 6, 7, 9). They simply reiterated what God had said—bare, unadorned, but powerful! When it comes to encouraging other believers to trust the Lord and serve him, we don't have to be clever and inventive. Just patiently and kindly speak Scripture into someone's life, and watch its power at work. Second, here we find the way godly people should respond to authority: with submission, prayer, and encouragement. Is this pattern apparent in the way you respond to the leadership God has placed in your life?

During the days of the judges, a young boy named Samuel lived at the Lord's house in Shiloh. One night he heard a voice calling to him, and he thought that it was his guardian, Eli. After going to Eli three times to see what he wanted, the old priest realized that Samuel was hearing the voice of God. He told the boy, 'Go, lie down, and if he calls you, you shall say, "Speak, Lord, for your servant hears"' (1 Sam. 3:9).

What are you doing with God's word? Are you receiving it? Submitting to it? Acting on it? Encouraging others with it? Ignoring it? Disobeying it? Rejecting it? When God speaks, he wants you to know and do his will. That's why he has given you the Scriptures. Will you open your Bible and lift your heart in prayer to say, as Samuel did, 'Speak, Lord, for your servant hears'?

4

Rooftop Revival
Joshua 2:1-24

Rahab said to the men, 'I know that the LORD *has given you the land, and that the fear of you has fallen upon us, and that all the inhabitants of the land melt away before you. For we have heard how the* LORD *dried up the water of the Red Sea before you when you came out of Egypt, and what you did to the two kings of the Amorites who were beyond the Jordan, to Sihon and Og, whom you devoted to destruction. And as soon as we heard it, our hearts melted, and there was no spirit left in any man because of you, for the* LORD *your God, he is God in the heavens above and on the earth beneath.'* (Josh. 2:9-11)

I love a good spy story. Whether it is an Alistair MacLean novel, a classic film like *The Spy Who Came in from the Cold*, or the real-life drama of Aldrich Ames, I am fascinated by the covert operations, the intrigue, the tension and suspense. Joshua 2 is a *great* spy story. Here we find the elements of a classic tale of espionage. Two men from Israel with concealed identities sneak into the city of Jericho. Their cover is blown, and a search party deploys directly under the king's authority. And what's a good spy story without a beautiful woman? Rahab, *femme fatale*, Jericho's Mata Hari, concealed the spies under stalks of flax and turned traitor to her own people.

As Israel prepared to march westward into Canaan, Joshua did what any good general would do: he reconnoitred the situation.

Sending his spies to Jericho was not due to a lack of faith. The Lord had not yet revealed to Joshua the unique plan of attack for the first battle (cf. 6:1-7). On Joshua's part, he simply acted prudently to prepare for whatever might lie ahead. God would fight for Israel, but Israel would have to wield both wisdom and the sword.

The basic plot line of the narrative looks like this: two Israelite spies hide out at the house of a prostitute named Rahab. Though a search party looks for them, Rahab willingly hides the men, transfers her allegiance to Israel, and sends the spies away safely. As a result of this covert mission, 'Operation Flax Stalk', Rahab's family came to be a part of Israel. Yet this chapter does much more than simply offer an etiology for some Canaanite co-existence among God's people. The spies' mission was to find out about the conditions of the land. What was the geography like? What were the people like? What could the Israelites expect to face once they crossed the Jordan River? That was the spies' purpose, a fact that both the opening and closing verses of the chapter confirm.

As a result of their reconnaissance, the spies discovered that the people of Canaan were afraid. They had heard about the great things God had done for Israel, and their hearts melted within them. Though the various nations shared a common sense of dread, each nation reacted very differently to it. Later in the book, we will discover that fear led the Gibeonites to surrender without as much as a skirmish (Josh. 9:22-27) while others turned against Israel with a brutal ferocity (Josh. 10:1ff.). In the case of Rahab, however, her fear led eventually to her conversion and the rescue of her family. Knowledge of the Canaanites' fear provided encouragement to the spies, and thus to Israel as a whole, to march forward to conquer. As we follow the action in Joshua 2, we will see God's saving acts both compel and strengthen the faith of his people.

Rahab's deception: implicit faith

While most of this chapter consists of dialogue between Rahab and the spies, the first seven verses give us an introduction and overview of the situation. From east of the Jordan, at a place called Shittim, Joshua launched a scouting mission into Canaan. Shittim had played a significant role in Israel's wilderness wanderings. When camped there years earlier, the men of Israel committed immorality with the women of Moab and worshipped Baal rather than the Lord (Num. 25:1-9). For their sin, 24,000 Israelites perished. Now, back at a place that held strong memories of sin and suffering, a chastened and repentant nation is ready to follow the Lord.

Like Moses thirty-eight years earlier, Joshua realized the necessity of assessing the situation at hand. A secret mission[1] was in order to prepare for the coming invasion. Joshua sent two men to spy out the land, especially Jericho (verse 1). No sooner do we learn their destination than we discover that they went to Rahab's house. Why that particular house? Did they dash into a dark alley to avoid detection and find themselves in the red light or, in this case, the 'red rope district'?[2] Whatever brought them to Rahab's door, for their part it was a smart move. Two strangers in town staying at the local brothel would be neither unusual nor noteworthy. It was a good cover. 'They went where they could easily "get lost", where they could find shelter with some degree of freedom. There is no place like a harlot's house for people coming and going. There is no indication whatever that they went there for any immoral purpose; this simply does not exist in the story.'[3]

Though Rahab's house was a good choice for a hideout, something went terribly wrong. The text never indicates how, but in some way it was discovered who these men were ('of Israel'), what they were up to ('to search out the land'), and where they were staying ('your [Rahab's] house'). A good cover was blown, and the news went straight to the top. Someone informed the king of Jericho about their presence. Who told on these men? A nosey neighbour? A sycophant skulking in the streets looking for some way to gain the king's favour? The text passes over that detail without the slightest mention. It obviously isn't important. The main thing to know is

---

[1] The LXX omits the word *secretly* perhaps because the underlying Hebrew term *heresh*, occurs only here in the Old Testament and the translators did not understand its meaning.

[2] P. Bird, 'The Harlot as Heroine: Narrative Art and Social Presuppositions in Three Old Testament Texts,' *Semeia* 46 (1989): 130, n.34. Quoted in Hubbard, *Joshua*, 126.

[3] Francis A. Schaeffer, *Joshua and the Flow of Biblical History* (Wheaton: Crossway, 2004), 79.

that the king immediately dispatched a search party to look for these nefarious visitors (verses 2-3).

Upon arriving at her house, the king's officers informed Rahab that the two men who, as they thought, had sought her services were not just a couple of lonely strangers in town. They had come to scout out the land in preparation for the upcoming Israelite invasion. They demanded, therefore, that she hand them over to the proper authorities (verse 3).

With the search team inquiring at Rahab's door, the air grew thick with tension. How would she respond to their demand? Before we learn the answer to that question, the narrator takes us behind the scenes. We can begin to guess what Rahab will say because she had already hidden the spies (verse 4). Was she tipped off that the king's men were coming? Perhaps. I'm more inclined to think, however, that the text places some emphasis here on her having already hidden the men to indicate that she knew what their business was about and was willing to join sides with them. Though these two men had come to a prostitute's house, they were not a part of her clientele.

That, of course, is not what she tells the king's men. When asked about the Israelites she replied, 'Sure, there were a couple of guys here.' But not to blow their cover further, and in keeping with what one would expect from the selfishly anonymous sex trade she adds, 'but I don't know where they were from' (verse 4).

The ruse continues as Rahab pretends to cooperate and 'explains' what happened next. 'It was dark and time for the gate to close, so the men left town. But they couldn't have gone too far. I'm sure that if you hurry you can catch them' (cf. verse 5). Her story was entirely believable and, with the added flourish of 'they just left', the men of the search party conclude that they shouldn't waste time chatting on the doorstep. Rahab's diversion tactics went without a hitch, and she was quickly rid of the inquirers.

Meanwhile, back on the rooftop, verse 6 provides us with more details about how Rahab hid the spies, a fact already mentioned in verse 4. These undercover agents were under cover. Earlier Rahab had arranged stalks of flax on the roof, apparently to dry them, so she used these to conceal the men.[1]

---

[1] 'Some evidence confirms its [flax] cultivation in pre-Israelite Canaan, but the

The king's troops pursued the spies on the logical route toward the fords of the Jordan River (verse 7a). If the men had come from Israel's camp on the eastern side of the river, then the search party naturally assumed that, having obtained whatever information they came for, the spies would head back to the camp with their report.

Where is Rahab, spiritually, in all of this? Clearly she evidences a new commitment and a radical shift in loyalty. Rather than siding with her king, she acts on behalf of enemy agents. Hebrews 11:31 identifies her friendly welcome of the spies as an indicator of her faith: 'By faith Rahab the prostitute did not perish with those who were disobedient, because she had given a friendly welcome to the spies.' This occurrence of her name in Hebrews 11 aligns her with other great men and women of faith such as Abraham, Sarah, and Moses. It is clear that the New Testament recognizes her actions as those of a true believer.

That raises the question, however, 'What are we to make of Rahab's deception?' Do we condemn her lie but praise her faith? This was Calvin's solution to the dilemma. He recognized the mixed nature of her response. No one's actions, motives, or faith are ever completely pure. Rahab was right to believe God was on Israel's side but wrong to deceive the king's men.[1]

On the other hand, is it possible to see Rahab's actions as part-and-parcel of war's necessary subterfuge? Were Rahab's deeds any different from Corrie ten Boom's family hiding Jews from Nazi Stormtroopers during World War II?[2] If members of Al-Queada came to your door and demanded to know the whereabouts of your family, would it be a sin to say, 'They're not here'? These ethical

reference here may simply be to wild flax that Rahab harvested and laid out on the roof to dry. Wild flax is typically scarce, so its availability as a hiding place here suggests a providential stroke of good luck. The piles happen to be there just when they are needed.' Hubbard, *Joshua*, 117-18.

[1] 'And still the act of Rahab is not devoid of the praise of virtue, although it was not spotlessly pure. For it often happens that while the saints study to hold the right path, they deviate into circuitous courses.' Calvin, *Comm. Joshua*, 47.

[2] The fascinating account of the ten Boom family, their Christian commitment, and their willingness to conceal Jews in their home in Holland during World War II may be found in Corrie ten Boom, *The Hiding Place* (Old Tappan, NJ: Revell, 1971).

questions are never easy to answer, and for every Christian arguing for one side of the issue, there is another Christian to defend the other side.[1] We should recognize Rahab's faith and thank God for it rather than trying to solve the conundrum of 'Was her lie a sin?' We should be thankful to God that those of us who live in Western nations have freedom of religion and are not faced with these kinds of decisions. We should also remember to pray for our brothers and sisters who suffer persecution and are forced to wrestle with similar dilemmas.

Not only should we ask where Rahab was during this time, we should also ask 'Where was God?' Verses 1-7 never mention the Lord but, like the book of Esther, his providential presence is unmistakable. God moves behind the scenes from Shittim to Jericho to the rooftop. Why did the spies go to Rahab's house and not another? How was Rahab able to be successful in her ruse? God was protecting his secret agents. Yet the fact that God was providentially controlling all of these events did not mean that the spies would be free from difficulties or immune to trying and stressful circumstances. They could, however, look back and testify to God's goodness to them every step of the way.

Isn't this the way we so often experience life? We look back at what has happened in our lives and see the hand of God at work. We may not know why certain things happen to us when they do any more than these spies knew who gave up their whereabouts. Providence can be puzzling, especially when we are going through a trial. Often it is only later that we can understand more of what God was doing. The Puritan, John Flavel, wrote, 'Sometimes providences, like Hebrew letters, must be read backwards.'[2]

Verse 7 concludes by informing us that as soon as the men of Jericho left the city in pursuit of the spies, the gate of the city closed for the night. The author intends for those words to grip us with dramatic intensity. Imagine the scene. Rahab may have been successful in temporarily hiding the spies, but now they're trapped! Two undercover agents hiding in a prostitute's house, and the city shut up as tight as a drum. This has all the makings of a great movie!

---

[1] For a survey of the various positions on Rahab's 'lie,' see Howard, *Joshua*, 106-12.
[2] John Flavel, *Works* (1820; repr. Edinburgh: Banner of Truth Trust, 2015), 5:284.

If the scenes of Joshua 2 were playing out before us as a film, then no doubt the sound track would at this point have reached a fevered pitch. Can you hear the fast tempo of the orchestra's string section and the clash of cymbals as the lock on the city gate slides into place with a thud?

Then, suddenly, the musical score modulates. The strings and percussion fade into the background as the strains of an organ grow louder, pumping out stanzas of 'Shall We Gather at the Rooftop?' At its nail-biting climax, this thriller turns into a church meeting!

Rahab's confession: explicit faith

'Before the men lay down', or before they went to sleep[1] under the stalks of flax, Rahab went back to the rooftop to speak with them (verse 8). Then, as suddenly as we learned of the spies' arrival at her house, we learn that Rahab has quite a grasp of Israel's theology.

The passage gives us no introduction to indicate what induced her confession of faith, but in verses 9-11 Rahab says some remarkable things. Here is the 'Jericho Confession of Faith.' First, she tells the men what she knows. She knows the name of God! He is not Baal or Anat or Chemosh or any of the other pagan gods of Jericho or Canaan. The God of Israel is the LORD, and he is sovereign and gracious. Her understanding of God's character becomes evident in the words 'the LORD has given you the land' (verse 9; cf. 1:2-3, 11, 15). As the owner of all things, a truth that becomes clearer in verse 11, he has the authority to dispose of the land as he wishes. And he wishes to give it to Israel.

The second thing Rahab knows is that 'the fear of you has fallen upon us, and all the inhabitants of the land melt away before you' (verse 10; Exod. 15:14-16; 23:27). A genuine alarm had struck the people of Canaan. In a remarkable turn of events from Israel's earlier history (Num. 13:28-29, 32-33), now the enemy quaked before them.

What would lead Rahab to these kinds of theological concepts and induce this kind of general dread among the population? Verse

---

[1] The Hebrew verb *shakab* can mean either to lie down or go to sleep. In certain contexts it can mean 'to sleep with' or 'have sexual intercourse.' There is no clear indication of sexual activity in this passage even though Rahab has been clearly identified as a prostitute.

10 answers the question: 'For we have heard how the LORD dried up the water of the Red Sea before you when you came out of Egypt, and what you did to the two kings of the Amorites who were beyond the Jordan, to Sihon and Og, whom you devoted to destruction.' The Canaanites knew about God's redemption of Israel from Egypt, and they knew about the Transjordanian conquest. These two pieces of evidence testify to the unstoppable power of God and his blessing on the military campaigns of the nation. Rahab effectively summarized all that the Lord had done for the people: the Exodus, which marked the beginning of Israel's journey from bondage while the defeat of the Amorite kings marked the end.[1] When the inhabitants of Jericho heard about these mighty saving acts of God for Israel, they lost all courage to fight. 'And as soon as we heard it, our hearts melted, and there was no spirit left in any man because of you' (verse 11a).

For Rahab, however, the effects of hearing about God's power went one step further. She was not just frightened by Israel's God. People were often afraid of the deities of competing city states. Rahab acknowledges more. She now recognizes that the Lord is the only God: 'for the LORD your God, he is God in the heavens above and on the earth beneath' (verse 11b). This description of God occurs three times prior to this in the Old Testament (Exod. 20:4; Deut. 4:39; 5:8). Each time it is a declaration of God's 'exclusive claims to sovereignty'.[2]

After confessing faith in the one true God, Rahab wants some assurance from these men that her loyalty to them will be repaid by rescuing her and her family when the invasion comes. She had saved their lives, now she asks for them to save her life and the lives of her family members. 'Now then, please swear to me by the LORD that, as I have dealt kindly with you, you also will deal kindly with my father's house, and give me a sure sign that you will save alive my father and mother, my brothers and sisters, and all who belong to them, and deliver our lives from death' (verses 12-13). Her request reflects the solidarity of the family unit that is often unappreciated in today's Western culture. She has put her faith in the Lord and asks that all her family come under the protection of that commitment.

[1] Hubbard, *Joshua*, 120.
[2] Howard, *Joshua*, 103.

The spies respond positively to this request but with one proviso, a condition they will later expand in verses 18-20. 'And the men said to her, "Our life for yours even to death! If you do not tell this business of ours, then when the LORD gives us the land we will deal kindly and faithfully with you"' (verse 14). They will save Rahab and her family if she doesn't reveal the reason they came to Jericho. Yes, she had dealt kindly with them. She displayed a loyalty one would expect from a marriage partner. Their instructions are for her to keep displaying this kind of fidelity to ensure their fidelity with her in turn and, ultimately, her rescue from the coming destruction.

What are we to make of Rahab's statements in these verses? Is she a conniving seductress who will say anything to save her own skin, or is she a genuine believer? As we noted earlier, Hebrews 11 recognizes her kindness to the spies as an evidence of faith. If her actions reveal her heart, then her words express her heart. The faith she displayed implicitly by hiding the spies she expresses explicitly in her confession.

Let us analyse her faith a little more. Knowledge of the Exodus and the events surrounding it indicate that Rahab understood something about God's power of redemption. The defeat of the Transjordanian kings testified to God's holiness and power. Her recognition of the Lord alone as God and her desire to be saved alive among his people clearly demonstrated a willingness to turn from her old life to the one true God. The sum of all of this is that, though couched here in Old Testament terms, Rahab came to saving faith.

Every Christian should know and believe the kernels of gospel truth that we find in Rahab's statements. God is holy and powerful. He will punish sinners (Heb. 9:27), but his power also makes a way of salvation through the person and work of his Son (Acts 4:12). The Lord alone is God, and those who turn to him for new life and confess him find salvation through the cross and resurrection of Jesus (1 Cor. 15:3-4). Everyone can experience the spiritual power of the Exodus through faith in Christ. To put these truths in explicitly New Testament terms, the apostle Paul wrote, 'if you confess with your mouth that Jesus is Lord and believe in your heart that God raised him from the dead, you will be saved. For with the heart one believes and is justified, and with the mouth one confesses and is saved' (Rom. 10:9-10).

Kent Hughes has served the Lord as a pastor and a leading Bible expositor in America. It was August 1955 when, as a twelve-year old boy, he went to summer camp in the Sierra Nevada Mountains and learned what it meant to confess Christ. Though under godly influences in his life and loved by the people of his church, he was still a stranger to grace. One evening the camp director, Verl Lindley, spent time with the campers going through key verses in the book of Romans to explain the gospel. Later that same night, Kent lay in bed with a flashlight re-reading those verses. As he went back over the promises of Romans 10:9-10, he believed the gospel. He believed that God had raised Jesus from the dead for him! He turned to the Lord and began confessing Christ as his Saviour, and he has been confessing him and preaching his word ever since.[1]

Have you ever confessed Christ? If not, isn't it time for you to turn, like Rahab, and trust in him? Perhaps you protest the idea that you need a Saviour just as much as a pagan prostitute did. 'Come on', you say. 'I'm not that bad!' Bishop H. C. G. Moule once countered that kind of objection by noting that everyone falls short of God's glory (Rom. 3:23). 'The harlot, the liar, the murderer are short of it; but so are you. Perhaps they stand at the bottom of a mine, and you on the crest of an Alp; but you are as little able to touch the stars as they.'[2]

Rahab's confession is also a confirmation of God's covenant with Abraham. A key part of that covenant was the promise of land (Gen. 15:18-21). But another crucial component was the guarantee that through Abraham all the nations of the earth would be blessed (Gen. 12:1-3). That promise finds its fulfilment in Christ who brings the Gentiles to faith (cf. Luke 2:32). In Rahab's conversion, we find a kind of firstfruits of that fulfilment. You and I are a part of the fuller harvest! God brought a Gentile (and a prostitute at that!) into his kingdom. Not only did she become a part of Israel, she was an

---

[1] Leland Ryken and Todd A. Wilson, eds., *Preach the Word: Essays on Expository Preaching: In Honor of R. Kent Hughes* (Wheaton: Crossway, 2007), 261-62.

[2] Handley C. G. Moule, *The Epistle of St. Paul to the Romans* (London: Hodder and Stoughton, 1894), 97.

ancestor of David and of David's great son, Jesus (Ruth 4:18-22; Matt. 1:1-6)!

One other element we should not overlook is the promise of the spies to Rahab. In response to her request and fidelity to them, they swore to 'deal kindly and faithfully' with her (verse 14). The words 'kindly and faithfully' translate two of the most important theological terms in the Old Testament. The sentence reads literally 'we will do with you loyalty and truth.' Loyalty is a covenant word, a word that means 'merciful faithfulness'. Truth is the revelation of God's character and purposes. The juxtaposition of these terms, which occurs several times in the Old Testament,[1] comes into the New Testament as 'grace and truth'. For example, 'And the Word became flesh and dwelt among us, and we have seen his glory, glory as of the only Son from the Father, full of grace and truth' (John 1:14). 'For the law was given through Moses; grace and truth came through Jesus Christ' (John 1:17). Joshua's secret agents promised to Rahab what all of God's people ultimately find in the Lord Jesus. All the promises of God find their 'yes' in Christ (2 Cor. 1:20). In him we have a Saviour who deals kindly and faithfully with us.

Rahab's rope: active faith

Having heard Rahab's newfound commitment to the Lord and his people, the spies set about their escape. Rahab's house was built into the city wall, perhaps a casement wall. As a result of its position on the city's periphery, a window provided access into the countryside. Using a rope, she let them down to freedom (verse 15). Her advice to the men was, 'Go into the hills, or the pursuers will encounter you, and hide there three days until the pursuers have returned. Then afterward you may go your way' (verse 16). Why the hills? They lay to the west of the city, the opposite direction the king's men went to search for them (verse 7).

Before the spies rappelled down the city wall and made their exit, the conversation turned again to the rescue of Rahab's family and the conditions she and her family must meet, an expansion on verse

---

[1] See, for example, Gen. 24:27; 32:10; Exod. 34:6; 2 Sam. 2:6; 15:20; Psa. 25:10; 40:10, 11; 57:3; 61:7; 85:10; 86:15; 89:14; 92:2; 117:2.

14. The men declare that they will be guiltless with regard to the oath that Rahab has made them swear (verse 17). In other words, they plan to keep their part of the bargain. But she must also do certain things. When Israel enters the land, she is to tie a scarlet cord in the window of her house, and she is to gather all her family under her roof (verse 18).

Once her family is in the house, it will be essential for them to stay there. Only if they remain with Rahab can the spies guarantee their safety. The spies promise to protect her family so long as they remain with her. If anyone goes outside, he or she will have to bear the consequences. The words are those of a blood-guilt oath. 'Then if anyone goes out of the doors of your house into the street, his blood shall be on his own head, and we shall be guiltless. But if a hand is laid on anyone who is with you in the house, his blood shall be on our head' (verse 19).

The spies then remind Rahab that she must not reveal what they have been up to. They reiterate that if the conditions are not met, they will not be held accountable for what happens to her or her family. If she breaks faith with them, then the deal is off. She is to remain faithful and thus demonstrate the genuineness of her commitment to Israel and the Lord (verse 20; cf. verse 14).

Rahab readily agreed to the conditions. 'And she said, "According to your words, so be it." Then she sent them away, and they departed. And she tied the scarlet cord in the window' (verse 21). After the spies left, we see how serious Rahab was and how intent she was to obey their instructions. She did not wait until the army of Israel is outside the gates of the city. She immediately tied the cord in the window. Rahab's deeds in these verses demonstrate that the faith she confessed in verses 8-14 was genuine. She demonstrated her faith by her works. In fact, James uses her as an example of doing just that. In chapter two of his letter, he argues that living faith, a faith that produces righteous actions, is the only true saving faith. He sees in Rahab just that kind of faith. 'And in the same way was not also Rahab the prostitute justified by works when she received the messengers and sent them out by another way' (James 2:25)? What she did proved the reality of what she professed.

In those closing moments at her house, Rahab seals her defection to Israel by lowering the spies down the city wall and tying the scarlet cord in the window.

On March 6, 1967, Svetlana Alliluyeva walked into the United States Embassy in New Delhi, India, and requested political asylum as a defector from the Soviet Union. You may never have heard of Svetlana, but you probably recognize the name of her father, Joseph Stalin, the Soviet Premier from 1941 to 1953. Why do people defect from their countries? Often several reasons come into play. For Svetlana, her father had forbidden a romance and marriage, and then the man she loved died. But at the bottom of it all was her longing for change and freedom. Once she arrived in America, she publicly denounced the actions of her father and became a naturalized citizen. She lived in Wisconsin until her death in November 2011. Svetlana swore her allegiance to another country for the freedom it offered.

Why did Rahab defect to Israel? Many motives may have weighed in her mind. As a prostitute, she lived on the lowest rung of the Jericho social ladder. But in the end she wished for life and freedom for herself and for her family. She defected from the enemy to join the people of the Lord and experience the life and liberty offered by God.

If you are not a Christian, this is exactly what you should do. You should defect! Why would you keep serving your sin and Satan when he offers you no true freedom and will lead you to eternal death? Isn't it time to desert, to run for freedom and liberty and peace? That's what Christ offers you in his gospel (Gal. 5:1; Rom. 5:1).

The final scene in the house also brings Rahab's scarlet cord to the foreground. What was this cord? Is it identical to the rope used in the escape? Perhaps, but the text uses different terms to describe these items. Was the scarlet cord an item of clothing or some accoutrement that served as a sign of Rahab's profession? These questions have no definitive answers. What we can say for sure is this—a scarlet cord would be easy to see and thereby enable the Israelites to identify Rahab's house and protect her and her family.

In addition, Rahab immediately tied the cord in the window and thereby indicated the hope she had that when the battle of Jericho commenced, the spies would keep their word.

Some interpreters have identified the cord in this story with the blood of Jesus. Both were red and associated with deliverance and safety. According to this interpretation, the cord was a type, a sign of salvation that prefigured the means of salvation, Christ's sacrifice on the cross. The text, however, gives us no indication that either Rahab or the spies made that kind of spiritual identification between the two. The cord was a sign of hope,[1] the sign of a promise, and all who gathered in Rahab's house under that sign would be saved. In that way, then, we may say that the cord points us to the assurance God gives us in his word that all who are in Christ are safe forever (cf. John 6:37; 10:28)!

The spies' report: emboldened faith

Following Rahab's advice, the spies fled into the hills and hid out for three days until the men pursuing them returned to the city. Their whereabouts were never discovered (verse 22). The Lord protected them throughout their mission. When the coast was clear, the two men returned to the Israeli camp and reported to Joshua (verse 23).

Verse 24 gives us the content of their report. 'And they said to Joshua, "Truly the LORD has given all the land into our hands. And also, all the inhabitants of the land melt away because of us."' Note the two vital elements that they learned from Rahab. First, they acknowledged that God has given them the land. Second, they reported that the people of the land melt away with fear because of Israel. Here was a great source of encouragement! As the warriors waited on the eastern banks of the Jordan, God was already on the move to bring victory to his people.

With 'Operation Flax Stalk' completed, the intelligence data the spies gathered would be put to good use. The spies had now seen what God could do! They saw the conversion of a Canaanite prostitute and an entire land trembling before them. God had confirmed and strengthened their faith. The nation was ready to move forward.

[1] Hubbard, *Joshua*, 126-27.

The proper response to Joshua chapter 2 is to sit back and marvel at the power of God. Providential power. Saving power. Protecting power. Overcoming power. Gracious power. The displays of God's powerful acts found here in the pages of holy Scripture ought to compel and strengthen our faith. Immerse your heart and mind in the Bible. Let God's word wash over you to confirm and embolden your faith. Find in the Scriptures the courage to step forward to victory in Christ!

5

Time to Go
Joshua 3:1-17

And Joshua said, 'Here is how you shall know that the living God is among you and that he will without fail drive out from before you the Canaanites, the Hittites, the Hivites, the Perizzites, the Girgashites, the Amorites, and the Jebusites. Behold, the ark of the covenant of the Lord of all the earth is passing over before you into the Jordan. Now therefore take twelve men from the tribes of Israel, from each tribe a man. And when the soles of the feet of the priests bearing the ark of the LORD, *the Lord of all the earth, shall rest in the waters of the Jordan, the waters of the Jordan shall be cut off from flowing, and the waters coming down from above shall stand in one heap.' (Josh. 3:10-13)*

The Jordan River and its spiritual imagery have played a significant role in our Christian hymnody. Out of the Welsh Great Awakening came William Williams' 'Guide Me, O Thou Great Jehovah.' With that great hymn we sing,

> When I tread the verge of Jordan,
> Bid my anxious fears subside;
> Death of death, and hell's Destruction,
> Land me safe on Canaan's side;
> Songs of praises, songs of praises
> I will ever give to Thee, I will ever give to Thee.

Samuel Stennett, an eighteenth-century Baptist pastor from England, penned the words,

> On Jordan's stormy banks I stand,
> And cast a wishful eye
> To Canaan's fair and happy land,
> Where my possessions lie.
> I am bound for the promised land,
> I am bound for the promised land;
> O who will come and go with me?
> I am bound for the promised land.

From the spirituals of the nineteenth century comes the haunting melody of 'Deep River.'

> Deep River,
> My home is over Jordan.
> Deep River, Lord.
> I want to cross over into campground.
>
> Oh, don't you want to go
> To the gospel feast;
> That promised land,
> Where all is peace?
>
> Oh, deep River, Lord,
> I want to cross over into campground.

The Jordan has played such a prominent role in our expressions of worship because we see a link, a common heritage and kinship, between the people of God in Israel and our own spiritual experience. It is as though we have joined them arm-in-arm to make the journey into the land. What was involved in that journey? What did it mean to Israel? And why is it of any concern to us? Why should Christians continue to sing about the Jordan? An examination of Joshua 3 will help us answer those questions.

The Jordan River served as one of the great boundary markers of the land of Canaan. Crossing the river into the land of promise is a major focus in the book of Joshua. In his opening speech to Joshua, the Lord said, 'Now therefore arise, go over this Jordan, you and all this people' (1:2). Chapter 3 now brings us to the actual event of that crossing and its significance for Israel.

We can easily divide this chapter into three major sections. The first six verses focus on the immediate preparation for crossing the

river. After relocating the camp, the officers and Joshua issue some
final instructions. The second section, verses 7-13, is in many ways
the heart of the chapter as the theological significance of the crossing
is unfolded before us. Finally, the event of the crossing itself serves
as the climax of the chapter as verses 14-17 describe what actually
took place.

Gordon McConville is right to describe the crossing of the Jordan
River as 'the most important single event in the book'.[1] Crossing
the Jordan demonstrates the miraculous power of the living God
and assures Israel that the Lord will give the nation victory over
its enemies. Its redemptive-historical significance, however, gives
it a more expansive message. From the vantage point of the New
Testament, we can see that crossing the Jordan typifies the work
of Christ which brings all believers into their inheritance in the
kingdom of God.

Preparation for the crossing

The spies returned from their mission to Jericho and reported to
Joshua all they had learned about the condition of the land and
its inhabitants. The Canaanites were confident that God had given
Israel the land, and they melted before the nation with fear (2:24).
With this favourable report to boost faith and morale in the camp,
Joshua is now ready to lead the people to victory.

The morning after receiving the report, Joshua got up early.[2]
The first task that lay before him was to move the Israelite camp
from Shittim to the banks of the Jordan. Israel had been camped at
Shittim (cf. 2:1; see also Num. 25:1; 33:49; Mic. 6:5; Joel 4:18), about
6 miles east of the river. Moving the entire entourage this distance
would have been a day's work, and having arrived at the Jordan they
set up camp once again and stayed there for three days (cf. 2a).

The temporal indicator 'at the end of three days' raises the
question as to whether these are the same three days referred to in
1:10, 11 or did Israel spend three days camped at the Jordan? It seems

---

[1] McConville and Williams, *Joshua*, 18.

[2] His early rising may be an indication of his eagerness to get the campaign
underway.

that this refers to three days they spent at the Jordan River. In that case, the three days of 1:10, 11 meant that they would leave Shittim within three days to go to the Jordan. These three days sitting on the banks of the Jordan would have given Israel time to contemplate just what lay ahead. The river was overflowing its banks (cf. verse 15), and there seemed to be no possible way to cross. The message 'no way to cross' would have been reinforced in the people's minds day after day as they encamped at the river's edge. The fact that they did not give up and turn back was in itself an evidence of God's grace, for God gives us the power and will to perform what he commands.[1]

At the end of the three days, the officers of the people went throughout the camp to prepare for the crossing. We have encountered these men prior to this in 1:10-11 where they had ordered the people to prepare food for the journey. Now they carry a different message among the tribes. 'As soon as you see the ark of the covenant of the LORD your God being carried by the Levitical priests, then you shall set out from your place and follow it' (verse 3). Once they caught sight of the ark on the move, the people were to break camp and follow. When the priests hoisted it to their shoulders and started to make their way forward, no one should hesitate.

Verse 3 contains the first reference in Joshua to the ark of the covenant, but throughout chapters 3 and 4 and at certain junctures in the conquest (especially chapter 6), it will play a prominent role. The ark is the chest God commanded Moses to make to house the Ten Commandments. It would later also contain Aaron's rod that budded and a pot of manna (Exod. 25:16, 21; 40:20; Heb. 9:4). The ark was not an idol; the Lord never intended it to be a picture of

---

[1] Calvin's comments at this point are significant. 'It is true, there were fords by which the Jordan could be passed. But the waters were then swollen, and had overflowed, so that they might easily prevent even men altogether without baggage from passing. There was therefore no hope, that women and children, with the animals, and the rest of the baggage, could be transported to the further bank. That, in such apparently desperate circumstances, they calmly wait the issue, though doubtful, and to them incomprehensible, is an example of faithful obedience, proving how unlike they were to their fathers, who, on the slightest occasions, gave way to turbulence, and inveighed against the Lord and against Moses. This change was not produced without the special agency of the Holy Spirit.' Calvin, *Comm. Joshua*, 58.

himself. It was, however, *the* symbol of God's presence in the midst of Israel. The ark also told the story of God's grace and forgiveness. Though it housed the holy law of God, the violation of which meant eternal damnation, the cover of the ark was called the 'mercy seat' (Exod. 25:17ff.). On the day of atonement, the high priest would sprinkle blood on it to symbolize God's forgiveness for all who had broken his commandments (Lev. 16:13-15). The ark, therefore, signified not just God's presence but his holy and gracious presence in the midst of his chosen people. From this point on in the story, this golden, holy chest will take centre stage. 'Watch for the ark! Follow the ark!' was the message.

Israel was not, however, to follow the ark too closely. 'Yet there shall be a distance between you and it, about 2,000 cubits in length. Do not come near it, in order that you may know the way you shall go, for you have not passed this way before' (verse 4). The distance of 2,000 cubits equals a little over half a mile. Maintaining this space would reinforce in the people's minds just how holy and transcendent God was, but it would serve another purpose as well. With the ark at such a distance ahead of the tribes, everyone could clearly see it. They needed to be able to keep their eyes on it in order to know which way to go. They had never travelled through this territory before. By keeping the ark ahead of them, they could easily detect any change in direction.

The clear lesson was that God was the leader of his people. The ark of the covenant represented him as he went before Israel. They got their direction from him. Their sole duty was to follow. Israel was ignorant both of the way and the final destination. Apart from a few spies, the people had never been in Canaan, and now a flooding river stood in their way. If God did not lead them, there would be no way forward. They would not know the path to pursue.

We no longer have the ark of the covenant, but the basic principles it taught remain the same. While we have no golden chest to follow, we do possess both what it contained and what it symbolized. It contained God's word and it pictured God's presence. Sometimes we might wish that a group of Levites would instruct us so that we could thereby be assured of God's will for us, but the reality is that we are not left without guidance any more than was Israel. When we need to know the way forward, we have the Scriptures that reveal to us the mind of God, and we have the Holy Spirit who uses the Bible to lead us in God's paths. 'When the people of Israel set out to cross the Jordan River at the beginning of their invasion of the promised land, *God himself went before them*, as must always be the case in any successful spiritual enterprise ... The only proper way to advance anywhere or at any time is by following God's lead. Only he can give victory.'[1]

Joshua then addressed the congregation and called on the people to consecrate or dedicate themselves to ritual purity, a holy frame of mind with a view toward holy actions. This kind of self-dedication to God prior to a special event prepared the bodies, hearts, and minds of the people to experience and receive what was about to happen. Several passages of Scripture highlight this concept. Moses consecrated the people prior to their receiving the law (Exod. 19:10, 14, 15). This also happened before they received God's gift of meat (Num. 11:18). Every Israelite was to consecrate himself before offering a sacrifice (1 Sam. 16:5). The theological basis for consecration is the holiness of God (Lev. 20:7). To encounter the holy God, one must be holy. Consecration would, in general, involve bathing, washing one's clothes, and abstaining from sexual relations. In this way the people prepared themselves to receive and participate in all that God was going to do. To consecrate oneself meant, however, more than just going through steps of ritual purity. It symbolized the preparation of the heart and indicated one's openness to what God was going to teach.[2]

Joshua clearly stated the reason the people were to consecrate themselves: 'tomorrow the Lord will do wonders among you' (verse 5). *Wonders* is a standard Old Testament word for miracles. God was about to perform some astounding feats for his people. They, therefore, must be ready to receive them. Old Testament expositor Dale Ralph Davis summarizes well the reasons for this kind of preparation: 'It is crucial that Israel recognize that what happens

[1] Boice, *Joshua*, 37.
[2] Woudstra, *Book of Joshua*, 81.

is indeed the Lord's work; and unless they have proper insight, expectancy, and preparation, they could see God's work and yet not understand its true value and significance.'[1] Spiritual preparation would sharpen their spiritual perception.

Next, Joshua turned his attention to the Levitical priests who would carry the ark (cf. Num. 4:15) and gave them their instructions. They were to lift the ark and carry it in front of the people (verse 6a). Though some time may have elapsed between Joshua issuing the command and the forward movement of the camp, the second half of verse 6 lets us know that the priests would indeed dutifully obey. At no point in the passage does anyone balk or even hesitate to follow through with what God had told them to do.

So what have we learned so far? Israel faced an impenetrable barrier to the promised land. They were, nevertheless, to consecrate themselves, keep their eyes on God, and be ready for him to do some miraculous things on their behalf. What he would do remained unclear, but the Israelites could rest assured that he would find a wary to fulfil his promises to them.

The Lord had hemmed in his people. Going back was not an option. Going forward was impossible. All they could do was seek to be holy, follow God, and trust that he would provide some way forward. Their forefathers had faced a very similar situation soon after leaving Egypt when Pharaoh's troops were in hot pursuit. Death lay behind them. The Red Sea stood before them. What were they to do? Moses' instructions were, 'Fear not, stand firm, and see the salvation of the LORD, which he will work for you today' (Exod. 14:13).

God often hems us into circumstances that are impossible for us to understand, unravel, solve, or even emotionally come to terms with. Fear grips us. Can you imagine the fear of facing the Red Sea or the raging Jordan? Movement either direction seemed impossible. When the Lord hems you in, he wants you to do two things. First, he wants you to be holy. Set apart the Lord God in your heart as holy (cf. 1 Pet. 3:15). Worship him. Love him. Pray that you will

---

[1] Dale Ralph Davis, *Joshua: No Falling Words. Focus on the Bible* (Fearn, Ross-shire: Christian Focus, 2000), 34.

not have harsh thoughts about God, the kind of wicked thoughts we are tempted to think when the pressures of our trials weigh us down and threaten to break us. Second, he wants you to keep your focus on him. Keep your eyes on the Lord by reading his word, and watch what he is doing. You have never been this way before. You don't know the way. It is time to trust his word and Spirit and wait upon him.

The theological significance of the crossing

The first six verses of chapter 3 provide us with a series of monologues. When we come to verse 7, the series continues but with an important shift in emphasis. Though verses 1-6 are not devoid of theology, as we have just seen, verses 7-13 take on a notable and specific theological emphasis. Joshua and the officers were the speakers in the preceding section, but now the voice of the Lord takes centre stage as he addresses Joshua (cf. 1:1). For a chapter and a half God has been silent as Joshua assumed command and sent out the spies. Now the Lord speaks again. 'Today I will begin to exalt you in the sight of all Israel, that they may know that, as I was with Moses, so I will be with you' (verse 7).

Why was God going to exalt Joshua in the eyes of the people? Because he had chosen him to be Israel's new leader, the mediator of his word, and the victor over the Canaanites. Joshua did not exalt himself or even ask for God to exalt him. The Lord alone had made this decision. The second half of the promise picks up on a theme first heard in chapter 1, 'Just as I was with Moses, so I will be with you' (1:5). 'The exaltation of Joshua is not for his own sake, but so that Israel may know that God is carrying out his purposes through him'[1] just as he had carried them out through Moses.

In the structure of redemptive history, God chooses to use certain men at key junctures to move his plan forward. Moses and Joshua were two such men. They were humble servants of God, but he made them great in the eyes of Israel in order to teach his people certain truths about salvation. This pattern finds its culmination in Christ when the prophecies of the old covenant reach their climax

---

[1] McConville and Williams, *Joshua*, 21.

in his cross and resurrection. Paul spelled this out for the church
in Philippi. Christ came as a humble servant and was crucified
(Phil. 2:5-8). But that was not the end of the story. As a result of
his humiliation, God exalted him. This is how Paul expressed it:
'Therefore God has highly exalted him and bestowed on him the
name that is above every name, so that at the name of Jesus every
knee should bow, in heaven and on earth and under the earth, and
every tongue confess that Jesus Christ is Lord, to the glory of God
the Father' (Phil. 2:9-11).

Just as God exalted Joshua to prove to Israel that he was using
him as his instrument of salvation and victory, so God the Father
has exalted his Son through his resurrection and ascension to
demonstrate that he accepted his work on the cross as payment in
full for the redemption of his elect. God exalted Joshua so that Israel
could see Jesus.

Having encouraged Joshua with this promise, the Lord
commanded him to have the priests carry the ark of the covenant
to the brink of the Jordan. When they come to the edge of the
water, they are to step in and stand still. Can you see how the Lord
is building the suspense among his people? Israel faces the flooding
Jordan. They are to watch for the priests and follow them. God is
going to do something wonderful. The priests are to walk right into
the waters of the river. If we are reading this text properly, we should
be moving to the edge of our seats waiting to see what God is going
to do next because the text is building and building to a climax.

As the suspense heightened, Joshua turned to Israel and addressed
the people: 'Come here and listen to the words of the LORD your
God' (verse 9). He summoned the people to draw near. They should
approach Joshua in order to hear what he has to say. But drawing
near is more than a physical movement to gain closer proximity. To
draw near reflects an attitude. It means to be diligent, to be earnest
and passionate about listening to God's word. This is the very same
approach we should always take when we have the occasion to hear
God's voice through the Scriptures. We have many opportunities
through daily reading, family worship, preaching, devotional books,
and commentaries to listen to the word of the Lord. We should take

full advantage of every opportunity we are given to draw near, to listen, and to heed the warning of Psalm 95:7-8, 'Today, if you hear his voice, do not harden your hearts.'

The message Joshua conveyed to Israel was a message of assurance. He promised them that they would come to know two things. First, they will know that the living God is in their midst. The people of Canaan worshipped a pantheon of pagan gods including Baal, Ashtoreth, Chemosh, and Anat. These gods, however, only lived in the imaginations of their devotees. The Lord, by contrast, is the living God, the God of all the earth (cf. verses 11, 13). Israel will know that he is with them, because he will do wonders among them (cf. verse 5). Their experience of his miraculous power will confirm Israel's faith and, as God would repeatedly warn, should serve to keep them from idolatry in Canaan (cf. Deut. 4:19; 17:3).

Second, they will also know that the living God is going to drive out their enemies. The seven nations listed in verse 10 are identical to the list in 24:11. Similar lists occur in the Pentateuch in connection with the land covenant promises (cf. Gen. 15:19-21; Exod. 3:8; 13:5; Deut. 7:1). Though not an exhaustive register of the land's inhabitants, these nations represent all of Canaan, the peoples whom God 'will without fail drive out from before you' (verse 10).[1]

Israel's entrance to the promised land was to be a faith-building experience. What God was about to do would assure them of what he could and would do in the future. This assurance would provide them with the spiritual strength they needed for the battles that lay ahead. Israel could move forward with confidence. They could face Jericho, Ai, Hazor, or any of the other Canaanite cities by looking back at what God had already done. The demonstration of his miraculous power would fortify their souls for battle.

Assurance functions in a similar way for us as Christians. When you know that you are a child of God, that the living Christ is your Saviour, you can face the trials and battles of life with the confidence

---

[1] The Hebrew text combines an infinitive absolute with a finite verb of the same root to read literally 'to dispossess he will dispossess'. This grammatical construction is one of emphasis to stress the absolute certainty of the action about to take place. For a fuller discussion of this construction and its significance, see Waltke and O'Connor, *Introduction to Biblical Hebrew Syntax*, 584-86.

that nothing can separate you from God's love. If God is for you, then nothing can be against you (Rom. 8:31-39). Assurance serves as a means of spiritual strength.

Having assurance, however, is not exactly the same as having faith. Assurance, in other words, is not of the essence of faith. A person may be a Christian and not be settled in his or her own mind and heart that things are right between him and God. The *Westminster Confession of Faith* explains that 'This infallible assurance doth not so belong to the essence of faith, but that a true believer may wait long, and conflict with many difficulties, before he be partaker of it.' That, of course, is not the ideal condition for the Christian life. So the Confession goes on to teach, 'yet, being enabled by the Spirit to know the things which are freely given him of God, he may, without extraordinary revelation, in the right use of ordinary means, attain thereunto. And therefore it is the duty of everyone to give all diligence to make his calling and election sure; that thereby his heart may be enlarged in peace and joy in the Holy Ghost, in love and thankfulness to God, and in strength and cheerfulness in the duties of obedience, the proper fruits of this assurance: so far is it from inclining men to looseness.'[1]

If you lack assurance, you should make every effort to come to a settled peace in your soul. One of the main ways to arrive at this peace is to focus on the promises of God, just as Israel did, just as the *Westminster Confession* encourages you to do. God promised to work miracles. Israel accepted that promise and marched forward in confidence. God has promised to save all who come to him through Christ (John 6:37; Heb. 7:25). If you have come to Christ as your hope of everlasting life, then embrace his promises as true of you. Be diligent to hear God's word, and stand upon it with confidence.

The suspense continued to build. Israel will know that the living God is among them, but how will they know? 'Behold, the ark of the covenant of the Lord of all the earth is passing over before you into the Jordan' (verse 11). To this point in the account, the ark has been called 'the ark of the covenant of the LORD your God' (verse 3) or simply 'the ark of the covenant' (verses 6, 8). Now the text adds

---

[1] *Westminster Confession of Faith*, 18.3.

an additional description, 'the ark of the covenant of the Lord of all the earth'. In verse 13, it is 'the ark of the LORD, the Lord of all the earth'. The Lord is the God of Israel, but he is also the sovereign of the universe (Psa. 97:5; Mic. 4:13; Zech. 4:14; 6:5). As Lord of all nations, he has the authority and power to dispossess them before Israel, drive them from the land, and give Canaan to his people as their inheritance.[1] The God of universal sovereignty would go before them *into* the river.

Joshua then called for Israel to select twelve men, one from each tribe (verse 12). The command is cryptic at this point in the narrative. These men will be the ones to gather the memorial stones, a point that will become clear in 4:2-3. For now it lends to the building suspense in the chapter.

Finally, we learn what is to happen in verse 13. When the priests carrying the ark step into the water, God will work his wonders (cf. verse 5). The river will cease to flow, and the waters north of the crossing will be dammed up like a dyke. Those flowing south of that point will go on their way. What God did for his people to bring them out of Egyptian slavery (Exod. 14:21-31), he would also do to bring them into the freedom of Canaan.

The crossing

The suspense that has been building now reaches its peak. Joshua finished his theological explanation of the crossing with the declaration, 'the waters of the Jordan shall be cut off from flowing' (verse 13). In the closing verses of the chapter, we see that promise fulfilled. Verses 14 and 15 provide the author with one last opportunity to heighten the anticipation. As the people pulled out from camp, the priests dipped their feet in the water's edge, but it was the time of the harvest flood, and the Jordan was a mighty, raging torrent due to the swell of melting snow and spring rains.[2] Yet the LORD is Lord of the harvest. He is Lord of the rivers and Lord of the seas (cf. Psa.

---

[1] Rahab clearly understood this truth when she confessed, 'For the LORD your God, he is God in the heavens above and on the earth beneath' (2:11).

[2] At flood stage, estimates of the river's width reach up to half a mile. Pitkänen, *Joshua*, 135.

29:3, 10; 33:7), and none of this would prove problematic to him.

When the priests stood in the Jordan, the waters stood. The text uses the same verb for both actions to draw the close parallel between the two events. The priests standing in the water was the cue for the water to stand up in a heap. God cut off the water (cf. verse 13). The author tells us that far north of where Israel was crossing, approximately 19 miles upstream at Adam,[1] a city near Zarethan, the waters stopped flowing. They dammed up as though held back by an invisible dyke. The water flowing south toward the Dead Sea rushed away leaving a wide swathe of dry land for Israel to cross.

What caused the waters to stop flowing? Should we attribute this to a landslide that temporarily blocked the river? Landslides that affect the river's flow are not unknown in that region.[2] While it is possible that God could have providentially timed a landslide to be his means of opening up the river to Israel, that need hardly be the case. God is the God who works wonders (verse 5). To believe in the God of the Bible is to believe in the miraculous. Besides, a landslide could hardly account for the instantaneous dry land Israel was able to traverse (verse 17). Like their forefathers, they had stood still to see the salvation of God (cf. Exod. 14:13). They had followed the Lord into the river only to see the wonder of his miraculous power part the waters and lead them into Canaan.

Joshua, Jesus, and the Jordan

Joshua 3 is clearly about the prominence and power of God to bring his people into Canaan, but how does this message fit into the bigger picture of redemptive history? Through the Jordan, God brought his people into the land he had promised them in the Abrahamic covenant. That is where the Israelites had been headed ever since they left Egypt. The Jordan was the path to reach their inheritance. The imagery of this passage, therefore, operates on two levels. On the first level, the inheritance (Canaan) represents all that believers have in Christ. In him, we are the heirs of everlasting life

---

[1] Most commentators identify the city of Adam with the city of Damiyeh. Woudstra, *Book of Joshua*, 87. See also Pitkänen, *Joshua*, 136-37.

[2] Woudstra, *Book of Joshua*, 87, n.33.

(Rom. 8:17; Titus 3:7). But our inheritance is not something that we earn for ourselves. Christ had to pass through death (the Jordan) to procure it for us.

We see this portrayed wonderfully in the chapter. When the priests carried the ark of God into the Jordan, the Lord himself parted the waters and made the way of access into the land. Jesus, our priest, the very presence of God with us pictured in the ark's mercy seat, did the same for us through his crucifixion. He bore the full brunt of Jordan's deadly force and pushed it back so that we might be safe. Christ has stepped into the brink of the Jordan by his suffering and death on the cross. All that death threatened, all of its terror and finality and despair he overcame so that we might be free from its bondage to move from slavery unto freedom and death unto life. Isn't this what the author of Hebrews meant when he wrote, 'Since therefore the children share in flesh and blood, he himself likewise partook of the same things, that through death he might destroy the one who has the power of death, that is, the devil, and deliver all those who through fear of death were subject to lifelong slavery' (Heb. 2:14-15)? Christ's sacrifice has opened up the way into everlasting life. The death of Jesus, therefore, becomes our assurance that the living God is among us and will, without fail, drive out every spiritual force and foe marshalled against us.

It was through this 'crossing of the Jordan' that God exalted the Lord Jesus. Earlier we noted the connection between the exaltation of Joshua and the exaltation of Jesus. Through the miracle at the river, Joshua would be made high in Israel's estimation (verse 7). How much more so would Jesus? As a result of his death, 'God has highly exalted him and bestowed on him the name that is above every name' (Phil. 2:9). The Lord has raised Jesus and placed him at his own right hand as Lord and Saviour to all who will believe on him. Have you ever experienced God's gift of salvation through Christ? Do you know what it is to have an inheritance in him, the hope of everlasting life?

In the introduction to his book *Excellence: The Character of God and the Pursuit of Scholarly Virtue*, New Testament scholar Andreas Köstenberger recounts the days and weeks leading up to his conversion. During that time Köstenberger was a graduate student studying economics in Vienna. He found himself under conviction of sin yet trying to self-reform, trying to *be* a Christian but not yet understanding the gospel. One day, while eating his lunch by the Danube channel, he had a remarkable experience. He writes:

> at that moment, I felt immobilized on one side of a vast, unbridgeable gulf, desperately wanting to cross over to the other side yet being completely unable to do so. Who would take me across the river? I knew I couldn't do it on my own; it took me several months before I realized that it must be Jesus. Finally, I gave up all resistance, intellectual and otherwise, and abandoned myself completely to my Lord, who took me and brought me safely to the other side by virtue of what he had done for me on the cross.[1]

If you are not a Christian, will you turn to Christ? He is the only one who can carry you safely across the river. He has stepped into the waters of death for you to open up the way to God.

---

[1] Andreas J. Köstenberger, *Excellence: The Character of God and the Pursuit of Scholarly Virtue* (Wheaton: Crossway, 2011), 20.

6

A Sermon in Stones
Joshua 4:1-24

'When your children ask in time to come, "What do those stones mean to you?" then you shall tell them that the waters of the Jordan were cut off before the ark of the covenant of the LORD. When it passed over the Jordan, the waters of the Jordan were cut off. So these stones shall be to the people of Israel a memorial forever.' (Josh. 4:6-7)

Nestled at the foot of Grandfather Mountain in western North Carolina lies a grassy field called MacRae Meadow. Each July thousands of tourists descend on that turf for the world's largest gathering of Scottish Highland clans. For a week the field is awash in a sea of tartans and colourful tents. The skirl of the bagpipes can be heard around the meadow during the day and around campfires at night. When the MacDonalds and MacLarens, Clan Lewis and Clan Ross, with many more beside, assemble for a week of games, education, entertainment, and heaping plates of steaming haggis, there is no better place to be!

But I have also been to the meadow in early spring. The crisp air, the bare trees, and the haunting stillness that lies over it present a stark contrast to the summer's festivities. Yet summer, spring, winter or fall two things in the meadow remain the same. Perched in distinct locations stand two cairns, piles of stones, erected as memorials. One cairn stands in memory of Agnes MacRae Morton, a founder of the games. The other is a clan cairn in which each stone represents

73

a different Scottish family. This second monument signifies that, though the names and relations are different, the people of Scotland and all their kith 'n kin from around the world have a common bond as a people of one land. The similarities between the clan cairn in MacRae Meadow and the tribal cairn set up at Gilgal are easy to see.

The events of Joshua 4 conclude the sequence that began at 3:1 as Israel moved their camp from Shittim to the edge of the Jordan River and three days later passed over into Canaan on dry ground. As we saw in the last chapter, crossing the Jordan River is the single most important event in the book, and that explains the reason Joshua gives an extended account of the occasion. Though chapters 3 and 4 cover the same event, they do so with two different points of emphasis. Chapter 3 focused on the ark of the covenant and the parting of the waters while chapter 4 turns the reader's attention to the twelve memorial stones Israel retrieved from the river.

Reading Joshua 4 is like using the fast forward and reverse controls on a CD or mp3 player. You may advance the player to listen to snippets of a later track only to reverse to an earlier song and listen to it in full. In this passage, the author will often jump ahead and refer to an event only to go back and fill in more details that led up to what he has already mentioned. For example, in 4:2 God commands Joshua to 'take twelve men from the people', but Joshua had already given that command back in 3:12. In 4:11, the ark passed over after all of the people made it safely to the other side. Later, however, in verses 15-18, we read the details of the priests carrying the ark up from the Jordan. This kind of narration, a literary technique called *prolepsis*, provides the author with a lively way to tell the story and underscores the most important aspects of what took place.

Through this back-and-forth retelling of the tale, the main point becomes clear. God instructed Israel to take twelve stones from the river and set them up in Gilgal as a monument. These stones from the Jordan would provide a means for remembering and testifying to the faithfulness and power of God. Furthermore, from a New Testament perspective, we can see that what God did for Israel he also does for the church. He provides many means by which we can remember his great works of redemption.

Stones from the Jordan

The opening words of chapter 4 tie the following events to those that precede them by an exact verbal repetition, 'When all the nation had finished passing over the Jordan' (verse 1; cf. 3:17). This double emphasis serves two purposes. First, it reinforces the fact that Israel did cross into Canaan on the bed of the Jordan River. Second, it calls attention to the fact that Israel is here first called a nation. Crossing the river was more than a means to get to the other side. It was a constitutive act. The people of God who wandered in the wilderness now become the nation of Israel with its own homeland to possess. Earlier passages in the Pentateuch refer to Israel's national status (Num. 14:12; Deut. 4:6-8), but they point to what God *will* do or what people *will* say about Israel. Israel officially becomes a nation when they step onto the western bank of the Jordan.

As the nation concluded its march into Canaan, we are introduced to another speech from the Lord to Joshua (cf. 1:1; 3:7). God tells his commander to select twelve men, one from each tribe, for a task.[1] Chapter 3 alluded to these men in verse 12 but never gave any explanation as to why Joshua should set them apart. Now it becomes clear just what they are to do. Once these men have been chosen, Joshua is to command them each to take a stone from the place where the priests stood in the river-bed on dry ground and to carry the stones to the place where they will set up camp for the night (verse 3). Having received his instructions from the Lord, Joshua summoned the tribal delegates (verse 4) and gave them specific instructions to follow. 'Pass on before the ark of the LORD your God into the midst of the Jordan, and take up each of you a stone upon his shoulder, according to the number of the tribes of the people of Israel' (verse 5).

From these instructions it becomes clear that the stones accomplished two things. First, they represented the entire nation of Israel. Joshua appointed a man from each of the twelve tribes. Each man in turn selected a stone to symbolize his tribe. The concluding phrase of verse 4 ('a man from each tribe') is repeated from verse 2,

---

[1] The command in Hebrew is plural. Though directed through Joshua, it was a message for the entire nation. Later, in verse 4, it will become clear that Joshua was personally responsible for appointing the men.

underscoring the representative character of the men and the stones they carry to the river-bank. In addition, the verbs translated 'bring them over' and 'lay them down' are terms that repeatedly describe Israel in the book. They are to make the stones *pass over* and cause them to *rest*, just as God's people would do (verse 3).

Second, the stones testify to the faithfulness and miraculous power of God. The tribal representatives took the stones from where the priests stood. The Lord wanted Israel to see the closest possible connection between those rocks and the miracle that had taken place. These were the stones from where the ark-bearing priests stood firmly on the Jordan's dry river-bed (verse 3). They represented the dried-up Jordan in the clearest possible way.

To this point in the narrative the instructions are rather pedestrian. Choose men, pick up stones, and take them to the river-bank. In verse 6, however, Joshua begins to unfold the purpose for this enterprise. These stones were to serve as a sign for the people. When the children ask their parents about the stones, they would serve as a means of instruction, a sign pointing to a greater truth. This is, after all, what signs do. They point to something else.

Several years ago my family and I visited the Grand Canyon. As typical tourists, we stopped and took pictures of the large sign at the park entrance. But what would you think if that had been the end of our vacation? 'How was our trip? Well, we saw the Grand Canyon National Park sign, took some pictures, bought T-shirts, and headed home.' You would be right to think that we had lost our minds. We did not travel all that way to see the park sign. The sign pointed us to something greater. It told us that we were at the Grand Canyon, but it was the canyon itself that we wanted to see.

These river-rocks pointed to something other than themselves. They were to direct people's attention to the great act of God when he dried up the flooding Jordan. These stones would guide people's minds and hearts to reflect on the historical event of the crossing, and they would provide a ready-made teaching opportunity when their children began to ask about them. That becomes clear in the rest of verse 6.

In anticipation of Israel's future settlement in Canaan, and with the implication that parents would bring their children to the

Jordan to see the sight of the crossing, verse 6 supplies us with the first question of the 'Canaan Catechism': 'What do those stones mean to you?'[1] The question implies that the stones have a personal significance. They do not just mean something; they mean something to *you* the parents. Even though years and generations may pass, Israel's connection to the memorial cairn and its significance was to have a personal meaning to everyone who identified himself as a member of the covenant nation.

What is the answer to the 'catechism' question? 'The waters of the Jordan were cut off' (verse 7). Twice the verse repeats the phrase for emphasis. The waters of the river *were cut off, were cut off.* The passive voice turns our attention away from the waters *per se* to the One who cut them off from flowing. They were cut off before the ark. We might well say that verse 7 is a summary of chapter 3.

Yet these stones were also more than a sign. They were a memorial to Israel forever (verse 7). As a sign, they pointed to God's faithfulness and power. As a memorial, they served a sacramental purpose. The stones not only helped Israel recall the Jordan crossing, they also helped later generations participate in all the benefits of the crossing, as the recollection of their great heritage provided a means of strengthening their faith. As they looked at the stones and heard the story, they could exercise faith in what God had done to bring his people into the land of promise. By believing that good news, the coming generations could identify themselves with all that God

[1] The stones at Gilgal were not the only thing Israelite children were to ask about. The entire Passover celebration was to be a teaching moment as they inquired into its significance. In Exodus 12:26-27, Moses instructed Israel to be prepared 'when your children say to you, "What do you mean by this service?" you shall say, "It is the sacrifice of the LORD's Passover…"' After they left Egypt, the Lord had each Israelite family dedicate the firstborn of their flocks, herds, and even of their family, to God. 'And when in time to come your son asks you, "What does this mean?" you shall say to him, "By a strong hand the LORD brought us out of Egypt, from the house of slavery."' (Exod. 13:14). Israelite children were also to ask about the law. 'When your son asks you in time to come, "What is the meaning of the testimonies and the statutes and the rules that the LORD our God has commanded you?" then you shall say to your son, "We were Pharaoh's slaves in Egypt. And the LORD brought us out of Egypt with a mighty hand"' (Deut. 6:20-21). All of these questions and answers relate, in one way or another, to the Exodus.

had done through this miracle. They could enjoy all the blessings their fathers had received when they crossed into Canaan.[1]

Children have a natural curiosity. They love to ask questions. 'What?' and 'Why?' are some of the first words in their rapidly expanding vocabulary. Parents and teachers need to find ways to channel that curiosity to inquire about the most important things. One of the primary ways to accomplish that is to use the signs and memorials that God has given us. Just as the Lord appointed stones from the Jordan to remind Israel of his great acts, he has also provided certain means or tools for the church to use, primarily the word of God and the sacraments.

How can any of us remember God's great acts in redemptive history? We are removed from the crucifixion and resurrection of Christ by almost two thousand years. Yet we remember them because we have a memory book, the Bible. When the apostle Peter wrote his second letter, one of his primary purposes for putting his words on paper was to provide a way for his readers to remember the truths he had taught them: 'Therefore I intend always to remind you of these qualities, though you know them and are established in the truth that you have. I think it right, as long as I am in this body, to stir you up by way of reminder, since I know that the putting off of my body will be soon, as our Lord Jesus Christ made clear to me. And I will make every effort so that after my departure you may be able at any time to recall these things' (2 Pet. 1:12-15). The Scriptures vividly and sufficiently portray everything that a Christian needs to know and remember for his or her walk with God (see 2 Tim. 3:16).

The sacraments also help us to remember. Both baptism and the Lord's Supper are signs that turn our attention to the work of Christ when he offered his broken body and shed blood for our salvation so that we might be cleansed from sin and engrafted into his body, the church. Jesus himself instructed us to take Communion in remembrance of him (1 Cor. 11:24-25). By these signs and memorials

---

[1] 'Remembering was a way for future generations to participate in the great acts that God had done for Israel.' Madvig, *Joshua*, 269. 'The notion of remembering in Hebrew is more than a calling to mind. It involves a remembering with concern; it also implies loving reflection and, where called for, a corresponding degree of action.' Woudstra, *Book of Joshua*, 92.

we can know what took place in the past; and by remembering, by recalling with faith and appropriation, we can participate in them. Parents, therefore, need to use these means of grace to instruct their children. There are many ways to accomplish this. Why not discuss the sermon or the Communion service at Sunday dinner? Ask, 'What did you understand about the message? What did you not understand?'

Our children should ask questions, and we should provide them with opportunities to ask them. Catechetical instruction is an excellent way to do this. Catechisms did not originate with the Roman Catholic Church, though many evangelicals mistakenly think that they did. Catechetical instruction involves a question and answer method of teaching which comes straight from the Bible as Joshua 4 clearly attests. In his good providence, God has given the church an excellent tool in the *Westminster Shorter Catechism* to instruct children (and adults) in the fundamentals of the faith.

This kind of grounding in the faith can shape an entire life. In an article entitled 'Is the Shorter Catechism Worthwhile?', Princeton theologian Benjamin B. Warfield writes,

> We have the following bit of experience from a general officer of the United States Army. He was in a great western city at a time of intense excitement and violent rioting. The streets were over-run daily by a dangerous crowd. One day he observed approaching him a man of singularly combined calmness and firmness of mien [bearing], whose very demeanour inspired confidence. So impressed was he with his bearing amid the surrounding uproar that when he had passed he turned to look back at him, only to find that the stranger had done the same. On observing his turning the stranger at once came back to him, and touching his chest with his forefinger, demanded without preface: 'What is the chief end of man?' On receiving the countersign, 'Man's chief end is to glorify God and to enjoy him forever'—'Ah!' said he, 'I knew you were a Shorter Catechism boy by your looks!' 'Why that is just what I was thinking of you,' was the rejoinder.

Warfield concluded, 'It is worthwhile to be a Shorter Catechism boy. They grow up to be men. And better than that, they are exceedingly apt to grow to be men of God. So apt, that we cannot afford to have them miss the chance of it.'[1]

For parents to instruct their children, however, the means of grace must first mean something to them. The word, the sacraments, prayer, and worship must play a significant enough role in the life of the family that one can, when asked, easily sit down with a son or daughter and say, 'I would love to answer your question.' The spiritual truth that lies behind all of this is that you can never lead a person beyond where you are in your own walk with the Lord. And that applies not only to parents but to elders, teachers, leaders, and anyone who wants to exert influence for the kingdom of God.

Joshua made the instructions clear, and in verse 8 the twelve stone-bearers comply: 'And the people of Israel did just as Joshua commanded and took up twelve stones out of the midst of the Jordan, according to the number of the tribes of the people of Israel, just as the LORD told Joshua. And they carried them over with them to the place where they lodged and laid them down there.' One of the most interesting features of this verse is that it attributes the action of removing the stones and transporting them to Gilgal to 'the people of Israel', not just the twelve men. This is another way that the text stresses the solidarity of the tribes and their representatives.

A second cairn?

The fact that the tribal delegates obeyed Joshua is not surprising. The theme of obedience runs through these chapters (cf. 1:10, 16; 2:21; 3:6, 14). But the fact that Joshua goes into the midst of the Jordan, where the priests have been standing, and sets up a twelve-stone monument is an unexpected turn of events (verse 9). Some commentators believe that ultimately only one memorial existed and that what we find in Joshua 4 are two different accounts that have been combined into one text.[2] In other words, ancient Israel

---

[1] B. B. Warfield, 'Is the Shorter Catechism Worth While?' in *Selected Shorter Writings of Benjamin B. Warfield,* ed., John E. Meeter (Phillipsburg: P&R, 1980), 1:383-84.

[2] David Howard does not believe the text is conflated, but he does believe that the most likely meaning of the passage is that there was only one stone memorial. Howard, *Joshua,* 136. Pitkänen believes 'that there has been some kind of confusion,

possessed a 'river memorial' text and a 'Gilgal memorial' text and elements of both are evident here. The text as it stands, however, reads clearly.[1] Joshua set up two monuments, one in the Jordan River and one on the western bank. And though we have not had previous indications that a second cairn would be erected, that should not deter us from seeing that as exactly what happened. The author goes on to point out that this monument in the Jordan was still standing when the book of Joshua was written. It was a verifiable, historical witness.

Why were there two memorial cairns (verses 9, 20)? This question has puzzled commentators for centuries, and a definitive answer may not be available. I would like to suggest, however, that these two monuments are analogous to the two tables of the law. People often assume that the Ten Commandments were given on two stone tablets in order to have room to contain all of the words. Popular depictions of Moses holding the tables of the law often show them numbered 1-5 on the first and 6-10 on the second. Old Testament scholar Meredith Kline, however, has argued that the two tables were two copies of the covenant. A covenant always involved two parties, and each party required a copy of the covenant stipulations. In the case of the Ten Commandments, one copy was for God and the other was for Israel.[2] While the parallels are not exact, these two piles of stones, like the two tables or copies of the law, served as a reminder or memorial both to God and Israel of what the Lord had done. The one, buried under the waters of the river, remained unseen by human eyes. It was God's cairn. It was his monument of covenant faithfulness and witnessed to the fact that at one time the

---

and the verse should refer to the stones that had been taken out of the Jordan.' Pitkänen, *Joshua*, 138.

[1] The NIV indicates that there was only one pile of stones by supplying three words to its translation of verse 9: 'Joshua set up the twelve stones *that had been* in the middle of the Jordan at the spot where the priests who carried the ark of the covenant had stood. And they are there to this day.' This translation, however, represents an interpolation.

[2] Though Meredith Kline does not identify the Jordan monuments with the tables of the law, the broad contours of the concept I have suggested come from his article 'The Two Tables of the Covenant.' *Westminster Theological Journal*, 22 (1960): 133-46.

river-bed had been dry. The other cairn at Gilgal was the people's copy. It was a memorial to them that God kept his promises to give Israel the land. Two tables of stone were given to Israel by their first mediator, Moses. Now two piles of stones, given by the new mediator, Joshua, serve as testaments to the covenant-keeping faithfulness of the Lord.

The first major section of the chapter concludes with a reminder that the water stood still so long as the priests stood still in the river: 'For the priests bearing the ark stood in the midst of the Jordan until everything was finished that the LORD commanded Joshua to tell the people, according to all that Moses had commanded Joshua' (verse 10).

Interlude on unity and faithfulness
Following the concluding explanation in verse 10a, the text presents us with an interlude that runs to the end of verse 14. The major focus of the chapter is on the memorial stones, but here the author adds a few more details of the crossing. Far from being out of place or the result of a conflated text, this brief interlude provides the author with another opportunity to highlight two major theological themes of the chapter, namely, unity and faithfulness, from a different perspective.

Joshua first 'fast forwards' the text to tell us that the people passed over in a hurry and, when that was complete, the ark and the priests passed over as well (verses 10b-11). More details appear in verses 15-18. He then 'rewinds' to verse 12 where we learn that Reuben, Gad, and half of Manasseh remained true to their commitment and obeyed the word that Moses spoke to them. These two and a half tribes passed over before the sons of Israel armed and ready for battle, having mustered 40,000 troops (verses 12-13). These statements connect back to 1:12-15 where Joshua had reminded them of their obligations to go into Canaan proper to help the rest of Israel fight and obtain their land. That, in turn, was the outworking of Moses' instructions in Numbers 32:20-27.

The inclusion of this brief account of the two and a half eastern tribes crossing the Jordan with the rest of Israel allows us to see that Reuben, Gad, and half of Manasseh took their responsibilities seriously. They had been blessed by the Lord and already possessed their land, but that did not mean they had nothing left to do. Grace-filled religion is not duty-free religion. The Transjordanian tribes knew what God required of them, and they were faithful to their obligations. Taken in the larger context not only of Joshua but the earlier defeat of Sihon and Og (Num. 21:21-35), we see that God's faithfulness had likewise inspired and instilled faithfulness in his people. This report also solidifies the emphasis on unity in the passage. The twelve stones for the twelve tribes included stones to represent the tribes that lived east of the Jordan as well.

The second feature of the interlude is God's exaltation of Joshua. The Lord promised Joshua that he would exalt him in the eyes of the people (3:7). After Israel crossed the Jordan on dry ground, that is exactly what he did. 'On that day the LORD exalted Joshua in the sight of all Israel, and they stood in awe of him just as they had stood in awe of Moses, all the days of his life' (verse 14). The Israelites had for decades heard about the crossing of the Red Sea and how God had used Moses as his great servant. Now they have seen the Lord do the very same thing with Joshua. As a result, from that point on they gave him the same admiration they had given Moses.

Two things happen as a result of verse 14. First, God once again proved his faithfulness. He promised to exalt Joshua, and he did. But, second, the Jordan crossing solidified Joshua's leadership over the nation. He had been giving orders to prepare for the conquest (1:10-3:1), but now he moves beyond the role of general to that of covenant mediator and national leader.

Out of the Jordan

If we follow the analogy of listening to a CD or mp3 player, we have already heard a few notes of the track we are about to play. Verse 11 introduced the fact that the priests bearing the ark passed over before the people. Now we get more of the details.

The full account begins with God's voice. This is the second divine speech in the chapter (cf. verse 1). The Lord continued to speak to Joshua and use him as the mouthpiece of revelation (verse 15). 'Command the priests bearing the ark of the testimony to come up out of the Jordan' (verse 16), and Joshua dutifully complied (verse

17). Reminiscent of chapter 3, this account of the exit from the river builds to a climax, though admittedly faster than the previous chapter. 'And when the priests bearing the ark of the covenant of the LORD came up from the midst of the Jordan, and the soles of the priests' feet were lifted up on dry ground, the waters of the Jordan returned to their place and overflowed all its banks, as before' (verse 18).

The emphasis is that the priests and the ark were the means God used to part the river. That significance came out clearly in the study of chapter 3. The priests and the ark are types or picture-prophesies of the Lord Jesus Christ, our priest, the very presence of God with us. Jesus passed through death (represented by the waters of the Jordan) to bring us into our inheritance. After the priests climb out of the river onto the western bank, the Jordan resumes its course as a flooding torrent. The picture is complete but, by means of the monuments, not forgotten. In the same way, the work of Christ is finished, but the Holy Spirit works through the word of God and the sacraments to make it ever fresh and new to the soul that believes.

Camped at Gilgal

The final scene in this chapter takes us from the Jordan River to Israel's first camp in Canaan. Several points in these closing verses are very important to note.

The first item is the date. All of this happened on the tenth day of the first month.[1] That should grab your attention. If I said to you, 'Let us meet for coffee on December 24th', what is one of the first things that would likely pop into your mind? 'Why, that is Christmas Eve!' That is exactly what is supposed to happen when you read verse 19. 'This is day ten of the first month.' 'Hey, wait a minute. That is just four days before Passover!' In fact, it was the very day Passover preparations were to begin (Exod. 12:2-3).

Further on in the text we read that Israel set up camp on the east border of Jericho. When we put all of these pieces together,

---

[1] The first month of the Hebrew calendar goes by the name of either Abib or Nissan and corresponds roughly to March–April.

our reaction should be something like this: 'Wait a minute! Jericho is where Joshua sent the spies. It is going to be the first city the Israelites attack. The people of Jericho know that they are coming. It is kind of hard for a nation to move in next door and not be noticed. But it is close to Passover, and that takes lots of preparation. Surely Israel is not going to position themselves like sitting ducks on the plains of Jericho and then take time to celebrate Passover. The nation has forward momentum. The people are eager. You have got to strike while the iron is hot. You cannot waste your time with worship. There is too much work to be done!' What will Israel do? It becomes evident in chapter 5 that the people were willing to 'waste' the time.

Israel set up their camp 'at Gilgal on the east border of Jericho' (verse 19). Gilgal will become the base of operations for the southern campaign and the first land distribution (see Joshua 10, 14).[1] Joshua set up the twelve stones from the Jordan at Gilgal as well. He built the memorial cairn (cf. verse 20 with its parallel in verse 9). Representatives of the tribes carried the stones to the campsite, but it was the leader who put them in place. Joshua symbolically united the people as twelve separate stones became one monument, a monument to commemorate the mighty saving act of God at the Jordan.

The memorials God has given us, especially the sacraments of baptism and the Lord's Supper, display the same underlying theological truth. Christ Jesus unites his people by baptizing every believer into one body and feeding every believer with one bread. Both the baptismal font and the Communion table underscore the fact that our greater Joshua fulfils the saving work of God by bringing elect people from every tribe and nation together as one.

After constructing the cairn, Joshua again addressed the people. The words are essentially repetitive of verses 6 and 7. Those earlier instructions, however, were directed specifically to the twelve tribal representatives. Now the instructions are for everyone. 'And he said to the people of Israel, "When your children ask their fathers in

[1] Bill T. Arnold and H. G. M. Williamson, eds. *Dictionary of the Old Testament Historical Books* (Downers Grove, IL: InterVarsity Press, 2005), 335.

times to come, 'What do these stones mean?' then you shall let
your children know, 'Israel passed over this Jordan on dry ground''"
(verses 21-22). When your children ask in the future, 'What about
these stones?', the proper response is 'The Lord is faithful.'

Fathers were also to fill out that explanation by telling their
children just how all of this came about. It was the Lord their God
who dried up the waters before them. What he did to the Jordan
was what he had done to the Red Sea (verse 23; Exod. 14:26-29).
Though the parallels are clear, this is the first time the text makes
an explicit connection between the two events. Joshua spoke from
personal experience when he said, 'which he dried up for *us* until *we*
passed over', but he used the plural pronouns to refer to the nation
present before him. Though, with the exception of Caleb, none of
them were born at the time, because of the covenant relationship
that existed for all of God's people, what happened to the forefathers
happened to them. Once again the text underscores the solidarity
of the nation, a solidarity that runs through the ages, not merely
through the physical descendants of Abraham who share his DNA
but the spiritual descendants who share his faith (cf. Rom. 4:9-12).[1]

Why did the Lord do all of this? The chapter ends with two
purpose-statements. He dried up the Jordan 'so that all the peoples
of the earth may know that the hand of the LORD is mighty" (verse
24a). The miracle had a universal purpose. That was certainly the
effect the Red Sea crossing had. When the spies visited Jericho, they
learned that the inhabitants of the land trembled because they had
'heard how the LORD dried up the water of the Red Sea before you
when you came out of Egypt' (2:10). If an event four decades old

[1] 'Moreover, because the covenant by which God had adopted the race of
Abraham was firm in an uninterrupted succession for a thousand generations, the
benefit which God had bestowed on the deceased fathers is, on account of the unity
of the body, transferred in common to their children who were born long after. And
the continuation must have more strongly awakened their attention, inasmuch as
posterity were in this way reminded that what had long ago been given to their
ancestors belonged to them also. The answer of the parents would have been coldly
listened to had the divine favour been confined to a single day. But when the sons'
sons hear that the waters of Jordan were dried up many ages before they were born,
they acknowledge themselves to be the very people towards whom that wonderful
act of divine favour had been manifested.' Calvin, *Comm. Joshua*, 74-75.

had that kind of impact, how much more force would the recent crossing have. The word quickly spread throughout Canaan that Israel had traversed the flooding Jordan on dry ground, a fact which could only be explained in terms of the Lord's miraculous power. The second purpose was for God's own people. Yes, the nations should know God's power, but Israel should 'fear the LORD [their] God forever' (verse 24b). The surrounding pagans may be struck with wonder, but the Lord's people should worship.

As we reflect on the memorial cairns at Gilgal and in the Jordan, we should pause to ask ourselves, 'How do we react to the mighty, saving acts of God in Christ?' Do we use the means that the Lord has given to us, the Scriptures and the sacraments, to remember those great deeds? Do we seek to use these means to instruct our children and our congregations? The God of our salvation gives us frequent reminders both of our former wanderings and estrangement as well as the unity and reconciliation we have in Christ. We must use the means he has provided to worship him and to recall frequently that Christ is the one, true source of everlasting joy.

7

The Art of Spiritual Warfare
Joshua 5:1-12

As soon as all the kings of the Amorites who were beyond the Jordan to the west, and all the kings of the Canaanites who were by the sea, heard that the LORD had dried up the waters of the Jordan for the people of Israel until they had crossed over, their hearts melted and there was no longer any spirit in them because of the people of Israel. At that time the LORD said to Joshua, 'Make flint knives and circumcise the sons of Israel a second time.' (Josh. 5:1-2)

*T*he Art of War, written sometime between the 5th and 3rd centuries B.C., by one of China's leading generals and military strategists, Sun Tzu, consists of thirteen chapters which cover the fundamental tactics of warfare. Sun Tzu covers all of the basics of combat strategy from laying plans and manoeuvring troops to assessing terrain and using spies. This tactical treatise is one of the most influential military texts of all time.

Though written about a thousand years before Sun Tzu, one might well attach the title *The Art of War* to the book of Joshua. We read from chapter 1 onwards how Israel's great general had prepared to lead his troops to victory. In chapter 5, Joshua stands on the brink of the first battle in Canaan. Israel had just crossed over the Jordan River into hostile territory. Encamped on the plains of Jericho, they could easily see the impressive, fortified city they were soon to engage. What would they do next?

Had Joshua read Sun Tzu's tactics, he would have found this advice for laying plans for battle: 'When we are near, we must make the enemy believe we are far away; when far away, we must make him believe we are near.'[1] That is wise counsel, but Israel could hardly hide since they were in plain sight of the city. Furthermore, in planning offensives, Sun Tzu advised, 'Thus the highest form of generalship is to balk the enemy's plans; the next best is to prevent the junction of the enemy's forces; the next in order is to attack the enemy's army in the field; and the worst policy of all is to besiege walled cities.'[2] If giving away your position is poor strategy and attacking a walled city is the worst policy a general can follow, then Joshua clearly had two strikes against him.

As the Bible makes clear time and time again, however, God's ways are not man's ways. Though *The Art of War* contains a great deal of military wisdom, the Lord has a way of turning our ideas upside-down in order to show us that sometimes our best wisdom is folly and God's foolishness turns out to be wiser than we could have imagined (see Isa. 55:8-9; 1 Cor. 1:25). That is certainly what happens in Joshua chapter 5.

Now that Israel had safely made it to the western bank of the Jordan River, it must have seemed that a battle was imminent and that the people were ready, but, in fact, they were not yet ready. Their lack of preparedness, however, had nothing to do with marshalling troops or engaging in a few more practice manoeuvres. Before the Israelites could begin to conquer the land of promise, the Lord had to prepare them spiritually. Situated within easy striking distance of Jericho, Israel stopped their forward march, camped, circumcised the soldiers, and celebrated the Passover. These actions, which seem at first like utter folly, unfold for us the ways of God. Worship comes before war. In order to serve God, we must first honour him. Worship prepares us for warfare.

This truth works its way out in the passage in three ways. First, the chapter opens by describing *the setting of worship* in verse 1. Second, two further scenes narrate *the acts of worship*: circumcision and the

---

[1] *Sun Tsu on the Art of War*. Translated by Lionel Giles. http://www. artofwarsuntzu.com/LionelGilesTranslation.htm (accessed 4 June 2015).
[2] *Ibid.*

celebration of the Passover. Third, the overall context describes *the delay of worship*.

The setting of worship—poised for victory

Chapter 5 begins with a comment which forms a bridge between the events that had just occurred and those that are about to occur: crossing the Jordan had an unexpected, miraculous impact on the surrounding peoples. 'As soon as all the kings of the Amorites who were beyond the Jordan to the west, and all the kings of the Canaanites who were by the sea, heard that the LORD had dried up the waters of the Jordan for the people of Israel until they had crossed over, their hearts melted and there was no longer any spirit in them because of the people of Israel' (verse 1). The reference to all the kings of the Amorites on the west side of the Jordan and all the kings of the Canaanites by the sea or the Mediterranean is an all-inclusive description akin to an American saying, 'east and west of the Mississippi'. A general sense of dread fell upon all the people when they heard that the Lord had dried up the Jordan (during flood stage at that!) so that Israel could pass over on dry ground.

All of the Canaanite leaders quaked in their sandals at what God had done for his people. They had never experienced such an event. What kind of God must this be who pushed back the rushing waters of the river and created a dry path to cross? The inhabitants of the land were overcome with fear. Earlier, Israel's hearts had melted when they contemplated going up against the giants of the land (Deut. 1:28). But now, just as Rahab had described (see 2:11), not one of Israel's enemies had the courage to fight. God's mighty actions were a clear indication that he himself was engaging in psychological warfare.[1]

At this point one can begin to see contrast in the text. Fear mounted in Jericho as Israel camped on the outskirts of the city. No doubt the people's fear kept them inside the city and prevented them from attacking Israel. This, in turn, has allowed God's people time to worship. The Lord's miraculous rescue from the waters of the Jordan provided Israel with an opportunity to pause, rest,

---

[1] Pitkänen, *Joshua*, 149.

reflect, and honour their God. Salvation led to worship, as it always should. To put this truth in New Testament terms, justification, a right standing with God, always leads to sanctification, a growing godliness in one's life. Worship is a key component in that growth.[1]

The acts of worship—celebrating the sacraments

What kind of worship did Israel conduct? Two rites occupied the people's time, one of which was ancient, the other of which was of more recent origin. The first ritual they observed was circumcision. Though other peoples of the Ancient Near East practised the procedure, God appointed this rite to be a sign of his covenant with Israel's patriarch, Abraham (Gen. 17:9-14). The removal of the male foreskin became a permanent reminder that God had promised to bless Abraham, make of him a great nation, and bring blessing to all the world through him (cf. Gen. 12:1-3; 17:1-8). The removal of the foreskin also symbolized the removal of the 'flesh' and hence it became an emblem of spiritual rebirth. It was important to have both a circumcised body as well as a circumcised heart or spirit (Deut. 10:16; Jer. 4:4).

In order to carry out the procedure, the Lord commanded Joshua to 'make flint knives and circumcise the sons of Israel a second time' (verse 2). Flint knives reflect the antiquity of the event. During later times iron would have been the preferred metal for such an implement.[2] With these knives, Joshua circumcised the sons of Israel 'a second time'. These final words of verse 2, 'a second time', are somewhat puzzling. How could someone be circumcised more than once? The explanation appears to be that though the fathers of these

---

[1] On the ways in which worship cultivates spirituality see the brief but excellent treatment by Joel R. Beeke, *Piety: The Heartbeat of Reformed Theology* (Phillipsburg, NJ: P&R, 2015).

[2] The description of these knives as 'flint' occurs only one other time in the Old Testament when Moses's wife Zipporah used such a knife to circumcise her son (Exod. 4:25). 'Here is another parallel between Moses and Joshua: When called to lead the covenant people out of Egypt, Moses had to restore the covenant of circumcision in his own family (Exod 4:24-26).' Madvig, *Joshua*, 273. It has also been suggested that the term translated 'flint' refers to a ceremonial knife and not its composition. An ancient tradition says that these knives were buried with Joshua.

men had been circumcised (verse 5), the current generation had not. Their fathers' circumcision would have been the first circumcision. Theirs was now the second. Joshua obeyed the Lord and followed through on the commands of verse 2. He did exactly what God told him to do, and the place where he circumcised the men became known as *Gibeath-haaraloth*, a transliteration from Hebrew which means 'the hill of the foreskins'.

Why did Joshua have to circumcise these men? Parents were to have their boys circumcised at eight days old (cf. Gen. 17:12), so why had this not been taken care of years before? The explanation occurs in verses 4-7. Though the men who came out of Egypt had been circumcised, they neglected to do the same for their sons (verse 5). Because of their rebellion, that circumcised generation perished in the wilderness (verses 4, 6). They did not believe that God was able to defeat the Canaanites, and for that reason they were fearful and refused to enter the land (see Num. 13:25-14:12). They walked by fear instead of by faith. Their disobedience kept them from enjoying the blessings of the promised land, and their infidelity also kept them from performing their duty to see that their sons bore the sign and seal of the God's covenant of grace. It was the children of these men whom Joshua circumcised (verse 7). Since their fathers had failed, the Lord turned to Joshua to fulfil his will.

What is it about this passage that is so startling and spiritually searching? The men who came out of Egypt had the sign of the covenant, but having the sign was no guarantee of their spiritual faithfulness. They had circumcised bodies but lacked circumcised hearts (cf. Deut. 10:16; Jer. 4:4). Religion that consists merely of external ceremonies, rites, and rules lacks the power to change the heart. The law can show us our sin, but it is powerless to make us love Christ (cf. Rom. 8:3). It takes regeneration, a new heart, a new will to delight in obedience. Baptism, church membership, and a host of other outward religious expressions must not be automatically equated with salvation. It is possible to possess the sign and seal of the covenant and to do the kinds of things that Christians are expected to do and yet remain in spiritual darkness.

It is a shame to any generation when the children display more godliness than their parents, but experience demonstrates that this is often the case. It happened in Israel. It happens in the church. Parents have a duty to see that their children receive the sign and seal of the covenant in Christian baptism and to raise them in the light of God's covenant promises. A child should never be left on his or her own to try to follow Christ. Parents must take the lead to encourage their sons and daughters towards spiritual maturity. The wilderness generation had failed in their spiritual duties to their children. This sober realization should send us all to the foot of the cross to seek God's grace so that we might not fail and to seek his forgiveness for the ways in which we have.

After Joshua finished circumcising the men, they stayed in camp and did not proceed further in the campaign until they were healed (verse 8), a recovery period that lasted for several days. When Shechem wanted to marry Jacob's daughter, Dinah, the sons of Jacob stipulated that he, along with his father, Hamor, and all of the men in his city had to be circumcised if the Israelites were to intermarry with them. The men were willing to comply with the requirement, but three days later they were still sore and unable to defend themselves when attacked by Simeon and Levi (see Gen. 34). In other words, the healing time required would have been longer than three days. Most likely, it would have been closer to a week before the men could resume normal activities.

The most significant outcome of this event was not just that it applied the sign of the covenant to those who had been denied it, but it also prepared them to enter battle ceremonially clean. Circumcision on the plains of Jericho served to roll away the reproach of Egypt (verse 9). In fact, it was this 'rolling away' that gave the place its new name, *Gilgal*, which comes from the Hebrew verb *galal*, to roll. What was the 'reproach of Egypt'? It could refer to the disgrace of being uncircumcised. A parallel use of the term *reproach* occurs in Genesis 34, again with Shechem's request to marry Jacob's daughter Dinah. Jacob's sons told Shechem that they could not give their sister to someone who was uncircumcised. To do so 'would be a disgrace to us' (Gen. 34:14). Not being circumcised meant not being marked as set apart to God which was a shameful reproach. For an Israelite (or someone who married into the people

of Israel), anyone who did not receive this rite was looked upon as
being no different than a Gentile; and that was a reproach. Thus,
by submitting to circumcision, the men on the plains of Jericho
no longer bore the disgrace of Egypt. They were clearly set apart as
distinct from the world.

On the other hand, this reproach may have been the scorn and
taunts heaped upon God's people by the Egyptians. Scoffing words
like 'God brought you out of Egypt but he cannot take you into
Canaan', may have been directed against Israel.[1] It seems most
likely, however, that the reproach of Egypt is a broad expression
that includes everything involved in the shame and disgrace of
having been slaves in that land.[2] Now that God marked his men
with circumcision, the disgrace of Israel's past life of slavery was now
and forever removed.

Shame and reproach are powerful tools. The world wields them
and so does Satan. Sometimes we find these tools in the hands of
those closest to us. You may feel the burden of shame because of
some sin or spectacular failure in your life. Perhaps your sense of
disgrace comes from the way someone has sinned against you or
abused you. Misdeeds, mistreatment, or harsh words have left you
feeling useless. The gospel, however, rolls away guilt and shame.
As a believer, you can overcome the disgrace of sin by refusing to
identify with your old life outside of Christ. New life in Christ, the
reality that circumcision points to, rolls away shame. To be justified
in Christ results in God seeing you as righteous as his only Son.
Justification, not shame, should be the defining characteristic of the
believer's life. If you are in Christ, his righteousness is yours. It has
been imputed or credited to you. Likewise, the gospel, rather than

[1] Several Old Testament scholars believe this is the proper interpretation. These
include Howard, Jr., *Joshua*, 151 and Hubbard, *Joshua*, 182-83. DeGraaf comments
that God 'told Joshua that he was to name that place *Gilgal,* which means *turning,*
for there the Lord had turned away from the people the reproach of the Egyptians.
While the Israelites wandered for 40 years in the wilderness, the Egyptians said that
the Lord had indeed led them out of Egypt but added that they would all die in the
wilderness because the Lord could not bring them into Canaan.' S. G. DeGraaf,
Promise and Deliverance. Trans. by H. Evan Runner and Elisabeth Wichers Runner
(St. Catharines, ON: Paideia Press, 1977), 1:398.
[2] McConville and Williams, *Joshua*, 27.

the failures and sins of the past, defines you and tells you that you are one with the Saviour!

If you labour under a weight of shame, guilt, and disgrace, let the place where you are become your Gilgal. Turn your heart to Christ and say, 'Lord, let me see myself in you. Roll away the shame I feel and no longer let sin and failure be the defining features of the way I see my life or the way anyone else sees it. Since I am in Christ, let my life reflect the glory of your grace, and let my heart rejoice in the assurance of sins forgiven.' That day on the plains of Jericho the Lord rolled back the humiliation and derision of Egyptian bondage by the act of circumcision. Today, through the work of Christ, God can roll back the reproach of sin and guilt from you.

Passover

Following the circumcision of the new generation of soldiers, the people of God celebrated their first Passover in Canaan. Verses 10-12 give us a compact version of the events surrounding the celebration and the subsequent feast of Unleavened Bread. This condensed account highlights several events associated with the festivities.

First, verse 10 points out the timing. The celebration took place on the date God prescribed (Exod. 12:6; Lev. 23:5; cf. Num. 9:5). The Lord brought his people to Gilgal at just the right time. The text laid the groundwork for anticipating this back in 4:19, 'The people came up out of the Jordan on the tenth day of the first month, and they encamped at Gilgal on the east border of Jericho.' With the crossing of the Jordan just four days before one of the major dates on the Hebrew calendar, we can see the Lord's orchestration of all these events. The significance becomes even clearer when you realize that the tenth day of the first month was the day Israelites chose their Passover lamb (Exod. 12:3). Second, Israel kept the Passover on the plains of Jericho, camped within plain sight of the enemy. They took their stand for what was most important in the life of the nation, and they did so without shame.

The Passover was the Old Testament parallel to the Lord's Supper. As a sacrificial meal, the celebration involved slaying a lamb and subsequently roasting and eating it. The Lord's Supper is not a sacrificial meal in that most literal sense, though it is a meal looking back to a sacrifice. Instead of slaying a lamb, at Communion we remember the Lamb who was slain for our sins, the Lord Jesus Christ (John 1:29; Rev. 5:9, 12; 13:8). Paul stated this truth as plainly as possible: 'Christ, our Passover lamb, has been sacrificed' (1 Cor. 5:7). At the Lord's table we feast on Christ. We do not literally eat Christ's body or drink his blood, but when we eat the bread and drink the cup, we receive by faith the benefits of the Saviour's life and death. We literally eat bread and drink wine, but spiritually we feast on the person and work of the Lord Jesus.

The *Westminster Larger Catechism* explains this truth very well. Question 170 asks, 'How do they that worthily communicate in the Lord's supper feed upon the body and blood of Christ therein?' The answer?

> As the body and blood of Christ are not corporally or carnally present in, with, or under the bread and wine in the Lord's supper, and yet are spiritually present to the faith of the receiver, no less truly and really than the elements themselves are to their outward senses; so they that worthily communicate in the sacrament of the Lord's supper, do therein feed upon the body and blood of Christ, not after a corporal and carnal, but in a spiritual manner, yet truly and really, while by faith they receive and apply unto themselves Christ crucified, and all the benefits of his death.

Israel's celebration of the Passover was also an expression of faith and a means of assurance. By sitting on the plains of Jericho, having just crossed the Jordan on dry ground, the Passover reminded the people that the same God who brought them out of Egypt would certainly bring them into the full possession of Canaan. The Lord's Supper should work the same way for Christians. As we use the elements to remind us of Jesus's life and death, we should cling to the promise that he who died and rose again for our salvation will bring us safely to heaven. Israel could no more fight their battles without assurance than can you. The person best suited to engage in spiritual warfare is the one who knows he or she fights in the victory Jesus has already won.

Next, the Israelites ate parched grain and made unleavened cakes. Though what we read in verse 11 is not a celebration of the feast of firstfruits, it does anticipate it (see Lev. 23:10; Deut. 26:1-2).[1] The following day, the second day of the feast, the manna ceased. For forty years God had fed his people with this flake-like, seed-like bread that tasted similar to wafers made with honey (Exod. 16:13-30). Each day, with the exception of the Sabbath, Israel gathered this bread from heaven as God provided for them throughout their time in the wilderness. Each day the Lord sustained the lives of his people in a barren wasteland to preserve them and to teach them how dependent they were upon him. Moses wrote, 'And he humbled you and let you hunger and fed you with manna, which you did not know, nor did your fathers know, that he might make you know that man does not live by bread alone, but man lives by every word that comes from the mouth of the LORD' (Deut. 8:3).

The manna, just like the Passover, was a picture of Christ. The Lord Jesus tells us that the bread from heaven was really an object lesson all about him. In John 6, after the Jesus fed the 5,000, large crowds followed him and said, 'Then what sign do you do, that we may see and believe you? What work do you perform? Our fathers ate the manna in the wilderness; as it is written, "He gave them bread from heaven to eat"' (John 6:30-31). Jesus replied, '"Truly, truly, I say to you, it was not Moses who gave you the bread from heaven, but my Father gives you the true bread from heaven. For the bread of God is he who comes down from heaven and gives life to the world." They said to him, "Sir, give us this bread always." Jesus said to them, "I am the bread of life; whoever comes to me shall not hunger, and whoever believes in me shall never thirst"' (verses 32-35). The lesson is not difficult to see: just as food gives us physical energy and strength, so too Christ gives us the spiritual energy we need to go on day after day, the strength to believe and pursue holiness as we wander as 'pilgrims through this barren land' on the way to glory.

---

[1] 'After the Passover, they eat unleavened bread and parched grain. The logic of this is simply that these are natural foods for a people newly arrived, on the march, in a land which they have not had time to cultivate. There is, nevertheless, an echo of the idea of firstfruits, which became a regular seasonal offering, but which are associated with the first entry to the land in texts that deal with them (Lev 23:10; Deut 26:1-2).' McConville and Williams, *Joshua*, 28.

With the wilderness phase of Israel's instruction over, God would now provide for them another source of sustenance—the produce of the land of Canaan. 'The lesson taught by the manna (Deut. 8:3) had been sufficient. God's pedagogy could now resort to other means, namely those of ordinary providence.'[1] By stopping the manna, God let the people know that their wanderings had ceased. They had come home to the land of promise to establish a permanent place for the worship of the Lord and to await the coming of Messiah.

The delay of worship—waiting on the Lord

Now, having looked at the text in some detail, we need to step back and look once again at the big picture. Circumcision and Passover each carried significant theological weight and spiritual lessons in and of themselves. God designed them that way. But look at where he places these two events in the book of Joshua—on the brink of the conquest. Before Israel could fight against their enemies they must first worship their God. Worship prepared the nation for war. We do not learn to fight spiritual battles by studying the art of combat. We learn to engage in the conflicts of the soul through worship of the Almighty.

In this passage, Israel did two things that, humanly speaking, were foolish. First, the soldiers weakened themselves. I refer you back to the events of Genesis 34 when the men of Shechem submitted to circumcision so that Hamor's son could marry Dinah, Jacob's daughter. The men were sore, unable to fight, and were thus easily defeated by Simeon and Levi. How easy it would have been for the army of Jericho to overcome Israel during this time. What general would hamper his troops on the eve of battle? Yet this is precisely what Joshua did in obedience to the Lord. Second, the Israelites took time to focus on the Passover meal and the feast of Unleavened Bread. Plotting strategy for the upcoming battle was not their first priority.

Israel made themselves vulnerable in the face of the enemy. No one likes to feel defenceless, but imagine how the Israelites felt. These events did not happen on the plains of Moab or in the Sinai

---

[1] Woudstra, *Book of Joshua*, 103.

peninsula. Israel worshipped on the plains of Jericho in full sight of the enemy and within easy striking distance. How contrary all this is to the western way, especially the western approach to Christianity. We are people of action. Give us a job to do, a siege mound to build, or a battle to fight. But what we can easily miss is that God instructs us first to rest. It is only after restful worship that you are truly ready to fight.

The Lord stresses this principle of *worship first* in the very way he has designed our week. When Jesus rose from the dead, he changed the Christian Sabbath from the last day of the week to the first. We call it the Lord's Day (cf. Rev. 1:10). Have you ever thought about the implications of that change? By placing his day as the first of the week, God calls us to worship him and rest our bodies to prepare us for what lies ahead in the following six days. The Christian life calls us to many activities, but where does the source of our energy lie? Wait on the Lord, then do his work. That is the divine order. Those who wait on the Lord receive his strength to do his will (Isa. 40:29-31). To say that worship is the key to spiritual warfare and service is not by any means an excuse for passivity but rather a plea to consider the proper priorities.

In his classic tale of the sea, *Moby Dick*, Herman Melville paints a scene of hurried action as sailors heave at the oars and hoist the sails to fight against the chaotic waters in their pursuit of the whale. But during this flurry of activity a lone sailor sits calmly. He does not rush about. He does not do anything, or so it seems. This man is the harpooner. Of him Melville writes, 'To insure the greatest efficiency in the dart, the harpooners of this world must start to their feet out of idleness, and not out of toil.'[1]

We must start our tasks from a position of calmness or rest and worship. Did not the psalmist write: 'Be still and know that I am God' (Psa. 46:10)? Isaiah reminds us, 'For thus said the Lord GOD, the Holy One of Israel, "In returning and rest you shall be saved; in quietness and in trust shall be your strength"' (Isa. 30:15).

---

[1] For this illustration I am indebted to Eugene H. Peterson, *The Contemplative Pastor* (Grand Rapids: Eerdmans, 1989), 24.

A thorough search of Sun Tzu's *The Art of War* reveals no mention of worship or rest or God. Such concepts seem foreign to a guidebook for battle. For Christians, however, what we find modelled for us in Joshua chapter 5 is the right approach to the art of *spiritual* warfare. In quietness and rest we find our strength. In worship we find our souls fortified for the battles that lie ahead.

8

The Lord's Commander
Joshua 5:13-15

When Joshua was by Jericho, he lifted up his eyes and looked, and behold, a man was standing before him with his drawn sword in his hand. And Joshua went to him and said to him, 'Are you for us, or for our adversaries?' And he said, 'No; but I am the commander of the army of the Lord. Now I have come.' And Joshua fell on his face to the earth and worshiped and said to him, 'What does my lord say to his servant?' And the commander of the Lord's army said to Joshua, 'Take off your sandals from your feet, for the place where you are standing is holy.' And Joshua did so. (Josh. 5:13-15)

'You are what you eat.' Or so we are told. The statement is used, of course, to encourage healthy eating; but one might well wonder, 'Who wants to be a turnip!' Aversions to turnip-like transformations aside, if healthy foods produce healthy bodies, then it is a good idea to eat a healthy diet. You are what you eat.

In a similar fashion and more importantly, 'You are what you worship.' In Psalm 115 the psalmist describes idols of silver and gold as the work of men's hands (verse 4). These idols have mouths, but they do not speak. They have eyes, but they cannot see. They have ears, but they cannot hear. The description continues and includes noses, hands, feet, and throats, yet no idol can smell, touch, walk, or speak (verses 5-7). This dumbness, deafness, and utter inability to act appears also in the lives of those who worship these lifeless images. 'Those who make them become like them; so do all who trust in them' (verse 8). An idolater is incapable of effecting any spiritual good. As the apostle Paul makes clear, 'whatever does not proceed from faith is sin' (Rom. 14:23).

A person does not have to bow down to a lump of wood or stone and call it his god in order to be an idolater. Any thing or any person that you elevate in your heart to the point that he, she, or it controls the way you act effectively becomes your god. And you become what you worship. If you worship yourself, you will be a proud person. If you worship money, you will be a greedy person. If you worship your perception of how things ought to be, you will be an angry person.[1] The focus of your trust and admiration, the source of your comfort and meaning, shapes the way you act and react to life.

Christians tend to toss around the word *worship* quite a bit. We believe in worship. We go to church to worship. We follow an order of worship. We sing hymns of worship. But do we realize that while we worship, God is also doing something in us? Worship brings honour and glory to the Lord, but it also shapes and moulds us into the people he wants us to be.

As Israel concluded their celebration of Passover and the feast of Unleavened Bread (Josh. 5:10-12), everything appeared to be set for the next move. The nation was well-positioned, well-rested, and well-prepared through the use of God's means of grace. But instead of moving directly to instructions for fighting at Jericho, chapter 5 concludes with an unusual scene unlike anything we find in the rest of the book. Joshua, somewhere near Jericho, encountered a man who identified himself as the commander of the Lord's army. At the feet of this man Joshua bows and worships, and that act of worship prepared Joshua to be the commander of Israel's army that God had called him to be.

The passage begins and ends with Joshua, which may lead us to think this text is primarily about him. He appears to be alone outside of Jericho. Perhaps he was meditating on the eve of the conflict. If

---

[1] For a thorough treatment of this theme, see G. K. Beale, *We Become What We Worship: A Biblical Theology of Idolatry* (Downers Grove, IL: IVP Academic, 2008).

so, this would be clear evidence of his spiritual-mindedness. On the other hand, his excursion to the city may have been to reconnoitre the situation. Perhaps, like Nehemiah, he went out alone to survey the scene (see Neh. 2:11-16). This would, no doubt, underscore the wisdom of a skilled leader. Furthermore, Joshua demonstrated great courage as he approached a man with a drawn sword when he did not know if the man was on the side of Israel or the Canaanites. Finally, we see in Joshua a man of deep humility as the passage concludes with his obedience. All of these elements are certainly in the text, and they definitely have a ring of relevance to them. Only one problem stands in the way: an approach to these verses that focuses primarily on Joshua's character misses the point of the text.

When we read our Bibles, and perhaps especially when we study to teach a Bible passage, our tendency is to rush to relevance. We know we should apply the Bible to ourselves in a practical way, but we tend to forget that the word of God is not first about us. For some reason we think that the Bible on its own is not interesting enough or exciting enough unless we can turn it into a book about us. When that happens, however, we usually miss the real point.

I do not doubt that Joshua was a spiritual, wise, courageous, and humble man. To one degree or another, most of that is suggested by the text. Yet the passage is predominantly about the commander of the Lord's army and Joshua's worship of him. The closing verses of chapter five continue the theme begun in the first twelve verses: worship prepares us for warfare. While the theme continues in verses 13-15, it does so by becoming more personal and individualized in Joshua's encounter with this commander, an encounter that forms the final step of preparation for Joshua before he leads Israel into their first Canaanite conflict. Joshua had not only to meet the commander of the Lord's army, but he also had to be brought to a place of reverence before him. To lead God's people, Joshua had to worship God's leader.

As we examine this passage, three steps will carry us right through these three verses: the man appears, identifies himself, and commands Joshua to remove his sandals.

The appearance of God's leader

Though Israel camped on the plains of Jericho (5:10), Joshua, apparently alone, ventured even closer to the city. We are tempted to ask, why was he there? Was he conducting reconnaissance? Having a quiet time to meditate on the eve of battle? Perhaps he was doing both, but the text simply does not tell us, and anything we say about this excursion would, therefore, be guesswork at best. This reminds us again that the emphasis of the text is not on Joshua but on the man he met.

As Joshua walked near Jericho, he looked up and 'behold, a man was standing before him with his drawn sword in his hand' (verse 13). When Joshua saw this man equipped to fight, he quite naturally identified him as a man of war. But who was this individual? Though his perception grew as the encounter continued, at first Joshua thought that this was just another soldier, though he was not sure whether this was a Canaanite or Israelite soldier. Is it possible for us with this meagre description to begin a process of identification? Yes, because only two other times in the Old Testament do we encounter characters with drawn swords, and in both passages the Scriptures identify these individuals as 'the angel of the LORD'.

The first instance occurs in Numbers 22. When Balaam was determined to accede to Balak's request to curse Israel, the angel of the Lord stood in his way. At first only Balaam's donkey could see him. 'And the donkey saw the angel of the LORD standing in the road, *with a drawn sword in his hand*. And the donkey turned aside out of the road and went into the field. And Balaam struck the donkey, to turn her into the road' (verse 23). Later, however, he understood what was happening. 'Then the LORD opened the eyes of Balaam, and he saw the angel of the LORD standing in the way, with his *drawn sword in his hand*. And he bowed down and fell on his face' (verse 31).

The second occurrence is in 1 Chronicles 21. When David decided to take a census of Israel, God was displeased. As a result, he sent a pestilence on Israel and 70,000 men died (1 Chron. 21:14). He also sent his angel to destroy Jerusalem. 'And David lifted his eyes and saw the angel of the LORD standing between earth and heaven, *and in his hand a drawn sword* stretched out over Jerusalem. Then David and the elders, clothed in sackcloth, fell upon their faces' (verse 16).

The wording of each of these texts is identical. With links to the only two other passages like this in the Old Testament, we can conclude that, though it may have taken him time to realize it, Joshua was standing face to face with the angel of the Lord. Israel had experienced the angel of the Lord's presence earlier when he protected them from Pharaoh's troops at the Red Sea crossing (Exod. 14:19). Furthermore, God had promised to send his angel before his people to lead and protect them. 'Behold, I send an angel before you to guard you on the way and to bring you to the place that I have prepared' (Exod. 23:20). The angel would precede the camp of Israel to the land of Canaan, a promise coupled with the assurance that once there the Lord himself would blot out all their enemies (Exod. 23:23).

The prominence of the angel of the Lord raises the question whether this was just one of the myriad of God's angels or was there something unique about this particular one? To answer that question we need to keep in mind a couple of things. Many people have come to associate angels with cherubic, winged infants, but that image is far from anything we find in the Bible. The term *angel* means *messenger*. The angel of the Lord is the Lord's messenger who often appears as a man, and in the passages cited above as a man of war.

In addition to the meaning of *messenger*, the Bible often presents this angel as the Lord himself. The angel of the Lord spoke to Abraham from heaven, and Abraham understood this to be an encounter with God (Gen. 22:11-12, 14). When Jacob blessed the sons of Joseph, he recounted the blessings of his own life. He referred to the God of his fathers as 'the God before whom my fathers Abraham and Isaac walked, the God who has been my shepherd all my life long to this day' (Gen. 48:15). He then immediately calls God 'the angel who has redeemed me from all evil' (Gen. 48:16). At the burning bush, the angel of the Lord appeared to Moses in a flame of fire. From that same bush God called out to Moses and later identified himself as the Lord (Exod. 3:2, 4, 6, 7). The patriarchs and early leaders of

Israel recognized this messenger of the Lord as the Lord himself, and
it will quickly become clear to Joshua that he has encountered God.
But that is to get ahead of ourselves. For now Joshua sees a warrior,
but with which army has he allied himself?

Apparently without trepidation Joshua walked up to the man and
asked, 'Are you for us, or for our adversaries' (verse 13)? The question
seems somewhat surprising since the man had a drawn sword in
his hand. This soldier was clearly prepared to fight, and Joshua
did not know who he was or on whose side he was. Israel's great
general was undoubtedly a brave man. Successful leadership requires
courage. No one can lead others if he is afraid of what may lie ahead.
Fear paralyses; faith steps forward to do what is necessary. Joshua
wanted to know, 'Are you here at Jericho to fight for us or to fight
against us?' This was the question foremost in his mind. Uncertainty
existed about this soldier and what he would do. Marten Woudstra
observed:

> Joshua's reaction to the appearance (*'Do you belong to us or to our
> enemies?'*) suggests that there is something ambiguous about it.
> Joshua's question serves to enhance the air of mystery surrounding
> the event and helps to prepare the reader for the significant disclosure
> that is to follow in v. 14.[1]

When Joshua approached the angel, he was prepared to fight if
necessary. What he was not prepared for was the response to his
question.

The identity of God's leader

To his inquiry about which side the soldier was on, Joshua received
a rather abrupt and startling 'No!' 'No; but I am the commander of
the army of the LORD. Now I have come' (verse 14).[2] Was this man

[1] Woudstra, *Book of Joshua*, 104-05.

[2] The LXX and several Hebrew manuscripts read 'to him' rather than 'no'. The
explanation for this is a case of Hebrew homonyms. The Hebrew word for 'no' is
lo' while the word for 'to him' is *lo*. Both sound exactly the same and are nearly
identical in spelling. Although it would seem natural for the text to read 'And he
said to him, "I am the commander of the army of the LORD,"' such a response
would not really be an answer to Joshua's question. On the whole the response 'no'
is the better reading and is maintained by almost all English Bible translations. The
New English Bible is a notable exception.

for neither side? Did he have no stake in the battle, no favoured allies in the fray? Certainly if he had come from God and was the angel of the Lord he would align himself on the side of Israel. Why this negative response? The answer of 'no' was not a statement of neutrality. The reply deflects Joshua's question in order to focus his attention on something more important. In other words, Joshua had asked the wrong question or at least he had not asked the most important question. The pertinent point at this juncture was not who is for whom. That question can be answered later. Something else must come first—the soldier's true identity.

Like Joshua, we often ask the wrong questions. We expect the Lord to have the same priorities and interests that we do. If something is important to us, then surely it must be on the top of God's list as well. We expect the Lord's agenda to be the same as ours. Many, if not most, of the problems we encounter in our Christian lives stem from our adoption of the wrong priorities. The Lord was on Israel's side, but the important issue at hand was not for whom this commander was fighting. The important issue was Joshua's worship. To live for Christ and serve him faithfully, worship must be our first priority.

After deflecting Joshua's question, the man identified himself as 'the commander of the army of the LORD'. The term 'commander' means *leader, chief,* or *ruler.* This title designates the one who leads troops into battle. The phrase 'commander of the army' occurs several more times in the Old Testament as a description of various generals. Examples include Sisera who was Jabin's general (Judg. 4:7; 1 Sam. 12:9), Abner, captain of Saul's army (2 Sam. 2:8; 1 Kings 2:32), and Shobach, the commander of Hadadezer's military (2 Sam. 10:16; 1 Chron. 19:16). Amasa took Joab's place and became the commander of David's forces (2 Sam. 19:14). After Zimri assassinated Elah, Israel made Omri, the army commander, king of the nation (1 Kings 16:16). Naaman was the army captain for the king of Syria (2 Kings 5:1). In each of these cases, the rank of commander designates someone who leads an army for a king. The angel of the Lord whom Joshua met came to him as the leader of God's army.

The phrase 'army of the LORD', however, is not in this instance a reference to Israel's troops but to God's angelic hosts, his heavenly forces. This description occurs, for example, in the psalms. 'The LORD has established his throne in the heavens, and his kingdom rules over all. Bless the LORD, O you his angels, you mighty ones who do his word, obeying the voice of his word! Bless the LORD, all his hosts, his ministers, who do his will' (Psa. 103:19-21)! Again we read in Psalm 148:2, 'Praise him, all his angels; praise him, all his hosts!' In the parallel structure of Hebrew poetry, 'his angels' in the first line are renamed 'his hosts' in the second.

God has a mighty, heavenly army that surrounds and protects his people. Perhaps the clearest example of this truth comes from the ministry of Elisha. The great prophet kept interfering with the battle plans of the king of Syria. God would reveal to Elisha what the king was going to do. The man of God would then send word to Israel's king who in turn would foil the Syrian king's plans. The Syrian ruler became furious, so when Elisha was at Dothan, he sent troops to surround the city and be done with this menacing prognosticator once and for all. The next morning, when Elisha's servant left the house, he saw the king's forces. 'Behold, an army with horses and chariots was all around the city. And the servant said, "Alas, my master! What shall we do?" He said, "Do not be afraid, for those who are with us are more than those who are with them." Then Elisha prayed and said, "O LORD, please open his eyes that he may see." So the LORD opened the eyes of the young man, and he saw, and behold, the mountain was full of horses and chariots of fire all around Elisha' (2 Kings 6:15-17). That day Elisha and his servant experienced the powerful and comforting truth of Psalm 34:7, 'The angel of the LORD encamps around those who fear him, and delivers them.' The Lord has an angelic army ready to do his bidding, fight his battles, and protect his people. The man with the drawn sword whom Joshua met outside Jericho stood at its head.

After identifying himself the commander says, 'Now I have come.' His declaration of having arrived, however, begs the question, 'Come for what?' The statement feels incomplete, but it is not. The announcement of his presence is enough. With the presence of the Lord there is salvation.[1] The commander's statement serves to

---

[1] 'The book of Psalms knows of a "coming" that is pregnant with redemptive meaning; see Psa. 40:8 (Eng. 7); 50:3; 96:13=98:9. Such instances are sufficient

assure Joshua of his presence with Israel's army. Now I have come so that you do not have to fight these battles alone. I will be with you. You do not have to face the enemy in your own strength.' The commander's appearance seems to be for Joshua's encouragement. Joshua could now lead Israel into battle knowing that the LORD's invisible army would ensure victory.'[1]

Some critics of the Bible have equated the conquest of Canaan with the genocides of Rwanda or Hitler's holocaust, but the war Israel was about to wage falls into a completely different category. One clear indication of that is this text. By appearing to Joshua as the leader of God's heavenly army, the angel of the Lord points out that behind Israel's battles lay a spiritual war, one fought in heavenly realms. For a soldier it would be easy to get caught up in the struggle of the battle and fail to recognize that something else was happening on a different level.[2]

Christians often fall into this same kind of distraction. We become so entangled in the problems we face, the discouragements and trials that come to us, that we seldom step back for a moment to ask if something more is happening. Do we face severe and bitter trials because a great deal of what God has called us to do involves spiritual warfare? It is true that we have to be careful not to attribute every bump in the road to the realm of the demonic. During the Welsh Revival in the early twentieth century, some Christians began to overemphasize the spiritual dimension. At that time, Jessie Penn-Lewis wrote *War on the Saints* from which many readers have concluded that Penn-Lewis saw a devil behind every chair leg! It is

---

to treat the words of the visitor to Joshua as in need of no further definition.' Woudstra, *Book of Joshua*, 105.

[1] The NET Bible on Joshua 5:14. 'The only remaining question is, how the Captain of the Lord's host can speak of having *now* come, seeing he had not deserted the people committed to his trust, and had lately given a matchless display of his presence in the passage of the Jordan. But according to the common usage of Scripture, God is said to come to us when we are actually made sensible of his assistance, which seems remote when not manifested by experience. It is therefore just as if he were offering his assistance in the combats which were about to be waged, and promising by his arrival that the war would have a happy issue.' Calvin, *Comm. Joshua*, 88.

[2] For a fuller explanation see chapter 10, 'Little Babies Too?'

true that we can become unbalanced in our Christian walk if we think of nothing but spiritual warfare.

On the other hand, spiritual battles with unseen forces are a reality. The apostle Paul informed us that 'we do not wrestle against flesh and blood, but against the rulers, against the authorities, against the cosmic powers over this present darkness, against the spiritual forces of evil in the heavenly places' (Eph. 6:12). No believer need fear these satanic troops, however, for in the gospel and the word of God, the Lord has equipped us with every piece of armour we need to fight in the victory of Christ's power (Eph. 6:10, 13-17a).

While it may be difficult at times for us to discern between trials that God has directly sent our way and the opposition to godly living that we face from the devil and his horde, Joshua was left in no doubt as to the underlying spiritual nature of the conflict that he and Israel faced. Nor was he left without the assurance that the commander of the Lord's army and the host of heavenly warriors would be there to fight on Israel's behalf. The next scenes at the battle of Jericho would prove just how much the Lord was doing for his people.

Upon hearing the angel's declaration, Joshua immediately reacts. Falling on his face to the ground, he bows low or worships and asks, 'What does my lord say to his servant' (verse 14). When he knew that this man was the Lord's commander, Joshua turned his attention from whether or not he would fight for Israel or their enemies. He was now concerned to hear what the commander would say to him. The second question Joshua asked was not intended merely to elicit information. Its essence was 'What do you want me to do? If you are the leader of God's army, what are your orders for me?'

Joshua asked a perfectly reasonable question. He was a man of authority used to giving orders (see Josh. 1:10ff.). By bowing low to the ground, he recognized the superiority of this sword-wielding commander, and he was willing to submit to his authority. If we look at other instances in the Bible where the Lord sent his angel to men, we discover that the angel of the Lord comes to reveal God and his plans and to bring the recipient of this revelation into submission to God's will. In the New Testament, we find that Christ does the very same thing for us. After expounding the glories and riches of God's grace in the Lord Jesus, Paul could appeal to his Roman readers to respond to his message with wholehearted dedication. 'I appeal to you therefore, brothers, by the mercies of God, to present your bodies as a living sacrifice, holy and acceptable to God, which is your spiritual worship. Do not be conformed to this world, but be transformed by the renewal of your mind, that by testing you may discern what is the will of God, what is good and acceptable and perfect' (Rom. 12:1-2).

The command of God's leader

What orders does the commander have for Joshua? Just one—take off your sandals. To remove one's sandals was a sign of respect, of reverence and humility. But why did the commander give this strange order at this juncture? Because sandals were inappropriate when standing on holy ground. The message the commander had for Joshua was the very same one the angel of the Lord had for Moses when he met his servant at the burning bush. While keeping the flock of his father-in-law, Jethro, Moses came to Horeb on the west side of the wilderness to a place called the mountain of God. 'And the angel of the LORD appeared to him in a flame of fire out of the midst of a bush. He looked, and behold, the bush was burning, yet it was not consumed. And Moses said, "I will turn aside to see this great sight, why the bush is not burned." When the LORD saw that he turned aside to see, God called to him out of the bush, "Moses, Moses!" And he said, "Here I am." Then he said, "Do not come near; take your sandals off your feet, for the place on which you are standing is holy ground." And he said, "I am the God of your father, the God of Abraham, the God of Isaac, and the God of Jacob." And Moses hid his face, for he was afraid to look at God' (Exod. 3:2-6).

Here we discover yet another parallel between Moses and Joshua. Time and again the text demonstrates the similarities between these two men to show the continuity between the leaders of God's people and thus of God's plan for his people. The important point to note, however, is that these words culminate the revelation of who this man with the sword is. Joshua was standing on holy ground because the presence of this individual had sanctified it.

As we reach the apex of this encounter, let us go back and put together the pieces of information we have been given. To begin with, this individual appears to Joshua as a man. This is a personal revelation. Next, from the drawn sword motif, we have identified him as the angel of the Lord, or more accurately the messenger who is the Lord. He is the leader of heaven's angelic forces. Furthermore, this person is so holy that he sanctifies the very ground on which he stands, so much so that he requires others to recognize this sanctity. The parallel with Moses' encounter at the burning bush makes it clear that this individual was the Lord God himself. From the vantage point of the New Testament, we can look at this passage and see that the commander of God's army was a pre-incarnate appearance of Jesus Christ.[1] He is the Lord's servant, the fullest expression of his holiness and power.

Before he led Israel into battle, the most important thing Joshua could do was worship the Lord. Worship prepares us for warfare. Joshua was a mighty man, a man of courage, wisdom, and spirituality, but the relevance of this text does not come from Israel's great general. It comes from the commander of the Lord's army. How should you respond to this passage? Take off your shoes! You are on holy ground! Worship Jesus Christ. That is what will prepare you to serve him and to fight against your temptations and trials because as you worship him you will become like him. You are, after all, what you worship.

---

[1] The term used for this in theological studies is *Christophany*.

9

Jehovah Fought the Battle of Jericho
Joshua 6:1-27

―――――――――

Now Jericho was shut up inside and outside because of the people of Israel. None went out, and none came in. And the LORD said to Joshua, 'See, I have given Jericho into your hand, with its king and mighty men of valour.' (Josh. 6:1-2)

One of the most well-known spirituals from the African-American tradition recounts the narrative of Joshua 6.

> Joshua fit the battle of Jericho,
> Jericho, Jericho;
> Joshua fit the battle of Jericho,
> And the walls come tumbling down.
>
> You may talk about your men of Gideon,
> You may brag about your men of Saul,
> There's none like good old Joshua
> At the battle of Jericho.

This spiritual sings the praises of Israel's great general who led God's people to victory in the promised land. Originating in the context of an oppressed people, the verses of this song held out the promise of triumph, if not in this world, then certainly in the next.

While I like this spiritual, I need to quibble a bit with its theology. It is true that God used Joshua to lead Israel into the land of Canaan. Certainly God repeatedly spoke with him to promote courage and give instructions. And there is no doubt that Joshua was a man of uncommon bravery and ability. But in the end, Joshua did not fight the battle of Jericho; Jehovah did. God brought down the impregnable walls of the fortified city. God led Israel to defeat the Canaanites. God gave the victory.

This astonishing truth, that the defeat of Jericho was a gift from the Lord that could be attributed only to him, is the unmistakable theme of this chapter. From the opening verse that leaves us asking how the city will ever fall to the closing curse on anyone who attempts to rebuild it, the clear lesson of Joshua chapter 6 is that God gives his people victory over their enemies. The big question is how does he do this? As you trace the narrative of the chapter, you will see that the Lord is on the move as the priests carry the ark of the covenant around the city, and you will discover that he moves in mysterious ways, powerful ways, and gracious ways to accomplish his ends.

God's mysterious ways

The chapter opens with a description of the besieged city. Every possible entrance had been closed, and no one dared leave the city nor was anyone allowed to enter (verse 1). From all appearances, it seemed that Israel was in for a long siege if they were to overthrow Jericho. The Lord revealed, however, that a complete reversal of events would occur in just seven days. His instructions in verses 3-5 outline the plan for victory, but before he lays out the plans for the overthrow of the city he gave Joshua a promise: 'See, I have given Jericho into your hand, with its king and mighty men of valour' (verse 2). The conquest of the city lay seven days in the future yet so sure and certain were God's purposes and plans that he could speak of it as already accomplished.[1] Both the king and his troops, called here the 'mighty men of valour' would fall before Israel. God repeatedly spoke to Joshua to reassure him with promises of his presence (1:5,

---

[1] The verb *nathanti*, translated 'I have given', is a prophetic perfect. Waltke also calls this a 'perfective of confidence'. Waltke and O'Connor, *Introduction to Biblical Hebrew Syntax*, 490. See also Ronald J. Williams, *Hebrew Syntax: An Outline*, 2nd edition (Toronto: University of Toronto Press, 1976), 30.

9; 3:7). Earlier the commander of the Lord's army declared, 'Now I have come' (5:14), a further commitment to encourage Joshua. With the presence of the commander of heaven's angelic forces, the armies of Canaan would prove powerless before Israel. The Lord wanted his general to know that he was not alone and that success was certain.

The victory was assured, but the method for securing it was most unusual. Israeli archaeologist Yigael Yadin, in his book *The Art of Biblical Warfare*, lists five ways to capture a walled city. You can go over the wall, under the wall, through the wall, surround the city and starve out the inhabitants, or use some sort of trickery, like the Trojan horse, to gain entry.[1] Those strategies make perfect sense, but God had Joshua follow none of them. Instead, in the words of William Cowper, the Lord 'moves in a mysterious way his wonders to perform'.[2] Unlike these typical ways of conquering a walled city, Israel's army was to march around the city walls once a day for six days (verse 3), and on the seventh day they were to encircle Jericho seven times (verse 4). These daily treks were not to be an unorganized meandering but a solemn procession. Seven priests were to bear seven ram's horns before the ark of the covenant. On the final day of the march, a blast from those horns will be a signal for the men of war to shout. At the moment the people cry out, the walls of the city will fall down flat, giving the soldiers access to the city. They can then advance straight into Jericho and capture it (verses 4-5).

This set of instructions was very unusual, but if you know anything about the God of the Bible, you know that you cannot predict his mysterious ways. Joshua knew the Lord, and he did not hesitate to obey by setting into motion the strategy for Jericho's demise. First he called for the priests who carried the ark, and then he arranged for seven other priests to carry trumpets made of ram's horns before the ark (verse 6). He instructed the people to 'Go forward. March around the city and let the armed men pass on before the ark of the LORD' (verse 7).

All of this marching must have looked like just so much foolishness to the people of Jericho. But God's mysterious strategies

---

[1] Yigael Yadin, *The Art of Biblical Warfare* (New York: McGraw Hill, 1963), 16.
[2] From William Cowper's hymn, 'God Moves in a Mysterious Way.'

are not confined to incidents like this in the Old Testament. He moves in mysterious ways when he defeats our enemies as well. Who are these adversaries that war against us? The Bible describes them in various ways. They are called 'principalities and powers' or demonic forces that fight against the children of God (Eph. 6:12; Col. 2:15). The world, the flesh, and the devil continuously assault believers. Death, which derives its fearful power from sin, is the great and final enemy (1 Cor. 15:26). Like Joshua, however, Christians have God's assurance that every foe will be defeated. Even death itself shall be destroyed!

The strategy God employs, however, is not what one might expect. He uses death to defeat death. But he does not use just any death or death as an abstract concept. He uses a real death that took place 2,000 years ago. Through his crucifixion, Jesus Christ suffered the penalty of our sins, but as God almighty, who offered up the perfection of his life as a sacrifice, he overcame the power of sin and death and defeated Satan. One of the clearest statements of this truth occurs in Hebrews 2:14-15: 'Since therefore the children share in flesh and blood, he himself likewise partook of the same things, that through death he might destroy the one who has the power of death, that is, the devil, and deliver all those who through fear of death were subject to lifelong slavery.'

How do we know this death had or has any saving significance? God raised Jesus from the dead. This truth stood at the heart of Peter's sermon on the day of Pentecost: 'Men of Israel, hear these words: Jesus of Nazareth, a man attested to you by God with mighty works and wonders and signs that God did through him in your midst, as you yourselves know—this Jesus, delivered up according to the definite plan and foreknowledge of God, you crucified and killed by the hands of lawless men. God raised him up, loosing the pangs of death, because it was not possible for him to be held by it' (Acts 2:22-24). Jesus' resurrection is the proof of his victory over all the forces of hell that were marshalled against us. The death and resurrection of Jesus Christ, what we commonly call the gospel (cf. 1 Cor. 15:3-4), is the means by which God rescues us from our sin and assures us of victory.

This gospel, however, is as foolish to the natural mind as marching around the walls of Jericho must have seemed to the Canaanites. The Lord knows that his plan for victory does not follow the patterns and standards of human thought. When Isaiah prophesied of God's compassion and the invitation to enter into the blessings of his salvation, he called upon Israel to submit to God's ways, the norms of his thought rather than their own imaginations: 'Seek the LORD while he may be found; call upon him while he is near; let the wicked forsake his way, and the unrighteous man his thoughts; let him return to the LORD, that he may have compassion on him, and to our God, for he will abundantly pardon. For my thoughts are not your thoughts, neither are your ways my ways, declares the LORD. For as the heavens are higher than the earth, so are my ways higher than your ways and my thoughts than your thoughts' (Isa. 55:6-9).

In the same vein, the apostle Paul wrote of the mysterious ways of the gospel that seem so foolish to the fallen mind: 'For the word of the cross is folly to those who are perishing, but to us who are being saved it is the power of God. For it is written, "I will destroy the wisdom of the wise, and the discernment of the discerning I will thwart." Where is the one who is wise? Where is the scribe? Where is the debater of this age? Has not God made foolish the wisdom of the world? For since, in the wisdom of God, the world did not know God through wisdom, it pleased God through the folly of what we preach to save those who believe' (1 Cor. 1:18-21). When Paul preached to the Athenians, some mocked his message (Acts 17:32). Later he defended his ministry before Festus by telling him how he had met the risen Christ and Festus replied, 'Paul, you are out of your mind; your great learning is driving you out of your mind' (Acts 26:24). The world continues to mock Christianity as the religion for the weak-minded. This is stock-in-trade reasoning for the unconverted, and it should come as no surprise to the believer. 'The natural person does not accept the things of the Spirit of God, for they are folly to him, and he is not able to understand them because they are spiritually discerned' (1 Cor. 2:14). That the death of Christ defeats sin and overcomes the power of death itself makes no sense to natural reasoning. The fallen and depraved mind rejects it. But for those who are willing to submit their thoughts to God's, for those who will come under the authority of Scripture as the revelation of God's mind for salvation, they experience victory over sin as surely as Joshua found victory over Jericho.

God's powerful ways

Joshua did not hesitate to set God's plan into motion, and the Israelites did not hesitate to obey either. They did exactly what Joshua commanded. A lengthy section of the chapter from verses 8-21 recounts the seven days of the 'siege'. The narrator tells the story in a highly repetitive, rather typical Hebrew fashion.

The first day of the procession the priests with the ram's horns started out ahead of the ark, blowing the trumpets as they went (verse 8). The armed guard took up the lead ahead of them, and a rear guard followed behind the ark (verse 9). The order of this procession is very important, and the text emphasizes it several times. First, armed men formed the forward guard and took the lead. Next came the priests with the ram's horn trumpets. The priests carrying the ark of the covenant followed them. Finally, the rear guard, another group of armed men, concluded the cavalcade.

The priests with the rams' horns continually blew them (verse 9), but Joshua commanded the people not to make a sound or say a word (verse 10). A time would come to give a war cry but only after Joshua said to do so. So by his orders Joshua 'caused the ark of the LORD to circle the city, going about it once'. At the end of the first day's procession, the priests and people returned to the camp and spent the night (verse 11).

The next morning Joshua rose early, indicating not just the time of day he got up but the eagerness, anticipation, and diligence with which he fulfilled his calling (cf. 3:1). The priests lifted up the ark, and the strange scene began to unfold once again. For the fourth time the text emphasizes the order of the march (cf. verses 4, 6-7, 8-9). The priests with the rams' horns marched before the ark. They were preceded by an armed guard at the fore and followed by an armed guard at the rear (verse 13). And for a second time the text stresses the continual sound of the trumpets (verses 9, 13). This constant blare along with the absolute silence of the people would have contributed to the eerie atmosphere surrounding Jericho. What could this blaring band of mute marchers mean? God was once again engaged in psychological warfare (cf. 5:1). He meant for this unsettling scene to do just that—unsettle the inhabitants of Jericho. With the second day's march complete, the soldiers and priests returned to the camp (cf. verse 11). Now that the processional order and the basic instructions are clearly in the reader's mind, the text simply notes that they kept up this same routine for six days (verse 14).

As this panorama unfolded day after day, it proved to be a demonstration that was both religious and militaristic. The military aspect is not difficult to see—an army surrounded a city. But what occupied the central place in the army's procession? The ark of the covenant. This symbol of God's presence went in the midst of the people, and as if its presence were not enough, the priests with the trumpets drew attention to it. The unmistakable lesson that comes from this order is that God stands at the centre of all his people's victories. The Christ-centred life is the life lived in the power of the gospel. No one can push God to the side and ever hope to achieve spiritual success. Preachers sometimes package 'the victorious Christian life' as a series of steps that one can follow as if it were a mathematical formula. If you simply add all of the parts of the spiritual equation together, you will experience triumph over sin. Of course God and the Holy Spirit are a part of the formula, but the believer is often left with the impression that the burden of the effort rests on his shoulders. The Christian life does not work that way. Of course Christians have responsibilities to strive for holiness; they have to exert effort in the mortification of sin. But at the end of the day success in our efforts and strivings for holiness results from living with the Lord Jesus at the heart of all we do.

Every event in the Jericho story builds to the climax of the seventh day. On that day everyone rose early (cf. verse 12), and only on that day Israel marched around the city seven times (verse 15). For the seventh circuit around the city walls, the strange blare of the trumpets fell silent. Then, from the silence, came one long blast and Joshua said, 'Shout, for the LORD has given you the city' (verse 16; cf. verse 5). At that moment the power of God brought down the wall of Jericho. It 'fell down flat' or 'it fell under itself'. God caused the wall to crumble under its own weight so that every Israelite soldier had a clear way to climb up over the rubble and capture the city! The wall fell. The soldiers went in. The city was theirs. The text mentions not one word about resistance on the part of the Canaanites.[1] The victory was total and complete.

'Shout' was not the only command Joshua issued that day. God gave Israel the city and they, in turn, were to give everything back to him. Known as the *ban* or the devotion to destruction, verses 17-21 provide detailed instructions to the army to destroy everything in Jericho. All the people and possessions in the city belonged to the Lord. Only Rahab and the family in her house were to be spared since she had hidden the spies (verse 17; cf. 2:15-21). The defeat of Jericho was a gift from God that could be attributed only to him (verses 2, 16). From this gift he demands that everything be devoted to him.

Since everything in the city belonged to the Lord, to take spoils of the conquest was to steal what was rightfully his property, and that would bring destruction and trouble on the camp (verse 18). On the other hand, the metallic items found in the city, those made of silver, gold, bronze, and iron were holy. They were set apart, not for destruction, but to be deposited into the treasury of the Lord (verse 19). Verse 24 calls this 'the treasury of the house of the LORD' and most likely refers to the collected possessions associated with the tabernacle. With the exception of these items for the treasury, the Israelites devoted everything to the ban: men, women, young, old, oxen, sheep, and donkeys. All of these they killed with the sword (verse 21). The battle of Jericho was the first battle in the land. Therefore, everything in the city was a kind of first fruits of harvest, dedicated completely to the Lord (Lev. 23:9-14).[2]

---

[1] 'The total silence about resistance on the part of the inhabitants emphasizes the impossibility of opposing [God's] word and also demonstrates that he really is with Joshua (1:5). In Jericho, the destruction of life is total, in contrast to Ai (8:2, 27). This makes Jericho the most complete example of the *herem* as it is prescribed in Deut 20:16-18.' McConville and Williams, *Joshua*, 36.

[2] On the ethical questions and theological significance of the *ban* or the so-called 'Canaanite genocide', see the following chapter, 'Little Babies Too?'

God owns everything by virtue of the fact that he is the creator. The cattle on a thousand hills are his, and he needs nothing from us. Indeed the world and its fullness belong to him (Psa. 50:10-12). Yet he has entrusted to each of us our lives as well as his gifts and blessings and asks that we dedicate them to him and use them for his glory. We are to give cheerfully and generously of our financial resources because Christ has given his all for us (2 Cor. 9:6-15). Such generosity ought to arise first from a complete commitment of our lives to Christ and, in turn, to his people (2 Cor. 8:5). Why should we be willing to devote ourselves to God in this way? Because of his great mercy shown to us in the Lord Jesus. This is Paul's plea in Romans 12:1: 'I appeal to you therefore, brothers, by the mercies of God, to present your bodies as a living sacrifice, holy and acceptable to God, which is your spiritual worship.' When the Lord gave Jericho into Israel's hand, he asked them to give everything back to him. Now that he has given us victory in Christ, he asks the same from us.

God's gracious ways

In the midst of all the chaos of battle, Joshua did not forget to save Rahab. He instructed the two spies who had found shelter in her house to make their way back there to rescue her and her family just as they had promised to do (verse 22). The young men returned to Rahab's home and spared her, her father, her mother, her brothers and all her family that was with her. They brought them out and settled them outside the camp of Israel (verse 23). The soldiers then set the city aflame. They burned everything in it except the silver, the gold, and the vessels of bronze and iron. Those they put into the treasury of the house of the Lord just as they had been instructed (verse 24; cf. verse 19).

Because Rahab had hidden the spies, Joshua saved her and all her house. At the time this account was written she and/or her descendants were still living in Israel as a part of God's chosen people. In the midst of the utter destruction of this Canaanite city, the story of Rahab stands out as a vignette of God's gracious mercy. She deserved to be destroyed along with everyone else. She too had been numbered among the enemies of Israel. She had not only been a pagan, but also a prostitute, an epithet difficult to overcome (cf. verses 17, 22, 25). Yet in his sovereign grace God chose to spare her. Her hiding of the spies did not earn her a place in Israel but rather evidenced a new commitment on her part to Israel's God. It was a work that demonstrated the reality of her faith (cf. James 2:25-26).

Grace lay at the basis of Rahab's rescue, but verse 23 stresses its import: 'So the young men who had been spies went in and brought out Rahab and her father and mother and brothers and all who belonged to her. And they brought all her relatives and put them outside the camp of Israel.' Why outside the camp? They were coming from a Gentile city. They were unclean and had to go through ritual cleansing prior to entering the Israelite camp. The significance lies, however, in what the spies did for them. They *put them* outside the camp'. The phrase is literally 'they caused them to rest'. The verb translated 'put them' occurs numerous times in Joshua to describe what God was doing for Israel. He was putting them or bringing them into a place of rest (see, for example, 1:13; 15; 21:44; 22:4; 23:1). What Israel did for Rahab reflected what God was doing for Israel. Israel provided rest for Rahab and her family just as the Lord was doing for his family. The story of Rahab was a microcosm of Israel's experience. The story that began with Abram, a pagan in Ur of the Chaldees (Gen. 11:31-32), and eventually led to redemption through the exodus and settlement in the land of promise was re-enacted in miniature with the rescue of this woman and her family.

Salvation always comes to a person by grace and the sovereign choice of God (see, for example, Eph. 1:4; 2:8-9). No one is spared the suffering of eternal punishment because he is a good person or she is a nice lady, and no one is damned to hell, no matter how great and horrible his or her sins may be, if those sins have been forgiven through the death of Jesus Christ on the cross. God's grace in the gospel comes to those who are not only undeserving but also ill-deserving. God owes us no favours. Because we are sinners, he owes us everlasting judgment. We deserve damnation for even just one of our sins (cf. James 2:10). Yet God reaches down to us in grace, he cleanses us with the blood of Christ, and by the work of the Holy Spirit he sets us apart, just as he did with Rahab, and says, 'You will be mine!'

God's faithful ways

The closing verses of Joshua 6 point back to Moses' instructions in Deuteronomy 13:12-16 about the curse of total destruction and to God's promise in Joshua 1:5 of his abiding presence. Later revelation demonstrates that God not only kept his promises to Joshua and to Israel, but he also remained true to his curses as well. After the destruction of the city, Joshua placed an oath on Israel regarding Jericho and anyone who would attempt to rebuild it. God would curse anyone who rose up and attempted to reconstruct the city. Laying the foundation would cost him his firstborn, and hanging the doors or gates of the city would lead to the death of his youngest (verse 26).

We know of one instance in biblical history when this curse was fulfilled. Ahab reigned over Israel for 22 years, and his monarchy was the pinnacle of wickedness in the land. The author of 1 Kings describes his reign this way: 'And Ahab the son of Omri did evil in the sight of the LORD, more than all who were before him … And Ahab made an Asherah. Ahab did more to provoke the LORD, the God of Israel, to anger than all the kings of Israel who were before him' (1 Kings 16:30, 33). Ahab's wicked reign bred a defiance of God's word and as a result, 'In his days Hiel of Bethel built Jericho. He laid its foundation at the cost of Abiram his firstborn, and set up its gates at the cost of his youngest son Segub, according to the word of the LORD, which he spoke by Joshua the son of Nun' (16:34). The destruction of Jericho was to be permanent. God kept his oath, and the curse that he pronounced through Joshua proved true.

The chapter ends, however, on a high note. The Lord was with Joshua (Josh. 6:27). That was the 'secret' to his success. God's presence is always the key to living successfully for him. Joseph rose to prominence as a godly man in Egypt because the Lord was with him (Gen. 39:2, 3, 21, 23). Ezra's journey from Babylon to Jerusalem was a success because 'the good hand of his God was on him' (Ezra 7:9). Nehemiah led Israel to rebuild the walls of Jerusalem because

God was with him (Neh. 2:8). Likewise, God was faithful to Joshua. The Lord had promised his presence from the very beginning (1:5, 9; 3:7; 4:14) and he was keeping every word of his promise. God's promised presence continues to be the church's assurance and the foundation of evangelism and missions. Jesus said, 'Go therefore and make disciples of all nations … And behold, I am with you always, to the end of the age' (Matt. 28:19-20).

Do you find it amazing that the God who spoke to Joshua still speaks to us today? God has given us his word, the Bible, so that you and I may still 'hear' him speak. Scripture is the unveiling of God's heart and mind to us. It pulsates with life and authority just as much as it did that day when God said to Joshua, 'See, I have given Jericho into your hand' (Josh. 6:2).

Because the Lord's mind is infinite and he understands all things comprehensively, his words and actions can seem very mysterious to us. We cannot comprehend his far-reaching plan in a single thought the way he can. We are limited to knowing bits and pieces, so to follow the Lord we are thrown back on his wisdom. This is the essential element of walking by faith and not by sight. God's ways do not always make sense to us, but are you willing to obey and follow him even when you do not fully understand? Are you willing to say, 'Lead me, Lord. Direct my paths according to your word.'

God's intention is to lead you, like Israel, into victory. What kind of enemies do you face? What kind of sin and temptation keeps you from living in joy? Do you believe that God's word is capable and complete to help you overcome your foes (see 1 Cor. 10:13)?

Of course we see the wisdom, power, and grace of God most fully in the work of the Lord Jesus Christ. God's wisdom and power meet at the cross. The Corinthian Christians were impressed by the philosophers and orators of their day, but to keep the believers from being swayed from the truth by the logicians and eloquent debaters who travelled from city to city, Paul reminded them that 'the word of the cross is folly to those who are perishing, but to us who are being saved it is the power of God' (1 Cor. 1:18). He goes on to explain, 'For the foolishness of God is wiser than men, and the weakness of God is stronger than men' (verse 25). That was the very reason the great apostle was not embarrassed to preach Christ. 'For I am not ashamed of the gospel, for it is the power of God for salvation to everyone who believes, to the Jew first and also to the Greek' (Rom. 1:16).

The work of Jesus Christ on our behalf demonstrates the ability of God to deal with our sin and death and bring us into everlasting life. Foolish and weak? Yes, that is how it appears. But Jesus, who was crucified in weakness, lives by the power of God (2 Cor. 13:4). Do you live in the life of Jesus? Have you been saved by his death?

In his prayer for the Ephesians, Paul asked the Lord to open the eyes of their hearts so that they might know 'what is the hope to which he has called you, what are the riches of his glorious inheritance in the saints, and what is the immeasurable greatness of his power toward us who believe, according to the working of his great might that he worked in Christ when he raised him from the dead and seated him at his right hand in the heavenly places, far above all rule and authority and power and dominion, and above every name that is named, not only in this age but also in the one to come' (Eph. 1:18-21). God has exercised the immeasurable greatness of his power to overthrow our enemies through the cross of Christ. He gave a foretaste of it at Jericho when the trumpets sounded, the people cried, and the wall fell. He will bring in the full manifestation of that power at the consummation when Christ returns.

On that great and final day a trumpet will sound once again, a cry will go up (see 1 Thess. 4:16), but more than a city wall will fall. John described it this way: 'Then the seventh angel blew his trumpet, and there were loud voices in heaven, saying, "The kingdom of the world has become the kingdom of our Lord and of his Christ, and he shall reign forever and ever"' (Rev. 11:15).

10

Little Babies Too?
Joshua 6:15-21

Then they devoted all in the city to destruction, both men and women, young and old, oxen, sheep, and donkeys, with the edge of the sword. (Josh. 6:21)

S ix million. As a number, I can define it as a six followed by six zeros. It is the sum of sixty multiplied by one hundred thousand. Yet I find it difficult to conceptualize what six million looks like. I cannot imagine six million pennies, certainly not six million dollars, let alone six million people. That vast number, however, corresponds to the number of Jews who were killed in Hitler's holocaust. Germany's *Führer* attempted to exterminate an entire race for his own personal and political gains, and he put millions of people to death, not just men but women and children as well, in cruel and vicious ways. The Nazi-led Jewish genocide scarred the twentieth century like no other crime.

Similar events occurred in Rwanda. In just over three months during the spring and summer of 1994 an estimated 800,000 Rwandans were slain as the Hutus conducted mass killings of the rival Tutsi tribe. The Rwandan genocide destroyed as much as 20% of the small, East African nation's population as fear, political plots, and pent-up hatred prompted the majority Hutus to turn on the minority Tutsis with ferocity.[1]

[1] For information about the Rwandan genocide see http://www.unitedhumanrights. org/genocide/genocide_in_rwanda.htm (accessed 23 June 2015).

Still closer in time and to our own experience were the events of September 11, 2001. The orchestrated attacks by Muslim extremists on the United States were acts of *jihad* or holy war. In the name of their god, *Allah*, terrorists struck at the vitals of American commerce and power in an attempt to wipe out, not a particular ethnic or racial group, but infidels who did not confess Allah as the only god and Mohammed as his prophet.

Each of these atrocities evoke within us feelings of sadness, disgust, and anger. That a demonic madman like Adolph Hitler could gas defenceless women and children seems beyond comprehension. To imagine one ethnic group wishing the complete extermination of another the way the Hutus did the Tutsis is difficult to grasp. The idea that young Islamic extremists would give their lives to take the lives of others for their religion boggles the mind. Yet how are these events of racial, ethnic, and religious slaughter different from the incidents of total warfare that we read about in the book of Joshua? When the Israelite soldiers scrambled over the ruined walls of Jericho, they put everything that breathed (with the exception of Rahab and her family) to the sword—men, women, old, young, soldiers, merchants, oxen, sheep, donkeys, kittens, puppies, and little babies too! How can we read this passage and others like it in the Old Testament and not be overcome with a feeling of revulsion? Is this the kind of material we want in our Bible?

The fact that the Lord, the God of Israel, commanded this wholesale carnage further complicates the problem. Joshua had no particular personal complaint with the Canaanites. He operated under direct, divine orders that God originally gave through Moses (see Deut. 20:16-18). The Jews slew the Canaanites and possessed their land. How do Christians reckon with this fact? Could these directives have come from the God who commanded mercy for the sojourner (Exod. 22:21; 23:9) and love for one's neighbour (Lev. 19:18)? Could this God who demanded the extermination of Jericho be the God and Father of the Lord Jesus? Can we justify keeping the book of Joshua in our Bibles and see it as a part of our Christian heritage, or should we purge it from the sacred record or at least ignore it like an embarrassing relative no one wishes to discuss? Should we conclude with C. S. Cowles that 'To attribute such atrocities to the actual intention and will of God ... poses insuperable difficulties for Christian theology, ethics, and praxis'?[1]

Some people read all the descriptions of indiscriminate slaughter as a certain kind of rhetoric, an overstatement for the sake of emphasis.[2] The language of violence serves to stress the necessity of following God, obeying his law, and forsaking idolatry. In other words, the massacre of the Canaanites is just overblown speechifying to say 'Buckle under the Lord's commands or else!' If this is the case, no one need be embarrassed by the text because it should not be taken literally any more than should the exaggerated threats of a parent who promises a slow and painful death to the child who does not clean up his room.

Another way to deal with this moral difficulty is to expunge the book of Joshua from our Bibles. In a Marcionite[3] manoeuvre, we could simply relegate the barbarism of this ancient document to a place in Ancient Near Eastern history without acknowledging its divine inspiration or granting it any religious authority. Joshua fought the battle of Jericho. What an interesting story. Now let us turn to Romans. Yet a fully Christian view of the Bible that sees each of its books originating by divine inspiration (2 Tim. 3:16) can never settle for cutting out vital parts of redemptive history. Unlike Thomas Jefferson, who was perfectly comfortable to take a penknife in hand and carve up his own version of holy writ, Reformed and evangelical Christians refuse to put forth their hand against the Scriptures lest, like Uzzah, we perish for violating God's holy boundaries (see 2 Sam. 6:1-8; cf. Deut. 4:2; 12:32; Rev. 22:18-19).

If we believe that we must keep Joshua wedged safely between Deuteronomy and Judges, we could opt to ignore it and hope no one asks about its ethical conundrums. Few Christians spend time reading the Old Testament. Perhaps it is best to let Joshua lie there, overlooked and unexplored. But surely we must refuse that course

[1] C. S. Cowles, *et al.*, *Show Them No Mercy: Four Views on God and Canaanite Genocide* (Grand Rapids: Zondervan, 2003), 15.

[2] See the discussion of rhetorical language in Hubbard, *Joshua*, 199-200.

[3] Marcion of Sinope (c. A.D. 85-160) was an early church heretic who rejected much of the Old Testament Scriptures and their teaching about the Lord God of Israel, and devised his own set of canonical Scriptures.

as well. We must honour the book of Joshua as the word of God, not just by retaining its place in the canon but by reading, studying, and believing it. If the Israelites saw the walls of Jericho fall by faith (Heb. 11:30), then we too must look to God in faith to help us understand the moral and ethical challenge of what took place after the walls fell. If faith comes by hearing (Rom. 10:17), then it is essential to look closely at the text of Joshua, to listen carefully to all that God has to say, to place Joshua within the larger context of the Old Testament, to tie it to the revelation of God in Christ that we have in the New Testament, and then draw from it the necessary theological conclusions that arise from such a study.

The day of the Lord

The six-day march around Jericho led inevitably to the climax of day seven. On the seventh day, and only on the seventh day, the Israelites circled Jericho seven times. The people rose up early, as the dawn began to break, and set out on their tour around the city (verse 15). We should exercise care not to overload numbers in the Bible with a significance they are incapable of bearing, especially in historical narrative, but Scripture often associates the number seven with God's presence or divine activity (see, for example, Gen. 2:2; Exod. 25:37; Rev. 1:4, 12; 3:1). The sequence of events that unfold around Jericho have an unmistakable pattern of six plus one, the pattern of the creation week. This seventh day became Israel's Sabbath of sorts as they entered their rest in the promised land. Seven days and seven times around the city on the seventh day also strongly hints at a delay. When the defeat of Jericho boiled down to a blast on the trumpet and a shout from the army, why did God have the soldiers encircle the city day after day? Was he perhaps delaying the overthrow of Jericho in order to give its inhabitants an opportunity to repent? Rahab had abandoned her former allegiance to the gods of Canaan. So had her family. Could others have done the same? Could others have sought refuge within the walls of Rahab's home and been rescued along with her? Perhaps the Lord delayed the destruction of Israel's enemies to give them time to turn from their wickedness. He has no delight in the death of the wicked (Ezek. 33:11). Destroying rebels never gives God a joyful glee. Whatever the reason might have been for this delay, when we reach verse 16, the delay is over. The moment of judgment has come. On the seventh time around the city walls, the priests blew the long blast (cf. verse 5) and Joshua shouted, 'Give the war cry because God has given you the city.'

Devoted to the Lord

Joshua provided specific instructions for the soldiers in verses 17-19 and defined what their task was to be once they were inside the city. Drawing on what Moses commanded in Deuteronomy 20:16-18, he issued the decree of the ban. Two words summarize the army's task: *devastation* and *deliverance*. The deliverance was for Rahab and her family. They alone were to be spared since she had hidden the Israelite spies (verse 17b). The remainder of the city and its inhabitants were to suffer the devastation of the ban. The term 'the ban' is often used to describe the Hebrew term *herem*, translated in the ESV as 'devoted to destruction'. Since the Israelite soldiers were forbidden to take any of the things devoted to the Lord, the items were 'banned', hence the origin of the term. The translation 'ban', however, inadequately explains the complex concept of the *herem* in Israel's holy war. We need to look closely at verses 17-19 to understand the multifaceted nature of this aspect of Israelite warfare.[1]

The term 'ban' or 'devoted to destruction' occurs throughout the Old Testament beginning in Exodus 22:20. To be under the ban is to be dedicated completely to God. In the case of Jericho's inhabitants, they were set apart for destruction. Joshua's instructions are clear—everything that breathes is to die (cf. verse 21). Israel had already carried out the ban on the eastern side of the Jordan River. Having vowed to devote to destruction the Canaanites led by the king of Arad (Num. 21:2-3), Israel followed through with their promise. Later they did the same to Sihon (Num. 21:21-30; cf. Deut. 2:34) and Og (Num. 21:31-35; cf. Deut. 3:6 and Josh. 2:10). Several hundred years after the conquest, the Lord demanded that Saul strike Amalek

---

[1] From the ninth-century B.C. Moabite Stone we have evidence that Mesha also used this term for military conquest. It appears, however, that the earliest use comes from the threats of the Old Testament. Pitkänen, *Joshua*, 162.

and destroy it completely (see 1 Sam. 15). In each of these cases, God required total warfare. Everyone, not just the soldiers or even all the men of fighting age and ability but all the people—men, women, young, old, even the livestock had to be killed.

After consigning everything and everyone in Jericho to total annihilation, Joshua solemnly warned the Israelites that they were not to take anything from the city for themselves. The command was absolute. 'Keep yourselves from the things devoted to destruction' (verse 18). The items were banned. Every Israelite was to stay away from the things found in the city because they belonged completely to the Lord. To take them was to steal what was rightfully his property, and such action would bring destruction and trouble on the camp.

The threat of danger hung over the soldiers when they entered Jericho. If they dared pilfer any of the goods they found, they would 'make the camp of Israel a thing for destruction' (verse 18). The ban would fall on Israel. Irrespective of religion or race, the Lord's ban condemns disobedience. When the verb 'to place under the ban' first occurs in the Old Testament it is a threat, not to the Canaanites, but to Israel. In Exodus 22, God's instructions in the Book of the Covenant direct his people to serve him and him alone. What should happen if an Israelite sacrificed to another god? 'Whoever sacrifices to any god, other than the LORD alone, shall be devoted to destruction' (Exod. 22:20).

That God is not a respecter of persons when it comes to this command becomes clear in the next chapter of Joshua. 'But the people of Israel broke faith in regard to the devoted things, for Achan the son of Carmi, son of Zabdi, son of Zerah, of the tribe of Judah, took some of the devoted things. And the anger of the LORD burned against the people of Israel' (7:1). Achan brought God's wrath down on himself and his family, and he brought destruction and trouble on the camp of Israel, by violating the command of verse 18. When we examine all that the Lord says here, what we discover is not some divine moral monster that derives sadistic pleasure from the slaughter of Jericho's citizens. The text confronts us with the Lord of heaven and earth whose holiness is impeccable. The passage does not present us with the Lord versus the Canaanites but with the Lord's holy hatred of sin.

The danger of the ban for Israel was not pious hyperbole. The nation suffered it, and not just in Achan's transgression. God would later send his messenger, a prophet called 'Elijah' because of the similarity to his Old Testament predecessor, to turn the hearts of Israel back to him and to lay upon Israel the peril of the ban if they refused to repent (Mal. 4:6). How did the people react? They rejected this 'Elijah', John the Baptist (cf. Matt. 11:7-14), and crucified the Lord Jesus Christ. As a result, the Romans invaded Jerusalem and devoted it to destruction in A.D. 70. God never makes idle threats because he never compromises his holiness. Only after the return of Christ and the establishment of his eternal and righteous reign will Jerusalem be free from the danger of the ban (Zech. 14:11).

While people and livestock met their end, the metallic items found in the city, those made of silver, gold, bronze, and iron were holy. They were set apart, not for destruction, but to be deposited into the treasury of the Lord (cf. verse 24). These belonged to God and would be used for the tabernacle and temple. Why did Joshua spare these materials? They are the kinds of items that could survive a fire (cf. verse 24). They are also items of lasting value. Their enduring quality and worth made them appropriate for the tabernacle and temple treasury. They were suitable items for building the house of God.[1] Other objects could also be devoted to God such as fields and livestock (see Lev. 27:21, 28), but once they became his possession they could not be redeemed for personal use.

Each of the verses in this section may easily be labelled with a term that summarizes their content: destruction (verse 17), danger (verse 18), and devotion (verse 19). These three terms also summarize the meaning of *herem* or the ban. If something is under the ban,

---

[1] Is it possible that Paul makes an allusion to this event when he describes the way God's New Testament house, the church, is to be built? Rather than worthless, perishable materials such as wood, hay, and straw, the minister of the gospel should build on the foundation of Christ with gold, silver, and precious stones. Only a temple made of these will withstand the fire (see 1 Cor. 3:10-17). Certainly the Lord rescued Rahab, and she became precious building material for the house of the Lord as an ancestor of David and ultimately of Jesus himself (Matt. 1:5ff.).

God claims absolute and exclusive rights to that person or item and may have it destroyed or set apart for his private use, hence the close correlation between the *herem* and holiness (cf. verse 19).

The destruction of Jericho

That the Israelite soldiers obeyed Joshua and carried out the indiscriminate killing presents us with the reality of this moral problem. No longer was it a threat; it became a fact. The people gave a war cry; the priests blew the trumpets; and as soon as the soldiers heard the blast of the shofar they shouted. At that the wall of the city fell down flat so that Israel's army could walk right into the city to capture it. With these events the story reaches its climax. Following the instructions of verses 17 and 18, the soldiers devoted everything to the ban—men, women, young, old, oxen, sheep, and donkeys. They slew them all with the sword, and afterwards burned the city and everything in it (verse 24). As the first battle in the land, Jericho was like the firstfruits of harvest, given entirely to the Lord (cf. Lev. 23:9-14).

With the implementation of the ban at Jericho, God answered the question, 'Can the paganism, the immorality, the iniquity, and idolatry of Canaan coexist peacefully with the Israel of God?' God made a comprehensive claim to Jericho and its inhabitants in order to judge them and protect Israel. God's holiness demands the punishment of sin and provides for the protection of his people.

Holy, Holy, Holy, Lord God Almighty

To describe and define the ban and the events at Jericho proves to be a relatively easy task. The words and concepts are quite clear. What is not so clear, however, is how to handle such a doctrine. How could a loving and merciful God ever demand such a horrible thing? Would the same Jesus who welcomed and blessed little children (Mark 10:13-16) have them slaughtered? Is God selfish and vindictive? Every parent knows that soon after a child can say 'Mama' or 'Dada' he or she quickly learns to say 'Mine!' Is the God of the Old Testament childish, hoarding his 'toys' so that no one else can have them? Can you and I worship that kind of God? Would God ever tell someone today to do something like this? Were the

Crusades not a mistake after all? Can we become avenging prophets
like Hudson, Ohio's abolitionist John Brown, taking justice into our
hands and justifying bloodshed in the process? Are holy war texts
appropriate Scripture for modern conflicts like Northern Ireland
witnessed during 'the Troubles' between Protestants and Roman
Catholics? To answer these questions we must look at the context
and underlying theology of these incidents, but never for a moment
think that an analytical treatment is an attempt to gloss over or
ignore the horror of the scenes.

These events have first of all to be put into their historical context.
Canaan was not an idyllic setting of happy, close-knit families living
in peace and harmony, planting their flower gardens and spreading
love and joy until those nasty old Israelites came along.[1] God
had delayed the destruction of the Canaanites for four centuries,
as he told Abraham, because their iniquity was not yet complete
(Gen. 15:16). For four hundred years the Canaanites kept sinning
grievously against God as though they were filling a bucket with
their transgressions. What kind of sins were they guilty of? Blatant
idolatry mingled with immorality (Deut. 23:17-18; cf. Num. 25:1-
2) and child sacrifice (Deut. 12:31; 18:10). Canaanite worship was
disgusting on several levels, but before we look down our long,
refined, modern noses at the ignorance and barbarism of ancient
peoples, we should pause to reflect and realize that the modern West
is no different. We worship the god Lust and sacrifice our children as
an inconvenient by-product of our religion. Burn them on the altar
to Molech or have them aborted at a local clinic, the sin is the same.

Not only must we face the reality of the historical setting, but
we also have to come to grips with the Bible's theology. God is
God. He owns all things because he is the creator of all. He has
the right to give life and to take it. God's character is holy and just,
and though we may not understand why the Lord does what he
does, the failure lies in our finitude and sinfulness not in his nature.
Whatever God does is just because he is just. This was John Calvin's
position. Commenting on the slaughter at Jericho he wrote, 'The
indiscriminate and promiscuous slaughter, making no distinction

[1] McConville and Williams, *Joshua*, 111.

of age or sex, but including alike women and children, the aged and decrepit, might seem an inhuman massacre, had it not been executed by the command of God. But as he, in whose hands are life and death, had justly doomed those nations to destruction, this puts an end to all discussion.'[1]

The Canaanites kept adding to their sins until the tipping point came and their 'bucket' could contain no more. As in the days of Noah, God saw their wickedness and determined it was time to judge. When the Lord flooded the earth, 'He blotted out every living thing that was on the face of the ground, man and animals and creeping things and birds of the heavens. They were blotted out from the earth' (Gen. 7:23). God executed his own watery *herem* because he 'saw that the wickedness of man was great in the earth, and that every intention of the thoughts of his heart was only evil continually' (Gen. 6:5). In Joshua 6, he carried out a military *herem* to accomplish the same purpose. God is holy. God's holiness demands that he hate sin. His holy hatred of sin will not allow him to overlook the violations of his law. The Lord must judge sin. Moses stated this explicitly in Deuteronomy 9:4-5: 'Do not say in your heart, after the LORD your God has thrust them out before you, "It is because of my righteousness that the LORD has brought me in to possess this land," whereas it is because of the wickedness of these nations that the LORD is driving them out before you. Not because of your righteousness or the uprightness of your heart are you going in to possess their land, but because of the wickedness of these nations the LORD your God is driving them out from before you, and that he may confirm the word that the LORD swore to your fathers, to Abraham, to Isaac, and to Jacob.'

The God who judges is also the God who protects. By wiping out the Canaanites and their way of life, the Lord endeavoured to preserve Israel from becoming influenced by the sins around them. The events at Baal Peor, recorded in Numbers 25, earlier testified to how easily the Israelites were led astray into idolatry and immorality. What would happen if they were surrounded by it? When Moses preached his final sermon to Israel, he justified the

[1] Calvin, *Comm. Joshua*, 97.

complete destruction of Israel's enemies for this very reason. 'When
the LORD your God brings you into the land that you are entering to
take possession of it, and clears away many nations before you, the
Hittites, the Girgashites, the Amorites, the Canaanites, the Perizzites,
the Hivites, and the Jebusites, seven nations more numerous and
mightier than yourselves, and when the LORD your God gives them
over to you, and you defeat them, then you must devote them to
complete destruction. You shall make no covenant with them and
show no mercy to them. You shall not intermarry with them, giving
your daughters to their sons or taking their daughters for your sons,
for they would turn away your sons from following me, to serve
other gods. Then the anger of the LORD would be kindled against
you, and he would destroy you quickly. But thus shall you deal with
them: you shall break down their altars and dash in pieces their
pillars and chop down their Asherim and burn their carved images
with fire' (Deut. 7:1-5). God protects his people. He protects his
church by calling believers to separate from lawlessness because light
and darkness can have no fellowship. The temple of God is no place
for idols (2 Cor. 6:14-7:1). Though separation from unbelief looks
vastly different for the church than it did for Israel, the underlying
principle remains the same.

In close conjunction with God's hatred of sin, the destruction
of Jericho and other Canaanite cities gives us a small glimpse of
what will happen at the second coming of Jesus Christ. The *herem*
of Israel was limited to a specific time, place, and purpose because
God was establishing his kingdom on earth. He could not allow the
pagan practices of the land to coexist with his rule in Israel.

When Christ returns to establish the full manifestation of God's
eternal kingdom, he will fulfil the spiritual lessons of that ancient
theocracy. He will not allow anything unclean to enter his kingdom
either. John's vision in Revelation 19 of a rider on a white horse
portrays the Lord Jesus Christ as 'Faithful and True', the executor of
the final *herem*. 'From his mouth comes a sharp sword with which
to strike down the nations, and he will rule them with a rod of iron.
He will tread the winepress of the fury of the wrath of God the
Almighty. On his robe and on his thigh he has a name written, King

of kings and Lord of lords … And I saw the beast and the kings of the earth with their armies gathered to make war against him who was sitting on the horse and against his army. And the beast was captured, and with it the false prophet who in its presence had done the signs by which he deceived those who had received the mark of the beast and those who worshipped its image. These two were thrown alive into the lake of fire that burns with sulphur. And the rest were slain by the sword that came from the mouth of him who was sitting on the horse, and all the birds were gorged with their flesh' (Rev. 19:15-16, 19-21).

When the Lord Jesus returns to deal with his enemies, his holy war against sin will make Joshua's conquest look like the proverbial Sunday School picnic. Those who wish to describe the God of Joshua as a moral monster must deal with Jesus the Conqueror. The God of Joshua and Jesus are the same God. They possess the same holiness and intolerance of sin. Is it any worse for the Lord to use the army of Israel to judge his enemies than it is for him to judge them directly?

These events, foreshadowed by Joshua and fulfilled in Jesus show us just how seriously we should take sin and indicate just how vigilant we must be to deal with our own sin. The apostle Paul calls upon every believer to mortify, to put to death, his or her sins by the power of the Holy Spirit: 'For if you live according to the flesh you will die, but if by the Spirit you put to death the deeds of the body, you will live' (Rom. 8:13). He repeats this same command to the church in Colossae: 'Put to death therefore what is earthly in you: sexual immorality, impurity, passion, evil desire, and covetousness, which is idolatry' (Col. 3:5). As Christians, we must engage in a full-scale assault on our sinful desires. In his classic work on the doctrine and practice of mortification, the Puritan John Owen wrote, 'Do you mortify; do you make it your daily work; be always at it whilst you live; cease not a day from this work; be killing sin or it will be killing you.'[1] If the ban executed at Jericho teaches us anything it is that nothing can be tolerated in our lives that opposes God. What

[1] John Owen, *Of the Mortification of Sin in Believers. Works,* edited by William H. Goold, (1850-3; repr. Edinburgh: Banner of Truth Trust, 1987), 6:9.

deeds of the flesh do you coddle rather than kill? What do you allow in your life that depletes your spiritual strength? What sin do you need to face off with the sword of the Spirit and hack to pieces the way Samuel dealt with Agag (see 1 Sam. 15:33)?

Where do you get the power to kill sin? At the place where sin was slain. The Lord Jesus who executes holy wrath against sin became the object of that wrath (see Isa. 53:6-12; 2 Cor. 5:21). God's holiness and justice meet in Christ and his crucifixion. The ban fell on Jesus so that God might be just and the justifier of the one who believes on him (Rom. 3:26). Both salvation from sin and the power to mortify our sins come from Calvary where the curse fell on Christ that the blessing might flow to us. Do you know this Saviour? Are you living and fighting in his power to put to death your sins or is sin killing you?

II

Achan Lost the Battle of Jericho
Joshua 7:1-26

Then Joshua said to Achan, 'My son, give glory to the LORD God of Israel and give praise to him. And tell me now what you have done; do not hide it from me.' And Achan answered Joshua, 'Truly I have sinned against the LORD God of Israel, and this is what I did: when I saw among the spoil a beautiful cloak from Shinar, and 200 shekels of silver, and a bar of gold weighing 50 shekels, then I coveted them and took them. And see, they are hidden in the earth inside my tent, with the silver underneath.' (Josh. 7:19-21)

Many medieval kingdoms abounded in intrigue, conspiracies, mayhem, and even murder. In the late fourteenth century, Richard II of England had his cousin Henry Bolingbroke exiled after Bolingbroke supposedly made treasonous remarks against the monarchy. The following year, 1399, while Richard was on a military campaign in Ireland, Henry returned from exile and, supported by a former Archbishop of Canterbury, Thomas Arundel, confiscated lands, destroyed much of Cheshire, and had himself declared King Henry IV. Upon Richard's return from Ireland, Henry had him imprisoned, where he later died in suspicious circumstances for reasons unknown.

Two hundred years later, against that backdrop, William Shakespeare wrote *Henry V*, an historical play that focused on incidents in the king's life just before and after the Battle of Agincourt.

In Act 4, Scene 1, on the eve of the battle, Henry looks back on the misdeeds of his father and pleads for God's forgiveness lest his troops fear and be decimated in the ensuing conflict. Henry prayed:

> O God of battles! steel my soldiers' hearts;
> Possess them not with fear; take from them now
> The sense of reckoning, if the opposed numbers
> Pluck their hearts from them. Not today, O Lord,
> O, not today, think not upon the fault
> My father made in compassing the crown!
> I Richard's body have interred anew;
> And on it have bestow'd more contrite tears
> Than from it issued forced drops of blood:
> Five hundred poor I have in yearly pay,
> Who twice a-day their wither'd hands hold up
> Toward heaven, to pardon blood; and I have built
> Two chantries, where the sad and solemn priests
> Sing still for Richard's soul. More will I do;
> Though all that I can do is nothing worth,
> Since that my penitence comes after all,
> Imploring pardon.

Although the king sadly sought forgiveness based on the good works he had done and was still attempting to do, he understood that prayer was the best preparation for battle and that unconfessed sin would lead to defeat. If only Israel had realized that before they sought to conquer the city of Ai!

Israel suffered a mysterious defeat when they first went up against Ai. As Joshua reflected on that loss, the Scripture account confronts us with what we need to know to solve the mystery of Israel's surprising loss. How could Jericho fall so easily and yet the smaller, weaker city of Ai rout Israel's forces and send them back to their camp to cower in fear? The answer was sin, sin concealed and unconfessed. Once you read that story, the mystery of Israel's loss is not so mysterious after all. The opening words of Joshua 7 are dark with direct disobedience, covetousness, and greed. These sins, sins we often overlook in ourselves, justify, and in some cases even glorify, provide the backdrop for this discouraging defeat and its horrifying conclusion.

Broken faith

'Israel broke faith in regard to the devoted things. ... And the anger of the LORD burned against the people of Israel' (verse 1). Those few words summarize the situation and give us the bottom line that explains Israel's defeat at Ai. When the walls of Jericho fell, God gave explicit instructions about the spoils of the battle. He claimed possession of the people, animals, and everything else within the city boundaries. Everything in Jericho belonged exclusively to God. It was to be destroyed by the sword and fire (6:21, 24) or put into the treasury of the Lord's house (6:19, 24). He, therefore, warned the soldiers not to steal: 'But you, keep yourselves from the things devoted to destruction, lest when you have devoted them you take any of the devoted things and make the camp of Israel a thing for destruction and bring trouble upon it' (6:18). Achan blatantly disregarded this warning, and God fully enacted his threat.

The backstory of Achan's transgression and the subsequent story of Israel's defeat reveals the terrible consequences of sin. Sin angers God and hinders his work. As chapter 7 progresses, a number of underlying themes emphasize this basic truth. Sin ignites the wrath of God. It brings defeat to the people of God. It hinders the progress of the work of God and must, therefore, be dealt with by God.

Israel's victory at Jericho was one of the most astounding events in their history since the exodus. The Israelites were convinced that God was with them, but they were unaware that sin had entered the camp and compromised their future success. Sin was the one thing that could keep Israel from possessing the land and remaining in it. Sin became the great impediment to realizing fully the promises of God.

But ...

'But the people of Israel broke faith in regard to the devoted things, for Achan ... took some of the devoted things' (verse 1). The opening conjunction *but* draws attention to the contrast between Joshua's spiritual success (6:27) and what is about to be revealed of Achan's spiritual failure. In addition, the information in verse 1 explains the rest of the narrative. Without verse 1, verses 2-5 make no sense against the backdrop of the unbroken chain of success found in Joshua chapters 1-6. The first verse prepares us for what we are about to read, but Joshua had access to the information only after the fact, which explains his actions in verses 6-9.

Achan's thievery was a direct violation of the commands Joshua had given in 6:17-19. His were the actions of but one man. God, however, viewed them as the sin of the nation. It was, therefore, '*the people of Israel* [who] broke faith' and as a result, 'the anger of the LORD burned against *the people of Israel*'. Israel, like the church, was the body of God's people. Paul described the church as one body composed of many members: 'For just as the body is one and has many members, and all the members of the body, though many, are one body, so it is with Christ. For in one Spirit we were all baptized into one body—Jews or Greeks, slaves or free—and all were made to drink of one Spirit' (1 Cor. 12:12-13). Each member is responsible for his or her own sin (cf. Ezek. 18:20), but because of the close unity of God's people, disease in one part of the body affects the whole body. Israel existed as a corporate solidarity so that the sin of one became, in essence, the sin of all. Achan's sin affected not just himself. He 'robbed the whole nation of the purity and holiness which it ought to possess before God'.[1] No one ever sins in isolation.

Having established the background for what unfolds in the rest of the chapter, verses 2-9 spell out the defeat that Israel suffered at the hands of the men of Ai. It was a loss on the field of battle, but it was also a loss in the hearts of Israel's leadership. Military defeat led to spiritual turmoil.

Joshua's approach to the battle of Ai was different than that of Jericho. In the case of the latter, he had specific instructions from the Lord. He did not presume, however, that this battle would be the same, so he sent a reconnaissance team from Jericho to Ai (verse 2). The report that the spies brought back was encouraging. The population of Ai was small. Joshua need not, therefore, send all the troops to fight. A small force of two or three thousand men would be sufficient (verse 3).

Following the advice of his scouts, Joshua sent up the larger of the two suggested numbers, about three thousand men, but they soon

---

[1] Woudstra, *Book of Joshua*, 120.

fled before the enemy (verse 4) who pursued them 'and chased them before the gate as far as Shebarim' (verse 5). Then, at the descent, the men of Ai killed about 36 Israelites. Though this was not a high casualty rate percentage wise, a little over 1%, for the nation and its leaders the loss was great. That Israel could not stand before the men of this city proved to be a huge source of discouragement: 'The hearts of the people melted and became as water' (verse 5). The reaction of the Israelites now mirrored the earlier response of the Canaanites whose hearts had melted (2:11; 5:1). The tables have now turned. Things were not the way they were supposed to be.

How did Joshua and the elders of Israel react to this surprising and discouraging turn of events? They tore their clothes, fell on their faces, and put dust on their heads (verse 6). These were classic signs of mourning in ancient Israel. Joshua and the elders were hurt and bewildered. They had gone from hope and confidence to defeat and despair in one day. In his distress, Joshua cried out to the Lord: 'Alas, O Lord GOD, why have you brought this people over the Jordan at all, to give us into the hands of the Amorites, to destroy us? Would that we had been content to dwell beyond the Jordan! O Lord, what can I say, when Israel has turned their backs before their enemies! For the Canaanites and all the inhabitants of the land will hear of it and will surround us and cut off our name from the earth. And what will you do for your great name' (verses 7-9)?

The defeat at Ai overwhelmed Joshua emotionally and spiritually. He began to question God. 'Why have you brought us here to destroy us?' Was not this the same voice of unbelief heard from the Israelites early on in their journey when they faced difficult obstacles (Exod. 16:1-3; 17:1-3; Num. 14:1-4)? After raising the question, Joshua concluded that Israel would have been better off to remain on the eastern side of the Jordan. He began to experience regret, the attitude we often adopt when we face obstacles and begin to question the wisdom of God. Joshua 'appears to have forgotten God's promises that no one would be able to withstand Israel and that he would be with his people (1:5-9). He concluded that God intended to destroy Israel, and he did not consider the possibility that there might be sin in the camp.'¹ God uses trials, obstacles, and setbacks to grow our faith, to deepen our experience of grace, and sometimes—as in the case of the first battle of Ai—to reveal our sin.

Joshua's distressed state of mind not only led him to question God but also to raise questions in his own mind as to how he would respond now that Israel had suffered a defeat (verse 8). What would he say to the people after all that had happened up to this point? His mental anguish also caused him to lose perspective. He began to believe that the loss at Ai would lead to the rest of the Canaanites surrounding Israel and cutting them off (verse 9). Joshua was afraid that God would not follow through on his promises. They 'will cut off our name', he said. 'And what will you do for your great name?' (verse 9). Joshua feared for Israel's survival and God's glory. The Lord promised to bring Israel into full possession of the land. If they failed, if their enemies were victorious, then the loss would defame the name of God. Nothing less than God's faithfulness to his covenant and the glory of his character were at stake. Though Joshua battled fear and unbelief in his own heart, he knew to take his distress to the Lord. He questioned what God was doing, but he did not keep his questions to himself where they could fester and breed further discontentment and eventually bitterness with the Lord. He cried out to God in prayer. Joshua's posture points us to where every hurting and confused believer needs to be—on his knees, on his face before God. The psalmists, often confused by their circumstances, took their pain to God (Psa. 10:1; 22:1; 44:23-24; 74:1, 11; 80:12; 88:14; 115:2). And even when we do not know how to pray, the Holy Spirit has the ability to take our perplexed and painful attempts at prayer and transform them into groans too deep for words and bring them before the Father's throne (Rom. 8:26-30).

Commentators have suggested many reasons for Israel's defeat at Ai. Some read in the text an overconfidence after the astounding victory at Jericho. Others attribute the loss to a lack of prayer on the part of Joshua prior to the battle. Still others chalk it up to poor planning. But the real reason Israel lost the battle that day was the wrath of God against their sin.

¹ Howard, *Joshua*, 191.

Sin can stop the progress of God's work. Often we try to pass off the problems we face by blaming surface issues when the culpability is ours and our blame-shifting is only a vain attempt to cover our transgressions. When our sin is exposed, we often attempt to justify it by claiming it is not a 'big' sin. We are not guilty of robbery, like Achan, or adultery or significant deception (we only tell 'little, white lies'). But what about our sins of carelessness, bitterness, prayerlessness, or selfishness? Bitterness towards another Christian, or worse yet towards God, can delay and deter the Lord's work and take glory from his name just as easily as if you robbed a bank, bowed down to an idol, or were unfaithful to your spouse. Achan was a thief. He took something that belonged to God. But the essential nature of his sin was worldly selfishness and sinful self-centredness. What he wanted mattered more to him than what God wanted. What matters most to you?

Exposure

God's wrath brought defeat to Israel, but that is not the only way he reacted to the sin. He next moved to expose it because he will not allow a cover-up. Men may conceal their sin and hide it from others, but the Lord in his wrath will reveal it. God would not allow Joshua to blame him for Israel's problems. The answer to Joshua's *Why?* (verse 7) is not *God has been unfaithful* but *Israel has sinned* (verse 11). The Lord rebuked Joshua for his mourning and misplaced blame (verses 7-9). Do not blame God. The fault lay with the people.[1] Joshua did not know that someone had sinned. He did not have the advantage of reading verse 1 of this chapter. What he did know and should have relied on was the fact that God can never lie (cf. 1 Sam. 15:29; Rom. 3:4; Heb. 6:18). But the Lord knew the sin that had been committed, and he knew who had committed it.

When I was a child, one of my favourite books was Laura Ingalls Wilder's *Farmer Boy*. Wilder narrates many stories about her husband, Almanzo, and his experiences of growing up on a farm

---

[1] Compare this to the statements found in Josh. 7:1. Though Achan was the guilty party, the indictment of Israel throughout this chapter underscores the solidarity of the people as one covenant nation.

in New York State. In one of the stories Almanzo, along with his siblings, had to keep house while their parents were away visiting relatives. One day they cleaned the parlour, the nicest room in the house. While the children were working, Almanzo began to argue with his sister, Eliza Jane, and in a split-second of anger, he threw a brush covered with black stove polish at her. It missed her but hit the white and gold wallpaper on the parlour wall! A couple of days after his parents returned home, visitors arrived and Almanzo's mother showed them into the parlour. Almanzo dreaded what was about to happen. When his mother saw the spot on the wall, he was going to be in serious trouble and punished accordingly. His parents and guests went into the parlour and invited him in as well. Almanzo sat among the adults and stared at the wall but could not find the spot where the blacking brush had done its damage. The next day he crept back into the room for a closer look. Where the brush had hit the wall there was now a very carefully cut and pasted patch of wallpaper covering the spot. He later discovered that his sister had covered the black mark to keep him from getting into trouble. Neither of them ever mentioned it to their mother, and she never knew. It is common for people to believe that if they are careful enough, like Eliza Jane with paper and paste, they can cover their sin and no one will ever know. But God knows. And that is the sobering truth. You may be very clever in concealing your wrongdoing from everyone, but you will never be successful in hiding it from God.

Charges

How had Israel sinned? The Lord handed down an indictment with five specific charges: 1. the people transgressed God's covenant which he had commanded them; 2. they took from the devoted things; 3. they stole; 4. they deceived; 5. and they placed the stolen goods among their stuff (verse 11). The Lord had given Israel the land, but he had not given them everything in the land. Some things belonged exclusively to him. The sins enumerated in the indictment explained the victory of the men of Ai and were the reasons the nation could not stand before its enemies (verse 12). The Hebrew soldiers turned their backs and fled because the tables had turned.

Achan had taken some of the items devoted to destruction, and now Israel became 'devoted for destruction'.

Achan's sin was thievery, but its essence was unbelief. By coveting and stealing he said to God, 'I don't believe you have given me all that I need. I do not believe that your provisions are sufficient.' Unbelief had led to defeat on other occasions in Israel's history. When the nation first rejected the report of the spies but later decided to go to battle, the Canaanites defeated them (Num. 14:45). In the early chapters of Judges, the nation as a whole turned to idolatry: 'So the anger of the LORD was kindled against Israel, and he gave them over to plunderers who plundered them' (Judg. 2:14). Nothing will bring judgment upon a Christian more quickly than the turning of his heart away from God's word and failing to trust it.

After handing down his indictment, the Lord concluded: 'I will be with you no more, unless you destroy the devoted things from among you' (verse 12). This statement may at first seem to contradict other passages of Scripture. God must remain everywhere or cease to be God. Omnipresence is an essential characteristic of deity. Though you soar as high as heaven or plunge as deep as hell, you cannot escape the presence of the Lord (cf. Psa. 139:7-12). Heaven and hell, however, demonstrate the great contrast between the blessing of God's presence and the curse of his 'absence'. By God's 'absence', I mean the reality of his divine presence without the blessing of his divine beneficence. Though God had promised to be with Israel and with Joshua (1:5, 9, 17; 3:7), sin threatened his withdrawal. The stolen items had to be destroyed or God would no longer go with Israel's army. The final words of verse 12 remain a stern warning for all. If we allow sin in our lives, then we will forfeit the blessing of fellowship with the Lord.

Joshua continued to lie before the Lord in grief, but it was time for him to deal with Achan's sin, so once again the Lord told him to get up (verse 13). As Israel's leader, Joshua has a responsibility to expose the sin that has so adversely affected the nation. God called for Israel to sanctify themselves: 'Consecrate the people and say, "Consecrate yourselves for tomorrow"' (verse 13). They could not proceed further in the conquest without holiness. No sanctification, no blessing. No blessing, no victory. No victory, no land. The command for consecration is identical to the one Joshua gave just prior to crossing the Jordan (see Josh. 3:5). After the sin of Achan and the defeat at Ai, the Lord has Israel to go back to the beginning, back to the basics. Repent; dedicate yourself afresh to do God's will. 'Consecrate yourselves for tomorrow' because there will be a tomorrow. God has a future for his people because he has a purpose and plan to fulfil. Defeat proved no reason to abandon the cause. If there was repentance, if there was consecration, then there would be hope.

The people were to consecrate themselves because on the morning of the following day God planned to reveal the offender. The Lord outlined his method in verses 14 and 15. He will begin by bringing near the twelve tribes of Israel and selecting one of them by lot. He will then proceed to narrow down the tribe by clans, then by households, and finally by individuals until the guilty person is identified.[1] What will happen once the culprit is caught? 'And he who is taken with the devoted things shall be burned with fire, he and all that he has.' Why? The Lord states two reasons: 'because he has transgressed the covenant of the LORD, and because he has done an outrageous thing in Israel' (verse 15).

With the procedure established, verses 16-21 describe the narrowing-down process as it unfolded the next day.[2] From the tribe of Judah the clan of the Zerahites was taken. From the clan of the Zerahites the household of Zabdi was taken. From the household of Zabdi the selection procedure culminated with the identification of Achan (verses 16-18). After the text names Achan, he is then identified by a reverse statement beginning with his father, expanding to including his clan, and concluding with his tribe. He is Achan the son of Carmi, son of Zabdi, son of Zerah, of the tribe of Judah (verse 18). The text narrows down and then broadens back

[1] Note the emphasis of the text: It is the Lord who will narrow down the selection process. Three times the text repeats the phrase 'that the LORD takes'. Joshua, however, will be his instrument in the process (verse 16).

[2] Now for the third time we are told that Joshua rose early (3:1; 6:12; cf. 8:10). The verb *shakam* indicates not just the time of day (early as opposed to late) but suggests diligence and purpose as well.

out to leave Achan as the focal point. This arrangement not only places him squarely in the middle, but it also links him with all of the people of Israel, and we see the solidarity of God's people emphasized once again (cf. verse 1).

Once sin is uncovered, the right response is confession: 'Then Joshua said to Achan, "My son, give glory to the LORD God of Israel and give praise to him. And tell me now what you have done; do not hide it from me"' (verse 19). Sin dishonours God; confession, however, brings glory to his name. The command 'Give glory to God' occurs seven times in the Old Testament and three time in the New. It can mean to praise God as in Psalm 115:1. Other times, however, such as 1 Samuel 6:5, Jeremiah 13:16, and John 9:24 it appears to be almost equivalent to 'tell the truth'. When Joshua demanded Achan's confession, he wanted him to come clean about what he had done. He had hidden the items he took from Jericho; it was now time for the hiding to stop. The essence of confession is 'coming clean' before God. Only when we confess our sins and seek the Lord's remedy for cleansing can we expect to find pardon (Psa. 32:5; 1 John 1:9).

Achan responded: 'Truly, I have sinned against the LORD God of Israel, and this is what I did' (verse 20). He realized that his sin was against God. No matter who else may be involved and no matter how many people have to face the consequences, the major factor in any sin is that it is a transgression of God's law. David sinned against Bathsheba when he committed adultery with her. He sinned against her husband, Uriah, when he had him killed. But when he came to confess his sin, Israel's king cried out: 'For I know my transgressions, and my sin is ever before me. Against you, you only, have I sinned and done what is evil in your sight' (Psa. 51:3-4). When conviction grips a person's heart he becomes sorry, not for the consequences of sin but for the fact that his sin has been an offence to the Almighty himself. This is the godly sorrow that leads to repentance (cf. 2 Cor. 7:10).

When Achan confessed his sin, he listed the three descending steps that led to his fall. He *saw* a beautiful cloak from Shinar, 200 shekels of silver, and a bar of gold weighing 50 shekels. He then *coveted* them. He desired them and wanted them for his own in spite of the prohibition God had given. Once his sight had stirred his passions, he *took* them and hid them in the ground inside his tent (verses 20-21). These three movements from temptation to sin are as old as the Fall itself. Eve took the same three steps: 'So when the woman *saw* that the tree was good for food, and that it was a delight to the eyes, and that the tree was *to be desired* to make one wise, she *took* of its fruit and ate, and she also gave some to her husband who was with her, and he ate' (Gen. 3:6). I saw, I desired, and I took are the three steps to destruction.

As it turns out, the real battle of Jericho raged not in its streets but in the heart of one man. The city itself fell with no resistance. The trumpets blasted, the people shouted, and the walls fell. In the midst of the city's capture, however, a new foe arose, looked Achan in the eye and said, 'Aren't these things beautiful? Wouldn't you like to have them?' Rather than seeing the enemy for who he was, Achan looked back and said, 'They are beautiful, and I would like them very much.' He saw the clothes, the gold, the silver, and then he wanted them. He coveted them. The text uses the same word that occurs in the prohibition of the tenth commandment, 'Thou shalt not covet' (Exod. 20:17; Deut. 5:21). Achan knew God's moral law, but he willfully disobeyed. He had heard Joshua's admonition before he pillaged Jericho, yet he deliberately took some of the devoted things in spite of the warning. He knew the difference between right and wrong, but knowledge was not enough. It never is. Merely knowing the right thing to do will not give you the power to do it. Achan knew God's law, but he did not delight in it. He let a look become lust, and lust became larceny.

'I saw, I coveted, and I took.' That is a description of sin's operating system. That is the way sin 'boots up' in your heart. It begins with a look, either with your eyes or your imagination. If you do not counter that look, that passing thought, that desire with another look, another thought, another desire, then the first look will lodge in your mind and entice you to come back for more. Your mind is the battlefield for temptation, and what passes through your thoughts is all-important. If you do not renew your mind

by the gospel mercies of God (Rom. 12:1-2), if you do not live in
the realm of greater delights (Psa. 1:1-2), then the battlefield will
become overrun with adversarial thoughts. Soon they will seem too
many and too strong to resist. Surrendering and siding with the
enemy will offer a much easier path and a more pleasant outcome,
or so you think. If you do not love God's law and God's ways and
delight in the word of God more than in the passing pleasures of
sin, you will never overcome the temptations that look you in the
eye and say, 'You want it, don't you?' When sin starts to 'boot up'
in your heart, it is time to reach down and pull the plug. Cut off its
source of power. The apostle Paul instructs us, 'make no provision
for the flesh, to gratify its desires' (Rom. 13:14b). Rather, reconnect
to another power source, a greater power source: 'Put on the Lord
Jesus Christ' (Rom. 13:14a). Consider yourself dead to sin and alive
to God (Rom. 6:5-14).

God's wrath deals with sin

Israel's initial defeat at Ai was the consequence of Achan's sin, but it
was not the punishment for it. This chapter is about God's burning
anger, but as God deals with sin we can also see his marvellous grace.
Without exposing and punishing the transgression, the work could
not go forward. When God poured out his wrath on Achan and his
family, the door was opened for further victory.

With God's indictment (verse 11) and Achan's confession (verses
20-21), it only remains to present the hard evidence. The location
of the contraband was now known, and Joshua sent messengers
to retrieve it. They found everything just as Achan had described.
He had hidden it just as he said (verse 22).[1] The messengers then
returned with the goods and spread them out before the Lord
(verse 23). Their action was significant for two reasons. First, they
presented the articles as evidence in the case. God's identification,
Achan's confession, and the items themselves served as the necessary

---

[1] In English we use various synonyms for the word *hide*. For example, if you
wish to hide something, you may *conceal* it, *secrete* it away, or *cover* it up. Hebrew
possesses several different words for *hide* as well. The particular verb Achan uses
(*taman*) occurs in Joshua only here and in the Rahab story. Rahab hid the spies
(2:6). Achan hid the spoils (7:21-22). The first evidenced faith, the second unbelief.

witnesses to secure his condemnation. Second, the items belonged to the Lord, and the messengers were bringing them back to their rightful owner.

Throughout this chapter there has been a strong emphasis on the verb *take*.[1] Achan took, the messengers took, and finally Achan and all that he had was taken to the valley of Achor (verse 24). The Lord then enacted the ban against him. Because he took from the devoted things, everything that he owned was devoted to destruction. This chapter is full of poetic justice. Achan had brought trouble to Israel then God brought trouble to him. Joshua began with a question, 'Why did you bring trouble on us' (verse 25)? He knew what Achan had done, but why? No answer was forthcoming. The only answer had already been given in verse 21: 'I saw, I coveted, and I took.' The fate of Achan, his family, and his possessions was the same as Jericho's—death and conflagration: 'And all Israel stoned him with stones. They burned them with fire and stoned them with stones' (verses 25).

This horrific scene contains more than a little irony. Achan wanted a small portion of the spoils of war, and in the end he lost everything. He sacrificed his family's safety and the success of the work of God on the altar of immediate gratification. It was just one sin, but one sin can destroy you. That is the reason you have to be vigilant against all sin.

Achan's one sin destroyed him, but it affected others as well. His children lost their lives, possibly because they were accessories after the fact. But 36 soldiers also died, and Israel suffered a humiliating defeat—all because of the sin of one man. Our lives have far-reaching consequences. Our sin can bring destruction to our families and to our churches. That should terrify everyone who reads this and it should drive us all to the foot of the cross for grace, mercy, and the way to escape when temptation comes (1 Cor. 10:13).

Not a few commentators compare the events of Joshua 7 to those of Acts 5 and the deceit of Ananias and Sapphira. In Acts 5, the early church was growing by leaps and bounds. The progress of the

---

[1] The Hebrew verb is *laqah* and occurs in verses 1, 11, 21, 23, and 24. Cf. 6:18. 'Taking' is a key theme in the chapter.

gospel was one of unstoppable, Spirit-empowered success, and then Ananias and Sapphira lied. They sold a piece of land, gave a *portion* of the proceeds to the church, but said that they had given *all*. And God judged them for their lie. The work of God continued but not until after this dreadful intermission into its progress and not until the guilty parties were dead (Acts 5:1-11).

Israel raised up over Achan and the others a great heap of stones (verse 26). At the time the book of Joshua was written the piles of stones were still there, a sobering reminder of what had happened (cf. 4:9; see also 6:25). After the death of Achan, and only then, did God turn from his anger. The chapter closes with an etiological statement: 'Therefore, to this day the name of that place is called the Valley of Achor' (verse 26). The name *Achor* means 'trouble', and a more appropriate name could not have been chosen for that was what Achan had brought on the nation.

But there is something more in verse 26 that we dare not ignore. When Israel executed Achan, 'then the LORD turned from his burning anger'. God poured out his wrath on Achan, and his anger was pacified. We use the theological term *propitiation* to describe this truth. When God poured out his burning wrath on Achan, the door opened for further victory. In chapter 8 Israel wins the second battle of Ai. The Lord's anger has to be appeased for there to be a future for his people. And when his wrath is placated, the way forward opens. That, in summary, is the gospel. I am not arguing that Achan is a type of Christ, far from it. But what this chapter teaches about the wrath of God against sin and his wrath meted out in judgment reveals the essence of the crucifixion. As Jesus hung on the cross of Calvary, he bore our sins and appeased God's wrath on our behalf (1 Pet. 2:24; Rom. 3:25; 1 John 2:2; 4:10).

The shadow of the cross hangs over this chapter. We know that because the concluding events took place in the Valley of Achor. This is not the only passage in the Bible where this valley is mentioned. Hosea prophesied about this very same place: 'Therefore, behold, I will allure her, and bring her into the wilderness, and speak tenderly to her. And there I will give her her vineyards and make the Valley of Achor a door of hope. And there she shall answer as in the days

of her youth, as at the time when she came out of the land of Egypt'
(Hos. 2:14-15). Achor had been a place of desolation when Achan
sinned, but God promised to bring Israel back to the land after the
captivity and make that same valley a place of hope. The Lord once
again committed himself to Israel in faithfulness (Hos. 2:20). That
second exodus prepared the way for Christ to come and accomplish
his 'exodus' on the cross (cf. Luke 9:31) and open the door of hope
for all who trust in him.

Have you hidden some sin in your life? Oh, I know it is just a
little sin and it does not really matter. Or does it? At the end of the
day there are only two things you can do with your sin—attempt to
conceal it (a fruitless effort in the long run) or confess it. If you are
willing to acknowledge your transgressions and bring them to the
cross of Christ, you will find there a just and loving God who has
already poured out his wrath on his Son. And you will find there an
open door of hope which no man can shut.

12

Ambush at Ai
Joshua 8:1-29

And the LORD said to Joshua, 'Do not fear and do not be dismayed. Take all the fighting men with you, and arise, go up to Ai. See, I have given into your hand the king of Ai, and his people, his city, and his land. And you shall do to Ai and its king as you did to Jericho and its king. Only its spoil and its livestock you shall take as plunder for yourselves. Lay an ambush against the city, behind it.' (Josh. 8:1-2)

'Ambush at Ai' sounds more like the title of an old western movie—something along the lines of 'Gunfight at the OK Corral'—than it does a Bible message. If we were to let our imaginations run with the title, we could envision Joshua and the Israelites topped in white hats as they ride off to fight the bad guys west of the Jordan. On the other side, the Canaanites, coiffed with black Stetsons, waylay the Israelites with six-shooters drawn and spurs a' jingling! Yet the ambush at Ai, far from resembling the climactic scene of a cowboy movie, represents a significant turning point in the history of Israel's conquest of the promised land. Israel's first attempt to defeat the city of 12,000 inhabitants proved disastrous. Unknown to Joshua and Israel's other leaders, flagrant and debilitating sin had entered the camp. Achan, the son of Carmi, had taken some of the spoils from Jericho, and his blatant disregard for the word of God cost him his life, his family (7:24-25), and the lives of about 36

159

Israelite soldiers (7:5). Though he thought he had covered up his sin (literally! see 7:21), God revealed Achan's transgression and identified it as the cause of Israel's initial defeat at Ai.

In Joshua 8, however, Israel's failed first attempt to overthrow the city turns, through the guidance of God and the use of military tactics, to a complete victory for the Lord's people. One could easily overlook this strategic chapter by either combining it with chapter 7, and thus seeing it as nothing more than a happy conclusion to a very unhappy beginning, or by sweeping over the text as an interesting bit of Hebrew history without pausing to see the theological statements, links, and implications that the passage presents. Joshua 8 lays out more than a battle plan; it is a religious event undertaken at the command of God. From the opening words of 'And the LORD said to Joshua' (verse 1) to the concluding heaps of stones left to mark the defeat of Ai and its king (verses 28-29), the presence and power of God pervades this chapter as he commanded and Israel obeyed. As Israel dutifully followed God's word, he used his power in conjunction with their planning to achieve his purpose and gave Ai into their hands. The story of Ai's eventual conquest recounts events that entail both divine sovereignty and human responsibility as the way in which God accomplishes his will.

Fear not!

The chapter opens with God's message of peace and assurance, and how Joshua needed to hear those words! The initial defeat at Ai had left the leaders of Israel on their faces in humiliation and sorrow. Prostrate before God, they had torn their clothes and put dust on their heads as they mourned their first loss and began to question the Lord (7:6-9). As the story unfolded, however, it became apparent to all that the sin of Achan had brought defeat to the nation (7:10-26). But those events are now in the past, even if it is the not-too-distant past. Joshua dealt with Achan's sin. God poured out his wrath on that act of wickedness and then turned back from his wrath (7:26). Through judgment Israel was forgiven. The sin had been put away and it was no longer time to mourn; it was time to move.

The forward movement of Israel's troops and subsequent victory began with a message from God: 'The LORD said to Joshua, "Do not fear and do not be dismayed"' (verse 1a). These words no doubt took Joshua's thoughts back to events on the plains of Moab just a few days or weeks earlier. Joshua's commission had included a call to steadfast bravery: 'Have I not commanded you? Be strong and courageous. Do not be frightened, and do not be dismayed, for the LORD your God is with you wherever you go' (1:9). These words echoed the repeated calls to courage that the Lord gave through Moses as he prepared Israel for the conquest. Moses, for example, reminded Israel: 'See, the LORD your God has set the land before you. Go up, take possession, as the LORD, the God of your fathers, has told you. Do not fear or be dismayed' (Deut. 1:21). Later he encouraged bravery in battle through the assurance of God's presence: 'It is the LORD who goes before you. He will be with you; he will not leave you or forsake you. Do not fear or be dismayed' (31:8).

God had not changed. Now that his wrath had been appeased, Joshua and the men of Israel have no reason to cower in fear. Israel's army could proceed with confidence because God promised, 'See, I have given into your hand the king of Ai, and his people, his city, and his land' (Josh. 8:1b). Joshua was, therefore, to take all the army and go up to Ai. One of the interesting features of God's instructions is his emphasis on *all the fighting men*. The text stresses this description again in verses 3 and 11. Earlier, when Joshua had sent a reconnaissance team to Ai, their recommendation was, 'Do not have all the people go up, but let about two or three thousand men go up and attack Ai. Do not make the whole people toil up there, for they are few' (7:3). That advice may have seemed reasonable at the time, but it reflected the opinion of men not the instruction of God. Israel set out on their own without divine directions. The conquest of the city was not the task of merely a handful of soldiers. The overthrow of Canaan was the responsibility of everyone (cf. 1:12-15):[1] 'So Joshua and all the fighting men arose to go up to Ai' (8:3).

God's purpose was to give the king, the people, the city, and the land into Israel's hands. He, therefore, promised a comprehensive

---

[1] 'This phrase "all the people of war" is found in the Old Testament only in the Book of Joshua (8:1,3,11; 10:7; 11:7). These uses seem to emphasize the unity of the entire nation in doing battle (cf. the concern for unity in 1:12-15), even though it was most likely only men who actually engaged in the battles.' Howard, *Joshua*, 203.

conquest as a divine gift. Three additional times in this chapter the
Lord stresses that he will give the city into Joshua's hand (verses 1,
18) and into the hand of Israel (verse 7). There should be no doubt
or concern over this battle since God would see to it that all he has
promised would soon take place.

Almost like Jericho

The specific instructions for taking the city contained three distinct
features. First, Israel was to do to Ai as they had done to Jericho
(verse 2). This meant the destruction of all the inhabitants and
conflagration of the city. Second, while Israel was not allowed
to take anything from Jericho (6:17-19), here the instructions are
different. The spoil and livestock could be taken as plunder for the
people. From this point on the soldiers are allowed to plunder the
cities and use their goods. Had Achan only waited! How often do we
rush to take the things that we want when the Lord wishes to give
us so much more if only we will be patient and trust him. Third, the
Lord gave specific instructions for the method by which they were
to take the city. Israel was to 'lay an ambush against the city, behind
it' (verse 2).

The opening verses set the agenda and tone for the rest of the
chapter. With the call to courage, the confidence God gave through
his promise, and the conquest he guaranteed by Israel's strategic use
of an ambush, he combined the elements of divine sovereignty and
human responsibility from the beginning and gave his people the
assurance they needed to persevere.

A strategy overview

Joshua immediately set out to obey the Lord. Verse 3 summarizes
his actions: he chose 30,000 elite troops, called here *mighty men of
valour*,[1] and sent them out by night. Some have raised the question
whether or not Israel could have mustered such a large army in the
wilderness. It is possible that the term often translated *thousand* may
not refer to a specific number but to a unit of soldiers (for example,

---

[1] The troops from Reuben, Gad and half of the tribe of Manasseh were called
mighty men of valour (1:14). The Lord also used this phrase to describe the soldiers
of Jericho (6:2).

a platoon). So it could be that Joshua took 30 platoons or 30 units of soldiers for the task.[1] But it may be a literal number. In either case, he organized the soldiers to take the city.

Joshua charted a simple plan of attack. The army would divide into two groups. One division was to position itself behind and not very far from Ai and wait to ambush it (verse 4). The second division, led by Joshua, would approach the city fully expecting the men of Ai to come out to meet them just as they had done a few days before (cf. 7:4-5). And similar to the prior encounter, Joshua and his troops will flee (verse 5). The quick retreat on Israel's part was to serve as a ploy to give the soldiers of Ai a false sense of security. Just as Israel had fled from their prior attempt to defeat the city so, it would appear, they were doing again. Joshua and his forces planned to draw the men of Ai far away from the city (verse 6). With the city left unprotected, the Israeli soldiers lying in wait can then ambush the city and take possession of it because the Lord their God will give Ai into their hand (verse 7). As soon as the ambush troops captured the city, they were to set it on fire (verse 8).

The summary of Israel's strategy once again clearly combines God's sovereignty and man's responsibility. The military plan involved an ambush and eventually a pincer movement to cut off all the troops of Ai. But it also included the promise of the divine appointment and the gifting of the city to Israel. The Lord was at work behind the scenes, but none of his actions absolved Israel's army from making its plans and situating its troops to secure the best possible advantage for victory.

The execution of all of the plans was to be done 'according to the word of the LORD' (verse 8). Joshua then concludes his instructions with the words: 'See, I have commanded you.' The Lord speaks, and Joshua is his mouthpiece. Everything was done 'according to the word of the LORD' in contrast to the advice of men (7:3). When Israel first attempted to conquer Ai, the record is remarkably silent regarding the voice of God. The text gives no indication that Joshua or any of the rest of the Israelites sought his direction. They simply

[1] Pitkänen, *Joshua*, 172. Holladay lists the third meaning of *'elep* as 'military unit, subdivision of tribe.' William L. Holladay, *A Concise Hebrew And Aramaic Lexicon of the Old Testament* (Leiden: Brill, 2000), 18.

spied out the land and devised what they thought to be the best possible plan of action. Now, however, Israel is careful to do just as the Lord said because they have seen the terrible consequences of disobedience.[1]

After Joshua completed his instructions, he sent the troops out by night and they went to the place where they were to lie in ambush and stayed there. They positioned themselves between Bethel and Ai, just to the west of Ai (verse 9). The planning stage for the battle concluded, however, with a rather odd note about Joshua's sleeping arrangements: 'but Joshua spent that night among the people' (verse 9). Why would Scripture care to tell us where Joshua slept? Because the Lord wants us to see this leader as one who lives among his people rather than standing aloof from them. Joshua also slept among the people because he was a part of the decoy troops not the ambush unit that had just left the camp. The decoys had the most dangerous task and, though his own life may be on the line the next day, he would not shirk his duties. This kind of dedication should remind us of our greater Joshua who not only sleeps among his people and is with them in the toughest battles, but who has promised to be with them even to the end of the age (Matt. 28:20; cf. Heb. 13:5).

Déjà vu?

When we arrive at the third segment of the story (verses 10-17), a close reading of the text begins to raise a number of questions. How is the account recorded in these verses related to what is written in verses 3-9? Are the 5,000 soldiers mentioned in verse 12 additional troops to the 30,000 stated in verse 3 or is the smaller unit a subset of the larger?[2] Was the night Joshua spent with the people (verse 9) and the night he spent in the valley (verse 13) two separate nights or two parts of the same night? Commentators have approached this passage from several different angles, including emendations to the

[1] 'In vv. 7-8, religious concerns are visible again. This time, Ai fell to the Israelites because God was involved, in contrast to the first time, when he was not (see on v. 1). It was at God's command that Israel would take Ai (v. 8) and with his help (v. 7). The unfolding of the story in the rest of the chapter shows that the Israelites strictly obeyed God's commands this time.' Howard, *Joshua*, 204.

[2] Calvin combined the two for a total of 35,000 soldiers. Calvin, *Comm. Joshua*, 123.

Hebrew text. It seems best, following David Howard's lead, to read
verses 3-9 as a summary with verses 11-13 functioning as a flashback
that covers verses 3 and 10. The main events then resume in verse
14.[1] Hebrew narrative often does not follow a sequential order of
events, so to read the text in the way Howard suggests poses no
problems from a literary standpoint. And it preserves the interpreter
from suggesting changes to the Hebrew text where no manuscript
evidence to support such changes exists.

Following this approach to the text's structure, we can proceed to
summarize the more detailed account of the events. Joshua and the
troops with him approached the city of Ai and camped on its north
side, with a ravine lying between the Israelite camp and the city
itself (verse 11). Of the 30,000 troops that Joshua had mustered, he
took approximately one sixth of them, or about 5,000 men, and sent
them west of the city to lie in wait for the ambush (verses 12, 13).[2]
Verse 13 ends as verse 9 had, referring to the place Joshua spent the
night. Since verses 9 and 13 refer to the same night, it appears that
Joshua stayed with the army north of the city but then, sometime
during the night, made his way down into the ravine (cf. verse 11) to
prepare for the battle.

As soon as the king of Ai saw the Israelite encampment, he and
his soldiers set out to fight, unaware of the ambush forces positioned
west of the city (verses 14). Joshua and the troops he led feigned
defeat and retreated in the direction of the wilderness (verse 15). This
ruse was the genius of Joshua's plan. The soldiers of Ai took the bait,
pursued Israel, and were drawn away from the city (verse 16). With

---

[1] The text itself contains internal markings that indicate this is the proper
way to read the story. 'Verse 11 begins with a disjunctive, circumstantial clause
construction and thus introduces the retrospective account of vv. 11-13. The signal
that this account is concluded—and the main narrative is resuming—comes at
the beginning of v. 14, which begins with the paragraph marker *wayehi* ("and it
happened"), followed by a stage-setting time reference in a subordinate clause
("when the king of Ai saw") and a normal resumptive verb form.' Howard, *Joshua*,
200-01. See also pp. 205-06.

[2] The text presents the ambush troops as waiting *behind* the city (verses 2, 4, 14)
and to its *west* (verses 9, 12). With the main forces camped north of the city (verse
11), *behind* the city would appear to be toward the south. It seems, however, that
west of the city is *behind* it from the perspective of the Israelite camp near Jericho.

all of the men from Ai and Bethel joining in the pursuit, the city was left wide open and vulnerable to attack (verse 17). Ai's earlier victory had left the people over-confident that they could easily defeat Israel again.

The tables turned

With the soldiers drawn away from the city, the Lord commanded Joshua to stretch out his javelin toward Ai for the city had been given into Israel's hand (verse 18). That simple act alerted the ambush brigade positioned west of the city to attack (see verses 18, 19, 26). But Joshua's stretched-out spear played a more important role than just a signal. Joshua resembled Moses who stretched out his staff to perform miracles in Egypt (Exod. 7:19; 8:5, 6, 16, 17; 9:22, 23; 10:12, 13, 21, 22), to part the Red Sea (Exod. 14:16, 21, 26, 27), and to fight with Amalek (Exod. 17:8-16). Both Moses and Joshua resembled the Lord who redeems his people with a stretched-out arm (Exod. 6:6; 7:5; 15:12). Joshua's extended javelin became a symbol of God's hand stretched out in power on Israel's behalf.[1] Like Israel's earlier victory over the Amalekites and David's later victory over Goliath, there was to be no doubt that the battle belonged to the Lord (1 Sam. 17:47).

When the Israelite soldiers lying in ambush received the sign, they rose quickly, ran into the city, captured it, and set it on fire (verse 19; cf. 7:20). When the men who had pursued Israel in the direction of the wilderness looked back, they saw smoke rising from the fires of Ai and realized what had happened—they had been tricked! Left without strength to turn one way or the other, they found themselves trapped between the burning city and the Joshua-led forces who then turned on them (verse 20). Death and destruction were inevitable and inescapable. The soldiers' demise at the hands of Israel served as a portent of God's judgment to come—inevitable and inescapable. When he turns to bring down his condemnation, no one will have the strength to flee (Rev. 20:11-15).

---

[1] 'As Israel appears to flee, Joshua stretches out his sword towards Ai, in a sign that it is Yahweh who reigns over the events.' McConville and Williams, *Joshua*, 43. The traditional translation of *kidon* is *javelin*. Holladay notes, however, that the Qumran materials suggest a 'short sword for cutting and thrusting.' *Concise Hebrew Lexicon*, 156.

When we reach verse 21 it is as though the camera has swung around to film the battle from the opposite direction, and we see the same events unfold from the Israelite's perspective. With smoke rising from the city, Joshua and his brigade could see that the ambush had been successful. With the city under Israel's control, Joshua turned his men to attack their pursuers. The ambush troops then left the city to pursue the men of Ai and trapped them on both sides. Leaving them nowhere to flee, the Israelites destroyed everyone. Not one soldier survived (verse 22). Israel then captured the king of Ai and brought him to Joshua. This final note from verse 23 was, in the words of one commentator, 'an action that signals absolute victory (verse 23; cf. 10:26-27; 1 Sam. 15:8)'.[1]

Complete destruction

The final paragraph of the Ai narrative details for us the complete destruction of the city itself. The word *all* is the key term, and the text repeats it five times regarding Ai in verses 24-26. After the Israelite forces slew everyone in the field, they returned to the city and destroyed it. Israel struck *all* of the inhabitants, *all* of them to the very last with the edge of the sword (verse 24). *All* who fell that day, the total number of men and women, was 12,000. Those were *all* the people of Ai (verse 25). Finally, Joshua kept his javelin outstretched until he had devoted everyone, *all* the inhabitants of Ai, to destruction (verse 26). Israel did to Ai just as they had done to Jericho, and that is a key theological point in this chapter. The city was an offering to the Lord. Destroyed because of its wickedness (like Jericho), Ai became a sacrifice that testified to the holiness of God and his ownership of all things. In the case of Ai, God allowed Israel to take the spoil and livestock, but the underlying principle remained the same: the enemies of God's righteous kingdom had to be judged. Rather than being fuelled by spiteful vengeance or blood-thirsty aggression on Israel's part, everything happened 'according to the word of the LORD that he commanded Joshua' (verse 27; cf. verse 8).

---

[1] Hubbard, *Joshua*, 234.

Joshua's concluding acts at Ai delineate the final scenes of total warfare. He burned the city, made it a heap of ruins (verse 28), and executed its king (verse 29). Joshua hung the king on a tree until sunset. This probably means that he impaled the king on a spike,[1] a further display of the *herem* or the ban. The sight of the impaled king reminded Israel that the people of Canaan were under the curse of God. Moses, by the inspiration of the Spirit, had written: 'And if a man has committed a crime punishable by death and he is put to death, and you hang him on a tree, his body shall not remain all night on the tree, but you shall bury him the same day, for a hanged man is cursed by God. You shall not defile your land that the LORD your God is giving you for an inheritance' (Deut. 21:22-23). At sundown Joshua, in obedience to the stipulations of this law, ordered that the carcass be removed from the tree and thrown at the gate of Ai. Over the king's corpse was raised 'a great heap of stones, which stands there to this day' (verse 29). Like the earlier cairns of the conquest (4:20-21) and the grave of Achan (7:25-26), this stone pile memorializes God's hatred of sin and his determination to be the sole king and ruler of his people.

Lessons from Ai

The account of the second battle and ultimate conquest of Ai highlights both God's sovereignty and man's responsibility. Entailed in these twin truths, however, are a number of other lessons. One of the main principles evident in this account is that God will accomplish his purposes in spite of man's sin. And the Lord will do this because he triumphs over sin. His purposes and plans cannot ultimately be thwarted (Job 42:2). The initial defeat at Ai left Joshua questioning the Lord. Is evil more powerful than God? Will Satan's forces triumph in the end? Has God made some mistake (cf. 7:7-9)? The answer to all of these questions was and remains a resounding 'No!' Sin wreaks havoc with people's lives. It harms their fellowship with God and gets them off the track of pursuing his purposes. About that there can be no doubt. Sin is contrary to God's will. It is

[1] This is Hubbard's opinion. *Ibid.,* 235.

'any want of conformity unto, or transgression of, the law of God'.[1] But sin cannot stop the purposes of God in working out his perfect plan.

I never reflect on this truth without thinking about the life of Alexander Whyte, one of Scotland's premier preachers of the nineteenth century. Whyte had been born out of wedlock and raised by his single mother, Janet Thompson. Though Whyte had been born illegitimately, and thus his parents were out of God's will for their purity, the Lord still fulfilled his plan to raise up a great voice for Christ. Had Whyte's parents sinned? Yes. Could they be excused for their sin? No. Did God have a plan to bring Alexander Whyte into the world and make him a mighty instrument in his hand? Yes. Can all of this be grasped and fully understood by the human mind? No. We are left to marvel at the wisdom, grace, goodness, and power of our sovereign Lord!

Belief in the sovereignty of God does not mean, however, that our obedience or disobedience is inconsequential. Israel followed the word of God, and as the Israelites obeyed and did everything 'according to the word of the LORD' God brought them victory. Christians should never think of obedience as one option among many; we should consider it the *only* course to follow. Scripture repeatedly attaches blessing to obedience (see, for example, Deut. 28:1-14; Psa. 1:1ff.; Prov. 8:32; James 1:25). Obedience never *earns* blessing. The gospel teaches that we must live and die by grace alone. Obedience is, however, the means God uses to bring blessing into our lives. The Israelites experienced success in the second attempt to defeat Ai because they followed God's instructions. Success for the believer comes the same way (cf. Josh. 1:8). The Bible may seem old-fashioned and irrelevant to our culture, but it is still the only guide to the knowledge of God and his will (2 Tim. 3:16-17).

The ultimate victory of the Israelites at Ai also demonstrates to us that God is a God of renewed opportunities. Though Israel had transgressed his law, the Lord did not give up on his covenant people. He corrected them; he dealt with their sin; but he also forgave and brought his people back to Ai to experience his triumph. Perhaps

[1] *Westminster Shorter Catechism*, Answer 14.

some sin from your past continues to rise up and haunt you. You have confessed it to God and sought the cleansing of Jesus' blood, but the memory of your transgression and the feelings of guilt that accompany it seem to hover over you like a spectre. When you think about your past, you may conclude that God will never be able to use you. Your emotions may say, 'You're worthless', but grace says, 'You're forgiven.' Guilt may say, 'God has no place for you', but the gospel says, 'The steadfast love of the LORD never ceases; his mercies never come to an end; they are new every morning; great is [his] faithfulness' (Lam. 3:22-23).

God's ways

When we compare the first two victories recorded in Joshua, it becomes evident that God does not always work the same way to accomplish his goals. He gave both Jericho and Ai into Israel's hands, but he did so in two very different ways. Victory at Jericho consisted of marching around the city and waiting for the walls to fall. The triumph at Ai involved military tactics and strategy. God gave the success in both instances, but one victory looked very unlike the other. God works in different ways in our lives as well. This is especially true with regard to our salvation. While the gospel remains the same and justification is always by faith alone in Christ alone, the circumstances and experiences of Christians differ considerably. When I was a young believer, I listened to testimonies of others, and they all seemed so different from mine. 'Was I really a Christian?' I wondered. I finally realized that I was being foolish. God has created us as unique individuals with distinctive personalities, often placed us in vastly different circumstances, and we should not expect every testimony to sound the same.

Though God works in different and often mysterious ways throughout history, in the end, his kingdom will triumph. Chapter 8 opened with the words, 'Do no fear and do not be dismayed. ... See I have given into your hand the king of Ai, and his people, his city, and his land' (verse 1). This promise sounds very similar to one that Jesus gave to his disciples: 'Fear not, little flock, for it is your Father's good pleasure to give you the kingdom' (Luke 12:32). We might well wonder, given all the wickedness we see in the world around us and the remaining sin we find within us, if we will lie defeated like the soldiers who first attacked Ai or be victorious like Joshua and his ambush unit? The answer lies in the cross of Christ. Since Jesus has triumphed over all sin through his death and resurrection, and since he will fully manifest his kingdom when he returns, we need not fear. He who has begun a good work in us will bring it to completion on that great and final day (Phil. 1:6).

Covenant Renewal
Joshua 8:30-35

———

*At that time Joshua built an altar to the L*ORD*, the God of Israel, on Mount Ebal, just as Moses the servant of the L*ORD *had commanded the people of Israel, as it is written in the Book of the Law of Moses, 'an altar of uncut stones, upon which no man has wielded an iron tool.' And they offered on it burnt offerings to the L*ORD *and sacrificed peace offerings. And there, in the presence of the people of Israel, he wrote on the stones a copy of the law of Moses, which he had written.* (Josh. 8:30-32)

N ow that the Israelites had achieved victory at Ai, they would have naturally assumed that they were to proceed to the next battle in their overthrow of Canaan. But Joshua and the nation did the unexpected; they paused. This is not the first time a surprising halt occurs in the narrative. After crossing the Jordan, Israel camped within sight of Jericho to perform the rite of circumcision and celebrate the Passover (see Josh. 5:1-12). Why the unexpected stop? The nation pursued far more than a military campaign. The battles they fought were the Lord's battles, and it was essential that they be prepared spiritually to act as his agents to subdue the land of promise. Both in Joshua 5, before the battle of Jericho, and here, after the battle of Ai, Israel paused for renewal.

Renewal is an essential element of spiritual progress. The apostle Paul commands Christians to be renewed in the spirit of their minds (Eph. 4:23). Our goal should be for inward renewal day by day

(2 Cor. 4:16). Renewal entails a fresh start and fresh hope. Israel had failed at Ai, but God in his mercy brought his people from defeat to victory. Before the people pressed on, however, they needed to reaffirm their resolution to follow the Lord. This ceremony was not, however, Joshua's last-minute idea. As early as Deuteronomy 11 God commanded Israel to do this: 'And when the LORD your God brings you into the land that you are entering to take possession of it, you shall set the blessing on Mount Gerizim and the curse on Mount Ebal' (Deut. 11:29).

The Israelites were to renew the covenant after they entered Canaan as a reminder of who God is and what their relationship to him must be if they were to keep their inheritance in the land. Since Israel had recently done a royal job of bungling their efforts to secure the land, this proved to be an opportune time to return to the basics of spiritual life, which is the essence of covenant renewal. Covenant renewal is an intentional return to the fundamentals of our relationship with God so that we might remember his commitment to us in Christ and so that we might reaffirm our commitment to him. We return to the basics of our relationship with God so that we might move forward into the future.

Worship through sacrifice

What did it look like when God's people renewed their commitment to the Lord? As Israel paused outside of Ai, the anticipated event unfolded in several distinct actions. It began with worship at the altar. 'Then' (NIV) or 'At that time' (ESV) 'Joshua built an altar to the LORD' (Josh. 8:30). These introductory words connect the ceremony described in the following verses with the events that had just taken place. Israel had recently gone from astonishing victory to devastating defeat and back to victory again within a brief period of time. The nation had ridden a spiritual roller coaster that brought Joshua and the elders from lying prostrate before the ark of the covenant (7:6) to marching the people some twenty miles north of Ai to gather around that same ark and rededicate the nation to God.

Joshua built an altar to the Lord on Mount Ebal, and established an atmosphere of worship. From where did Joshua get this idea?

Moses had prescribed the ritual in Deuteronomy 27. Before Israel
ever entered the land, they had received God's instructions to make
their way to Mount Ebal and its nearby neighbour, Mount Gerizim,
to renew the memory of the covenant and to recall their covenant
obligations to follow God's law.

From the very beginning of this effort, therefore, Scripture guided
Joshua as he set about to erect the altar 'just as Moses the servant
of the LORD had commanded the people of Israel, as it is written in
the Book of the Law of Moses' (verse 31).[1] Since the debacle at Ai,
where the text makes no mention of God at all, Joshua has been
keen to point out that the Israelites would claim victory only if they
followed the will of the Almighty (cf. 8:8, 27). He carefully built
the altar exactly as Moses prescribed: 'And there you shall build an
altar to the LORD your God, an altar of stones. You shall wield no
iron tool on them; you shall build an altar to the LORD your God of
uncut stones. And you shall offer burnt offerings on it to the LORD
your God' (Deut. 27:5-6; cf. Exod. 20:24-25).

Uncut stones have never been chiselled or shaped by the hand
of man. They are stones as they naturally exist. Why did God put
this restriction on the building materials? It may have been to avoid
the appearance of making a carved image for worship, an act clearly
forbidden by the Ten Commandments (Exod. 20:4).[2] Hubbard
believes it is difficult to discern the intent of the regulation. He writes,
'The purpose for the prohibition of reworked stones is uncertain. In
my view, if the physical alteration of the stones transmits defilement
(likely), the preference for unaltered ones serves to preserve the

[1] The expression 'the book of the law' occurs several times in Joshua (1:8; 8:31, 34;
23:6; 24:26). Twice it is simply 'the book of the law' (1:8; 8:34). Twice it is 'the book
of the law of Moses' (8:31; 23:6). Once it is 'the book of the law of God' (24:26).
The phrase 'the book of the law' occurs at both the beginning and the end of the
book of Joshua, and the words of Joshua were added to the book of the law (24:26)
indicating that Joshua clearly saw what he wrote to be Scripture and on equal par
with the words of Moses. It raises the question, however, as to what it refers to
specifically. It seems to refer to Deuteronomy (Deut. 29:21; 30:10; 31:26; 2 Kings
14:6; 22:8, 11). Nehemiah read the book of the law (Neh. 8:1, 3, 18; 9:3). The phrase
'book of the law' only occurs once in the New Testament in Galatians 3:10 where
the apostle Paul quotes from Deuteronomy 27:26.
[2] Woudstra, *Book of Joshua*, 147.

holiness of space set aside for God.' He adds, 'Other scholarly
suggestions include: to keep out Canaanite influences from Israelite
worship; to avoid luxury; and to maintain a semi-nomadic lifestyle.'[1]
Since using tools profaned the altar, it appears that God did not
want Israel to use cut stones in order to keep the altar free from the
work of man. The worship of God through sacrifice should not be
associated with man's efforts or, as Francis Schaeffer described it,
'humanism'.[2]

We can never approach God through our own works. Even our
best endeavours fall far short of his perfections (see Isa. 64:6). If
we listen to God's word as Joshua did, however, and are careful to
follow his instructions, then we may come to him with confidence
(Eph. 3:12) because we approach God through the work of his Son,
Jesus Christ, and not through the efforts of our own hands. That is
the lesson—another sermon in stones—not just for Israel but for us
to learn as well.

After raising the altar, the people of God offered burnt offerings
and peace offerings on it. Of the numerous sacrifices available
to Israel, these two were fundamental for the covenant renewal
ceremony. Moses recorded the regulations for the burnt offering,
sometimes called the *holocaust* offering, in Leviticus 1. After the
chosen animal was sacrificed, a priest used its blood to make an
atonement or covering for sin. He then burnt the entire carcass
on the altar. Nothing was saved for food or implements. The fire
completely consumed it. As the substitute for the worshipper, the
blood of the animal was poured out for forgiveness and its entire
body consigned to the flames symbolized the Israelite's complete
dedication to God.

The peace offering, also called the fellowship offering, was similar
to the burnt offering in that it consisted of the death of the animal

[1] Hubbard, *Joshua*, 254-55.

[2] 'This special altar was not to have any works of man upon it. In this way, it was
different from the brass altar that was commanded for the tabernacle. When God
gave the Ten Commandments, he wanted the people to understand and never to
forget that an altar does not have value because of what people do to it. In other
words, this was a complete negation of all humanism.' Schaeffer, *Joshua and the
Flow of Biblical History*, 130-31.

as a representative of the individual and the shedding of the animal's blood. The peace offering differed, however, in that the worshipper kept part of the meat from the sacrifice and used it for a meal (Lev. 3; 7:15, 30-34). This meal represented the restored fellowship of the Israelite and his God. The peace offerings also included thank offerings (Lev. 7:12-15) as a means of giving praise to God for his goodness.[1]

Israel offered these sacrifices on Mount Ebal, the mountain of curses (Deut. 27:9-26). At the very place where God's people rehearsed the penalties inflicted on all those who break his law, at the place where the guilt and burden of sin would be felt intensely, there the Lord made provision for forgiveness and communion with him. This scene provides us with a beautiful representation of the gospel. Where was the weight of sin's curse felt the most? Where did God's judgment fall with such intensity that the sun was darkened so that no one could witness the agony of the awful exchange? At the cross, the very place where, through the sacrifice of Christ Jesus, God held out his mercy. On the mountain where the curses fell, God offered a lamb as the terms of peace. The law calls men and women to holiness: 'You shall therefore be holy, for I am holy' (Lev. 11:45). But no one is perfectly holy. The altar on Mount Ebal reminded Israel of God's grace and his provision for restoration.[2] In New Testament terms, this is the message of John: 'My little children, I am writing these things to you so that you may not sin. But if anyone does sin, we have an advocate with the Father, Jesus Christ the righteous. He is the propitiation for our sins, and not for ours only but also for the sins of the whole world' (1 John 2:1-2).

The fact that this ceremony began at an altar points us unmistakably to the fact that for Christians renewal begins at the cross. When an Israelite brought a ram or lamb to sacrifice, he placed his hands on the victim's head, leaned his weight on the beast, and confessed his sins. He symbolically transferred his guilt to the sacrifice. Now that Jesus has born our sins on the cross, we can return to him with our

[1] J. Barton Payne, *The Theology of the Older Testament* (Grand Rapids: Zondervan, 1962), 387.
[2] Schaeffer, *Joshua and the Flow of Biblical History*, 130.

confession and ask him to cleanse us from all defilement because he has made the atonement. If, like the church at Ephesus, you have lost the passion of your first love for Christ (see Rev. 2:4), flee to the feet of a crucified and risen Jesus to rekindle the flame. Confess your sins, and find forgiveness.

That, in turn, enables you to become a kind of whole burnt offering as you consecrate your life to God. Is that not what the gospel calls every believer to do? In Romans 12, Paul urged to the Christians in Rome to become living sacrifices: 'I appeal to you therefore, brothers, by the mercies of God, to present your bodies as a living sacrifice, holy and acceptable to God, which is your spiritual worship. Do not be conformed to this world, but be transformed by the renewal of your mind, that by testing you may discern what is the will of God, what is good and acceptable and perfect' (verses 1-2). He based his plea on 'the mercies of God'. What are they? The entire summary of the gospel that he gave in the first eleven chapters! The only logical response to the gospel is whole-hearted dedication to the Lord Jesus Christ. If Jesus gave his all for you to secure your eternal salvation, why would you hold anything back from him?

In 1872, evangelist D. L. Moody travelled to the United Kingdom to meet with and learn from other Christian workers. One day in Willow Park he sat on a bench with fellow evangelist Henry Varley. Varley turned to Moody and said, 'The world has yet to see what God will do with and for and through and in and by the man who is fully consecrated to Him.' It proved to be a turning point in Moody's ministry. He said to himself and to the Lord, 'I will be that man!'[1] Will you be that man, that woman, that boy, or that girl? Can you say that you are consecrated to God? Have you given yourself entirely to Jesus Christ as your Lord and Saviour? If you cannot affirm that statement, what are you holding back from God? Why are you holding back from God? Where will your reluctance lead you? What will it do to your soul and to your life?

Renewing your covenant with God also entails a renewal of your fellowship with other Christians. While we do not bring bulls and

[1]   http://www.christianitytoday.com/ch/1990/issue25/2510.html   (accessed   30 June 2015).

goats to church for sacrifices, we do share a fellowship meal. As a family we sit at the Lord's Table and feast with him. Each time you take Communion, the sacrament serves as God's means to call you to renew your commitment to the Saviour and enjoy all of his goodness. Those who receive the supper by faith are 'made partakers of his body and blood, with all his benefits, to their spiritual nourishment, and growth in grace.'[1]

The transcription of the law

The covenant renewal ceremony consisted not only of worship at the altar but it also involved the transcription of the law. After the sacrifices were offered, Joshua wrote a copy of the law of Moses. He wrote the law on stones in the presence of all the people. Stones have already played an important role in the book of Joshua. After Israel crossed the Jordan, Joshua built a cairn at Gilgal as a sign and in anticipation of a time when the children would ask 'What do those stones mean to you' (4:6)? A mound of stones was raised over Achan's grave (7:26) as well as that of Ai's king (8:29). The reference to stones in verse 32 leaves us asking, 'Which stones do you mean?' Are these the stones of the altar? Grammatically that is possible. Those are the only stones that have been mentioned so far in the immediate context. If we look back, however, at Deuteronomy 27 where Moses first outlined this ceremony, Israel was to set up two stones, cover them with plaster, and write the law upon them (verses 2-3). Since Joshua scrupulously followed the other directions Moses gave, the only reasonable conclusion is that he did here as well.[2]

We are left, however, with a second question: What did he write? The text says 'the law of Moses' (verse 32), but what did that entail? It is unlikely, indeed most likely impossible, that he could have written an entire book from the Pentateuch and certainly not all five books. The law that he wrote on the two stones may reflect the two tablets of the law that Moses carried down from Mount Sinai. In that case, Joshua wrote the summary of the law that we commonly

---

[1] From the *Westminster Shorter Catechism*, Question and Answer 96.

[2] Pitkänen, following Driver and Craigie, points out that plastering stones for writing was an Egyptian practice. Pitkänen, *Joshua*, 86. Joshua and Caleb would likely have had first hand experience of this kind of stone writing.

call the Ten Commandments. It is also possible that he wrote the Commandments and the document that follows them, a combined collection known as 'the book of the covenant' (Exod. 20:1-23:33). Whichever portion of Scripture he wrote, Joshua was careful to transmit the word of God. He copied the law that had already been given to Israel. Joshua conveyed the text; he did not create it.

These standing stones, like the other cairns found in the book, served as a memorial, a solemn reminder of God's actions. They also provided Israel with another copy of the word of God for all to see and read. This in itself was a great blessing. Every copy of God's word is precious. God's ancient people did not own personal copies of the Torah. And only since the Protestant Reformation have ordinary Christians had access to the Scriptures in their native language. How great is our advantage to have the Scriptures so easily accessible! Do not take that blessing for granted.

All Israel

The renewal ceremony involved all of Israel. In addition to the expression 'all Israel', the text enumerates the kinds of people who were there: sojourners or aliens as well as native-born Jews. The group also included its notable leaders: elders, officers, and judges (verse 33). This emphasis appears again in verse 35 where Joshua read all of the law 'before all the assembly of Israel, and the women, and the little ones, and the sojourners who lived among them'. It is important to see this ceremony as a corporate event rather than an individualistic one.

The priests who carried the ark had been situated at Shechem between Ebal and Gerizim. The ark here has its full name: 'the ark of the covenant of the LORD' (verse 33) and stands, along with the altar, as the focal point of the events. Moses was very specific when he gave directions to Israel. Six tribes were to stand at Mount Ebal—Reuben, Gad, Asher, Zebulun, Dan, and Naphtali. The remaining six, namely Simeon, Levi, Judah, Issachar, Joseph, Benjamin, positioned themselves on Mount Gerizim (Deut. 27:11-13). John Calvin pointed out the significance of this arrangement: 'The intervening space was occupied by the Levites with the ark of the covenant, that the Lord might be surrounded on all sides by his own people.'[1]

The text again mentions the command of Moses, the Lord's servant (cf. verses 31, 35). References to Moses occur five times in these verses. Everything that happened was 'just as Moses the servant of the LORD had commanded'. The entire ritual rings out again and again 'the word, the word, the word'. Scripture plays a central role in the revelation of and establishment of the covenant. In fact, God's covenant with Abraham is Scripture. It is his word of promise. Without God's word, how else would we know that God is our God and that we are his people? Without his initiative to tell us, we would remain in ignorance, sin, and death. Scripture not only reveals the Lord's faithful and binding promises, but it also tells us how to live in covenant faithfulness as we follow our God. The reason for it all is 'to bless the people of Israel'. 'In short, this ceremony serves a single purpose, to bestow on the people Yahweh's blessings. As the words of Joshua's reading cascade like a waterfall on the people below, they drench them in the power of God to bless.'[2]

The reading of the law

After transcribing the words of the law on the stones, Joshua read them aloud. This was the third and final phase of the ceremony. Situated as they were between Mounts Ebal and Gerizim, the Israelites found themselves in a natural amphitheatre where the people could easily hear Joshua.[3] He read 'All the words of the law', which is further defined as 'the blessing and the curse'. This is likely a specific reference to the blessings and curses listed in Deuteronomy 27:9-28:68. He was thorough: 'There was not a word of all that Moses commanded that Joshua did not read' (verse 35).[4]

---

[1] Calvin, *Comm. Joshua*, 134.
[2] Hubbard, *Joshua*, 258.
[3] Schaeffer, *Joshua and the Flow of Biblical History*, 128.
[4] Moses used these words to make a covenant with the people, a covenant between Israel and God in addition to the covenant he made with them at Horeb. Horeb, Moab, and now Shechem became the key locales for God's interactions with his people.

When the people of Israel heard the blessings and the curses, they were reminded of their solemn obligation to follow the Lord wholeheartedly. Israel was to repeat this kind of covenant renewal service in seven-year cycles. During the Feast of Booths in the year of Jubilee all Israel was to assemble and hear God's word so that they may 'learn to fear the LORD' (see Deut. 31:9-13). Fear or reverence is the proper response to God's law. Those who hear it ought to tremble at its threats and rejoice in the promises. Covenant renewal reminds us that we are obligated to obey God as well. We owe our obedience to him, not out of a servile fear but stemming from a loving relationship. The greatest summary of the covenant is the Ten Commandments, but how do they begin? With redemption. *I have brought you out of Egypt, therefore obey me.* Grace enables and encourages duty.

Joshua read aloud to all the assembly of Israel. The final words of the passage emphasize once again the corporate nature of the ceremony. The text clearly stresses the involvement of all Israel. Not only does Joshua refer to 'all the assembly' but he further refines his description so that the reader understands this does not refer to just the men. It included the women, the small children, and the resident aliens (verse 35). The people who received the word included the socially disadvantaged as well.[1] Covenant renewal involves all of God's word for all of God's people.

The Bible contains other examples of covenant renewal. In Nehemiah 8, Ezra read the law of God and explained it to the exiles who had returned to Jerusalem. He taught the Scriptures, and the Israelites responded to what they heard. This is the essence or core of covenant renewal. Abraham Kuruvilla defines it as 'the reading and exposition of the biblical text in a corporate, ecclesial context, an event mediated by the preacher, [which] culminates in application that readjusts the congregation to their God and his demands, and restores them in proper relation to him, thus reaffirming their status as those purchased and delivered by God.'[2]

---

[1] 'Hess (1996: 172) notes pertinently that verse 35 specifically mentions groups that are weak in respect of power (women, children and sojourners).' Pitkänen, *Joshua*, 191.

[2] Abraham Kuruvilla, *Privilege the Text: A Theological Hermeneutic for Peaching* (Chicago: Moody, 2013), 99.

Covenant renewal takes place as God's people gather around God's word. This is one of the primary reasons Christ has placed the church at the centre of his plan for spiritual growth. Well-rounded Christian nurture cannot occur in isolation from other believers. Edification, the use of spiritual gifts, united praise and prayer all require the gathered assembly of God's people.

The elements of covenant renewal found in Joshua 8 are exactly what we need if we are to renew our own walk with God and pray for him to revive our hearts and his church. As we hear the gospel preached, we must be brought again and again to the person and work of Christ as the foundation, not only for salvation but for discipleship as well. We must also have the word of God taught and applied clearly so that we might know his will. And we must receive the Lord's word in the context of his people.

14

Obligated by Oath
Joshua 9:1-27

So the men took some of their provisions, but did not ask counsel from the LORD. *And Joshua made peace with them and made a covenant with them, to let them live, and the leaders of the congregation swore to them.* (Josh. 9:14-15)

A roller coaster provides a good metaphor for the Christian life with its ups and downs of spiritual highs and lows. At times, you probably feel that you are riding a roller coaster in your own journey with God. No sooner do you experience a success than you plummet to a failure. The difference between a roller coaster and your spiritual life, however, is that at least you can anticipate the descent with a roller coaster! You are fully aware that the long click, click, click climb to the top will result in a sudden, heart-swallowing, stomach-churning plunge on the other side. The spiritual life, on the other hand, does not always come packaged with built-in anticipation and forewarning. Often we find ourselves tumbling into temptation and trouble before we know what is happening.

Israel experienced something of a spiritual roller coaster ride after they entered Canaan. From heights of victory at Jericho to the crushing low of their initial defeat at Ai (along with the revelation and punishment of Achan's sin), back again to triumph at Ai and the covenant renewal at Mounts Ebal and Gerizim, Israel has climbed to heights of joy and plummeted to the depths of despair. Then came the Gibeonites.

The conclusion of chapter 8 is a spiritual pinnacle in the book. Yet no sooner did the Israelites reach this high point in their experience than they fell into the Gibeonites' deception. Israel compromised with the Canaanites because they failed to seek the counsel of God. Joshua 9 is about the sin of disobedience, but it is also about more than disobedience. It is about compromise, but it is also about more than compromise. It is about Israel's lack of prayer, but it is also about more than their lack of prayer. Bible readers often look at passages of Scripture like this and see various truths or principles that the text contains but fail to see their inter-connectedness. It is like looking at a recipe and seeing apples, sugar, flour, and shortening and yet failing to see 'apple pie'.

We have to try to look for the big picture, the 'finished product', the 'pie' of Joshua 9. Sin, compromise, lack of prayer—all of these ingredients are important, yet the emphasis of the chapter is on Israel's swearing an oath to the Gibeonites and keeping that oath at all costs. The men of Gibeon asked Israel to make a covenant with them (verse 6). Joshua made a covenant and swore to them (verse 15). This binding oath affected Israel's subsequent actions because they spared Gibeon for the sake of the pledge they swore (verses 18, 19, 20). It is in this truth—the making and keeping of oaths—that the message of the chapter is to be found. When you take an oath or make a vow, God expects you to keep it even though you may have made the vow to your own disadvantage.

An oath made sinfully

The first half of the chapter is about an oath made sinfully. A Canaanite coalition that included kings from far and wide, from the hill country and the lowland and from the area east of the Jordan and as far west as the Mediterranean Sea, amassed itself against Israel. The alliance consisted of six different people groups: the Hittites, the Amorites, the Canaanites, the Perizzites, the Hivites, and the Jebusites. Though these peoples often fought among themselves, their kings rallied them to form a united front against a common enemy—Israel. Fear motivated this alliance. These nations had heard reports about the conquests of Jericho and Ai, and their hearts melted within them (cf. 5:1; 7:5). If those great cities had fallen, they could not afford to stand by and wait for Joshua and his troops to show up outside their city walls. As a result, the pagan powers of the land combined their armies and mounted an aggressive opposition to the people of God.

This reaction to Israel's victories should not surprise us. They were, after all, facing an invading army intent on complete conquest. Yet from another angle their reaction is the common response of the world to the people of God. The Lord Jesus tells us to expect opposition, hostility, and persecution: 'If the world hates you, know that it has hated me before it hated you' (John 15:18). The apostle John wrote, 'Do not be surprised, brothers, that the world hates you' (1 John 3:13). Why did these nations fear Israel so? They knew that Israel's presence in the land threatened their lives. They knew that Joshua left no survivors at either Jericho or Ai, which did not bode well for the future, and they could not sit idly by. People today fear the power of God and the presence of authentic Christianity, not because they believe they will lose their lives but because the presence of a genuine, biblical faith threatens their lifestyle. And so they lash out with anger; they oppose and fight the truth.

Though our historical situations differ from that of ancient Israel, the attitude of the world toward God and his people remains the same. When you find yourself in a conflict for being a Christian, remember that the opposition you face from others is not so much directed at you as it is at God. This Canaanite coalition mounted an armed resistance to Israel because they opposed Israel's God. Rather than submit to him they fought against him. When people hate you and persecute you for being a Christian, it is because they hate God. You happen to be his representative and the closest target at the time.

The Gibeonites heard the same reports about Jericho and Ai as had the other nations, but they chose a very different response. Rather than aggressive opposition, they opted for cunning deception. We discover in verses 4 and 5 a well-thought-out and elaborate ruse.

By taking clothing, shoes, and accessories that were old and worn-out, as well as dry and crumbly food, the men of Gibeon disguised themselves to make it appear as though they had come from a far country.

With their disguises in place, the Gibeonites approached Joshua in the camp at Gilgal and requested that he and Israel make a covenant with them. Their request indicated that they knew something about Israel's law. The Lord had told Moses that he could not make a covenant with any of the inhabitants of the land (Exod. 23:32; Deut. 7:2), but if those who lived in cities far away were willing to submit to Israel, they could co-exist in a peaceful relationship (Deut. 20:10-18). Somehow the people of Gibeon knew that this was Israel's policy. And so they set about to convince Joshua and the leaders of the nation that they were indeed from a very distant land and, therefore, Israel could safely swear an oath to them.

Israel had a clear obligation, however, not to enter into treaties with the people of the land. The close proximity of Gibeon would have prevented any kind of alliance. 'Perhaps you live among us', they said (verse 7). The Gibeonites responded with a vague, non-committal reply. 'We are your servants', they said. Joshua, with far less subtlety retorted, 'Who are you? And where do you come from?' (verse 8).

In response to those direct questions, the Gibeonites' deception became more direct, more explicit, and more pious. They claimed that they had made a long journey from a far country because they had heard about the Lord and all that he had done in Egypt as well as to Sihon and Og on the other side of the Jordan (verses 9-10). Sin is never more disgusting than when it attempts to put on a spiritual face. What was missing from their report? They did not mention Jericho and Ai. Why not? Apparently this would have been a dead give away that they lived near by.[1]

The Gibeonites then proceeded to recount their rehearsed lies. They told how their elders had sent them on this journey and how they had started out with new clothes and fresh food (verses 11-13). With their plan to deceive in full swing, they presented the evidence

[1] Howard, *Joshua*, 226.

of their long expedition. 'Look at our bread. Look at our wineskins, shoes, and clothes. Is this not enough to convince you that we are telling the truth?' The Gibeonites filled their story with half truths. They had heard of Israel's conquests; their elders had sent them on the journey; they did take clothes and provisions with them. Israel had a right to the whole truth from the Gibeonites, but they did not get it.[1]

Deception was not the only sin that occurred in this incident; Israel was guilty of presumption. Having heard the Gibeonites' story, they responded in verses 14 and 15 by examining their provisions. What Israel failed to do was to ask counsel from the Lord. Marten Woudstra calls Israel's reaction to the Gibeonites 'naïveté'.[2] Dale Davis refers to it as 'the trouble with common sense'.[3] Israel presumed that they could evaluate the evidence, size up the situation, and make a decision regarding this treaty without seeking the counsel of God.

As a result, 'Joshua made peace with them and made a covenant with them, to let them live, and the leaders of the congregation swore to them' (verse 15). These three expressions: (1) made peace, (2) made a covenant,[4] and (3) swore to them, stress the strength of the agreement Israel entered. The Gibeonites got what they wanted: a solemn oath sworn by Israel that they would not slaughter the Gibeonites. While the men of Gibeon reached their goal, Israel failed at what should have been their first priority. They failed to

[1] Howard, *Joshua*, 226.

[2] Woudstra, *Book of Joshua*, 157.

[3] Davis, *Joshua: No Falling Words*, 75.

[4] The expression 'made a covenant' is literally 'cut a covenant' (*wayyikroth lahem berith*), an expression that refers to the sacrificial ceremony that took place when two parties entered into a covenantally binding agreement. By literally cutting animals, placing the parts in two piles, and passing between them, the parties in the agreement said, in effect, 'May it be done to me as has been done to these animals if I fail to live up to my terms of the covenant.' This is sometimes called a self-maledictory oath. See Genesis 15:7-21 and Jeremiah 34:17-20. For further explanation, see O. Palmer Robertson, *The Christ of the Covenants* (Phillipsburg, NJ: P&R, 1980), 7-15, 128ff., and Peter J. Gentry and Stephen J. Wellum, *Kingdom Through Covenant: A Biblical-Theological Understanding of the Covenants* (Wheaton: Crossway, 2012), 248-58.

seek God and his glory. They failed to pray. They failed to walk by faith and not by sight.

The concluding words of verse 14, that Israel 'did not ask counsel from the LORD', clearly indicate that prayer would have prevented this sinful alliance. Had they only asked for insight and wisdom, God would have given it. He would have revealed the devious plot. God is willing and able to answer prayer and to use prayer to guide us into his will, but we are quick to sell God short when it comes to this means of grace. We don't really believe that prayer accomplishes anything and that's evident by how little we actually pray. But how much do we forfeit when we fail to pray? James makes it clear that we have not because we ask not (James 4:2). The problem is not unanswered prayer but rather unasked prayer. We must 'Ask, seek, knock,' Jesus said (Matt. 7:7), and watch God work!

An oath kept faithfully

Both Gibeon and Israel sinned when they entered this treaty, but once the oath had been made it had to be kept. Three days after their encounter, Joshua and the other Israelite leaders realized their mistake. News reached them that the Gibeonites were their neighbours, and rather than living far away they lived among them (verse 16). When Israel set out to find them, they reached their cities (Gibeon, Chephirah, Beeroth, and Kiriath-jearim) on the third day (verse 17). The distance between Gibeon and the Israelite camp at Gilgal was only 19 miles. 'Why did you deceive us?' Joshua asked (cf. verse 22). 'We were afraid that we would be destroyed', they replied (cf. verse 24). Fear led Gibeon to deception. Their sin is understandable—they did not want to die—but it is not excusable.

For Israel, on the other hand, self-reliance led to presumption. Their sin is understandable as well—the evidence was compelling— but it is not excusable either. Natural fears, sincere efforts, or logical conclusions never excuse sin. Both Gibeon and Israel did wrong when they formed their alliance, and even though the oath was made sinfully, still, it had to be kept faithfully. And that is exactly what Israel did.

Israel kept their oath to Gibeon in two ways. *First*, they spared the Gibeonites. Israel's army would not attack and kill them (verse 18).

Not everyone was happy with this situation. Many of the Israelites wanted to destroy them, and they murmured against their leaders for ever making a covenant with them in the first place. Despite this, the leaders stood firm (verse 19).

Second, in chapter 10, Israel protected the Gibeonites. When Adoni-zedek, the king of Jerusalem led a coalition to attack Gibeon, the Gibeonites called on Israel to come to their aid and they did. God honoured Israel's faithfulness and fought for them against Adoni-zedek and the others. He cast down great hail stones and threw the Canaanites into a panic (10:6-11). As a result, Israel won the battle and Gibeon was spared.

Why were the Lord's people so intent to keep this oath, and why did the Lord honour it? Because it was an oath sworn in his name (see verses 15, 18, 19, and 20). It would have been easy to justify breaking this treaty.[1] Joshua and the others could have reasoned that since they made the treaty under false pretences its terms were not binding. On the other hand, they could have concluded that, since they had not sought divine guidance about the matter, it was not God's will for the Gibeonites to live and, therefore, have slaughtered them. Yet they honoured their oath because to break it was to go against one's word of guarantee and, worse yet, to dishonour God's name. Since they made promises to the people of Gibeon, Israel could not renege on their obligations. Had they done so, God's wrath would have fallen upon them. So Israel allowed Gibeon to live. If you take notes in your Bible, may I suggest that next to verse 20 you pen the words, 'Two wrongs don't make a right.'

This oath continued to bind Israel into the future. During King David's reign the land suffered from a famine that lasted for three years. When David prayed and sought an answer from God, the Lord revealed that he was punishing Israel because Saul had broken the covenant with Gibeon and sought to destroy them (2 Sam. 21:1-9). God takes oaths and vows seriously even if we were wrong to have made them.

---

[1] 'Contrary to the human impulse to lie and justify oneself, an impulse indulged far too commonly, the leaders did not deny that they had done this … but they are powerless to make any changes.' Howard, *Joshua*, 229.

Israel's oath represented a compromise with the pagans of the land. They swore to their own detriment, but God honours those who honour their vows. In fact, by honouring our vows we draw close to the Lord. In Psalm 15:1 David asks, 'O LORD, who shall sojourn in your tent? Who shall dwell on your holy hill?' The multifaceted answer to that question includes that person 'who swears to his own hurt and does not change' (verse 4). The psalm describes and praises a man who makes a vow and then, even though he has to suffer for it, does not break his word.

This is what Jesus did for us in the covenant of redemption. We use the phrase 'covenant of redemption' to describe the arrangement or agreement, if you will, between God the Father and God the Son for our salvation.[1] The Father promised to give the Son a people for his own possession. The Son promised to come and die to redeem those people from their sin so that he might present them to the Father as his spotless bride. Jesus emphasized this covenant in his high priestly prayer in John 17. The Lord Jesus Christ entered into a bond and swore to secure our salvation even though it meant suffering and death for him. He swore to his own hurt and yet did not turn back.

If we take seriously the work of Christ for our salvation, then must we not also take seriously the vows that we take as Christians? If you are married, then you once stood before God with your true love and said, 'I do.' And now perhaps you wish you had not. Marriage vows have become cheap in our society. They are easily abandoned for 'irreconcilable differences'. If anyone ever had 'irreconcilable differences' with a spouse, then surely it was the Rev. James Fraser of Alness, a Scottish minister who lived in the eighteenth century. His most famous work is entitled *A Treatise on Sanctification*. Alluding to his domestic circumstances, Sinclair B. Ferguson writes, 'In the case of this work a little biographical knowledge increases our appreciation of the author and enhances the credibility of his exposition.'[2] What was Fraser's marital situation?

[1] For a discussion of the historical development of this doctrine, see John Murray, *Collected Writings, Vol. 4: Studies in Theology* (Edinburgh: Banner of Truth Trust, 1982), 234-38.

[2] Sinclair B. Ferguson, Foreword to James Fraser, *A Treatise on Sanctification:*

He was a godly and well-respected minister, but his wife turned out to be just the opposite. The details of his home life are sketchy, so whether he was deceived, made a poor choice, or was converted after his marriage is not known. What is known is that his wife treated him horribly. John Kennedy describes her as 'a cold, unfeeling, bold, unheeding wordly (*sic*) [worldly] woman.'[1] She didn't try to hide her ill treatment of him, and the people of his parish tried to help him as much as they could. She often denied him food at home, and one friend arranged to leave food for him at a certain place near where he walked so that he would not go hungry. Here was a godly man caught in a miserable situation. What was he to do? What did he do? He honoured his vows to God and to his wife. His marriage was very difficult, but he left a Christ-honouring testimony and a book on the doctrine of sanctification that Christians read and study to this very day.

You may have sworn to your own disadvantage, but honour Christ in keeping your vows and God will honour you. Becoming a member of a church also involves taking vows, and unfortunately these are often treated lightly as well. But what you have promised, you have promised in the sight of God, and you should take your membership vows as seriously as you do the vows you took to your spouse.

An oath honoured graciously

What have we seen thus far in this chapter? An oath made sinfully and an oath kept faithfully. In the final verses we find an oath honoured graciously. The grace and mercy of the Lord shine through this chapter just as they do in the story of Rahab in chapter 2. God is so powerful, sovereign, wise, and loving that he overcame the sin of the Gibeonites *and* the sin of Israel. *First*, the Gibeonites were allowed to live. The oath Israel made saved their lives.

An Explication of Romans Chapters 6,7, and 8:1-14 (Audubon, NJ: Old Paths Publications, first published 1774; reprint of 1897 rev. ed., 1992), v.

[1] John Kennedy, *The Days of the Fathers in Ross-shire* (Tain, Ross-shire: Christian Focus, reprint 1979), 43. The other details in this illustration from Fraser's life are from Kennedy as well.

Second, not only were the Gibeonites allowed to live, but they were also allowed to serve. Verses 22-27 are an elaboration of verse 21 and explain how the Gibeonites became Israel's and God's servants. It is true that Joshua told them they were cursed (verse 23). The curse meant that they were to be servants to perform the most menial tasks. But the curse was also a blessing. They served God at the tabernacle; though they were assigned the tasks of chopping wood and carrying water, with God there are no menial tasks. Every opportunity to serve him is a great privilege. The psalmist wrote, 'For a day in your courts is better than a thousand elsewhere. I would rather be a doorkeeper in the house of my God than dwell in the tents of wickedness' (Psa. 84:10).

If we trace the trail of Gibeon through the rest of the Old Testament, we can see some of the other privileges that they had. The city of Gibeon became a city of the Levites. David put the tabernacle in Gibeon (1 Chron. 16:39). Solomon offered burnt offerings there (1 Kings 3:4), and there the Lord appeared to him (1 Kings 3:5). When the Israelites returned from Babylon, Gibeonites were among them, it appears fully assimilated into the nation, helping to rebuild the walls of Jerusalem in service to the Lord (Neh. 3:7; 7:25).

But we need to expand this a little further. First, the curse upon and continuance of Gibeon highlights the difficulty Israel faced with the continuing presence of Canaanites in the land. By the time you reach the end of the book the conquest is complete, and Israel owns all of the land God promised. But their ownership was not without complications. God's people lived in the land but still faced the pressure of ungodly influences. How were believers to live side-by-side with unbelievers? How are we to live in what is effectively a post-Christian, pagan society? Many things could be said about this topic from the establishment of a Christian counterculture, which in essence is what the church should be, to relational evangelism, where we try to understand our neighbours so we can help them to understand Jesus.

Many of these issues, however legitimate they may be to discuss, would take us far from the text of Joshua. How does Joshua resolve the dilemma of the Gibeonite presence? He begins by pronouncing a curse upon them. That does not seem to be any kind of solution at all, but it is where he must begin. They are, after all, Canaanites. They are on Israel's hit list,[1] and they have devised and perpetrated an elaborate deception. None of that can be ignored.

Still, Israel had sworn an oath to them in the name of God, and that cannot be ignored either. To solve this dilemma, Joshua allows them to live in Israel with the status of resident aliens, not native-born Israelites but connected to Israel and to the Lord by covenant.[2] The Gibeonites are assigned a menial task for a magnificent God. They are promoted from certain death to the privilege of working in the very courtyard of the tabernacle. They went from cowering in fear for their lives to watching the gospel portrayed day by day as the lambs and bulls and goats were slaughtered for people's sins. God brought good out of evil. Do not make the mistake of thinking that God needs evil to accomplish good. He does not need darkness as a backdrop to shine the majesty and brightness of his glory. But God is so good and so gracious and so powerful that he overrules our foolishness and sin and from it accomplishes his grand purposes.

God can take the most unlikely people and make them the trophies of his grace. That is our hope for our neighbours, and that is also key to understanding how we relate to them. Give them the gospel. Tell them that God can bring blessing out of cursing. Take them to Calvary and tell them of Christ. Tell them about the place where the ultimate curse fell and where the greatest blessing flowed.

In our culture vows are made and broken every day. 'Promises, promises. Talk is cheap', says the scoffer. But as a Christian you must realize that your word means something, not just to the person to whom you gave it but to God. You may have made a vow to your own disadvantage, but God expects you to keep it. He will give you the strength to keep it because he has pledged himself to you in Christ. His mercy will triumph over your pain and bring glory to him in spite of your sin. That is the wonder of God's amazing grace!

[1] Hubbard, *Joshua*, 281.
[2] Hubbard, *Joshua*, 288.

15

The Day the Sun Stood Still
Joshua 10:1-15

At that time Joshua spoke to the LORD in the day when the LORD gave
the Amorites over to the sons of Israel, and he said in the sight of Israel,
'Sun, stand still at Gibeon, and moon, in the Valley of Aijalon.' And the
sun stood still, and the moon stopped, until the nation took vengeance on
their enemies. Is this not written in the Book of Jashar? The sun stopped
in the midst of heaven and did not hurry to set for about a whole day.
(Josh. 10:12-13)

'Time flies when you are having fun, but it sure drags by
when you are fighting a battle!' I doubt Israel ever had
a saying like that, but if they did it no doubt would
have owed its origin to Joshua chapter 10. Along with the battle of
Jericho, the miracle of the sun halting its course while Israel fought
the Amorites is one of the best known incidents in the book. This
is also a much-discussed and debated passage. Do Christians really
believe the sun stood still?

During the 1970s, a story attributed to Harold Hill of
Baltimore, Maryland, supposedly a NASA consultant at the time,
circulated in Christian circles. According to the account NASA
computers, working to calculate future orbital positions for the
stars and planets, discovered a missing day in the past. A scientist
on the team remembered the story of Joshua's long day from

Sunday school and informed his workmates that this must be the explanation.[1]

I first heard that story as a young teenager and was overawed at the remarkable accuracy of Scripture. Since then I have have discovered that the story is not true. It is a Christian urban legend, and cannot be substantiated by any evidence. That revelation, however, has not shaken my faith in Scripture. The authority of the Bible depends upon its source, the Holy Spirit, and so does its authentication. If the NASA story were true, it would possess a 'wow' factor. But that it is not true does not lessen the truthfulness of God's word or the power of Joshua chapter 10.

Joshua's long day, the day the sun stood still, is the highlight of the story that began in chapter 9. After foolishly and sinfully entering a pact with the Gibeonites, Israel not only spared their lives and incorporated them into the tabernacle workforce, they also took on the responsibility of protecting them as the nation's vassals. In chapter 10 we learn that Adoni-zedek, king of Jerusalem, led an alliance of kings to attack Gibeon (verses 1-5), and thus when the need for protection arose, Joshua did not hesitate to fulfil his obligations when he was called upon to do so. Could he, however, count on God's help to protect these devious Canaanites? Israel failed first at Ai and a second time with Gibeon. Would they be left on their own to face the Amorites?

Joshua 10 is devoted to the account of Israel's southern campaign that began with this face-off at Gibeon. This chapter is both a military report and a theological treatise. Its theme is prominent, occurring near the beginning of the chapter in verse 14 and again at the end in verse 42: 'The LORD fought for Israel.' Here we see the grace, commitment, power, and promises of God summarized in one succinct statement. To the question 'Will Israel be left to face the Amorites alone?' the clear answer is 'No.' In spite of their failures and setbacks, the Lord fought for his chosen nation, and he fought for them miraculously. The Lord never forsakes his children, even when they have failed him. He brings his resources to bear on

[1] Robert C. Newman, 'Joshua's Long Day and the NASA Computers: Is the Story True?' available online at http://www.reasons.org/articles/joshua-s-long-day-and-the-nasa-computers-is-the-story-true (accessed 7 July 2015).

each situation they face so that he might bring them, in the end, to ultimate victory.

The battle day

If you look closely at Joshua 9, 10, and 11, you will notice that each chapter begins the same way: 'And it happened when they heard.'[1] 'They' are the Canaanites, and what they heard were the accounts of Israel's victories. As the news of Israel's conquests spread throughout Canaan, fear spread alongside it. Here the text focuses on Adoni-zedek the king of Jerusalem. He heard the spreading reports of Israel's victories and the Gibeonite league with Israel (verses 1-2). The last piece of information only increased his fear. Though Jerusalem would later become a very important city in biblical history, at this point in time it is an unpretentious town, nothing in comparison with Gibeon, which the text describes as a royal city,[2] even greater than the city of Ai. Furthermore, all of Gibeon's men were warriors. Once you put those pieces of information together, the first two verses give us some insight into Adoni-zedek's thinking: 'If Gibeon gave up without a fight, what hope does anyone else have?'

Because he feared Israel and their power, Adoni-zedek sent a message to Hoham king of Hebron, Piram king of Jarmuth, Japhia king of Lachish, and Debir king of Eglon, four monarchs who ruled within a 30-mile radius southeast of Jerusalem. He pled for help: 'Come up to me and help me, and let us strike Gibeon. For it has made peace with Joshua and with the people of Israel' (verse 4).[3] Heeding Adonai-zedek's message, the coalition amassed its forces, marched up to Gibeon, encamped against the city, and fought against it (verse 5). Notice carefully how the text lists all five kings in verse 3 and then again in verse 5. Why are these identical lists

---

[1] Though the wording in the ESV and other English translations vary, the opening phrase for each chapter is identical in Hebrew: *wayyehi kishmoʿ*, 'and it happened as [the subject] heard …'

[2] A royal city—'that is, the heavily fortified capitals of kings who ruled city-states (cf. 1 Sam. 27:5).' Hubbard, *Joshua*, 292.

[3] 'His message that Gibeon has "made peace with Joshua and the Israelites" (v. 4b) captures the sizeable threat that an Israelite-Gibeonite force poses. As in 9:1-2, these royal war plans also make a fateful decision—the rejection of Yahweh—and sharply contrast the Gibeonite approach.' Hubbard, *Joshua*, 292.

placed so close together? Does the author think that two verses later we have already forgotten who Gibeon's enemies were? Hardly. He lists all of the kings twice to say, in essence, that Gibeon's survival is unlikely. Take a good look at the odds. It is five against one.

Five-to-one odds did not look good to Gibeon, and they sent a message to Joshua at the Israelite camp in Gilgal. It consisted of a four-fold plea. First, 'Do not relax your hand from your servants.' This was no time to rest. Gibeon's plea was based on the fact that they were now Israel's servant and in need. Second, they needed help urgently. 'Come up to us quickly.' Their third petition was 'save us' and the fourth, 'help us'. There is no sharp distinction between the meaning of these two final phrases. The Gibeonites repeated the request for emphasis. Why did Gibeon issue such an urgent plea? 'For all the kings of the Amorites who dwell in the hill country are gathered against us' (verse 6).

How should Israel respond to this plea? With faithfulness. They were now bound to the Gibeonites by a solemn oath and covenant. Integrity called for Joshua to go to their aid: 'So Joshua went up from Gilgal, he and all the people of war with him, and all the mighty men of valour' (verse 7). These words reflect a bit of irony in the passage. Gibeon was a city of great warriors (verse 2), but they pleaded with Joshua for help. In response, Joshua took up his army ('all the people of war') and 'all the mighty men of valour' (cf. 1:14; 6:2; 8:3). In other words, Israel, a nomadic people, could muster a greater army than the established city-states of the land. The city of great warriors looked to Israel for help. Israel would join the Gibeonites to fend off this coalition and make the contest five against two. Though the odds had improved in their favour, victory was still unlikely for Israel. If the Lord did not fight for them, they would be doomed.

The judgment day

Whether at Gilgal or somewhere along the way to Gibeon, the Lord spoke to Joshua, bolstering his confidence and assuring him of victory: 'Do not fear them, for I have given them into your hands. Not a man of them shall stand before you' (verse 8). To begin with, the Lord charged Joshua not to fear.[1] The same command occurred in 8:1 as the Lord encouraged Joshua to approach Ai a second time (cf. also verse 25 and 11:6). War is a fearful thing. My father fought in Europe during World War II, and he maintained that a soldier who was not afraid on the battlefield was either a liar or a fool. But in this instance, as at Ai, Joshua could fearlessly lead his men into battle with a divine guarantee of the outcome.

Joshua's confidence was based on God's two-fold promise. The first thing the Lord said was 'I have given them into your hands.'[2] Note the expression 'I have given.' The battle had not begun, yet the Lord expressed the victory in the past perfect tense. This is often called the 'prophetic perfect' because though the event lay in the future, it was so certain as to be a done deal. Israel's enemies were already their possession. The second thing God promised was 'Not a man of them shall stand before you.' Neither their sheer numbers nor their military prowess would prove successful. These final words of the promise recall Joshua's initial commission to lead Israel into Canaan. God had said to him, 'No man shall be able to stand before you all the days of your life. Just as I was with Moses, so I will be with you. I will not leave you or forsake you' (1:5).

Joshua's commission remained the same and the promise remained the same, because God remained (and still remains) the same. The Lord had not changed and neither had his commitment to his people. Even today, God's presence, along with his loving faithfulness, remains the source of comfort and courage to drive out fear and doubt when the enemy attacks. How can we be assured of God's love and loyalty? First, by his promise. Jesus said, 'I am with you always, to the end of the age' (Matt. 28:20). This statement, a close parallel to Joshua 1:5 and 9, guarantees for us the abiding presence and power of the Lord. Second, we can know that he is with us when we use the sword of the Spirit (his word), the shield of faith, and all of the armour he provides to fend off Satan's attacks

[1] The literal translation of the phrase is 'do not fear because of them'. 'Because of them' (*mehem*) is an accurate reflection of the causal (*min*), though Waltke points out that with verbs like *fear* it can be difficult to distinguish cause and origin. Waltke and O'Connor, *Introduction to Biblical Hebrew Syntax*, 213.

[2] See the very similar statement about Jericho in Joshua 6:2.

and extinguish all of his flaming darts (see Eph. 6:10-18). Scripture is our source of comfort because it is God's living voice that tells us what is true. Faith shields our hearts because by it we listen to the Lord's voice and rely upon all that he has said.

With God's word to encourage him, Joshua marched his troops the 19 miles from Israel's camp at Gilgal, all in one night, and came upon the Amorite coalition suddenly (verse 9). The Amorites were taken by surprise when the Israelite army showed up that morning. Even more surprising is the fact that God used Joshua's surprise attack to launch his own surprise attack. The Lord threw the Amorites forces into a panic before Israel (verse 10). This was the first step in God's battle for his people. It was also the very same thing the Lord had done to Pharaoh's troops when they tried to cross the Red Sea in pursuit of Israel: 'And in the morning watch the LORD in the pillar of fire and of cloud looked down on the Egyptian forces and threw the Egyptian forces into a panic, clogging their chariot wheels so that they drove heavily. And the Egyptians said, "Let us flee from before Israel, for the LORD fights for them against the Egyptians"' (Exod. 14:24-25). God has always fought for his people, and he always will.

Next, in rather rapid succession, the text unfolds a series of events that led to the overthrow of the Canaanite coalition. God struck them, pursued them, and struck them. An interpretative choice has to be made in verse 10. In the English Standard Version, the text reads, 'before Israel, who struck them ... chased them ... and struck them....' But the ESV footnote provides an alternate translation. Instead of reading the text 'who' it can also be translated 'and he', in which case God would be the one doing the pursuing and striking, and I believe that is the best rendering of the text.[1] The Lord is the subject of these verbs. He is the one who struck and chased the Amorites. The wording of verse 10 further strengthens the point of the entire chapter that it was the Lord who fought for Israel.

---

[1] Both the NIV and the NRSV identify the pronoun as a reference to Israel. The NASB takes it to refer to God and capitalizes 'He.' The LXX does this as well and supplies the word *kurios*, 'Lord.' The NEB follows the singular reading of the Masoretic text rather than the Syriac and Targum plurals, but identifies the 'he' as Joshua.

This does not mean, however, that Israel played no role in the battle. Verse 11 makes it clear that the Israelites also chased the Amorites and killed them with the sword. The Israelites were in hot pursuit, while the Lord was in cold pursuit! He threw down large hailstones from the sky all the way from the ascent of Beth-horon to Azekah, a distance of about 20 miles. The expression is one of deliberate forethought and purpose. The text does not say that hailstones fell from the sky. That happens all the time and is not at all unusual. But during this battle, where God was already actively attacking Israel's enemies, he threw down hailstones with intentional purpose and obviously with great accuracy because the hail killed more Amorites than the Israelites did in hand-to-hand combat.

The battle that raged that day in southern Palestine was more than a skirmish over land. It was a battle of cosmic proportions. What the Lord did to the Amorite coalition that day pointed to his judgment in the past and his judgment in the future. First, it recalled the seventh plague when God rained down hail on the Egyptians and destroyed their crops: 'The LORD sent thunder and hail, and fire ran down to the earth. And the LORD rained hail upon the land of Egypt' (Exod. 9:23). He judged Pharaoh and the land of Egypt for their refusal to comply with his command. Second, this hail storm in Joshua 10 was a harbinger of greater judgment to come. In Revelation 8:7, the first of seven angels sounded his trumpet, 'and there followed hail and fire, mixed with blood, and these were thrown upon the earth. And a third of the earth was burned up, and a third of the trees were burned up, and all green grass was burned up.' This judgment clearly parallels Exodus 9 with its combination of hail and fire. But it too is only a portent of things to come. At the sound of the first trumpet, God destroys only a third of the earth, trees, and grass. He restrains his hand but warns of greater judgment to come.

When we reach Revelation 16, the bowls of God's wrath are poured out on the earth. The seventh and last bowl is the final judgment (verses 17-21). When an angel poured out this bowl, a loud voice came from the temple, from the throne itself saying, 'It is done!' The end has come and along with it lightning, thunder, a great earthquake, 'And great hailstones, about one hundred pounds each, fell from heaven on people; and they cursed God for the plague of the hail, because the plague was so severe' (Rev. 16:21).

What God did to the Amorites that day between the ascent of Beth-horon and Azekah he will do on the last day to all of his enemies. With intentionality and accuracy, with righteousness and wrath, he will judge. Just as God judged the Amorites, but protected his people in the battle, so too he will do on the day of judgment. The only way to be saved on that day is to be safely shielded in Christ.

If you are in Christ, then the promises God gave to Joshua apply to you as well. There is no reason for you to fear anything or anyone who rises up in opposition to you or the work of God. The Lord assures us that even our last and worst enemy—death—will be destroyed (1 Cor. 15:26). That is the assurance that our Joshua, the Lord Jesus, had when he went to the cross, and it is the comforting words of confidence he gave to his church: 'I will build my church, and the gates of hell shall not prevail against it' (Matt. 16:18).

The longest day

Prior to this battle we have seen Israel commit two glaring sins: Achan's thievery and presumption regarding the Gibeonites. Now we are about to see the Lord work a stupendous miracle. 'Joshua spoke to the LORD' (verse 12). Having heard God's voice (verse 8) and seen God's power in the storm (verse 11), he was emboldened to pray an amazing prayer in the sight of all Israel: 'Sun, stand still at Gibeon, and moon, in the Valley of Aijalon.' Apparently sensing the need for more daylight, Joshua prays a brief, beautiful, poetic appeal to God. From our vantage point, it is a non-traditional prayer. It does not begin with 'Our Father' or even end with an 'Amen'. Technically it is an apostrophe, an exclamation addressed to someone or, in this case, some things (sun and moon) not immediately present. Joshua addressed these heavenly bodies as if he were God himself. He commanded the sun and he ordered the moon to do his bidding. What we witness in verse 12 is Joshua as God's man speaking as though he were the God-man, for he is indeed a type of Christ.

Since, however, he is only a type and not the fulfilment, he intended these words, and God regarded them, as a prayer.[1]

In response to Joshua's declaration, 'the sun stood still, and the moon stopped, until the nation took vengeance on their enemies'. The author then asks the rhetorical question, 'Is this not written in the Book of Jashar?' (verse 13). Apparently the lines of poetry at the end of verse 12 and the beginning of verse 13 are a quotation from the Book of Jashar, an Israelite book of songs.[2] Having stated the poetic form of Joshua's prayer and referenced it to the Book of Jashar, the text plainly states the outcome of the prayer: 'The sun stopped in the midst of heaven and did not hurry to set for about a whole day' (verse 13).

How are we to explain what we read in verses 12 and 13? Should we take it literally? Can we be expected to believe that the earth actually stopped rotating around the sun for almost 24 hours? Would that not result in all kinds of catastrophes for the earth as we know it?[3] As Bible scholars have examined this text and wrestled with these questions, the solutions they have proposed may be classified into four basic categories.

---

[1] 'At that point Joshua exercised authority over the natural course of things as a type of the Christ, who exercises authority over all creation. In that sovereign rule, Christ sees to it that the cause of His people is victorious and executes judgment upon His enemies.' DeGraaf, *Promise and Deliverance*, 1:409.

[2] The only other reference to the Book of Jashar is 2 Sam. 1:18. The Book of Jashar appears to have been a book of poetry and songs that possibly included epics. Some scholars have conjectured that it may have included the Song of Deborah (Judg. 5) and the Song of Miriam (Exod. 15:21). 'The provenance of the work has been the topic of considerable discussion. The comparatively poor state of preservation of the OT quotations indicates the antiquity of the material itself. There can be no doubt about the authenticity of the extracts from the work. Their linguistic affinities suggest that the book originated in the late Armana period; additions were made at least until the time of Solomon. It seems to have had some affinity with the Book of the Wars of the Lord (Num. 21:14), and both compositions may have commenced at approximately the same time.' James Orr and R. K. Harrison, 'Jashar, Book of', *International Standard Bible Encyclopedia*, rev. ed. (Grand Rapids:: Eerdmans, 1982), 2:969-70 .

[3] Bernard Ramm, *The Christian View of Science and Scripture* (Grand Rapids: Eerdmans, 1955), 157-58.

The first view we might call the 'poetic language' view. This position states that we should not take these words literally. They are written as poetry and should be read as such. John Bright calls it the Oriental use of poetic imagery.[1] Other passages in the Old Testament contain similar expressions that we do not take literally. For example, Judges 5:20 reads, 'From heaven the stars fought, from their courses they fought against Sisera.'[2] In essence, all Joshua is praying for here is enough time to finish the battle. We could summarize his prayer as 'Let me get the job done before it gets too late.'

A second view believes that what occurred here was a prolongation of light. This may have resulted from a slowing or stopping of the earth's rotation by means of a great catastrophe or a refraction of the sun's rays. This was Calvin's view as well as more modern scholars such as Marten Woudstra, and Gleason Archer.[3]

The third view is a bit of a twist on the tradition because it holds that what happened here was actually a prolongation of darkness. This was the position of the eminent Bible scholar of old Princeton, Robert Dick Wilson, a great defender of Scripture. Wilson discovered that a Babylonian word meaning 'eclipse' had the same root as the word translated 'stand still' in verse 12. Wilson thus translated the passage, 'Be eclipsed, O sun, in Gibeon, And thou moon in the valley of Aijalon!' Because Israel's enemies worshipped the sun and moon, such an eclipse would have terrified them and helped Israel to get the upper hand.[4] Another variation of the 'prolonged darkness' view is that Joshua prayed for a lengthened night in order to facilitate a surprise attack.[5]

[1] John Bright, 'Joshua' in *The Interpreter's Bible*, volume 2 edited by George Arthur Buttrick, *et al* (New York: Abingdon-Cokesbury Press, 1951), 605. Keil and Delitzsch also hold this view. C. F. Keil and F. Delitzsch, *Commentary on the Old Testament: Joshua, Judges, Ruth*, trans. James Martin (Peabody, MA: Hendrickson, 1989), 108.

[2] For similar passages see Psa. 18:10; 24:6; 114:46; Isa. 34:3; 55:12; Amos 9:13; and Micah 1:3.

[3] Calvin, *Comm. Joshua*, 161-62, and *Survey of Old Testament Introduction*, rev. ed. (Chicago: Moody, 1974), 279.

[4] Robert Dick Wilson, *Princeton Theological Review*, 16 (1918): 46-54.

[5] Hugh J. Blair, 'Joshua.' *The New Bible Commentary: Revised*, edited by D. Guthrie and J. A. Motyer (Grand Rapids: Eerdmans, 1970), 243-44.

The 'omen view' is the fourth approach to interpreting this unusual scene. This interpretation states that Joshua was looking for an unusual astronomical incident in which the sun and moon would align in the same sky. This would be a frightening omen to the Amorites but a sign of God's good pleasure to Israel.[1]

So which view is correct? I believe the answer is found in verse 14: 'There has been no day like it before or since, when the LORD heeded the voice of a man, for the LORD fought for Israel.' What a day! There has never been a day like it. Only once has the sun stood still in the sky and delayed to set. The clearest reading of the text, in my opinion, is that God prolonged the light by slowing or stopping the earth's rotation. What about the disasters that would occur in a situation like that? Well, if this was a miracle of altering the rate of the earth's rotation, then overcoming the catastrophic results would also be a miracle and certainly not a problem for the Lord! To some that explanation will sound like a pious cop-out. But is it? Once we read the opening words of Genesis 1, 'In the beginning God', anything is possible. If we believe in God, then the only God worth believing in is the one who has created all things by the word of his power and who, by that same powerful word, rules over all his creation.

Could there be anything more amazing? Well, if there is, it is the reason the sun stood still—the LORD heeded the voice of a man![2] God willingly complied with Joshua's request. Why was he so ready to do as asked? Because 'the LORD fought for Israel'. What a great contrast this is to chapter 9 where Joshua failed to call upon God. Now, in answer to prayer, God works his mighty power. This is the same God who fights for us as we assail our spiritual enemies, and he uses prayer as the energizing force behind the battle. We are to put on the whole armour of God, 'Praying at all times in the Spirit, with all prayer and supplication' (Eph. 6:18).

[1] 'Consistent with ancient Near Eastern beliefs, Joshua seeks an omen—an extraordinary alignment of sun and moon in the same sky that Israel reads as favourable and/or the Amorites as unfavourable.' Hubbard, *Joshua*, 296.

[2] 'Strikingly, while the cosmic scale of the text's claims are what amaze modern readers, what stuns the narrator is the terrestrial scene—that Joshua prays and (unbelievable!) Yahweh obeys ... by fighting for Israel (v. 14).' Hubbard, *Joshua*, 295.

What more can we say about this passage? Apart from talking about God's power, a passage like this does not seem particularly relevant. And that is one reason so many Christians virtually ignore the Old Testament. After all, we experience hail storms but they hardly seem of cosmic or eschatological import. Furthermore, I have never seen the sun stand still, and I do not really expect to. Those kinds of miracles were for long ago and far away. Joshua's long day may be an interesting story, fascinating in some respects, but little more. Surely it is not relevant for or applicable to you and me.

Let us analyse that attitude for a moment because it occurs often in the church. First, it reveals an all-too-western attitude toward, not only the Bible, but all of life. If what I read or what I do, or what I buy does not demonstrate its immediate usefulness to improve my life, make me happy, fulfilled, or more skilful, then it is not worth my time. Joshua 10 tells me nothing about being a better spouse, a better parent, how to improve my daily schedule, feel happier, or make more money, therefore it is insignificant and unimportant.

I will grant you that texts from Joshua 10 will not show up in a parenting seminar. Your counsellor is not likely to turn to this chapter to help you be a better wife or husband. You will not find much here about living the Christian life in a secular workplace. So where does this passage leave us? What should it do to us and for us? It should leave us marvelling at the grace of God to Israel and to Gibeon. It should leave us startled and amazed at the power of God as he rules over hail storms and sunshine. It should leave us humble before the Lord who rules the universe. It should remind us that the God who used his miraculous power to rescue Israel still uses his miraculous power to save his people. From Jesus' virgin birth to his glorious resurrection, God exerted his power over creation to accomplish our redemption. Joshua 10 should draw us to Jesus and then cast us down on our faces to wonder at and worship our great God!

You see, the Bible is not ultimately about you and me. It is about God. And I wonder, have we ever considered that marvelling at and worshipping the Lord is the primary means of shaping us into the spouses, parents, and people we need to be? You never lose out in your marriage or with your children or with your boss or your parents or your friends until you have first lost out with God. As it turns out, worshipping the God who miraculously fought for Israel is the most relevant and practical thing you can do.

With the battle over and Israel victorious once again, Joshua, and all Israel with him, returned to the camp at Gilgal (verse 15). God had not failed in his promises. He never does. That day in southern Palestine, the Lord demonstrated his amazing power. There has never been a day like it before or since. It was the battle day, the judgment day, the longest day, the day that, in spite of their failures and setbacks, the Lord fought for Israel.

The LORD is a Man of War
Joshua 10:16-43

And Joshua captured all these kings and their land at one time, because the LORD God of Israel fought for Israel. (Josh. 10:42)

'The LORD is my strength and my song, and he has become my salvation; this is my God, and I will praise him, my father's God, and I will exalt him. The LORD is a man of war; the LORD is his name' (Exod. 15:2-3). With those words, Moses led Israel to praise God for his triumph over Pharaoh's army after he drowned the Egyptians in the Red Sea. This is the first time in the Bible that God is portrayed as a warrior, but from this point on it becomes a prominent theme in biblical theology.

For example, during David's ongoing conflicts with the Philistines, the Lord fought for him. After achieving victory at Baal-perazim, David said, 'The LORD has burst through my enemies before me like a bursting flood' (2 Sam. 5:20). When the Philistines again spread out their armies in the Valley of Rephaim, the Lord told David to delay his attack until he heard 'the sound of marching in the tops of the balsam trees'. He could then rouse his troops to fight because 'the LORD has gone out before you to strike down the army of the Philistines' (2 Sam. 5:24).

When Jehoshaphat, a ninth-century B.C. king of Judah, fought the Moabites, Ammonites, and Meunites and the Lord gave him victory, 'the fear of God came on all the kingdoms of the countries when they heard that the LORD had fought against the enemies of Israel' (2 Chron. 20:29). The prophet Nahum proclaimed the Lord to be a mighty warrior who would destroy Nineveh (cf. 1:8; 2:13). John the apostle saw visions of Christ mounted on a white steed (Rev. 19:11). From the Saviour's mouth proceeded a sharp sword which he used to strike down the nations (verse 15). He is called 'Faithful and True, and in righteousness he judges and makes war' (verse 11).

These few passages give us glimpses of the divine warrior motif throughout Scripture, but nowhere do we see it displayed more clearly than in Joshua 10. The theme of this chapter is set out clearly in verses 14 and 42: 'the LORD fought for Israel'. God's clash with the Canaanites explains Israel's success in battle. In spite of Israel's failures and setbacks, the Lord still exerted his power in covenant faithfulness to see that his people overcame their foes. The chapter then focuses on informing us about the ways in which God fought for Israel.

Before we look at those ways, however, we need to look at how the narrative is structured. The long-day account concluded: 'So Joshua returned, and all Israel with him, to the camp at Gilgal' (verse 15). At this point it seemed as though the battle was over, and indeed it was. But the account of the battle was not complete. The chapter ends with a repetition of the same event expressed in identical words: 'Then Joshua returned, and all Israel with him, to the camp at Gilgal' (verse 43). Verses 15 and 43 both refer to the same return to Gilgal.[1] The first fifteen verses give a summary of the day's events with a focus on the miracle of the sun and moon while verses 16-43 give an expanded version of the story that fills in more of the details. In the first part of the chapter, verses 1-14, the Lord fought miraculously. He exercised his omnipotence to make the sun and moon stand still (verse 13). But he fought for Israel in other ways as well, and it is those other ways that we see emphasized in the remainder of the chapter.

[1] Davis calls this 'the summary-expansion pattern of Hebrew narrative'. *Joshua: No Falling Words*, 86-87.

The Lord fought justly

With verse 16 the account of the five Amorite kings who led the coalition of rebellion resumes (cf. verses 3-5). Both the kings and their armies fled from Israel, but the leaders stayed together as they made their getaway and hid themselves in the cave at Makkedah (verse 16). We find Makkedah mentioned only in the book of Joshua, and primarily in this chapter (verses 10, 16, 17, 21, 28, 29).¹ Geographically it lay in the Shephelah or lowlands of Judah. Joshua called the place where the kings hid themselves '*the*' cave at Makkedah. If not the only cave near the town, it was evidently the prominent cave that everyone could readily identify. It did not take long for a report of their whereabouts to reach Joshua (verse 17). The Israelites found them tucked away in the cave, and their hopes of escaping detection vanished.

Once these men were found, Joshua gave orders to imprison them in the cave by rolling large stones to cover its entrance and to appoint men to guard the cave in order to assure that no one escaped (verse 18). The rest of the soldiers, however, were to move on in pursuit of their enemies. Their responsibility was to attack the rearguard of the fleeing armies and not allow them to enter their cities (verse 19). An attack on the rearguard would draw the rest of the armies back to reinforce their troops. If they reached their respective cities, they could hole up within the city walls and make the battle much more difficult. There was really no danger of that happening, however, because the Lord had given Israel's enemies into their hands (verse 19c). This is another example of the 'prophetic perfect'. The outcome of the battle was already certain, so certain in fact that it could be spoken of as accomplished. Once God has spoken, you can be sure that his word will be fulfilled to accomplish his purposes (cf. Num. 23:19; Isa. 55:10-11; Rom. 3:4).

Also note that God was gracious in his actions on behalf of Israel. He was *giving* their enemies into their hands. The Lord described Israel's earlier victories with the same language, first at Jericho: 'And the LORD said to Joshua, "See, I have given Jericho into your hand, with its king and mighty men of valour"' (6:2); and then at Ai: 'And

---

¹ The other two references are Joshua 12:16 and 15:41.

the LORD said to Joshua, "Do not fear and do not be dismayed. Take all the fighting men with you, and arise, go up to Ai. See, I have given into your hand the king of Ai, and his people, his city, and his land"' (8:1). At no point could or should Israel ever assume that their victories in the conquest were due to their expertise or power. God handed over their enemies one by one and gave Israel success in battle so that he might give them the land (cf. 1:3). Gave, gave, gave, equals grace, grace, grace! God's loving intervention reminded Israel, and should remind us as well, that all we have is due to the unmerited goodness of God. We cannot claim to deserve one thing that we possess, especially the blessings of salvation and forgiveness. Christians are graced people and should, in turn, grace others with demonstrations of God's goodness.

The army of Israel eventually returned to Joshua at Makkedah, but not until the soldiers had finished striking the Amorites with a great blow that wiped them out and left only a ragtag remnant to return to their fortified cities (verse 20). Israel, on the other hand, did not lose a single soldier in the pursuit. All returned safely. Furthermore, 'Not a man moved his tongue against any of the people of Israel' (verse 21).[1] God gave such favour to his children that they were free from all threats and dangers, even barking dogs!

Once the remainder of the army made its way back to the camp at Makkedah, the time had come to deal with the imprisoned kings. Joshua commanded that the cave be opened and the kings be brought to him (verse 22), and the prisoners were brought out of their make-shift jail (verse 23). Now, for a third time the text lists the five kings: the king of Jerusalem, the king of Hebron, the king of Jarmuth, the king of Lachish, and the king of Eglon (cf. verses 3, 5). The previous lists emphasized the size of the coalition and the odds that Gibeon faced. The present list serves as a roll call for execution.

Joshua summoned the men of Israel to gather around. He then had his chief military officers come forward to where the kings were lying prostrate and place their feet on the victim's necks. Why did Joshua have them do this? It was a symbolic act to demonstrate the

---

[1] A similar expression occurs in Exodus 11:7, 'But against any of the children of Israel shall not a dog move his tongue, against man or beast: that ye may know how that the Lord doth put a difference between the Egyptians and Israel' (KJV).

complete subjugation of the Amorites to Israel. To conquer your enemy is to tread him down. By placing their feet on the necks of these kings there remained no doubt about who had won.[1]

These actions foreshadowed what Jesus would one day do. One of the great Messianic prophecies occurs in Psalm 110:1, 'The Lord says to my Lord: "Sit at my right hand, until I make your enemies your footstool."' When Peter preached on the day of Pentecost, he interpreted this passage to refer to the victory that Christ achieved through his resurrection (Acts 2:33-36), a victory to be fully realized at his return. Paul, quoting Psalm 8:6, concurred in 1 Corinthians 15:24-27, 'Then comes the end, when he delivers the kingdom to God the Father after destroying every rule and every authority and power. For he must reign until he has put all his enemies under his feet. The last enemy to be destroyed is death. For "God has put all things in subjection under his feet."' That day at Makkedah Israel's military leaders experienced a sign of greater things to come. They caught a glimpse of the coming victory of Jesus. When Christ, the one whom John calls 'Faithful and True', returns, he will strike down the nations and subdue them and rule them with a rod of iron (Rev. 19:11-16). On that day, every knee will bow to him and every tongue will confess that he is Lord (Phil. 2:9-11).

Joshua also used this event as a teaching opportunity for his generals. Just as God had called him to be strong and brave, he gave the same message to his leaders. Along with the encouragement came the promise: 'For thus the Lord will do to all your enemies against whom you fight' (verse 25). When these men placed their feet on the necks of the Amorite kings, they saw God's promise in verse 8 fulfilled in a very literal way: 'Not a man of them shall stand before you.' The fulfilled promise was meant to bolster their faith for the future battles they were about to face. The simple message is that the faithful God would continue to be faithful. God can be relied upon. Israel will triumph. They will inherit the land. Look at what the Lord has already done!

[1] 'A widespread ancient custom called for victorious kings to put their feet upon the necks of conquered enemies (see also Deut. 33;29; 1 Kings 5:3; Psa. 110:1).' Woudstra, *Book of Joshua*, 178.

Is this not the essence of Paul's argument in Romans 8? We need not worry that anything or anyone will deprive us of the everlasting love and security of God. Neither the flesh nor sufferings nor height nor depth nor anything we can imagine will separate us from who we are and what we have in Christ Jesus. Paul's exact words are 'If God is for us, who can be against us?' (verse 31). How does Paul know this? He continues in the very next verse: 'He who did not spare his own Son but gave him up for us all, how will he not also with him graciously give us all things?' (verse 32). God has been faithful to give us his Son. He will be faithful to bring us to glory. It is the same God, the same grace, and the same argument that Joshua preached to his men.

Israel's victory was, however, more than symbolic. After the military chiefs placed their feet on the enemies' necks, Joshua executed the kings, hung them on five trees, and left them on display until evening (verse 26) just as he had done to the king of Ai (8:29). The message was very clear to the Israelites who, steeped in the theology of Deuteronomy, witnessed these events. They knew full well that everyone who was hanged on a tree was under the curse of God (Deut. 21:22-23). Joshua complied with the law and, in order not to defile the land, had the bodies removed and thrown back into the cave. The place these five pagan kings thought was their refuge became their grave. There is a sobering lesson in that as well. If we do not find our safety and security in God alone, the idols we trust will destroy us. The place we sought sanctuary will become our sepulchre.

To seal off the entrance, the Israelites placed large stones at the mouth of the cave, 'which', the author notes, 'remain to this very day' (verse 27). The concluding words of verse 27 have become a familiar phrase by now. This is the eighth time the book states this or a very similar phrase, and this is the fourth time it is used in connection with a pile of stones (see 4:9; 7:26; 8:29). These rock piles (either purpose-built (4:9) or makeshift (7:26; 8:29)) have become memorial cairns to commemorate God's victories. First it was a victory over the barrier of the flooding Jordan, then Jericho, then Ai, and now these five armies and their kings. These cairns were functioning, may I say, 'sacramentally'. They were perpetual reminders to the people to encourage their faith and spur them on to faithful obedience. I refer to their function as sacramental because baptism and the Lord's Supper are to operate in essentially the same way for Christians. The water of baptism and the bread and wine of the Lord's Supper are constant reminders to the gathered church of God's faithfulness, and they are means to encourage and build up the faith of believers and urge us onward to greater spiritual growth.

God fought for Israel and thus for Gibeon. The odds were not favourable, but the motto 'You and God make a majority' was never proved to be more true than in this battle. Never be afraid to stand for and to do what is right because God is on the side of his people. Pressure to conform and compromise can be great, but God is greater still.

We have seen in verses 16-27 these five kings set apart for special treatment. They did not die in battle. They were imprisoned in the cave at Makkedah until the battle was over, then Joshua summarily executed them for their war crimes. The twentieth and now the twenty-first centuries have seen more than their fair share of war crimes trials. After World War II many criminals were tried at Nuremburg. Though these trials took place over sixty years ago, the crimes are still fresh in our memories. To the list of names such as Hermann Goring we could add Slobadan Milosevic and Sadam Hussein. Charles Taylor, the former president of Liberia, was convicted of war crimes in Sierra Leone. In all of these cases the men were charged with crimes against humanity. The five Amorite kings, however, were charged with crimes against Deity. By rebelling against Israel, they had rebelled against the Lord himself. Do you realize that every sin is a crime against Deity? Every act of disobedience, every hateful word, every bitter thought, every gossiping story, every lustful look is an act of cosmic treason.

One of the reasons these kings received such special and severe treatment was that they led their people into this rebellion. They bore an even greater responsibility than their troops. God judges more severely those who lead others into wickedness. Jesus pronounces a severe woe on anyone who causes one of his little ones to sin (cf. Matt. 18:1-9). That should lead us to ask ourselves, What are we doing with our sphere of influence? Are we persuading people to love and follow Christ or do our words and our jokes and our insinuations draw them away from the paths of righteousness?

The Lord fought successively

After he dealt decisively with the Amorite kings, Joshua turned his attention to the city of Makkedah itself. He captured the city, struck it and its king with the edge of the sword, and devoted it to destruction (verse 28). This is the basic, recurring pattern that you discover in the remainder of the chapter.

Joshua, and all Israel with him, then passed on from Makkedah to Libnah. This journey required them to travel nine miles north and west. They fought against Libnah, and the Lord gave the city and its king into Israel's hand (verses 29-30). Israel then turned south from Libnah and journeyed five miles to Lachish where they laid siege to the city and captured it (verses 31-32). Horam king of Gezer came to help Lachish, but Joshua struck him and his people and left none remaining.[1] Eglon, where the army next focused its attention, lay seven miles southeast of Lachish. Once again Israel laid siege to the city and captured it (verses 34-35). The battle at Hebron required Joshua to proceed twelve miles northeast. Again he and the Israelite soldiers were successful in battle (verses 36-37). Joshua and the army then turned back to Debir.[2] From the description it would appear that the army altered its course and moved back toward the southwest. As with all the other cities, this one also fell at Israel's hand (verses 38-39).

Why would the Lord give us this highly structured, almost formulaic account of six battles? In this section, God is doing three

[1] Younger demonstrates that these verses form a chiasm with Gezer as the pivot point, the point of emphasis. 'Israel never conquered Gezer (16:10), so the chiasm singles out the event as a major and especially memorable one, given the city's ancient importance.' K. L. Younger Jr., 'The "Conquest" of the South (Jos. 10:28-39),' *BZ* 39 (1995): 255-64 (esp. 259-64). The quotation comes from Hubbard, *Joshua*, 302. Howard also points out this structure. He also sees the focus in this section on seven cities. Howard, *Joshua*, 256-57. Though seven are mentioned, Gezer is connected to its king, Horam. The city itself was not defeated, only the king and the army that came up with him.

[2] Modern attempts to identify the location of Debir have proved inconclusive. It is possible that it lies about eight miles southwest of Hebron.

things. First, he reminds us that grace explains triumph. Victory has a way of making us feel self-confident. The Israelites did, after all, fight the battles. They had experienced the blood, sweat, and tears of gruelling hand-to-hand combat. Their efforts, though necessary, were not, however, the ultimate cause of success. Had God not been on the side of his people, they would surely have perished. The metrical version of Psalm 124 captures this truth so well.

> Now Israel may say, and that truly,
> If that the Lord had not our cause maintained;
> If that the Lord had not our right sustained,
> When cruel men who us desired to slay
> Rose up in wrath, to make of us their prey;

> Then certainly they had devoured us all,
> And swallowed quick, for ought that we could deem;
> Such was their rage, as we might well esteem.
> And as fierce floods before them all things drown,
> So had they brought our soul to death quite down.

> The raging streams, with their proud swelling waves,
> Had then our soul o'erwhelmed in the deep.
> But blessed be God, who doth us safely keep,
> And gave us not a living prey to be
> Unto their teeth and bloody cruelty.

Second, God recounted the consistency of his triumphs. The never-failing purpose of God marched on city after city. The official record of these battles presents us with a formula for conquest. If you analyse this report, after the initial battle at Makkedah the following six-part pattern emerges from the text:

(1) statement of troop movement,

(2) siege of and/or battle waged against the target city,

(3) capture of the city (this sometimes includes the king, the citizens, and even the surrounding towns),

(4) the city is struck with the edge of the sword,

(5) Israel destroyed every person,

(6) the formula concludes with a comparison statement (Joshua did this 'as he had done to …')

Observe, however, the way the comparison statements progress as the victories increase. Up to this point everything is compared to Jericho and/or Ai (9:1; 10:1). Even the conquest of Makkedah and Libnah are recounted in these terms ('as he had done to the king of Jericho' verses 28, 30). But after those two battles each proceeding victory becomes the standard for the next. In other words, there began to be so many victories and such a demonstration of God's power that the next victory was just like the one before it. No longer does Israel think solely in terms of Jericho or Ai, but they see God's remarkable power in every encounter with the enemy.

Third, God records what he is willing and able to do for his people. The Lord fully intends for us to find encouragement in passages like this. The account of the southern conquest provides us with a wonderful demonstration of God's omnipotence and omni-competence. If we take time to look at the details of Scripture and to do the hard work of meditating, we may find this text and others like it are just as heart warming as John 3:16. You and I do not have to face Canaanites, but in reality we face more formidable foes. We are engaged in a battle 'against the rulers, against the authorities, against the cosmic powers over this present darkness, against the spiritual forces of evil in the heavenly places' (Eph. 6:12). The triumphs recorded here remind us of the God who will help us in the fight. We have a storehouse of strength in the Lord, and we must avail ourselves of that power if we are to overcome. God so loved Israel that he gave them the land. God so loved the world that he gave us his Son. And God so loves his people that he will give us victory over every adversary and safely bring us home to heaven.

The Lord fought thoroughly

The concluding verses of the chapter summarize this third major campaign of the conquest. The description moves from regions to boundaries to kings.[1] To summarize Joshua's victory the text lists four geographical areas that he struck: the hill country, the Negeb or desert area to the southwest, the lowland, and the slopes. This is a description of all of the southern country and includes a much

---

[1] Howard, *Joshua*, 258.

greater area than the six cities listed in verses 28-39. Joshua struck the people and their kings. In carrying out this campaign, he fully obeyed the Lord by enacting the ban. Everything that breathed he devoted to destruction (verse 40).

Verse 41 offers the summary with four additional descriptions: 'from Kadesh-barnea as far as Gaza, and all the country of Goshen, as far as Gibeon'. Though you and I read this as a simple sentence consisting of four names of far-off places, the account encompasses a large area of land extending from the border of Judah in the south at Kadesh-barnea (cf. 15:3) to Gibeon as the northernmost point of conflict in this campaign, a distance of about 100 miles. Joshua captured all these kings and their lands at one time. There was a thorough and consistent victory 'because the LORD God of Israel fought for Israel' (verse 42). Joshua and the troops then returned to the camp at Gilgal (verse 43).

In this passage we are presented with the complete conquest of southern Canaan. Yet in other places we find clear statements of on-going resistance (cf. 11:22; 14:12). Not everyone was driven out (13:2-6; 15:63; 16:10; 17:12-13; cf. Judges 1). Are these somehow contradictory statements? Not at all. On 10 May 1940, the Nazi army invaded France. The Battle of France consisted of two major operations called 'Case Yellow' and 'Case Red'. In less than two months, on 22 June, an armistice was signed, and the Axis powers had won a remarkable victory. But that did not mean everyone suddenly swore allegiance to the German National Socialist Party. The French Resistance, known as the Underground, sought to hinder the Germans in any way they could. Germany had conquered France, but there were still strong pockets of resistance, and the French people as a whole wanted to rid their country of all Nazi troops.[1]

That situation parallels what we find here: a conquered land yet on-going resistance. This is an important point to keep in mind because it plays a significant role in the Bible's theology. From one perspective Israel continued to struggle with Canaanites in the land, but from another perspective, the theological perspective, the land

---

[1] I am indebted to David Howard for this very helpful analogy. Howard, *Joshua*, 259-60.

belonged to God's people. It was his covenant gift to them, and a picture of so much more to come, because the Lord fought for Israel. The Lord fought miraculously when the sun stood still. But he continued to fight justly, successively, and thoroughly as he kept every promise of his word. This powerful, faithful, covenant-keeping God is 'our God for ever and ever: he will be our guide even unto death' (Psa. 48:14 KJV).

The on-going conditions in Canaan mirror what every Christian finds in his or her heart. Christ has conquered sin in our lives. He is our king. But pockets of resistance known as remaining sin continue to rise up in rebellion. Like Israel's enemies, it must be struck down and destroyed. The apostle Paul reminds us that it is our duty to put sin to death (Rom. 8:13; Col. 3:5). We have the responsibility to deal the death blows to temptation, but we fight in a power not our own. We struggle, resist, and gain victory in the power of Christ as we consider ourselves dead to sin and alive to God through the Saviour's finished work (Rom. 6:11).

17

Canaan's Last Stand
Joshua 11:1-15

And all these kings joined their forces and came and encamped together at the waters of Merom to fight against Israel. And the LORD said to Joshua, 'Do not be afraid of them, for tomorrow at this time I will give over all of them, slain, to Israel. You shall hamstring their horses and burn their chariots with fire.' (Josh. 11:5-6)

Born in 1839, this Ohio native graduated last in his class at West Point. Such a standing from the United States Military Academy would have gained him an assignment at some remote post except for the fact that he graduated just as the War between the States began. The Union army was looking for officers, and it was judged that even this vain prankster would do. Though his prior academic performance did not bode well for an illustrious career, he became a cavalry commander, associated himself with several well-known and important officers, and proved to be a capable leader. After the war ended, his next assignment was in the Dakotas and Montana territory where he fought in the Indian Wars of the 1870s. Though he overcame his poor standing at West Point and gained a stable position and standing in the army, he is most remembered for the disastrous outcome of his final conflict—the Battle of Little Bighorn.

In late June 1876, General George Armstrong Custer faced a coalition of Plains Indians made up of Lakota, Northern Cheyenne, and Arapaho. Led by Sitting Bull, Crazy Horse, and Chief Gall, this tribal alliance soundly defeated Custer's troops, killing over one third of the 700 soldiers of the Seventh Cavalry. Custer, as well as two of his brothers, a brother-in-law, and a nephew were also killed in the battle. This, the most famous conflict of the Great Sioux War of 1876, became known popularly as 'Custer's Last Stand'. A coalition, a conflict, and a final defeat—those are the elements we find in Joshua 11:1-15, except in this case it is the story of 'Canaan's Last Stand'.

Since chapter 6 and the battle of Jericho, we have been following the movements and the battles of Israel's army as it made its way from central Palestine to the south to conquer that entire region. Now, for the third time, the Israelites faced an alliance of city-states. This time, however, they were from the north and were led by Jabin, king of Hazor. Chapter 10, the southern conquest, and chapter 11, the northern conquest, are parallel in many ways. Much of the wording is similar if not identical, and the overall military strategy is comparable as well. In chapter 11, the main battle took place in one location, in this case at the waters of Merom (verse 7). This was followed by the pursuit of the enemy as he fled for safety (verse 8). Finally, the Israelites turned back for a final mop-up campaign which involved capturing and destroying the cities of the region (verses 10-14).

The study of Israel's battles and the ensuing extermination of many cities presents us with a great deal of bloodshed and destruction. These are difficult chapters filled with hard realities. In the minds of many people, including some professing believers, the events are far from anything remotely Christian. Joshua appears to be a pagan, blood-thirsty warrior. As Reformed and evangelical Christians, however, we accept the book of Joshua as a part of the canon of Scripture and, indeed as a vital part of God's unfolding revelation. How should we understand and explain battle after battle in coherent and Christ-centred theological terms? Is that possible or even desirable? We get significant help to understand this chapter, and indeed the entire conquest of the land, from the words of verse 20, 'For it was the LORD's doing to harden [the Canaanites'] hearts that they should come against Israel in battle, in order that they should be devoted to destruction and should receive no mercy but be destroyed, just as the LORD commanded Moses.' The text throws us back upon God and his actions. The overthrow of Canaan is not to be explained in terms of marauding Israelites and land-hungry leaders but in terms of a holy, just, and sovereign God.

We have seen evidence of God's sovereignty all along as he exerted his power over the waters of the Jordan and parted them so that Israel could cross into Canaan on dry ground (chapter 3). We saw it at the fall of Jericho when, with a trumpet blast and shout from the people, God caused the walls to come tumbling down (chapter 6). We also witnessed the sovereignty of God in the amazing miracle of the long day when the Lord made the sun to stand still (chapter 10). But in chapter 11 the emphasis on God's sovereignty becomes even more explicit. The Lord ruled over the hearts of the Canaanites to make them obdurate and resistant to Israel. But God exercised his sovereignty in other ways as well.

Sovereign grace

As God's rule and power work themselves out in the account of the northern conquest, chapter 11 begins with another display of sovereign grace. In verses 1-3, we encounter yet another military alliance, the third coalition Israel has had to face (cf. 9:1-2; 10:1-5). The pattern we have seen in the previous chapters continues as the news of Israel's victories spread throughout Canaan and the inhabitants began to react (see 9:1; 10:1). Jabin, king of Hazor, heard about Joshua's victory over the Amorite coalition and the cities of southern Canaan. With this impressive victory, the army of Israel must be taken seriously, so Jabin wastes no time in taking the lead and organizing the next coalition to resist its advance. Hazor was the most prominent city in Palestine at that time, even though it lay in the far north about ten miles beyond the Sea of Galilee. So it comes as no surprise that Jabin initiated this action and played a leading role in the events.[1]

[1] Madvig, *Joshua*, 308. With regard to Hazor, 'its remains can be found on a huge mound, more than two hundred acres in area, about eight miles north of the Sea of Galilee. Biblical and extrabiblical evidence alike point to its having been a large and strategic city.' Howard, *Joshua*, 265.

Jabin contacted Jobab king of Madon (cf. 12:19) as well as other kings from the surrounding areas. The scope of the alliance included Jabin and Jobab, the only two kings identified by name, but the coalition also consisted of the king of Shimron (cf. 19:15), the king of Achshaph (12:20; 19:25),[1] and kings from various areas of northern Canaan (verse 2). Then, in a sweeping summary of the rest who were involved, the author reminds us of the major people groups Israel faced in this military alliance. They were the Canaanites, the Amorites, the Hittites, the Perizzites, the Jebusites, and the Hivites (cf. 9:1). It is unusual to find the Jebusites listed along with these others from the north of Palestine because they are usually associated with the city of Jerusalem in the south. Either there were Jebusites who lived in the north, which is very likely, or the author throws them into the list for good measure to stress how widespread the opposition was that Israel faced. In either case, what we find in these opening verses is a large and impressive alliance.

This list of kings and people groups is significant for two reasons. First, because it summarizes all of Canaan, and it casts 'a dark cloud of impending doom over the Israelites.'[2] This gathering of Canaanites formed an imposing show of force. Second, because the list summarizes all of Canaan and is nearly identical to similar lists that occur earlier in Scripture in connection with God's covenant with Abraham, it serves as a reminder of the Lord's promise to the patriarch and his descendants that they would inhabit this land. For example, in Genesis 15 we read, 'On that day the LORD made a covenant with Abram, saying, "To your offspring I give this land, from the river of Egypt to the great river, the river Euphrates, the land of the Kenites, the Kenizzites, the Kadmonites, the Hittites, the Perizzites, the Rephaim, the Amorites, the Canaanites, the Girgashites and the Jebusites"' (Gen. 15:18-21).

Later, when the Lord appeared to Moses at the burning bush and said, 'I have surely seen the affliction of my people who are in Egypt and have heard their cry because of their taskmasters. I know their

---

[1] Archaeologists have been unable to make a clear identification of Madon, Shimron, and Achshaph. Pitkänen, *Joshua*, 232. It is possible that Madon may have lain just a couple of miles east of the Sea of Galilee.

[2] Howard, *Joshua*, 265.

sufferings, and I have come down to deliver them out of the hand of the Egyptians and to bring them up out of that land to a good and broad land, a land flowing with milk and honey, to the place of the Canaanites, the Hittites, the Amorites, the Perizzites, the Hivites, and the Jebusites' (Exod. 3:7-8). Between the promise and Israel's full possession of the land lay one final conflict. The land of promise that flowed with milk and honey was to flow once more with blood because the peoples of the northern alliance set themselves in defiant opposition to fight against Israel and the purposes of God.

Overwhelming odds and covenant promises

This third coalition proved to be the most populous of them all. Three times verse four repeats the word 'many' or 'much' to emphasize just how large and numerous a foe Israel faced. As these kings and their troops came out to fight they were 'a *great* horde, in number like the sand that is on the seashore, with very many horses and chariots' (verse 4).[1] Once again the wording of the text serves a double purpose. It emphasizes just how large this northern alliance was with its *many* people, *many* horses, and *many* chariots, but it also draws our minds back to the promises made to Abraham. When the Lord tested the patriarch and asked him to sacrifice his son Isaac, Abraham trusted God and passed the test. The Lord provided a ram as a substitute for Isaac (Gen. 22:1-14) and then spoke from heaven through his angel and said, 'I will surely bless you, and I will surely multiply your offspring as the stars of heaven and as the sand that is on the seashore. And your offspring shall possess the gate of his enemies, and in your offspring shall all the nations of the earth be blessed, because you have obeyed my voice' (Gen. 22:17-18).

Israel, who was to be like the sand on the seashore, faced an army described the same way. Joshua's report of the northern alliance contains these verbal allusions to the covenant promises. The wording of the text is no coincidence. The nations Israel was to dispossess are arrayed for a battle. The people of the covenant face a seemingly larger foe. This northern alliance led by Jabin forms, if you will, an anti-covenant coalition. Moreover, these enemies

---

[1] The Hebrew text of verse 4 repeats the adjective *rab*, 'many' three times.

came 'with very many horses and chariots' (verse 4). Israel's army consisted solely of an infantry. It was not equipped to face up to the speed and manoeuvrability of charioteers. With this new coalition forming such a large army and having such powerful means at their disposal, verses 4 and 5 raise the question, 'Can God's covenant purposes overcome these insuperable odds?'

The presence of chariots and horses also raised the issue of trust. The Lord forbade Israel's kings to multiply horses (Deut. 17:16) or trust in chariots, even though they would face such awesome forces in battle. God's people were not to rely upon the strength of conventional warfare; they were to trust in him. Now facing such a daunting threat, will the people of Israel continue to trust the Lord or will they cower in fear and rest content with only possessing the southern half of the land? This is the perennial issue that all of God's people face. Will we fear what we can see or trust the One who promises to be with us? Will we trust in odds or in God?

This is the believer's daily battle, the struggle to walk by faith and not by sight (cf. 2 Cor. 5:7). We face one level of reality in the world with all of its opposition and hostility to our faith and all of its temptations to allure us away from the Lord. Will we follow the path of least resistance or do the hard thing? Will we succumb to the pleasures that this level of reality offers us or will we look beyond what our eyes can see to the vaster, far deeper reality of God and his revealed will? In other words, will we bind our hearts to this world through sight or will we anchor our hope in the next world through faith in the promises of God (cf. Heb. 6:19)?

To anchor our hope we must return again and again to the word of God. This was the reason God told Joshua at the beginning to meditate on Scripture: 'This Book of the Law shall not depart from your mouth, but you shall meditate on it day and night, so that you may be careful to do according to all that is written in it. For then you will make your way prosperous, and then you will have good success' (1:8). We must engage in a constant repetition of the promises. We must rehearse again and again the essentials of our faith that they might become the fundamental building blocks of our daily lives.

All of the northern troops joined forces and camped 'together at the waters of Merom to fight with Israel' (verse 5). Their purpose was to destroy God's people. Can God's promises prevail? The people needed to remember the last time they encountered an impressive army with chariots. Pharaoh's forces chased the fleeing Israelites into the heart of the Red Sea only to be overcome as the Lord brought the walls of water crashing down on them. The last time Israel faced chariots, God left the chariots floating in the sea (see Exod. 14:26-29).

Victory for God's people

In a sense, God reminded Israel of that victory as he spoke once again (cf. 10:8). The Lord assured Joshua that he was there and that his word was active and powerful. The Lord did not stand on the sidelines watching the conquest of Canaan unfold. He was at the forefront of the action leading Joshua and his army into victory. Whenever Joshua faced a battle, the Lord reassured him of his presence and power by telling him not to be afraid (cf. 8:1; 10:8, 25; see also 1:6, 9), and that was exactly what he did once again on the eve of this battle. 'And the LORD said to Joshua, "Do not be afraid of them"' (verse 6). The Lord had already prepared Israel for the very situation they now faced by giving his word to Moses: 'When you go out to war against your enemies, and see horses and chariots and an army larger than your own, you shall not be afraid of them, for the LORD your God is with you, who brought you up out of the land of Egypt' (Deut. 20:1).

But the Lord did not give the command, 'Don't be afraid' without backing it up with divine reasons. Joshua need not fear because in twenty-four hours the Lord would give over the northern coalition into Israel's hands (verse 6). God's promise to give the Canaanites over to Israel once again highlights who was fighting these battles (cf. 10:14, 43). The Lord powerfully carried out the campaign of Canaan step by step. But here the expression is expanded. He will not only give them over, he will give them over *slain*.[1] It was as

[1] This is the first of only two occurrences of the verb 'slain' (*hll*) in Joshua. The other is in 13:22. Most of the time the expression for killing one's enemies is 'struck with the edge of the sword'. See the multiple occurrences of this phrase in chapter 10 (verses 28, 30, 32, 35, 37, 39).

though God himself wielded the sword before Israel's troops and handed over the Canaanite corpses to the advancing army. What was Israel's responsibility? The soldiers were to cripple the horses and burn the chariots. The 'very many horses and chariots' (verse 4) will prove to be no match for the Lord's foot soldiers.

If we count the command God gave Joshua at his commissioning, 'Be strong and courageous' (1:6, 7, 9), this is the seventh time the Lord has told Joshua not to be afraid. Over and over again he hears this same message from God because he needs to hear it over and over again. What do we learn from this? God's word never changes. It remains the same and comes with freshness and power to meet each new need. Do you experience the Bible like that? Do you experience the gospel like that? In the words of W. A. Williams's hymn,

'tis old, yet ever new.

Scripture *is* inspired. We do not believe that the Bible *was* inspired but that now it bears no life-giving vibrancy. It remains the breathed-out word of God, the only way the Holy Spirit speaks to us. This old book is not a dead book. It is living and active and powerful (Heb. 4:12).

With a word from God guaranteeing victory, 'Joshua and all his warriors came suddenly against [the northern alliance] by the waters of Merom and fell upon them' (verse 7). Merom became the central point of engagement in the northern campaign.[1] Located in upper Galilee, it was not a suitable place to use horses and chariots in battle.[2] Some place a little further south, like the plain of Esdraelon,[3] would be a much more ideal place to engage the Israelites. The waters of Merom was most likely the gathering place for the coalition to amass its troops before proceeding southward. Joshua, however, did

[1] Most likely located west of Kedesh in Galilee, the exact location of Merom has not been identified.

[2] 'The area of combat, the district of the waters of Merom, is about 4,000 feet above sea level, therefore an area in which chariots would find no room for manoeuvring. The author, however, is concerned chiefly to stress the divine assistance rendered to Israel during the combat.' Woudstra, *Book of Joshua*, 191.

[3] The Plain of Esdraelon is also known as the Valley of Jezreel and extends from Mount Carmel to Mount Gilboa.

not wait for the enemy to come to him. As a wise military leader, he knew to choose the time and place of the engagement according to his terms rather than reacting to the enemy's advances. So in a surprise attack, the Israelites came upon the Canaanites suddenly.[1] Joshua shared the attitude of David in Psalm 20:7, 'Some trust in chariots and some in horses, but we trust in the name of the LORD our God.'

When you take the lesson of verse 6 and combine it with verses 7 and 8, you see the wedding of divine sovereignty and human responsibility. God promised the victory *and* Joshua fought. In addition to divine sovereignty and human responsibility we also see human ingenuity. Joshua used wisdom to lead his troops into battle and to engage the enemy in a place where the latter was at the greatest disadvantage. None of these three facets of the victory are incompatible. We spend far too much time debating the sovereignty of God when it is not a debatable point. God is sovereign! Given the truth that God is in absolute control, what *we* need to do is to ask the Lord what *he* wants us to do. We should pray, 'What is my responsibility, Lord? What is the wisest course for me to take? Give me wisdom that I may do what is right.' Divine sovereignty should never stop us in our tracks. It should compel us forward to prayer and faithful obedience.

Once Israel engaged the battle, the Lord gave his people victory. The enemy was delivered over into Israel's hand. From the initial point of conflict, Israel pursued the Canaanites 'as far as Great Sidon and Misrephoth-maim, and eastward as far as the Valley of Mizpeh' (verse 8). The chase led the army to form two subgroups, one heading to the west near the Mediterranean coast and north beyond the Leontes River, and another going to the northeast toward the Valley of Mizpeh before turning south to attack Hazor (cf. verses 10-14).[2]

'And they struck them until he left none remaining' (verse 8). The last sentence in verse 8 displays a curious change in pronouns.

---

[1] See 10:9 for the only other occurrence of the word 'suddenly' (*pith'om*) in Joshua where it is also used to describe a surprise attack.

[2] Hubbard, *Joshua*, 328.

First, '*they* struck them'. The Israelite soldiers fought against their enemies. Second, they fought 'until *he* left none remaining'. The responsibility for victory once again falls upon the Lord. *He* gave them into the hand of Israel, and *he* left none remaining. Just as we saw in chapter 10, 'the Lord God of Israel fought for Israel' (verse 42; cf. verse 14).

This terse account of the battle wraps up by recalling Joshua's obedience to all that God had commanded. The Lord had said, 'hamstring their horses and burn their chariots with fire' (verse 6), and that was what Joshua did (verse 9). Full obedience from both Joshua and Israel is a recurring theme in the first half of the book (4:8; 8:31, 33; 10:40) and will occur three more times in this chapter (verses 12, 15, 20). God's blessing and Israel's obedience went hand in hand. We cannot expect the Lord to bless our endeavours if we are unwilling to do his will.

Israel did not deserve to win this battle nor any of the previous conflicts. Time and time again the text stresses that God gave the enemy into their hands (1:6, 13; 5:6; 8:7, 18; 9:24; 10:12, 30, 32). The Lord had been displaying his sovereign grace ever since the exodus. He did not bring his people out of Egypt because they were such a wonderful and pure people. Many, if not most of them, worshipped Egyptian idols. That is evidenced in the golden calf incident soon after their departure from Egypt (Exod. 32:1-6). They readily fell back into their old, pagan ways of religion. Why, then, did God rescue them from slavery, bring them through the wilderness, and give them Canaan? Simply because he, in his infinite goodness, chose to do so.[1]

Every spiritual blessing you and I have in Christ, comes to us on the same basis: pure, sovereign grace. No passage of Scripture presents this truth more clearly than Ephesians chapter 1. God chose us in Christ (verse 4); he predestined us to adoption as his children (verse 5); he redeemed us through Jesus' blood (verse 7), and lavished upon us the riches of his grace all because of his own good pleasure (verse 8). I own a number of study Bibles written from various theological persuasions and perspectives. One of them blatantly repudiates that

---

[1] On God's sovereign grace to Israel, see Geerhardus Vos, *Biblical Theology: Old and New Testaments* (1948; repr. Edinburgh: Banner of Truth Trust, 2014), 113-14.

any such thing as sovereign grace exists. When I read the particular note that denies the doctrine, I was shocked by the author's boldness and the glaring nature of his error. What other kind of grace is there but sovereign grace? If grace is really grace, if God is favourable to us and blesses us freely, not for any goodness in us or works done by us, then grace by its very nature is bestowed according to his good pleasure. Sovereign grace is the only grace there is!

Sovereign judgment

Having obeyed the Lord and dealt with the enemies' horses and chariots, Joshua turned the army back southward to attack Hazor and the other cities of the coalition. In verses 10-15, we find similar elements as occurred in the account of the conquest of southern Canaan: first, kings and their people were struck with the edge of the sword (verse 12; cf. 10:28, 30, 32, 35, 37, 39); second, the exercise of the ban in which every person in the respective city is destroyed (verse 14; cf. 10:28, 30, 32, 35, 37, 39); and third, Joshua's ongoing obedience (verse 15; 10:40).

But the text concentrates on the overthrow and destruction of one particular city. Hazor receives special attention. Jabin had led the northern alliance (cf. verse 1). That he had such influence over the region makes sense when we are told that 'Hazor formerly was the head of all those kingdoms' (verse 10). For this reason Joshua focuses his attention on that city and struck the king and all its inhabitants. He then set the city on fire.[1] This is the first time the text mentions the burning of Hazor, but that fact will be reiterated twice more in verse 13: 'But none of the cities that stood on mounds did Israel burn, except Hazor alone; that Joshua burned.' Having repeated for the third time that Joshua burned Hazor, the author is obviously at pains to stress this point. But why? It appears that Hazor received this unique treatment because it was the head of all the kingdoms of the northern coalition and because Jabin its king led the rebellion against Israel. In other words, conquer the head, and the rest will fall. Make an example of Hazor that all may fear.

---

[1] Hazor, along with Jericho and Ai, were the only cities that we have a record of Joshua burning.

Joshua then attacked all the cities that had joined with Jabin, like Shimron and Achshaph (cf. verses 1-3), captured them, struck them, and devoted them to destruction. By not burning these other cities, the Lord provided Israel with places to live, cities and houses that they did not build just as he had promised (Deut. 6:10-11). Though Israel was not allowed to take any of the spoils from Jericho (6:17-19), after that initial victory the Lord relaxed the stringency of the rule and let the people take livestock and other goods from the cities they conquered. So Israel took the plunder but allowed no one to live (verse 14). All of this was done according to the proper chain of command. The Lord commanded Moses, Moses commanded Joshua, and Joshua obeyed thoroughly leaving 'nothing undone of all that the LORD had commanded Moses' (verse 15).

Silence fell over these cities as every heart stopped, every breath ceased, and every cry was silenced by the sword. As you read the text you can almost feel the eerie hush of the judgment of God. The execution of the ban against the Canaanites reminds us that it is a fearful thing to fall into the hands of the living God (Heb. 10:31). God is a just and sovereign judge of all those who rebel against him. He is holy and must punish sin. But he is also full of love, and that is the very reason he sent the Lord Jesus—so that Christ might take the just punishment of God in our place so that you who trust in him and I may be forgiven. Christ bore our sins in his own body on the cross (1 Pet. 2:24). He died as our substitute to satisfy the wrath of God (Rom. 3:25; 1 John 2:2; 4:10). He died so that God might remain just and yet also be the justifier of all those who believe in Jesus (Rom. 3:26). The Lord's destruction of the northern alliance leaves us with no doubt as to his holy anger with sin. But the cross of Calvary and the empty tomb leave us with no doubt that his holy anger has been perfectly appeased by the work of Christ. Have you ever experienced the peace and forgiveness of God through Christ? Or do you await the judgment of the God who deals decisively with rebels?

Canaan's last stand provides us with yet another example of the remarkable power of God, the one who fights for Israel. It also presents us with a startling example of his sovereign grace and sovereign judgment. Under which do you fall?

18

Our Great Saviour
Joshua 11:16-23

So Joshua took the whole land, according to all that the LORD had spoken to Moses. And Joshua gave it for an inheritance to Israel according to their tribal allotments. And the land had rest from war. (Josh. 11:23)

The book of Joshua tells the story of God bringing his chosen people, whom he redeemed from Egyptian slavery, into the land he had promised to their forefathers. Israel did not, however, just walk into the land and inhabit its cities and villages. In order to possess Canaan as their own, they had to dispossess the nations who lived there. The first eleven chapters walk the reader step by step from the Israelite camp on the eastern bank of the Jordan River, across the river bed on dry ground, and through various military campaigns under the leadership of Joshua.

After defeating Jericho (6:1-27) and Ai (8:1-35), two major cities situated in central Palestine, Joshua led his troops on a southern campaign (10:29-43) and then turned his attentions north to conquer that area of Canaan as well (11:1-15). In the closing verses of chapter 11, we find a summary, not of the northern campaign from the immediately preceding section, but of all the conquest of Canaan. This passage brings to a close the major battles to overthrow the land of promise. As a summary or 'war wrap-up' as Davis calls it,[1] these verses stress the role of Joshua as Israel's deliverer. As you read the text it becomes immediately clear that Joshua is the Lord's instrument to bring Israel into the full possession of all that he has for his people.

Israel's army fought long and hard to secure its victories. It is also true, as chapter 10 repeatedly stressed, that the Lord fought for Israel. But it is no less true that Joshua played a key role as the leader of the nation and commander general of the army. Now, in 11:16-23 his role in history becomes even clearer. As Israel's leader, Joshua served as a type of the Lord Jesus Christ. In other words, Joshua, whose name means 'the Lord saves', was a picture prophecy of Jesus and all that he accomplished for our salvation. Just as Joshua led Israel to seize and occupy the land of promise, Jesus leads believers into the full possession of all their spiritual blessings.

To understand what God was doing through Joshua, and why it is important for us, we need to explore this passage and answer the simple question, 'How did Joshua bring Israel into the blessings God had for them?' The answer unfolds in three parts and points us to how Jesus brings us into the fullness of salvation. First, Joshua made war with the enemy. Second, he overcame Israel's greatest fear. And, third, he led Israel into rest.

Man of war

That God used Joshua to make war is the focus of verses 16-20 which offer us a summary of all that has happened in the ongoing conflicts with the Canaanites. The passage highlights the events geographically, militarily, and theologically. First, Joshua took all the land. The expression 'all this land' refers not just to the northern conquest in the immediate context but to all of Canaan and is a summary of the land conquered from the fall of Jericho until now. Similar to the account found in 10:40-42, the description of the land begins with a list of areas, then moves to boundaries, and concludes with a reference to kings.

The areas were 'the hill country and all the Negeb and all the land of Goshen and the lowland and the Arabah and the hill country of

---

[1] Davis, *Joshua: No Falling Words*, 99.

Israel and its lowland' (verse 16). The hill country of Judah runs north and south through south-central Palestine between the Dead Sea on the east and the Mediterranean Sea to the west. The Negeb refers to the region south and west of the Dead Sea and extends southward as the southernmost boundary of Israel. Goshen obviously does not refer to the locale in Egypt where Israel lived prior to the exodus (see Gen. 47:1-6). It was likely in southern Palestine near Anab and may perhaps be identified with *ed-Dahariyeh* (see 10:41 and 15:51). The lowland or the *Shepelah* is the area west of Judah and its hill country. It was called the lowland because it was lower than the Judean hills as the land slopes to the coastal plain toward the area occupied by the Philistines (see 11:2). The Arabah is the valley or rift that runs from the Sea of Chinnereth[1] in the north, down through the Jordan River valley, the Dead Sea, and ends at the Gulf of Aqaba in the south (cf. Deut. 2:8; 4:49; Josh. 11:2). The hill country of Israel and its lowland refers to the area north of the hill country of Judah west of the Jordan River valley and the lower elevations that slope down to the coastal plain.[2]

The next geographical indicators are the boundary markers: 'from Mount Halak, which rises toward Seir, as far as Baal-gad in the Valley of Lebanon below Mount Hermon' (verse 17). The reference to Mount Hermon marks the border in the far north and Mount Halak the south (cf. 12:7). Finally, verse 17 concludes by noting that Joshua 'captured all their kings and struck them and put them to death'. The text has emphasized this point all along as Joshua put to death the kings of Jericho (10:30) and Ai (8:29) and defeated the major coalitions arrayed against Israel (cf. 9:1-2; 10:16-28). In all of these places, Joshua captured the kings and executed them. A list of these kings can be found in 12:7-24. By putting these men to death, Joshua struck at the head of rebellion against God.

Though we can read these historical accounts in a matter of moments, we should not imagine that they took place within a day or two or even within a few months. It took Joshua a long time

---

[1] Throughout the history of Israel the Sea of Chinnereth was known by several other names as well such as Lake Gennesaret, the Sea of Galilee, and Lake Tiberias.

[2] Helpful maps of this area may be found in Herbert G. May, ed. *Oxford Bible Atlas*, 3rd edition (New York: Oxford University Press, 1984), 61-63.

(literally 'many days' verse 18) to overcome these kings.[1] How long did it actually take? In chapter 14, Caleb refers to the time period from when Moses first sent him to spy out the land to the time that he received his inheritance. Caleb was forty years old when he first went into Canaan to do reconnaissance (14:7). Following Israel's rebellion, the people wandered in the wilderness for forty years. When Caleb finally received the land promised to him, he was eighty five years old (14:10). That means, then, that the conquest of Canaan took at least five years. Throughout this long war, not one of the cities, with the exception of Gibeon (cf. 9:3-15), attempted to make peace with Israel. God's people took them all in battle (verse 19).

The first major emphasis that stands out in this summary is the comprehensive nature of the conquest. This is especially evident in the repeated use of the word 'all': '*all* that land', '*all* the Negeb', '*all* the land of Goshen' (verse 16), '*all* their kings' (verses 17, 18), 'they took them *all* in battle' (verse 19). Why do we find this stress in the text? To highlight for us the truth that God was fulfilling *all* of his promises. Later in the book, when Joshua summarizes what God did for Israel, he will say, '*not one word* has failed of all the good things that the LORD your God promised concerning you. *All* have come to pass for you; *not one of them* has failed' (23:14). You can rely upon God because he never forgets a single word that he has uttered. He does not get lost in the details and lose track of what is happening. He is steadily and systematically accomplishing his purposes step by step, both in the world at large and in your life in particular. He did it for Israel, and that is exactly what he is doing for you. God has promised to save *all* those who trust in Christ alone (John 10:27-29). He has promised to bring every believer into the full possession of every spiritual benefit that Jesus has to offer, culminating in eternal glory (Rom. 8:28-30). Your life may feel like a twisted mess of frustration, stress, and pain, but God is not lost in that mess. He is working in it and through it to bring you closer to himself and closer to the final goal.

[1] In the Hebrew text, the phrase 'many days' (*yamim rabbim*) stands at the beginning of verse 18 in order to stress the duration of the war.

The key feature of these verses is their stress on the role of Joshua. The army of Israel fought against its enemies (cf. verse 19), but the honour for the triumph is placed squarely at the feet of the leader: '*Joshua* took all that land' (verse 16). 'And [*Joshua*] captured all their kings' (verse 17). '*Joshua* made war for a long time' (verse 18). In verse 21, '*Joshua* came at that time and cut off the Anakim.' It was Joshua who 'took the whole land' and 'gave it for an inheritance to Israel' (verse 23). Why do these verses repeatedly make the same point? To demonstrate the way God fulfilled his promises. He accomplished his plan through his chosen leader. God brought Israel into the blessings of the promised land through the leadership and instrumentality of Joshua. This is where we see one of the striking parallels between Israel's great general and our great Saviour, the Lord Jesus Christ. Every promise of God is reliable because of the trustworthiness of Jesus. Christ is committed to do everything necessary to bring us to God. He is able to save completely all those who come to God through him because he not only died to save his people, he also continues to intercede for them at the throne of grace (Heb. 7:25). Everything the Lord promised Israel and everything he promises you and me culminates in Christ. The apostle Paul wrote to the church in Corinth, 'For all the promises of God find their Yes in him. That is why it is through him that we utter our Amen to God for his glory' (2 Cor. 1:20). God's final word is Jesus Christ (Heb. 1:1-2). He says 'Yes' to all of his promises in Christ. The believer's response is to be a heart-felt 'Amen.' And through God's 'Yes' and our 'Amen', the Lord receives all the glory!

A theological war

Verses 16-19 make it clear that Joshua accomplished a wide-ranging defeat of both the land and its leaders. Behind this comprehensive victory, however, lies a theological rationale. That is the focus of verse 20. Why were all these nations so ferocious when they attacked Israel? Why did no one other than the Gibeonites pursue peace? We know the Canaanites were afraid (2:11; 5:1; 7:5) and had a natural desire to preserve their lives, but behind this normal instinct for self-preservation lies a theological explanation. All of these great battles were fought because the Lord hardened the hearts of the Canaanites so that they would attack Israel. And that was for the purpose of destroying the Canaanites, devoting them to destruction, and showing them no mercy (verse 20).

In other words, God took the initiative to judge the inhabitants of Canaan by making their hearts obstinate and unwilling to submit to Israel or come to terms of peace. From their hardened hearts they turned viciously to attack God's people and resist his purposes. Yet we know that God did all of this so that he might destroy them. It was God's purpose to annihilate the Canaanites and to show them no mercy. He chose Israel as his people. He did not choose Canaan. He had mercy on Israel. He did not have mercy on Canaan. All of this falls under the purview of God's sovereignty. That Israel possessed the land and the Canaanites were killed and driven from their cities can be explained only in terms of sovereign grace and sovereign judgment. God's sovereignty is not a popular doctrine, but could the text be any clearer? 'It was *the LORD's doing* to harden their hearts.' He did this 'in order that they should be devoted to destruction and should receive no mercy but be destroyed' (verse 20). The only true and living God does as he pleases, and it is a fearful thing to fall into his hands (Heb. 10:31).

This was not the first time God hardened someone's heart. When the Lord sent Moses to address the king of Egypt and relay God's demand that he free Israel from captivity, 'the LORD said to Moses, "When you go back to Egypt, see that you do before Pharaoh all the miracles that I have put in your power. But I will harden his heart, so that he will not let the people go"' (Exod. 4:21).

God had already determined to harden the heart of Egypt's ruler. Paul used this Old Testament passage in Romans 9 to teach that God chose some for salvation and passed by others. The apostle wrote, 'What shall we say then? Is there injustice on God's part? By no means! For he says to Moses, "I will have mercy on whom I have mercy, and I will have compassion on whom I have compassion." So then it depends not on human will or exertion, but on God, who has mercy. For the Scripture says to Pharaoh, "For this very purpose I have raised you up, that I might show my power in you, and that my name might be proclaimed in all the earth." So then he has mercy on whomever he wills, and he hardens whomever he wills' (Rom. 9:14-18).

The only biblical way to explain the Canaanite conflicts with Israel is to speak in terms of God and his sovereignty over the lives and destinies of all people. He could have chosen the Canaanites and hardened the Israelites, but he did not. His choice was free and perfect according to the purpose of his will. The man, woman, or child who perishes in his sin cannot say that he deserves better, and the believer who lives through Christ can only say he deserves anything but the goodness he has received in Jesus.

Why does God harden people? Is he harsh and vindictive? Is he a cosmic bully? Not at all. Do not imagine that God came to people who lived in blissful, spiritual neutrality and cruelly said, 'I think I will harden your hearts.' The Canaanites were like everyone born into this world after the Fall.[1] They were born with depraved, rebellious hearts that were already hard toward God. God made harder what was already obdurate as an act of judgment in order that these people might ultimately be destroyed.

Does God harden everyone this way? No. Even though everyone is born depraved and spiritually dead toward God (see Eph. 2:1-3) not everyone is left to become harder and eventually perish. What God did with Israel, with Pharaoh, and with the Canaanites he continues to do. He has mercy on whom he chooses to have mercy, and others he hardens that they may continue in their rebellion and be judged.

Does it seem unfair to you that God should decide to save some and pass by others? I have a good friend named Chris who is a potter. Chris casts moulds for commercial pots, and he also makes bowls and vases that are beautiful works of art. I have been in Chris' studio a number of times but never once have I heard a pot argue with him. Never have I heard one say, 'I don't want to be a planter. I want to be a beautiful vase.' Nor have I gone into his studio and said, 'Chris, do not waste your time with those exquisite colours and intricate shapes for a vase, just make a plain brown pot.' Why

---

[1] With the exception of the Lord Jesus Christ, of course. He knew no sin, and that is the reason he could become a sacrifice in our place (2 Cor. 5:21). He was offered up as a lamb without blemish or spot (Heb. 9:14; 1 Pet. 1:19).

are there no arguments with the pottery? Why do I not decide what Chris makes and the way he makes it? Because when he goes into his studio to work, the things that happen, the forms that take shape, the colours that are mixed are all done according to his plan. Chris, not the clay nor his friends, runs the studio.

Is this not the way the apostle Paul responds to those who object to God's sovereign election and call him unjust? 'But who are you, O man, to answer back to God? Will what is moulded say to its moulder, 'Why have you made me like this?' Has the potter no right over the clay, to make out of the same lump one vessel for honourable use and another for dishonourable use' (Rom. 9:20-21).

As I have studied various commentaries written on this passage, it has been interesting to watch authors try to wriggle their way out of the clear implications of the text. Far too often Christians approach passages like this with the attitude of 'This verse cannot mean what it appears to mean because that is not the way I think God is.' With that attitude, we end up reducing the sovereign Lord of the universe into a benign god made in our image. But God is God! Our standard of justice must rise to meet his. He will not lower his standard to meet ours.

The doctrine of God's sovereignty is not to be the speculative playground of theologians. God intends it to raise the intensely personal question of your salvation. God intends you to ask, 'Am I one on whom the Lord has had mercy or am I being hardened for the day of judgment?' Which is it with you? Do you find your heart trusting in and loving the Lord Jesus or do you continue to cling to your sin and find your heart growing colder and harder to God as each gospel opportunity to receive and rest upon Christ alone for salvation passes by unheeded?

This passage serves to magnify God, his sovereignty, and his grace. This emphasis on God's sovereignty constitutes an essential part of what it means to be a Reformed Christian. In his delightful little booklet, *What is the Reformed Faith?* John R. de Witt writes,

> The Reformed faith is ... characterized by the insistence that God is to be known and worshipped as the sovereign God. Some would make this sovereignty the leading characteristic. There is a sense in

which that idea is correct, particularly when the Reformed faith is compared with other theological traditions, in which the grandeur and majesty of God are insufficiently appreciated or even lost to view. God, not man, is king!¹

The *Westminster Confession of Faith* stresses this important facet of God's character when it describes the Lord as 'the alone fountain of all being, of whom, through whom, and to whom are all things; and hath most sovereign dominion over them, to do by them, for them, or upon them whatsoever himself pleaseth.'² God's sovereignty is the bedrock of biblical faith, and that is why it is important to be in a church where the dominion, power, and authority of God are emphasized.

Overcoming fear

Not only did Joshua wage war, he also overcame fear: 'And Joshua came at that time and cut off the Anakim' (verse 21). The phrase 'at that time' occurred earlier in verse 10 as well as on two previous occasions in the book (5:2; 6:26). It is a generic time indicator, not a specific chronological marker. It refers to the time of the conquest in general. When Joshua defeated all of the other nations, he also cut off the Anakim from the hill country, from Hebron, Debir, Anab, the hill country of Judah and of Israel. He executed the ban against them destroying both the people and their cities. As far as Israel was concerned, it was a complete destruction. No Anakim were left within the territory, though some remained in the Philistine cities of Gaza, Gath, and Ashdod (verse 22).

Hebron, Debir, and Anab were all located in the area eventually allotted to Judah. Debir and Anab were very close to the land of Goshen, mentioned in verse 16 and perhaps included as a part of that land. Hebron was in the hill country of Judah, and both the hill country of Judah and of Israel are mentioned specifically here just as they were in verse 16. Since we already have a record that Joshua took all of that land and executed the kings, why do we have this

---

¹ John Richard de Witt, *What is the Reformed Faith?* (Edinburgh: Banner of Truth Trust, 1981), 9.
² *Westminster Confession of Faith*, 2.2.

separate account here? The answer lies in the specific reference to the Anakim.[1]

The Anakim were the descendants of Anak (Num. 13:22) who formed the supposedly undefeatable foe for Israel when the spies first searched out the land. After spending forty days travelling throughout Canaan to gather information about its people, geography, agriculture, and military strength, the spies returned with their report. Canaan was indeed a land flowing with milk and honey (Exod. 3:8, 17; Josh. 5:6). The cluster of grapes from Eshcol, which was so large it took two men to carry it, was proof enough of the agricultural abundance that was available. The spies related that the land was just as God had described it. 'However, the people who dwell in the land are strong, and the cities are fortified and very large. And besides, we saw the descendants of Anak there' (Num. 13:28).

Caleb, one of the spies who had seen the land and the enemies, believed that God was able to deliver the land and its people into Israel's hand. He 'quieted the people before Moses and said, "Let us go up at once and occupy it, for we are well able to overcome it"' (Num. 13:30). But his fellow-spies said, '"We are not able to go up against the people, for they are stronger than we are." So they brought to the people of Israel a bad report of the land that they had spied out, saying, "The land, through which we have gone to spy it out, is a land that devours its inhabitants, and all the people that we saw in it are of great height. And there we saw the Nephilim (the sons of Anak, who come from the Nephilim), and we seemed to ourselves like grasshoppers, and so we seemed to them"' (verses 31-33).

The Anakim were a very tall people (see Deut. 2:10, 21; 9:2) who struck fear in the hearts of the majority of Israel and kept them from possessing the land the first time they approached it. When

---

[1] This text is the first time the Anakim are mentioned in Joshua, but there are five more occurrences (14:12, 15; 15:13, 14 [twice]). References to the Anakim also occur in Judges 1:20; 8:26. After that we hear no more of them. 'In sum, this short account of the elimination of the Anakites is unusual in its harshness and thoroughness, a factor to be attributed, no doubt, to the Anakites' awesome reputation and their intimidating influence on Israel's attitudes heretofore.' Howard, *Joshua*, 275.

Moses recounted this scene in the opening pages of Deuteronomy, he recalled the words of the fearful Israelites: 'Where are we going up? Our brothers have made our hearts melt, saying, "The people are greater and taller than we. The cities are great and fortified up to heaven. And besides, we have seen the sons of the Anakim there"' (Deut. 1:28).

The story of the conquest ends where the fear began forty years earlier—with the Anakim. Israel thought the Anakim were the undefeatable foe but now, to cap off the story of God's gift of the land, we have the account of their defeat. It is reported here almost as an afterthought. 'By the way, remember the Anakim you feared so much? Joshua cut them off and devoted them to destruction as well.'

Though Israel feared these giants of the land, they posed no threat to God nor were they a foe too difficult to overcome. You and I should be able to see from this brief account that our fears pose no threat to God nor do they prove to be an obstacle for him. What are you afraid of? What the doctor may say on your follow-up visit? What your boss may say when he begins a conversation about tough times and down-sizing? What your spouse may say after you have had yet another argument? Uncertainty breeds fear. Will your doctor say, 'It is cancer'? Will your boss say, 'You are fired'? Will your spouse say, 'I am through with this relationship'? To overcome the fear of uncertainty we have to hold on to what is certain. If cancer kills me, heaven awaits me. If the boss fires me, I have a Father in heaven who owns the universe. If my spouse abandons me, I have a Saviour who has promised to seat me as his bride at the marriage supper of the Lamb.

Uncertainty breeds fear, and fear paralyses. It paralysed Israel. Forty years earlier the people were not confident that God could overcome the Anakim, so they refused to go into the land. If you let fear rather than faith dominate your life, you will never do anything for the Lord. You will never accomplish anything for Christ if all you do is sit around and list the reasons we cannot do anything for Christ. When Israel stepped by faith into the land of promise, believed God, and unsheathed the sword, God did amazing things.

Do not be afraid to step out on God's promises. You will discover that they provide a firm and reliable place to stand.

Rest

Finally, in verse 23, we see the third way in which Joshua led his people into the fullness of God's blessings. He gave them rest. The chapter closes with a summary within the summary of all that has happened since Israel approached Jericho in chapter 6: 'Joshua took the whole land, according to all that the LORD had spoken to Moses' (verse 23). We have encountered this final phrase ('according to all that the LORD had spoken to Moses'), or one very similar to it, a number of times already (1:7; 4:10; 8:31, 33; 11:12, 15). This recurring theme stresses two points. *First*, Joshua was very careful to follow the law of the Lord as Moses had prescribed it. The conquest unfolded according to divine dictates not the whims of a man. *Second*, by connecting the work of Joshua with the word of Moses, the Lord demonstrated to Israel that Joshua was the worthy successor of his prophetic predecessor. God had promised to be with Joshua just as he had been with Moses, and as Joshua obeyed he experienced not only the blessings of the divine presence but he also exhibited the unified purpose of God that began with the exodus.

The land parameters set out in the God's covenant have now come under the domination of Israel (see Num. 34:1-15). Notice again who the main actor is in the passage. It is Joshua. He was God's chosen instrument for bringing Israel into their covenant blessings. Joshua not only took the land, he also gave it to the twelve tribes of Israel according to their allotment. Chapters 13 through 19 give a detailed description of each tribe's portion. 'More immediately, this verse ends the section of the Israelites' encounter with the Canaanite peoples (chaps. 9-11). It functions as a "hinge" verse, looking back to summarize the conquests and looking forward to anticipate the inheritance of the land.'[1]

'And the land had rest from war' (verse 23). The verb translated 'had rest' occurs in Joshua only here and in 14:15.[2] But the book

---

[1] Howard, *Joshua*, 276.

[2] The verb is *shaqat* and is used exclusively in Joshua to describe rest from war. In both 11:23 and 14:15, 'the land' is the subject of the verb.

has much more to say about rest than just what we find in these two verses. Joshua contains a theology of rest. In fact, *rest* is one of the most significant theological terms in the book, though the concept is usually expressed by a different term.[1] God had promised a place of rest through Moses (1:13, 15). When crossing the Jordan, the priests rested their feet in the river and the waters parted (3:13). To commemorate the occasion, Israel took stones and 'rested' them in two piles as memorials (4:3, 8). Rahab's family was rescued from Jericho and made to rest outside the camp of Israel (6:23). Then, in the concluding chapters of the book, the Lord gave his people rest from their enemies and rest in the land of promise (21:44; 22:4; 23:1). For Israel *rest* meant no more wandering and no more war.[2] Rest meant home and the cessation of conflict. To rest is to enter into the settled peace of what God has for his people. Peace in the land depicted salvation or rest in Jesus and the final experience of salvation in the new heavens and new earth in which righteousness dwells (2 Pet. 3:13).

All that God had for his people Joshua secured for them and distributed to them. As a result he brought the land into rest from war. Here again we see Joshua as the precursor for his namesake, Jesus. How does God give us every spiritual blessing? He had Christ secure the blessings for us by his death and distribute them to us by

---

[1] The usual Hebrew term is *nuah* and occurs in the following references: 1:13, 15; 3:13; 4:3, 8; 6:23; 21:44; 22:4; 23:1.

[2] 'Bound up with the land is the important question of "rest." Rest signifies the firm possession of the Promised Land, free from all threats (Dumbrell 1994, 54). This concept of rest finds frequent expression ([Deut.] 3:20; 12:9; 25:19) and is bound up with the notion of a pleasant life ([Deut.] 15:4; 23:20; 28:8; 30:16). Israel is to enjoy without threat the blessings of creation in her Eden-like situation. Like Adam in the garden, Israel is meant to enjoy the blessings of creation and to worship before God in ever-increasing awareness of the significance of the divine presence. Deuteronomy insists that only a correct view of Yahweh and a proper response to his gift can secure this rest. We are therefore not surprised to find that the important chapter 12, which deals with the centralization of the sanctuary, treats rest and sanctuary as interdependent notions (vv. 10-11). When Yahweh has given Israel "rest," he then "will make his name swell" at the central sanctuary, guaranteeing Israel's presence in the land.' William J. Dumbrell, *The Faith of Israel: A Theological Survey of the Old Testament*, 2nd ed. (Grand Rapids: Baker, 2002), 65-66.

his Holy Spirit. Joshua led Israel into rest in the land, but it was not a lasting peace or an eternal rest. It merely anticipated what Jesus would come to do:

> For if Joshua had given them rest, God would not have spoken of another day later on. So then, there remains a Sabbath rest for the people of God, for whoever has entered God's rest has also rested from his works as God did from his. Let us therefore strive to enter that rest, so that no one may fall by the same sort of disobedience (Heb. 4:8-11).

Do you long for rest? The rat race of modern western culture leaves us all exhausted. But biblical rest is more than physical restoration. Biblical rest is a far-reaching experience that is grounded in the work of Christ, entered into by faith, and reaches its consummation as heavenly rest in the presence of God. Have you come to rest in Christ for your salvation or are you still anxiously striving to work your way to God? Have you ever experienced the peace of rest in your souls? Jesus said, 'Come to me, all who labour and are heavy laden, and I will give you rest' (Matt. 11:28).

Joshua 11:16-23 presents us with a great Saviour and a great contrast. Our great Saviour is the sovereign Lord of the universe who hardens hearts, quells fears, and gives rest. The great contrast is between the people of Canaan and the people of Israel. It is the contrast between those who have hardened hearts and those who experience the peace of God. It is a contrast that continues to run through humanity. Some are obstinate and stubbornly resist God's salvation while others rest in Jesus. Which are you?

King of Kings
Joshua 12:1-24

Now these are the kings of the land whom the people of Israel defeated and took possession of their land beyond the Jordan towards the sunrise, from the Valley of the Arnon to Mount Hermon, with all the Arabah eastwards ... in all, thirty-one kings. (Josh. 12:1, 24b)

About the year A.D. 82, the Roman Emperor Domitian built an arch near the Roman Forum to commemorate the military victories of his older brother Titus, triumphs that included the siege and sacking of Jerusalem just a dozen years before in A.D. 70. Known as the Arch of Titus, it has served as a model for other monuments and could, at first glance, be mistaken for the *Arc de Triomphe* in Paris. The south panel of the Arch of Titus depicts in relief form the triumphal procession after the overthrow of Jerusalem. The lampstand or menorah from the temple's holy place can clearly be seen atop the shoulders of Roman soldiers. Did Domitian realize the profound symbolism of that scene? As Israel rejected their King and his gospel, the destruction of their capital, and more significantly their temple, resulted in the removal of light from God's ancient nation. The Romans carried away the lampstand from the temple as the Lord turned his apostles to carry 'the light of the knowledge of the glory of God in the face of Jesus Christ' to the Gentiles (2 Cor. 4:6; Acts 13:46).

What a contrast the Arch of Titus is to the literary 'Arch of Moses and Joshua' we discover in Joshua 12. Here stands a commemorative account of the victories of Israel's great leaders as they defeated king after king to bring the light of God to a darkened land.

Chapter 12 concludes the second major section of the book of Joshua. The first segment covered the details of Israel's entrance into the land and can be found in chapters 1-5. The second division describes the events of the conquest and covers chapters 6-12. While chapter 12 closes out this part of Joshua, the flow of thought could have easily moved from the end of chapter 11 to chapter 13 without a noticeable gap. Chapter 12 contains many familiar place names. But since the text has already covered the overthrow of many of these cities, why does the author take the time to go back over those places once again? What purpose does Joshua 12 fulfil in the book's narrative?

By cataloguing the conquered cities together in one place, Joshua once again gives us a view of the comprehensive nature of the conquest. God gave all the land to Israel (see 11:16-17). But that is not the particular focus of the chapter. This is a catalogue not just of defeated cities but of their kings as well. The emphasis lies on the monarchs of Canaan's city-states to remind us that Moses and Joshua conquered all of these kings because only one Sovereign can reign over Israel the people and Israel the land. The Lord will allow no rivals to rule the hearts and lives of his people.

Moses and the kings

A rather matter-of-fact style dominates the initial verses of the chapter: 'Now these are the kings of the land ...' The events recorded here take us back to Israel's earlier experiences found in the book of Numbers—Moses's victories over Sihon and Og, kings who reigned east of the Jordan River. The text describes their kingdoms as 'towards the sunrise, from the Valley of the Arnon to Mount Hermon, with all the Arabah eastwards' (verse 1). This area today overlaps southern Syria and parts of northern Jordan. What did Israel do in this place? Two verbs capture what the people and their leader, Moses, did to secure the land of promise. First, they *defeated* the kings or, more literally, 'they struck them'. In battle after battle, the army of Israel delivered blow after blow to bring these kings and their subjects to their knees. Second, Israel also *possessed* their land. They took the cities, villages, and territory of these monarchs for their own.

Sihon

After the general introduction provided by verse 1, the first king we learn about is Sihon, king of the Amorites. Sihon lived at Heshbon, a city primarily connected with his kingdom, though later in the prophets it is identified as a city of Moab (see Isa. 15:4; 16:8; Jer. 28:2, 34, 45; 49:3). He ruled over a large area, '… from Aroer, which is on the edge of the Valley of the Arnon, and from the middle of the valley as far as the river Jabbok, the boundary of the Ammonites, that is, half of Gilead, and the Arabah to the Sea of Chinneroth eastward, and in the direction of Beth-jeshimoth, to the Sea of the Arabah, the Salt Sea, southward to the foot of the slopes of Pisgah' (verses 2-3). All of this land, which lay east of the Jordan River, corresponds roughly to central Palestine down to the mid-point of the Dead Sea. Today it lies within the borders of the country of Jordan.

The immediate context of Joshua 12 offers no details of or rationale for the defeat of Sihon; for that we have to turn back to Numbers 21:21-26 (see also Deut. 2:26-37). As the Israelites wandered in the wilderness, it was their intention to pass quietly and peacefully though Sihon's territory. They requested that he allow them to travel along the King's Highway with the assurance that they would not turn aside to glean in the fields or vineyards, nor would they drink from the valuable water resources of the people. But Sihon refused their requests. Instead he mustered an army and went out to fight with Israel. Here is a clear example of the hard-heartedness of the people we found described in 11:20. In fact, this is exactly the way Moses described the conflict in Deuteronomy 2:30: 'But Sihon the king of Heshbon would not let us pass by him, for the LORD your God hardened his spirit and made his heart obstinate, that he might give him into your hand, as he is this day.'

Sihon and his troops paid dearly for their obstinacy. 'Israel defeated him with the edge of the sword and took possession of his land' (Num. 21:24) because 'the LORD our God gave him over to us, and we defeated him and his sons and all his people. And we captured all his cities at that time and devoted to destruction every city, men, women, and children. We left no survivors' (Deut. 2:33-34).

Og

From an established base of operations in the new territory, Moses sent spies to investigate Jazer. Israel 'captured its villages and dispossessed the Amorites who were there' (Num. 21:32). The army then turned its attentions to Bashan and its king, Og. Og was 'one of the remnant of the Rephaim, who live at Ashtaroth and at Edrei' (verse 4). The Rephaim were an aboriginal people who lived east of the Jordan and, like the Anakim (see Deut. 2:10-11; Josh. 11:21-22), were famed for their height. In Deuteronomy 3:11, Moses remarked that Og slept in a giant bed that was thirteen feet long and six feet wide! This big man with the little name ruled an area that extended from Mount Hermon in the north to Sihon's border in the south, approximately midway between the Sea of Chinneroth (called the Sea of Galilee in the New Testament) and the Dead Sea. Og 'ruled over Mount Hermon and Salecah and all Bashan to the boundary of the Geshurites and the Maacathites, and over half of Gilead to the boundary of Sihon king of Heshbon' (verse 5).[1]

Like the battle with Sihon, the details of Israel's conflict with Og also occur in Numbers 21 (see verses 31-35; see also Deut. 3:1-17). When Moses and Israel went up by the way of Bashan, Og and all his people came out against them to fight at Edrei. But God's message to Moses was, '"Do not fear him, for I have given him into your hand, and all his people, and his land. And you shall do to him as you did to Sihon king of the Amorites, who lived at Heshbon." So they defeated him and his sons and all his people, until he had no survivor left. And they possessed his land' (Num. 21:34-35).

---

[1] 'The location of Salecah is uncertain (MacDonald 2000: 152). The exact location of the lands of the Geshurites (and Maacathites; cf. 13:11) does not seem to be clear, even though MacDonald (2000: 154), based on earlier works, suggests they are located in the southern (and northern) segment(s) of the Golan, respectively.' Pitkänen, *Joshua*, 241.

Verse 6 places a marked emphasis on Moses' title 'servant of the LORD'. It is a common designation for Moses (see Deut. 34:5; Josh. 1:1, 13, 15; 8:31, 33; 11:12), but it occurs twice here to remind us that it was as God's servant that he led the military campaigns in the Transjordan. Moses was not a ruthless dictator or a land-hungry tyrant. He was God's man carrying out God's purposes. After he took the land of both Sihon and Og, Moses distributed it to Reuben, Gad, and half of the tribe of Manasseh. Though not the express purpose of the passage, this note served to remind God's people of their need for unity. Those who settled east of the Jordan were as much a part of the people of Israel as those who will settle to the west. This passage prompts us to remember the unity of the nation, which was a strong theme at the very beginning of the book (see Josh. 1:12-18).

The defeat of Sihon and Og occupy a significant portion of this chapter because the overthrow of those two kings played such an important role in Israel's history. Israel's initial victories bolstered their confidence in God. First, the former land of Sihon and Og became the location for Moses' greatest sermon, which we call 'Deuteronomy' (Deut. 1:4). The land that had once been occupied by pagans now resounded with the word of God.

Second, as the first kings conquered and the first land possessed by Israel, Heshbon and Bashan became a kind of first fruits of a coming harvest. The author went into detail about events that took place several years earlier to remind Israel that what God had started east of the Jordan he would complete in the west. Moses had earlier stressed this point in Deuteronomy 3: 'And I commanded Joshua at that time, "Your eyes have seen all that the LORD your God has done to these two kings. So will the LORD do to all the kingdoms into which you are crossing. You shall not fear them, for it is the LORD your God who fights for you"' (verses 21-22). He reiterated this point later as well in chapter 31: 'The LORD your God himself will go over before you. He will destroy these nations before you, so that you shall dispossess them, and Joshua will go over at your head, as the LORD has spoken. And the LORD will do to them as he did to Sihon and Og, the kings of the Amorites, and to their land, when he destroyed them' (verses 3-4). During the early stages of the conquest both Rahab (2:10) and the Gibeonites (9:10) recognized that the defeat of Sihon and Og was a portent of what the Canaanites could expect from Joshua and his troops.[1]

Third, like all of the victories Israel experienced west of the Jordan, the defeat of Sihon and Og was a gracious gift of God (see Deut. 2:33, 36; 3:3): 'And the LORD will give them over to you, and you shall do to them according to the whole commandment that I have commanded you. Be strong and courageous. Do not fear or be in dread of them, for it is the LORD your God who goes with you. He will not leave you or forsake you' (Deut. 31:5-6).

Few references to Sihon and Og occur outside the Pentateuch and Joshua, but two psalms celebrate the power of God over these enemies. After calling Israel to praise the Lord, the author of Psalm 135 writes, 'For I know that the LORD is great, and that our Lord is above all gods. Whatever the LORD pleases, he does, in heaven and on earth, in the seas and all deeps' (verses 5-6). What had God done?

> He it was who struck down the firstborn of Egypt, both of man and of beast; who in your midst, O Egypt, sent signs and wonders against Pharaoh and all his servants; who struck down many nations and killed mighty kings, Sihon, king of the Amorites, and Og, king of Bashan, and all the kingdoms of Canaan, and gave their land as a heritage, a heritage to his people Israel (verses 8-12).

In the very next psalm, 136, the psalmist appeals to God's people to thank the Lord for his goodness and his steadfast love that endures forever. What was the evidence of God's enduring love? He is the one,

> who struck down great kings, for his steadfast love endures forever; and killed mighty kings, for his steadfast love endures forever; Sihon, king of the Amorites, for his steadfast love endures forever; and Og, king of Bashan, for his steadfast love endures forever; and gave their land as a heritage, for his steadfast love endures forever (verses 17-21).

The motivation for God's defeat of Sihon and Og lay not in savage cruelty but in his steadfast, covenant love for his chosen people. And this Israel must remember.

---

[1] McConville and Williams, *Joshua*, 60.

Memory plays an important role in the Christian life as well. God
calls upon us to remember the Sabbath day to keep it holy (Exod.
20:8) and to remember our Creator in the days of our youth (Eccles.
12:1). When we sit at the Lord's Supper, we eat the bread and drink
the cup in remembrance of our Saviour (1 Cor. 11:24-25). For the
believer, this kind of memory is to be an act of faith. To remember is
purposefully to call to mind what God has done on our behalf and
use the memory of God's faithfulness to spur us on to continue to
trust him. Israel looked back to victories east of the Jordan River. We
look back to the greatest victory of all—the defeat of sin, death, and
hell by the sacrifice of the Lord Jesus Christ. When we remember
what he achieved through his suffering, we are encouraged to believe
that with him God will freely give us every other spiritual blessing
as well (Rom. 8:32).

Joshua and the kings

In verse 7, the topic of defeated kings continues but with three
noticeable distinctions. First, the text switches from Moses to
Joshua. Second, the geographical focus shifts from east of the Jordan
River to the land that lies to the west. Third, rather than focusing
on two kings and the details of their territory, the author supplies us
with a simple list of 31 kings.

The description of the land's borders and areas corresponds to
what is found earlier in 11:16-17.[1] To this is added six people groups:
Hittites, Amorites, Canaanites, Perizzites, Hivites, and Jebusites, a
list that closely corresponds to the groups God spoke of to Abraham
when he promised him the land (see Gen. 15:18-20; Deut. 20:17).

Beginning naturally with the kings of Jericho and Ai (verse 9)
and concluding with the king of the Goiim in Galilee (verse 23), the
remainder of Joshua 12 enumerates the monarchs Joshua defeated.
Though the text has mentioned a number of these kings already,
for example the kings of Jerusalem, Hebron, Jarmuth, Lachish, and

[1] 'Verse 7 gives the northern and southern limits of the territory that the Israelites
had taken, which are the same limits mentioned in 11:17, with the order reversed.
The verse looks backwards to the first half of the book when it states that Joshua
and the Israelites conquered the kings of the land, it looks forward to the second
half in stating that Joshua gave their land as an inheritance to the tribes, in accord
with their allotted portions (NIV: "tribal divisions").' Howard, *Joshua*, 280.

Eglon (verses 10, 11, 12; cf. 10:1, 3), here the record of their defeat is compiled in one account to serve as an official conquest list and reminder of all that God had done to help the Israelites overcome their enemies.

After listing Jericho, Ai, and Bethel (which was situated near Ai, cf. 8:17), the catalogue of conquered kings generally follows a south-to-north orientation.[1] As a general rule, cities in the south occur in verses 10-16a, cities in the central part of the land are listed in verses 16b-18, with the northern section covered in verses 19-24.[2] The grand total of fallen monarchs amounts to 33 (verse 24). Every ruler that stood up to oppose God's people has fallen.

The Lord and the kings

If you follow Israel's trek from the exodus, then the list of conquered kings in Joshua 12 will not take you by surprise. Upon leaving Egypt, the Lord struck Pharaoh's army at the Red Sea. In the aftermath of that divine victory, Moses sang what has become known as the Song of the Sea, a song that celebrates the Lord's authority and might. After recounting God's overthrow of Egypt's forces and celebrating his majestic holiness, Moses concluded,

> The peoples have heard; they tremble; pangs have seized the inhabitants of Philistia. Now are the chiefs of Edom dismayed; trembling seizes the leaders of Moab; all the inhabitants of Canaan have melted away. Terror and dread fall upon them; because of the greatness of your arm, they are still as a stone, till your people, O LORD, pass by, till the people pass by whom you have purchased. You will bring them in and plant them on your own mountain, the place, O LORD, which you have made for your abode, the sanctuary, O Lord, which your hands have established. The LORD will reign forever and ever (Exod. 15:14-18).

The settlement of Israel was to be a testimony to God's supreme sovereignty. Moses and Joshua, both of whom played such an important role in this chapter, were God's theocratic officers.

---

[1] Howard, *Joshua*, 281.

[2] Richard D. Nelson, *Joshua. The Old Testament Library* (Louisville: Westminster John Knox Press, 1997), 161 referred to in Howard, *Joshua*, 281.

They ruled over Israel under the Lord's direction.[1] The Lord was the king of his people. Immediately following the days of Joshua, however, the period of the Judges proved to be a cyclical series of spiritual disasters because there was no king to guide the nation in godliness. Old Testament theologian Willem VanGemeren notes that this troubled era demonstrated Israel's need for 'a centralized, self-perpetuating government that would be sensitive to the law of God, support the worship of God, bring unity to the tribes, and give Israel rest from her enemies.'[2]

Israel needed a king, and they began to desire one but not for the right reasons. They wanted a king in order to be like the other nations, but they did not want the rule of God (see 1 Sam. 8:1-9). Though the first king, Saul, proved to be a spiritual disaster for the nation, his successor, David, was the man God had chosen. David was a man whose heart sought the ways of the Lord (1 Sam. 13:14). He was not a king like the other nations had. David was the Lord's vicegerent.[3] He did not reign over Israel. He mediated the authority of God over the nation and thus proved to be a blessing to the people. In his last words, David recalled the Lord's promise to him:

> The God of Israel has spoken; the Rock of Israel has said to me: When one rules justly over men, ruling in the fear of God, he dawns on them like the morning light, like the sun shining forth on a cloudless morning, like rain that makes grass to sprout from the earth (2 Sam. 23:3-4).

Those parting words were to be programmatic for Solomon, David's son and successor. Earlier God had promised to raise up an heir for David, one to rule on his throne. This heir would build a house for God's name, and God in turn would establish his kingdom forever, be a father to him, and never let his love depart

---

[1] VanGemeren goes on to point out that 'the goal of the theocratic offices was that God's people may learn to live in harmony with the Lord, their Creator-Redeemer, and with their fellow Israelites. As long as they were living in harmony with their God and his covenant people, they expressed the covenant ideal: *the people of God*.' Willem VanGemeren, *The Progress of Redemption: From Creation to the New Jerusalem* (Carlisle, UK: Paternoster Press, 1988), 171.

[2] VanGemeren, *Progress of Redemption*, 195.

[3] One who acts or rules in place of another, having delegated authority.

from him (2 Sam. 7:12-17). We call this the Davidic Covenant. The more we read the Old Testament, and especially as we trace its lines of promise into the New, we discover that God's covenant was not just for Solomon and those who followed him as the kings of Judah. The Lord had something far-reaching in mind, a plan for mankind (2 Sam. 7:19).[1]

Jesus—the King of kings

Unfortunately, David and almost every one of his descendants bore a striking testimony to the disaster of moral failures. Neither David nor Solomon reigned in perfect righteousness. The 'instruction for mankind' (2 Sam. 7:19) that God gave was of a perfect king—Jesus, the King of kings! Jesus is the link between the Lord's covenant plan with David in the Old Testament and the kingdom of God in the New. The ministry of Jesus began with his preaching 'Repent, for the kingdom of heaven is at hand' (Matt. 3:2; cf. Mark 1:14-15). Matthew used the first three chapters of his Gospel to establish Jesus' identity as the long-awaited Messianic King. After Jesus announced the arrival of the kingdom, he continued the theme of kingship in the temptation account in which we see him enter the wilderness to confront and overcome the prince of the power of the air. Jesus Christ was not and is not a king in name only. He is not a figurehead or a puppet monarch. He is a king with authority and power.[2]

---

[1] David's response to God's promise was 'Who am I, O Lord GOD, and what is my house, that you have brought me thus far? And yet this was a small thing in your eyes, O Lord GOD. You have spoken also of your servant's house for a great while to come, and this is instruction for mankind, O Lord GOD' (2 Sam. 7:18-19)! In the phrase 'this is instruction for mankind', the term translated 'instruction' is *torah*. English translations have handled the translation of this noun in various ways: *manner* (KJV), *usual way of dealing* (NIV; NET), *custom* (NASB). God's *torah* is his teaching, what he reveals, in this case, to instruct everyone. 'With the realization that he had just been granted an everlasting dynasty, dominion, and kingdom, David blurted out in uncontainable joy: "And this is the Charter for all mankind, O Lord God!" Thus the ancient plan of God would continue, only now it would involve a king and a kingdom. Such a blessing would also involve the future of all mankind.' Walter C. Kaiser, Jr. *Toward an Old Testament Theology* (Grand Rapids: Zondervan, 1978), 155.

[2] 'The narrative of Matthew builds step-by-step to that point when Jesus straps on His kingly armour and goes to war with Satan as Israel's Champion!' Mark Dever

Throughout his earthly ministry, Jesus continued to display his kingly authority by proclaiming the word of God, healing the sick, and casting out demons. The greatest display of his sovereignty, however, was his death on the cross. In Pilate's Praetorium and on Calvary's hill, Christ's kingship was mocked. When Pilate questioned him, one of the main points under examination was his claim to be the king of the Jews (Matt. 27:11-14). Later that same day, the claim became a source of derision when Jesus was placed in the hands of a cruel Roman battalion, 'and they stripped him and put a scarlet robe on him, and twisting together a crown of thorns, they put it on his head and put a reed in his right hand. And kneeling before him, they mocked him, saying, "Hail, King of the Jews"' (Matt. 27:28-29).

The soldiers then led Jesus away to be crucified. When he hung on the cross, Pilate had a placard placed over his head that read, 'This is Jesus, the King of the Jews' (Matt. 27:37; John 19:20). What the enemies of the Lord did not realize was that as he suffered the pains of crucifixion, Jesus exercised his kingly authority.

> Pilate might not be interested [in Jesus's claim to a kingdom 'not of this world', cf. John 18:33-38], but to many who read these words when first they were published, and to many more who have read them since, they spoke and still speak of a King and a kingdom of enduring importance and authority. The title on the cross might be meant in mockery, but the theme of Christ reigning from the tree is central to Christian belief.[1]

What did Jesus do when he reigned from that tree? He bore our sins, he suffered in our place, he reconciled us to God. But he also, in the words of Colossians 2:15, 'disarmed the rulers and authorities and put them to open shame'. Is this not what we have prefigured for us in Joshua 12? Why does the author take the time to give us such a highly stylized list in verses 9-24: 'The king of Jericho, one; the king of Ai, one; the king of Bethel, one; the king of Jerusalem, one; the king of Hebron, one; the king of Jarmuth, one...'? His

and Greg Gilbert, *Preach: Theology Meets Practice* (Nashville: B&H Publishing, 2012), 66 (with obvious allusions to David's battle with Goliath (1 Sam. 17)).

[1] F. F. Bruce, *New Testament Development of Old Testament Themes* (Grand Rapids: Eerdmans, 1968), 31.

purpose is to count off the enemies, to list them and publicly put them to open shame as the victims of the conquest.[1] What Joshua did to the kings of Canaan, Christ did to the demonic powers. He disarmed them, put them to shame, and triumphed over them in the cross.[2] Paul's imagery in Colossians 2 is quite striking. When the emperor of Rome defeated an enemy, he would host a parade in which the conquered king and his armies were put on public display, exactly as we find depicted on the Arch of Titus. That spectacle of shame was intended to demonstrate to everyone the weakness of the vanquished and the strength of the victor.

The powers of hell could not defeat the Lord Jesus Christ when he died. Quite the opposite was the case. He squelched all demonic influence that attempted to thwart his plan to accomplish the salvation of his people. That is why God raised him from the dead. In the resurrection of Jesus, we see his victory parade as he exulted in triumph over all his foes. Joshua 12, in its own unique place in redemptive history, anticipates the resurrection and exaltation of King Jesus.

But Joshua 12 also points us further into the future of redemptive history. With the fall of these kings, their kingdoms (plural) became the kingdom (singular) of the Lord. That makes the conquest of the Canaanite kings a microcosm of the ultimate and final triumph of the kingdom of God. In Revelation 11, the seventh angel sounds his trumpet. As the seventh of seven trumpets, it is the last one to be blown, and with this last trump the Lord Jesus returns (see 1 Cor. 15:52; 1 Thess. 4:16-18). When that occurs, loud voices in heaven will announce, "'The kingdom of the world has become the kingdom of our Lord and of his Christ,'" then the voices in heaven echo the Song of the Sea, 'and he shall reign forever and ever' (Rev. 11:15; cf. Exod. 15:18).

---

[1] Hubbard sees the list as a stylized account to underscore 'how impressive and complete the Conquest is'. Hubbard, *Joshua*, 362. This is consistent with the point I make about their public shame.

[2] The ESV translates the third person pronoun at the end of verse 15 as 'him' referring to Christ but offers the alternative translation 'in it', referring to the cross (at the end of verse 14), in a footnote. I believe the footnote reflects the more accurate translation and have followed it in the exposition.

Why is Joshua 12 and its testimony to the kingship of Christ so important? Because of what it means for Christ to be king. There are two dimensions of this kingship that we need to remember.

First, as we look to the day when Jesus returns, we should think about his kingship on a cosmic level. He will come to rule over all creation with perfect justice. Our brothers and sisters in China, Iraq, Iran, Afghanistan, and countless other places will no longer be persecuted. Children will no longer be aborted. Money and coercion will be trumped by grace and truth. Creation will no longer groan under the burden of the curse (Rom. 8:20-22). There will be no more illness, no more disease, and no more death (1 Cor. 15:54-55).

Second, his kingship also exists on a very personal level. While we await the return of Christ for the full consummation of his reign, he is already the risen king (Acts. 2:29-32), but is he *your* king?

You may be a relatively new Christian and wonder what Christ's kingship means for your life. It means that first and foremost you live under the authority of his word. But remember, God is not a despot. Your king is also your loving, tender-hearted Saviour. What he demands of you in his word is not to burden you. Jesus calls for you to come to him, to take on his yoke, to learn about him because his yoke is easy and his burden light (Matt. 11:28-30). The kingship of Christ over your life frees you to obey by grace and thus to follow the path of blessing. It frees you from building your own kingdom so that you can invest in the kingdom of God.

In his poem, *Ozymandias*, Percy Bysshe Shelley wrote of a statue he had heard about, a broken effigy that remained not as a monument to a kingdom but as a testimony to the temporary nature of all earthly kingdoms.

> I met a traveller from an antique land
> Who said: Two vast and trunkless legs of stone
> Stand in the desert. Near them, on the sand,
> Half sunk, a shattered visage lies, whose frown,
> And wrinkled lip, and sneer of cold command,
> Tell that its sculptor well those passions read
> Which yet survive, stamped on these lifeless things,
> The hand that mocked them and the heart that fed:
> And on the pedestal these words appear:

'My name is Ozymandias, king of kings:
Look on my works, ye Mighty, and despair!'
Nothing beside remains. Round the decay
Of that colossal wreck, boundless and bare
The lone and level sands stretch far away.

Ozymandias had been someone! King of kings, or so he said. While the pedestal of his sculpture bade the Mighty to look on his works and despair, no works were left. All that remained were parts of a lifeless statue sunk in a sea of sand. This king of kings turned out to be just another man who met death and whose monument met the inevitable passage of time. The story of Ozymandias is the story of every earthly kingdom. For there is only one King of kings, and his name is JESUS.

20

Inherit the Land
Joshua 13:1-19:51

These are the inheritances that the people of Israel received in the land of Canaan, which Eleazar the priest and Joshua the son of Nun and the heads of the fathers' houses of the tribes of the people of Israel gave them to inherit. (Josh. 14:1)

If there is anything universally true about human experience, it is the deep and intense desire for security, stability, and hope. A person cannot live without hope. That hope may be temporary and transient like the man who perseveres through a tough project at work because he anticipates his vacation at the beach, or it may be something more long-term and enduring like the hope of having a family, getting an education, or embarking on a career. In either case, hope keeps us forward-focused and moving toward the future.

The opposite of hope is despair. It can be seen in the vacant eyes of those who see no reason for tomorrow. Much of the despair in today's world comes from a sense of rootlessness. If you want to shake up the security and stability of a person's life, let him lose a family member or give him no place to live. Let every day be uncertain and every night slept in a different location. Without roots, without home and family, a person soon loses any sense of belonging and, therefore, any sense of hope.

Yet the desire for hope and security extend beyond this life. We want to know that we will be safe for all eternity. We want to have the assurance that when we die we will go to heaven and everything will be alright. Children learn to pray,

> Now I lay me down to sleep,
> I pray the Lord my soul to keep.
> If I should die before I wake,
> I pray the Lord my soul to take.

But that child's prayer expresses the longing of many adults as well. God has placed eternity in our hearts (Eccles. 3:11), and everyone looks for immortality in someone or some thing. How can we know that we will be safe and secure for all eternity? How can we know that beyond the pale of death we will not wander helplessly forever? God has his ways of letting us know. He gives us means by which he leads us into the assurance of everlasting life. That is exactly what he did for Israel when he gave his chosen people the land of promise as their inheritance.

For over 400 years the Israelites had been a people without a country. Then, in one generation, they went from labouring slaves to wandering nomads to invading warriors—all in search of a land to call their own, a land promised to their forefathers. After the land of Canaan and its leaders had been conquered, the Lord assigned Joshua the task of dividing the territory among the tribes. Every acre was their proper inheritance, and every acre assured them of both God's faithfulness and of a greater land to come. Like the other symbols and types of old covenant religion, the land pictured for Israel and for us the rich inheritance that every believer has in Christ Jesus. It portrayed everlasting life in the new heavens and the new earth. To see this truth emerge from the text is akin to working a jigsaw puzzle. Several pieces of scriptural data have to be put together in order to see the big picture. Those pieces consist of certain key theological statements in the Scriptures (such as the text of Joshua 13:1-19:51), as well as the overall trajectory of the Bible, since we as Christians read the book of Joshua and every other Old Testament book in the clearer light of the New Testament.

An excursion through the land
To see how all of this works, we have to begin with an excursion through Palestine and that involves a survey of the contents of Joshua

13-19. We need to get the lay of the land in order to understand what transpires in this lengthy and significant segment of the book.

This section on land allotment begins the same way chapter 1 of Joshua begins, with a direct address from the Lord. Note the similarities between the two speeches: 'After the death of Moses the servant of the LORD, the LORD said to Joshua the son of Nun, Moses' assistant, "Moses my servant is dead"' (1:1-2). 'Now Joshua was old and advanced in years, and the LORD said to him, "You are old and advanced in years ..."' (13:1). The narrator sets up the background situation (Moses' death and Joshua's age) which is immediately followed by a direct proclamation from the Lord restating the same. Why this repetition? In both cases it is to emphasize the background against which the following events unfold. Moses' death became the backdrop for Israel's invasion of the land. Joshua's advanced age provided the setting for his apportionment of the land. Both Moses' death and Joshua's age point the reader to the inherent human limitations found in these stories. Moses was not the key to the promised land. He died before Israel ever crossed the Jordan. But Joshua is not the key to the land either. Though he led Israel through their initial victories, he was now an old man and there was still 'very much land to possess' (verse 1).

What was fundamental to Israel's full possession of Canaan? The presence of the Lord, their everlasting God. After outlining the land yet to be possessed (verses 2-6a), the Lord said, 'I myself will drive them out from before the people of Israel' (verse 6b; cf. 10:14, 42). Joshua's advanced age would not prove to be a barrier to Israel's reaching the final goal. With God, the Israelites could continue to drive out the inhabitants of the land and occupy all that the Lord had promised. Joshua's responsibility at this juncture was to divide the land among the remaining nine and a half tribes who would settle west of the Jordan (verse 7).

Before embarking on a description of the land that Joshua parcelled out, the remainder of chapter 13 (verses 8-33) describes the land that Reuben, Gad, and half of the tribe of Manasseh received on the western bank of the Jordan. This kind of excursus on the transjordanian tribes occurs several times in the book (see 1:12-15; 4:12; 22:1-9) to remind the reader again and again of the unity of

God's people. A mere river could not divide the tribes as brothers and must not divide them in their allegiance to the Lord (see 22:10-34). The land that those tribes received was just as much a part of the land of promise as the land taken on the eastern side of the river. It was all God's great gift, from the Great Sea to the Euphrates River. The unity of God's people is an important theme in the book because disunity ultimately denies the work of God, his work to give Israel the land and his work through Jesus on the cross. The Lord Jesus prayed that his people may be one just as he is one with the Father. Such unity among God's people bears witness to the world of the truthfulness of the gospel (John 17:20-23).

Though Chapter 14 begins with an introduction to Israel's inheritance west of the Jordan, the bulk of the chapter focuses on one man, Caleb, and the land that he received. One of the original twelve spies that surveyed the land some forty years earlier, Caleb had wanted to conquer Canaan at that time. His faith was rewarded by God's personal promise to him: 'But my servant Caleb, because he has a different spirit and has followed me fully, I will bring into the land into which he went, and his descendants shall possess it' (Num. 14:24). Caleb waited all of those intervening years to receive what God had for him. And all those years his devotion was evident because he wholly followed the Lord his God (Josh. 14:8, 9, 14). He walked by faith, and his faith was honoured.[1]

Chapter 15 covers the land allotted to Judah, first by describing its boundaries which reach southward to the border of Edom, north to En-rogel, east to the Dead Sea, and west to the Great or Mediterranean Sea (verses 1-12). This description is followed by a more detailed account of Caleb's territory, which lay within the borders of Judah (verses 13-19). It then concludes with a list of Judah's cities, a total of 114 plus many villages (verses 20-62). The one city the people of Judah could not inhabit was Jerusalem. It was occupied by the Jebusites, and at the time the book of Joshua was written Judah's soldiers had not been able to drive them out (verse 63; cf. Judg. 1:8, 21). Jerusalem would continue to be a city of mixed

---

[1] For a more detailed exposition of Joshua 14:6-15, see the following chapter entitled 'Whole-hearted.'

inhabitants, largely under Jebusite control, until David became king and took the city for his capital (2 Sam. 5:1-10).

The next two chapters, 16 and 17, describe the borders and towns belonging to the sons of Joseph, Ephraim and Manasseh. Following a summary in 16:1-4, verses 5-9 cover the borders and towns of Ephraim. But as in the case with Judah, Ephraim's success fell short of a complete occupation of its territory: 'they did not drive out the Canaanites who lived in Gezer, so the Canaanites have lived in the midst of Ephraim to this day but have been made to do forced labour' (verse 10).

Manasseh's allotment is recorded in chapter 17. Here we find a list of the clans of Manasseh (verses 1-2), the rightful inheritance for the daughters of Zelophehad (verses 3-6), and a description of the boundaries of the tribe (verses 7-11). But the persistent problem of Canaanites remained: 'yet the people of Manasseh could not take possession of those cities, but the Canaanites persisted in dwelling in that land. Now when the people of Israel grew strong, they put the Canaanites to forced labour, but did not utterly drive them out' (verses 12-13).

Judah, Ephraim, and Manasseh receive by far the most coverage in these chapters. We could speculate as to why this is the case. Certainly the people of Joseph requested more land because God had blessed them, and they were a numerous people (verse 14). The main reason, however, may have to do with the roles that Judah and Joseph played in the closing chapters of Genesis to preserve Israel during the early stages of their time in Egypt.[1]

Seven more

Finally, seven tribes remained that still needed to obtain their inheritance. Their allotment occurred in chapters 18 and 19. Joshua 18:1-10 sets the context for this remaining apportionment in two ways. First, it gives us a theological context regarding the tabernacle: 'Then the whole congregation of the people of Israel assembled at Shiloh and set up the tent of meeting there. The land lay subdued

---

[1] There is no doubt about Joseph's role. For a treatment of the importance of Judah's role, see Bryan Smith, 'The Central Role of Judah in Genesis 37-50.' *Bibliotheca Sacra* 162:646 (2005).

before them.' Second, Joshua gave instructions to men from each of the remaining tribes to map out the land. How were these tribes to receive their land? Joshua and Eleazar must divide it among them, but before they did so Joshua had each of the tribes supply three men to travel throughout the remaining territory to map it. They were to 'divide' and 'describe the land in seven divisions' (verses 5, 6) and bring the descriptions to Joshua. Excluding the tribes of Judah, Manasseh, Ephraim (verse 5b), the Levites (verse 7a), and those on the eastern side of the Jordan (verse 7b), the rest of the land remained to these seven tribes. In obedience to Joshua's instructions, the men went throughout the land, wrote a description of the remaining territory, and came back to Shiloh. There Joshua cast lots before the Lord and apportioned the land to the people (verse 10).

The first allotment went to Benjamin (18:11-28). Next, Simeon received his inheritance (19:1-9) followed by Zebulun (verses 10-16), Issachar (verses 17-23), Asher (verses 24-31), Naphtali (verses 32-39), and Dan (verses 40-48). The list concludes with Joshua's inheritance: 'By the command of the LORD they gave him the city that he asked, Timnath-serah in the hill country of Ephraim, And he rebuilt the city and settled in it' (verse 50). Finally, a summary statement caps off this account of allocations: 'These are the inheritances that Eleazar the priest and Joshua the son of Nun and the heads of the fathers' houses of the tribes of the people of Israel distributed by lot at Shiloh before the LORD, at the entrance of the tent of meeting. So they finished dividing the land' (verse 51).

That is a rather quick survey of the text but I want to point out two things from it.

First, this was real land for real people. The story of the Bible is not a story in the make-believe sense of that word. The biblical narrative is history. Many people approach the Bible looking for the timeless truths behind the husk of the text, but the text is the timeless truth. It is the voice of God that intersects history.

Second, Israel received what God had promised. In homiletic terms, that is 'the big idea'. All of the names and details of these seven chapters should impress upon us the faithfulness of God and the reliability of his word.

Hints and tensions

When you look back at the text and read it closely, you will see within it, however, certain themes, certain hints and tensions that point you beyond this middle-eastern land to something greater.

The first theme to notice is that this land is Israel's *inheritance* (14:1; 15:20; 17:4, 6; 18:4, 20, 28; 19:1, 2, 8, 9, 10, 16, 23, 31, 39, 48, 49, 51). To inherit something means to come into possession of an item by having it bequeathed to you. An inheritance is a gift, a possession handed down. It is something you did not earn yourself.

My wife and I have several clocks in our home. One, which I purchased for a few dollars at a local store, sits on my desk in the study. In the family room, however, stands a clock that I inherited. It belonged to my great-grandfather. It is my possession because he owned it and handed it down. God owned the land of Canaan. He fought for his people to drive out their enemies and to give the land as a grant. One day someone in my family will inherit the clock I received, and it will continue to be passed down through the generations as a family heirloom. And so it was with the land. The people were not to sell it. It was family land to be passed down from generation to generation.[1]

Next, the doling out of the land was a *religious act*. You can see this in a couple of different ways. First, who apportioned the land? Joshua did. True, he was not alone. Leaders and representatives from the tribes helped. But who else is named? Which other individual does the text stress? Eleazar the priest (14:1; 17:4; 19:51). Israel had an entire tribe, the Levites, devoted to the priesthood. Surely this tribe would receive the lion's share of the land. But that was not to be the case. In a brief excursus, the author noted that Levi received no inheritance: 'To the tribe of Levi alone Moses gave no inheritance. The offerings by fire to the LORD God of Israel are their inheritance, as he said to him' (verse 14). The point is made again at the end of the chapter: 'But to the tribe of Levi Moses gave no inheritance;

---

[1] 'The relationship between place and family is not accidental. The Israelite occupation of land is regularly called "inheritance" in Joshua (as in Numbers and Deuteronomy). However, inheritance by it nature does not stop at a single point, but is an ongoing issue for tribe, family, and clan.' McConville and Williams, *Joshua*, 72.

the LORD God of Israel is their inheritance, just as he said to them'
(verse 33). Chapter 14 emphasized: 'but to the Levites he gave no
inheritance among them. For the people of Joseph were two tribes,
Manasseh and Ephraim. And no portion was given to the Levites
in the land, but only cities to dwell in, with their pasture lands for
their livestock and their substance' (verses 3b-4).[1] Finally, in 18:7,
'the priesthood of the LORD is their heritage.' The Levites had a
place to live because God cared for their needs. He gave them food
to eat from select portions of the offerings (see, e.g. Lev. 2:3, 10; 6:16,
26, 29; 7:6). He gave them a task with which to serve him. And,
ultimately, he provided himself as their legacy. Levi's inheritance
was greater than real estate. This final statement offers a strong
theological hint of the kind of inheritance all of God's people should
expect in the end. No longer confined to a unique group among
believers, all Christians are believer-priests (cf. 1 Pet. 2:9), and our
inheritance, the reward for which we long, is nothing or no one less
that God himself!

Where did all of this occur? Gilgal had been Israel's base of
operations since entering Canaan, and so it is likely that the early
allotment took place there. At the beginning of chapter 18, however,
the location changed to Shiloh. Shiloh, introduced to us for the
first time in the Bible in this text, became the rallying point for
the nation.[2] Representatives, for surely that is the meaning of 'the
whole congregation', gathered there to set up the tent of meeting,

---

[1] This passage also explains how the numbering of the twelve tribes is
accomplished. Levi receives no inheritance (verse 3), which reduces the number
to eleven. Joseph, however, became two tribes through his sons, Manasseh and
Ephraim. With one son to stand for Joseph and the other to make up for Levi, the
grand total becomes twelve again.

[2] 'This opening verse is one of the most theologically pregnant in the book of
Joshua. The setting up of the tent of meeting at Shiloh clearly marks a significant
step in the progress of Israel towards fulfilling its destiny in the promised land. It is
the first reference to the tent of meeting in Joshua, though the closely associated ark
of the covenant was prominent in the narratives of entry to the land (Joshua 3-4). It
is also the first time that Shiloh has appeared as a place of special significance. The
conjunction of the two, however, now focuses attention on the nature of Israel as a
worshipping community in covenantal relationship with Yahweh.' McConville and
Williams, *Joshua*, 73-74.

another name for the tabernacle. The tabernacle represented the
very presence of God with his people. Built in the wilderness, this
tent became the centre of the nation's spiritual life. By erecting this
house of worship in Shiloh, centrally located in the hill country of
Ephraim, Israel had a central sanctuary in the land just as God had
commanded (Deut. 12:1-7).[1] The kings of the nations had perished
(see 12:1-24), but a King reigned over his land and people, and his
throne was in Shiloh.

How did the Israelites view their situation? As a success. 'The land
lay subdued before them' (verse 1b). The verb translated 'lay subdued'
occurs only thirteen times in the Old Testament. It was first used in
God's command to Adam and Eve to subdue the earth (Gen. 1:28).[2]
With the land of promise subdued before Israel, the people of God
were taking back the earth and bringing it back under the Lord's
dominion. What was lost in Eden was now being regained in part
and in principle for God's people to inhabit. A biblical theology of
the land does not begin with the conquest or even with the promise
to Abraham. The theology of the land begins with creation, with the
garden. In the fall, Adam and Eve lost the land God had given to
them. In the conquest, Israel gains the land God promised as a kind
of earnest or down-payment, the first fruits of more to come.

Already but not yet
That there is more to come can be seen in the already-but-not-yet
tension in the text. We can see this in several places. First, Israel
possessed the land (11:16-17; 18:1b). But Israel did not have all of the
land (13:1-7; 15:63; 16:10; 17:12-13). What happened? Are these texts

---

[1] The location will later change to Jerusalem under the leadership of David when
Israel achieved a post-Saul, unified and centralized monarchy (see 2 Sam. 6:1-23),
but from the time of the conquest until David, Shiloh was the central place where
Israel worshipped God (see Judg. 21:19; 1 Sam. 1:3, 24; 3:21).

[2] The Hebrew verb is *kabash*. In Moses' instructions to the western tribes
regarding their obligation to fight with the rest of Israel, twice there is a reference
to subduing the land (Num. 32:22, 29). To subdue means to bring someone under
your power whether it be a foreign nation (2 Sam. 8:11; 1 Chron. 22:18) or a slave
(2 Chron. 28:10; Neh. 5:5; Jer. 34:11, 16). The term can also be used for a violent act
of sexual conquest (Esth. 7:8). By his grace, God subdues or treads underfoot our
iniquities (Mic. 7:19).

contradictory? Israel conquered the land but did not conquer the land? Yes, Israel had occupied and owned the land in principle, but that did not mean there were no more skirmishes or battles to be fought. When an army invades another country, the invaders may prove to be victorious, but that does not preclude the formation of armed resistance, an 'underground' to resist, frustrate, and hinder the occupying forces. That was what happened in Canaan.

The initial report regarding land yet unconquered (13:1-6), the record of Jebusites in Jerusalem (15:63), Canaanites in Gezer (16:10), and yet more Canaanites in the cities of Manasseh (17:12-13) introduce into the text an eschatological, already-but-not-yet tension, much like we find in the New Testament. The victory has been achieved. Israel has seized the land. But the full manifestation is yet to be experienced. This parallels the believer's experience of salvation. Christ has finished his work. He, the righteous one, died once for all for the unrighteous so that he might bring us to God (1 Pet. 3:18).[1] By faith in this finished work we have been saved. But we look and long for the day of salvation, the day of his appearing when we will be saved from the very presence of sin (Titus 2:13). That will be the day we receive our inheritance.

The New Testament perspective

The already-but-not-yet tension spills over into the New Testament where we receive our fullest perspective on the land. A number of texts shed theological light on the subject. Since the promise began with Abraham, let us begin there as well. What did Abraham expect when God promised to give him the land of Canaan? He expected land! He took the Lord's promise literally. He sojourned in the land as a pilgrim only ever owning a small plot in which to bury his family (Gen. 23:17-20). He bought that land and buried Sarah there with the assurance that one day his descendants would own it all. When the patriarch heard God's promise, he expected dirt, fields, streams, mountains, forests, and rocks.

But was that all that Abraham expected? By its very nature, old covenant religion was a religion of types and shadows. Physical

[1] Anthony A. Hoekema, *The Bible and the Future* (Grand Rapids: Eerdmans, 1979), 13-22.

things and events pointed to much greater realities, and so it was with the land. When the Lord spoke to our father Abraham, he obeyed by faith. 'And he went out, not knowing where he was going. By faith he went to live in the land of promise, as in a foreign land, living in tents with Isaac and Jacob, heirs with him of the same promise' (Heb. 11:8b-9). Why did he step out in faith? Because 'he was looking forward to the city that has foundations, whose designer and builder is God' (Heb. 11:10). The land was a picture prophecy of the final destination, the celestial city, our heavenly home, the 'land that is fairer than day'.

Philip Hughes captured this truth so well when he wrote,:

> the New Testament makes it clear that Abraham and the other patriarchs did not seek in the physical land of Canaan their everlasting possession or interpret in a carnal manner the good things promised by God. Had they done so, they would have been bitterly disillusioned men. But the land of promise was an earthly sign pointing beyond itself to a heavenly reality, a pledge of the faithfulness of the promise concerning an everlasting inheritance, and a means to the inward experience even during this present pilgrimage of the blessings it portended.[1]

The apostle Paul described the land covenant in these terms: 'For the promise to Abraham and his offspring that he would be heir of the world did not come through the law but through the righteousness of faith' (Rom. 4:13). Paul knew that, as wonderful as its milk and honey were, the Lord covenanted to give to Abraham much more than just land. He promised him the *world*,[2] a promise

---

[1] Philip Edgcumbe Hughes, *Interpreting Prophecy: An Essay in Biblical Perspectives* (privately published, 1976), 43-44.

[2] Paul used the Greek term *kosmos*, which means 'the earth' or, in terms of the new heavens and the new earth, 'the universe'. Referring to the burial site of the patriarchs in light of this text O. Palmer Robertson wrote: 'So burial at Hebron, the premier peak for viewing the Land of Promise, suggests the hope of the patriarchs for resurrection from the dead. One day they will awaken from their tombs and look with new eyes on the land the Lord has given them, a land that has expanded under the new covenant to include the whole of the cosmos (Rom. 4:13).' *Understanding the Land of the Bible: A Biblical-Theological Guide* (Phillipsburg, NJ: P&R, 1996), 72-73. 'In the light of the Pauline teaching as a whole ... we cannot exclude from the scope of this promise, as defined by the apostle, the most inclusive

that reaches its ultimate fulfilment in the new heavens and the new earth (Rev. 21:1-8).

All believers, every spiritual son and daughter of Abraham, will inherit that land. But even now we have an inheritance. We do not have to wait for Christ to return to be assured of it. The land promise that points us to the renewed cosmos in the end also points us to Christ, the one in whom all of God's promises are confirmed (2 Cor. 1:20) and through whom they are realized. In Christ 'we have obtained an inheritance' (Eph. 1:11). The Father has qualified us 'to share in the inheritance of the saints in light' (Col. 1:12). Jesus came to be the mediator of the new covenant 'so that those who are called may receive the promised eternal inheritance' (Heb. 9:15). And God works his regenerating grace in our lives by the Holy Spirit so that we might 'be born again to a living hope ... to an inheritance that is imperishable, undefiled, and unfading,' an inheritance kept in heaven for us (1 Pet. 1:3-4).

We live in the already-but-not-yet tension that exists between the cross and heaven. We have been saved, but we await our salvation. The forces of hell have been overcome, but we engage in spiritual warfare. We are seated with Christ in the heavenlies, but we long for our heavenly home.

Do you have the assurance of a land awaiting you in the future? Do you have the hope of heaven? Is Christ your inheritance?

---

messianic purport. It is defined as the promise to Abraham that *he* should be heir of the world, but it is also a promise to his seed and, therefore, can hardly involve anything less than the worldwide dominion promised to Christ and to the spiritual seed of Abraham in him. It is a promise that receives its ultimate fulfilment in the consummated order of the new heavens and the new earth.' John Murray, *The Epistle to the Romans*, vol. 1 (Grand Rapids: Eerdmans, 1959), 142. On the promise of universal dominion to Christ, see Psa. 2:8 and 72:8-11.

21

Whole-hearted!
Joshua 14:6-15

'My brothers who went up with me made the heart of the people melt; yet I wholly followed the LORD my God.' (Josh. 14:8)

Where are you in your relationship with Jesus Christ? If someone could look into your heart, what would he see? Would he see a person who does not really know the Lord Jesus? Perhaps you know about him, but you do not have a saving knowledge of Christ. You have never closed with Christ by faith as he is offered to you in the gospel. Or perhaps he would see a professing believer who lives on the fringes of Christianity. You want to claim Jesus as your Saviour. You certainly want to go to heaven when you die. You want to hold on to Christ but you keep his demands at arm's length. Or would this individual with heart-penetrating insight see you as someone who is entirely and sincerely devoted to the Saviour? Do you have a testimony of resolute devotion to Jesus Christ?

As you read through Joshua 14:6-12 it becomes evident that the theme is 'Caleb wholly followed the Lord'. Though he freely confessed his dedication to God (verse 8), his was not a self-conceited evaluation of spiritual superiority. Moses acknowledged his commitment (verse 9), and Joshua did as well (verse 14). From every conceivable angle Caleb's whole-souled devotion was evident.

But what did it mean for him to wholly follow his Lord? A very wooden translation of the Hebrew yields the phrase 'I was full after', an idiom that means 'I remained loyal to' the Lord my God.[1] Caleb's loyalty was an expression of faith. To say that he wholly followed the Lord became a way to express his trust in God's word and his commitment to remain devoted to and rely upon all that the Lord had promised. It was this abiding faith in God that became the expressly stated reason that he received his inheritance (verses 9, 14), a portion of the land that, like all of the land of Israel, pointed to a greater place, a greater land, an eternal land—the new heavens and the new earth.

The times and circumstances of Caleb's experience were quite different from ours, but the heart of the text, the essence of its message, has not changed. Caleb received God's gracious gift of land because he trusted in the Lord, and he demonstrated the reality and living nature of his faith by remaining loyal to God. Without faith it is impossible to please the Lord (Heb. 11:6), and if you want his blessings, if you want all that he has for you in Christ, then you must receive them by faith alone. But true faith is a whole-souled commitment[2] that leads to a life of abiding loyalty.

Expressions of faith

Caleb spanned the chasm between the old generation that perished in the wilderness and the new generation that obtained the land of promise. He also stood as an example to the generations of Israel to come. Those who were to follow in the future would also have to whole-heartedly trust in God and follow him if they were to retain possession of the land (cf. Deut. 28:64-68).

The first major section of the Caleb story, verses 6-12, looks back at key events in the wilderness, but it also brings the reader up to

[1] This idiom (*mille' 'aharey*) also occurs in 1 Kings 11:6 where it is used to contrast Solomon's spiritual failure in his later days with his father's abiding faithfulness: 'So Solomon did what was evil in the sight of the LORD and did not wholly follow the LORD, as David his father had done.' See also the earlier reference to Caleb in Deuteronomy 1:36.

[2] John Murray's definition of saving faith is 'a whole-souled movement of self-commitment to Christ for salvation from sin and its consequences.' *Redemption: Accomplished and Applied* (1955; repr. Edinburgh: Banner of Truth Trust, 2009), 102.

the days of land allotment in Canaan. Caleb accompanied his fellow tribesmen from Judah to Gilgal to receive their inheritance. Gilgal is a significant place in the narrative of Joshua, especially in chapter 5, and is the main locale for the distribution of the western land prior to the location of the tabernacle at Shiloh (18:1).

Perhaps because he was the oldest living member of the tribe, Caleb spoke up first to claim his inheritance. He addressed Joshua and pointed back to events that they had both experienced as a reminder of the ways in which he had exercised faith in God's promises: 'You, you know the word the Lord spoke' (verse 6).[1] To paraphrase Caleb said, 'Of all people, Joshua, you, you are the one who is fully aware of what God promised me when you and I and the ten other spies returned from our reconnaissance trip into Canaan.' The historical account he referred to is recorded in Numbers 13-14. At that time about two years had passed since the Israelites had left Egypt, and the tribes camped at Kadesh-barnea. Moses chose Caleb, who was forty years old at the time, along with Joshua and ten other men (one from each of the twelve tribes) to spy out the land. After the spies returned from their exploration, Caleb brought a favourable report and encouraged Israel to forge ahead to conquer Canaan (Num. 13:30). He spoke all that was in his heart and challenged his brothers to believe the Lord, to trust him and obey (Num. 14:6-9a).[2] He wholly followed the Lord and wanted others to do the same.

Caleb's fellow spies, however, with the exception of Joshua, made the hearts of the people melt (verse 8). They frightened Israel with stories of rough terrain, fortified cities, and giants because they assessed the situation with the eyes of flesh rather than the eyes of faith. Note the great contrast Caleb highlights. When Israel invaded

---

[1] This is my translation to emphasize the second person independent pronoun *'attah*, 'you' followed by the suffixed or *qatal* verb *yada'ta*, 'you know'. See Cowley, ed. *Gesenius' Hebrew Grammar*, 437 (§135a).

[2] What did it mean for Caleb to speak all that was in his heart? 'Nothing more is meant than simply this, that he acted honestly according to the command given him, without gloss or dissimulation. He enlarges on the merit of his integrity, because though he was opposed by all his colleagues, with the exception of Joshua, he did not yield to their malice, nor was dispirited by their iniquitous conspiracy, but steadfastly pursued his purpose.' Calvin, *Comm. Joshua*, 195.

the land, the hearts of the Canaanites melted with fear (Josh. 2:9, 11, 24). That was the effect God intended. But initially the people of Israel had no strength or courage to press on and fight because of the faithless reports they had heard. Unbelief kept Israel from the land and led the nation to wander in the wilderness for forty years until all those twenty years old and older had died. Because they failed to trust in God's promises, the generation that came out of the land of Egypt never entered the land of promise.

Caleb, however, had a different spirit. He confessed, 'yet I wholly followed the LORD my God' (verse 8). In spite of how others reacted, he believed the word of God, and the Lord rewarded his faith. In the words of Matthew Henry, 'He kept close to his duty, and sincerely aimed at the glory of God in it. He conformed himself to the divine will with an eye to the divine favour.'[1] Caleb, therefore, reminded Joshua, 'And Moses swore on that day, saying, "Surely the land on which your foot has trodden shall be an inheritance for you and your children forever, because you wholly followed the LORD my God"' (verse 9). Moses' words reflected God's assessment of Caleb's attitude and actions: 'But my servant Caleb, because he has a different spirit and has followed me fully, I will bring into the land into which he went, and his descendants shall possess it' (Num. 14:24).[2]

Faith, then and now

Throughout the four decades of wandering in the wilderness, Caleb had witnessed the death of his contemporaries. One by one, they had passed into eternity until only he and Joshua remained. Throughout all those years his faith had not wavered. He persevered in believing, and his perseverance had brought him to that day. You can see a marked change in the text from Caleb's recitation of past events to his present experience. The key expression is 'and now'. It occurs twice in verse 10 and once in verse 12: *'And now,* behold,

---

[1] *Matthew Henry's Commentary on the Whole Bible* (Maclean, VA: MacDonald, n.d.), 2:77.

[2] The Lord spoke the words in Numbers 14:24, but Caleb referred to them as the words Moses swore. In verse 10, he referred to it as what 'the LORD spoke ... to Moses'. The theological point is that the Lord spoke through his prophet so that God's word is Moses' word and Moses' word is God's word.

the LORD has kept me alive, just as he said, these forty-five years since the time that the LORD spoke this word to Moses, while Israel walked in the wilderness. *And now*, behold, I am this day eighty-five years old … *So now* give me this hill country …'[1] God had been faithful. Caleb had not perished in the wilderness. He recognized and acknowledged the Lord's goodness that had preserved him throughout all those years. The passage of time had not abated his strength. At age eighty-five he had the vigour of a forty-year-old. His health had not diminished and neither had his faith!

The Lord had providentially preserved Caleb so that he might accomplish his will. God always provides the resources to accomplish what he calls us to do. He provided the physical stamina that Caleb needed. To take the land that he inherited meant a strenuous battle. He had to drive out the three sons of Anak (see 15:13-14). But God gave him the vigour to do it. The Lord will never call us to accomplish a task and then leave us to our own resources. The failure to grasp that truth kept Israel from invading Canaan forty-five years earlier, and it may deter you from stepping out in faith as well. Has the Lord called you to a task? Do you honestly believe that he will not also equip you for it? The gifts and calling of God are irrevocable in salvation (Rom. 11:29) and inseparable in service.

Having established the history that led up to this occasion, Caleb directly stated his request: 'So now give me this hill country of which the LORD spoke on that day, for you heard on that day how the Anakim were there, with great fortified cities. It may be that the LORD will be with me, and I shall drive them out just as the LORD said' (verse 12). Three important truths emerge from this verse.

First, faith did not change Caleb's circumstances, but it enabled him to face his circumstances with God. The territory was still rough; it was hill country. The cities were still large and fortified, fortresses as impenetrable as they had been all those years ago. And the giants, the Anakim, were just as tall as they had been, and they were still in the land. Nothing had changed. The same obstacles that Israel had faced forty-five years earlier were still present. When we trust in God, our difficulties do not disappear like a morning mist.

[1] Though the translation of the third occurrence varies slightly in the ESV ('So now'), the underlying Hebrew text (*we'attah*) is the same.

Faith does not dissipate our trials. Rather faith connects us to the power and help of God in the face of seeming impossibilities. The hindrances in the land did not deter Caleb in days gone by, and no reason existed for them to deter him now. His faith, like his body, was still strong.

Second, his past faith was a living faith and, therefore, a present faith. He did not just believe God in the past; he still believed him. True faith perseveres. It does not give up at the first bump in the road but rather clings to God who made the road and trusts that even the bumps are a part of his plan. I grew up in the Bible belt of the American South. In our town you did not ask someone, '*Do* you go to church?' You asked, '*Where* do you go to church?' Everyone was a 'Christian'. Yet, when you pressed someone for a testimony and asked, "Have you been converted? Has your life been changed by the gospel?' Some would reply, 'Well, I used to believe', or 'I used to be a Christian.' That would usually be followed by a story of some difficulty or doubt that steered them off the path. These people at one time professed the faith, but they did not persevere in the faith. A true and saving faith, however, does not talk merely about what it used to believe. Real faith *believes*. Had the professed Christians I spoke with genuinely trusted in Christ, they would have continued in the faith.

Faith is an abiding, present-tense reality. While people who do not know God should find that to be a deeply convicting truth, it can also be a comfort for those who struggle with assurance. People who have doubts about their salvation often try to relive a conversion experience. They will go back again and again in their minds to an event that happened long ago to dissect it, analyse it, and try to determine if it was genuine. But the salient question is not 'Did I believe back then?' I do not want to minimize the fact that people come to faith at a point in time, but, nevertheless, the issue is not *did* you believe but *do* you believe? If you trust in Jesus Christ *now*, then you began to trust him at some point along the way. If you do not trust him now, then any past experience you have had, however emotional it may have been, was not a saving encounter with the Son of God. Real faith refuses to let go of the Saviour.

Third, faith does not grant us instant gratification. We live in an 'I-want-it-now!' culture, but true faith waits. Caleb waited for forty-five years to receive his land. Every step he took in the wilderness he took by faith. Day after day he kept his focus on the Lord, on the future, and on the inheritance. How was he able to keep his spiritual focus for so long? He held the promise before him.

Promises

Six times in verses 6-12 Caleb emphasized God's promise to him. In verse 6 he referred to 'what the Lord said to Moses'. He was due what 'Moses swore' (verse 9), and 'just as [the Lord] said' (verse 10). Those three affirmations are followed by 'the Lord spoke this word to Moses' (verse 10), 'of which the Lord spoke' (verse 12), and 'just as the Lord said' (verse 12). Caleb appealed for his inheritance on the basis of God's promise. Faith is not an empty idea. It is not make-believe, and it is more than a positive feeling. Faith is the heart's positive response to the word of God. Faith has to have something to cling to or to stand upon, and that 'something' is the promise of the Almighty. Abraham's faith clung to the promise when God first spoke to him (cf. Gen. 15:6). Caleb anchored his own hope to the covenant that the Lord had made with Abraham. The patriarchal promises had given him the courage to want to invade Canaan all those years before, and that same firm and reliable basis of truth kept him going. In addition to the promise God gave Abraham, Caleb had the assurance that he would personally have a piece of property in the land. Even today, though the physical land aspect of the Abrahamic covenant has been fulfilled,[1] like Caleb, we are still heirs of that covenant and the promises made to Abraham, our father in the faith (see Gal. 3:7-9). Those promises continue 'to be the hope of the church'.[2]

The truth that fuelled Caleb's faith fuels ours as well, but we have the advantage to see the promises fulfilled in the Lord Jesus Christ. If we whole-heartedly cling to the Saviour, then we will receive our inheritance as well and on the last day, 'the King will say to those

---

[1] See chapter 20.
[2] VanGemeren, *Progress of Redemption*, 127.

on his right, "Come, you who are blessed by my Father, inherit the kingdom prepared for you from the foundation of the world"' (Matt. 25:34).

Note that God's promises are not just for the last day. They keep us going and growing day by day. If we want to mature in our faith, then Scripture must shape every area of our lives. God's word must focus our vision, inform our praying, and drive our ambition. If the Lord has promised the fullness of the Spirit (Luke 11:13), then that promise should shape how I look at my Christian walk and my service to others. If he has promised every spiritual blessing in Christ (Rom. 8:32), then I ought to pray to experience those blessings and to show the fruit of the Spirit in my life. We need a bigger vision of what God can do in and through us. To get that vision we must fill our hearts and minds with his promises and then let those promises drive our ambitions to be all that we can be for the Lord Jesus and do all that we can do to advance his kingdom.[1]

Against the tide

If you are going to wholly follow the Lord, you will have to stand against the tide. The faith exemplified in Caleb's life is a faith that believes God in spite of the attitude and actions of others. Though the other ten spies brought a negative report, they did not intimidate Caleb. He was a man who had the courage of his convictions. He never wet his finger and stuck it into the air to see which way the wind of opinion was blowing. The unbelief of the other spies grieved his heart because they were discouraging the people from trusting in and following God. Caleb said, 'We can do this! God has promised!' even though the others said, 'No way. Forget it. It will never work.'

Of A. A. Milne's *Winnie the Pooh* characters, Eeyore seems to be a favourite. Perhaps the reason is we can all relate to him so well. Eeyore is the eternal pessimist. His tag line is 'It wouldn't have worked anyhow.' The world is full of Eeyores when it comes to biblical faith. There will always be plenty of nay-saying to go around. Never expect faith to be the common attitude. Plenty of people will

---

[1] 'We need to live according to our promise-informed vision, and not according to the limits of our circumstances or our abilities—the puny promises of our mundane life.' T. M. Moore, *I Will Be Your God* (Phillipsburg, NJ: P&R, 2002), 29.

raise their voices with misgivings. Caleb and Joshua faced the odds of ten against two.

Whole-hearted commitment to Christ and his cause is often a lonely faith.[1] Caleb was in the minority, and that is not a comfortable place to be. Those who loyally follow Christ, however, often find themselves isolated or marginalized. Believers often find themselves alone at work, at school, and even at home. When the apostle Paul was imprisoned for the faith he wrote to Timothy, 'At my first defence no one came to stand by me, but all deserted me. May it not be charged against them! But the Lord stood by me and strengthened me' (2 Tim. 4:16). In the loneliness, God's voice must be the loudest voice we hear. Faith comes by hearing (Rom. 10:17), therefore we must give ourselves to Scripture, to read, meditate, memorize, and pray the very words of God as a means to stand strong when the ideas, opinions, and unbelief of others threaten to sweep us away.

The reward of faith
The great thing about faith is that, in spite of obstacles, setbacks, and the opposition of others, the one who believes always receives the reward. Three words best sum up the reward of faith as it is described in verses 13-15.

The first word is *blessing*. 'Then Joshua blessed him, and he gave Hebron to Caleb the son of Jephunneh for an inheritance' (verse 13). To bless someone involves much more than wishing him or her well. This was not Joshua's version of saying, 'Good luck!' When Joshua blessed Caleb, he called upon the Lord to empower him to take his possession. 'Blessing in the name of the Lord tapped into the power and resources of God himself.'[2]

Victory is the second word. 'Therefore Hebron became the inheritance of Caleb the son of Jephunneh the Kenizzite to this day, because he wholly followed the Lord, the God of Israel' (verse 14). Hebron became Caleb's property, but this involved more than a legal transfer, more than 'signing the papers'. Caleb did not receive his land without a fight. He not only had to drive out the three sons

[1] Davis, *Joshua: No Falling Words*, 116-17.
[2] Howard, *Joshua*, 330.

of Anak (15:14), but he also had to go up against the inhabitants of Debir (15:15).

The third and final term is *possession*. Verse 15 seems, at first, like an historical addendum to the story, but closer investigation reveals two significant issues. To begin with, Hebron was formerly called Kiriath-arba or the city of Arba, and Arba was the greatest man among the Anakim. The unbelieving spies feared the Anakim, but as a reward for his whole-hearted faithfulness Caleb received the city of their greatest giant.[1] God defeated the giant man and gave his city to a giant in the faith!

Hebron was 'an influential Canaanite city, located about nineteen miles south of Jerusalem in hilly but fertile terrain'.[2] It was also an old city that in earlier days had gone by the name *Mamre*. Abraham built an altar there, and nearby he purchased the cave of Machpelah in which to bury Sarah (Gen. 13:18; 23:1-20). The cave and the field surrounding it was the only land Abraham ever owned in Canaan. Eventually Abraham himself, Isaac, Rebecca, Jacob, and Leah were all buried there. It became the cemetery of hope, the ground where the bodies of the faithful were laid to rest while waiting for the promise to be fulfilled. Later, Hebron became David's first capital (2 Sam. 2:1-4a). What a fitting place for Caleb to inherit, and what a beautiful picture of our inheritance. Hebron was a picture of resurrection hope, a down-payment of greater things to come, and a signpost that pointed to the reign of a greater David, our King Jesus.

Then the land had rest from war (cf. 11:23). The entire affair opened with God's message for Joshua, 'Moses my servant is dead. Now therefore arise, go over this Jordan, you and all this people, into the land that I am giving to them, to the people of Israel' (1:2). Now Israel had entered the rest that the people longed for, and Caleb received the land he had patiently anticipated.

---

[1] Gordon McConville notes that 'Caleb's possession therefore corresponds perfectly to his illustrious reputation as the one who showed no fear of the giants in the land.' McConville and Williams, *Joshua*, 66.

[2] R. K. Harrison, *Numbers, The Wycliffe Exegetical Commentary* (Chicago: Moody, 1990), 205.

Dedication

Caleb's loyalty to God and his word represented a lifetime of dedication. We admire devotion when we see it. People who give themselves to a good task or pursuit in life and remain resolute in their endeavours should be acknowledged for their commitment and perseverance. Henry Martyn, an early missionary to India, demonstrated that kind of commitment to the cause of Jesus Christ in his life. When Martyn sailed for India in 1805, he struggled with leaving home. In the early nineteenth century, travelling to India meant that he might never see home again. After his ship docked in Cork, on the southern coast of Ireland, he recorded in his diary a calmness and resoluteness that had come over his soul. He wrote,

> After a long and blessed season in prayer, I felt the spirit of adoption drawing me very near to God, and giving me the full assurance of his love. My fervent prayer was that I might be more deeply and habitually convinced of his unchanging, everlasting love, and that my whole soul might be altogether in Christ. I scarcely knew how to express the desires of my heart. I wanted to be all in Christ, and to have Christ for my 'all in all',—to be encircled in his everlasting arms, and to be swallowed up altogether in his fulness. I wished for no created good, or for men to know my experience; but to be one with Thee, and live for Thee, O God, my Saviour and Lord.[1]

As Martyn ventured forth for India he, like Caleb before him, evidenced an unwavering commitment to follow Christ, a commitment that led him to give his life to spread the glorious news of Jesus. Thomas Babington Macaulay's *Epitaph* bears witness to the mark his life left.

> Here Martyn lies. In Manhood's early bloom
> The Christian Hero finds a Pagan tomb.
> Religion, sorrowing o'er her favourite son,
> Points to the glorious trophies that he won.
> Eternal trophies! not with carnage red,
> Not stained with tears by hapless captives shed,
> But trophies of the Cross! for that dear name,

---

[1] John Sargent, *The Life and Letters of Henry Martyn* (Edinburgh: Banner of Truth Trust, 1985), 97-98.

> Through every form of danger, death, and shame,
> Onward he journeyed to a happier shore,
> Where danger, death, and shame assault no more.[1]

Have you wholly followed the Lord? If you answer that question honestly, then you will have to admit that you have not. All of us have failed to believe his promises. We have not been willing to take the lonely stand of faith. We have let fear dominate our lives rather than the courage to believe God's truth. For this reason you and I need someone else from the tribe of Judah, a man greater than Caleb who believed God in the face of death, a man who was willing to stand alone outside the gate at that place called Calvary (Heb. 13:12), a man who was willing to suffer and endure the cross for the joy that was set before him, the promise of an inheritance given to him, the inheritance of a people. There is a man greater than Caleb, and he is called JESUS. Because he wholly followed the Lord, because he perfectly obeyed the Father, we can receive forgiveness for our failures by faith in him. For in every place you have failed, Jesus has succeeded. For every sin you have committed, Christ has earned for you a perfect righteousness. And he calls you to come, to commit your eternal soul into his hands that you might be saved.

---

[1] George Smith, *Henry Martyn: Saint and Scholar* (London: Religious Tract Society, 1892), 516, note 1.

22

Special Cities—
Gospel Truths: A Place of Refuge
Joshua 20:1-9

Then the LORD *said to Joshua, 'Say to the people of Israel, "Appoint the cities of refuge, of which I spoke to you through Moses, that the manslayer who strikes any person without intent or unknowingly may flee there. They shall be for you a refuge from the avenger of blood."' (Josh. 20:1-3)*

O ne of the great comforts we have as Christians is to know that the God we love and serve is sovereign. The psalmist proclaimed, 'Our God is in the heavens, he does all that he pleases' (115:3). From the New Testament, the apostle Paul affirmed that God 'works all things according to the counsel of his will' (Eph. 1:11). The Lord does everything according to his predetermined decree, and he always does what is right (Gen. 18:25). From our human vantage point, however, accidents happen. Events occur, often with horrific consequences, that we never planned or desired. At times unintentional acts can even result in the death of another individual. This reality lay behind God's appointment of certain cities as places of refuge to protect the innocent.

Throughout the conquest and distribution of the land, cities have played an important role. The Israelites faced formidable cities to conquer, like Jericho and Ai. Chapters 15 and 19 contain extensive lists of cities that Joshua, Eleazar, and the other leaders parcelled out to the various tribes. In chapters 20 and 21, however, the focus of the text turns to two sets of cities that provided special functions for the nation, cities whose names an Israelite would immediately associate with safety (chapter 20) and the Levites (chapter 21).

Joshua 20 gives us a list of six cities within Israel that served as places of protection for those guilty of manslaughter. Theses cities are commonly referred to as *cities of refuge*. They were special places because, in his mercy, God provided a sanctuary for a person who unintentionally caused someone's death. In a city of refuge, a manslayer could be spared capital punishment at the hands of the avenger of blood. These cities became a critical part of the structure of Israel's society, a society that in its ceremonies and its civic properties taught the people about God and pointed the people to God. These special cities served as tools to educate Israel about the way the Lord looked at life and death and to promote both mercy and justice in the land. The cities of refuge taught Israel, and teach us today, that God is a God of mercy and grace, and in his love he reaches out in pity and provides refuge and safety to all who will flee to his appointed place.

Accidents happen

Given the reality that human accidents resulting in death occur, the Lord spoke to Joshua[1] and had him instruct the people of Israel to appoint certain cities as places of shelter (verse 2a). This was not a new concept for God's people. The Lord had earlier given directions for these cities through Moses. In fact, several passages in the Pentateuch deal with the topic. For example, not long after Israel left Egypt, God instructed the people at Mt Sinai, 'Whoever strikes a man so that he dies shall be put to death. But if he did not lie in wait for him, but God let him fall into his hand, then I will appoint for you a place to which he may flee' (Exod. 21:12-13). This first, brief mention of a place to flee is later expanded in Numbers 35 where we

[1] The chapter begins with a direct address from the Lord to Joshua (verse 1). The last direct divine address occurred at the beginning of chapter 13 when the Lord gave Joshua the instructions for allotting the land. God now speaks again, and this will be the last time he addresses anyone in this way in the book. Hubbard, *Joshua*, 450.

find explicit instructions and scenarios laid out to cover the laws of manslaughter. Additional references occur in Deuteronomy 4:41-43 and 19:2-9. Cities of refuge were clearly important places to the Lord and hence their prominent place in the Mosaic legislation. For that reason, as soon as the land was securely in Israel's grasp, God spoke to Joshua to see that the cities were set aside and designated for this special use.

The Bible is a book of reality which recognizes the diversity of ethical situations we encounter in this world. Is it wrong to take the life of another person? That depends upon the context and circumstances. Scripture teaches the legitimacy of capital punishment and just war, but what about death caused in other contexts? Certainly pre-meditated murder is wrong. 'Thou shalt not kill' (Exod. 20:13; Deut. 5:17). But what if you do kill someone accidentally?

Several years ago, a gentleman I knew left a Wednesday night prayer meeting and headed home. Part of his drive was along a road with a few scattered houses and no street lights. It was dark, and he never saw the teenager he struck and killed. It was a terrible, heart-wrenching tragedy. But no one felt contempt for the man only deep sorrow because it happened unintentionally. Just a few years ago at a party in Detroit, a young woman walked up behind an off-duty police officer and gave him a hug. When she hugged him, his firearm discharged. The bullet pierced her heart and a lung, and she died instantly. Those are the kinds of situations, though certainly in more modern contexts, covered by the legislation in Joshua 20. These were not premeditated killings. They were not, in legal terminology, done with malice aforethought. But a death occurred, and that has to be acknowledged and dealt with in one way or another.

The purpose for these cities becomes clear in verse 3: 'that the manslayer who strikes any person without intent or unknowingly may flee there. They shall be for you a refuge from the avenger of blood.' If anyone strikes and kills his neighbour but does so accidentally, unintentionally, without forethought and planning, then that person should not have to bear the penalty of capital punishment. Instead, he should flee to one of the selected cities and find safety from 'the avenger of blood' (verse 3). This ominous sounding individual was not some sinister, black-hooded figure will a full-time occupation of avenging deaths and righting wrongs. The avenger was a relative of the deceased who had the right and responsibility to act on behalf of the family to pursue a murderer and to see that justice was done.[1] A person guilty of manslaughter, however, should be and could be kept safe from this individual and from the penalty of death.

When tragedy strikes

If you lived in ancient Israel and unintentionally caused a death, like the man I knew who struck the teenager or the police officer whose gun discharged, what would you do? Verses 4-6 set out the step-by-step procedure to follow. The first three steps are to be taken by the individual, steps that are described in the text in a series of succinct actions: he shall flee, he shall stand, and he shall speak. First, the individual would flee to the nearest city of refuge and explain his case to the elders who sat at the gate (verse 4a). As we will see in verses 7 and 8, there were six such cities in Israel so that no one would be under an undue strain to make it to his destination.[2] As soon as the death occurred, the responsible party was to make his way as quickly as he could to the nearest sanctuary.

The elders or leaders regularly heard cases and witnessed legal transactions at the city gate, the place that functioned as the court room (cf. Deut. 21:19; Ruth 4:1-2). They would hear the case and the individual's plea for asylum, take him into the city, and provide him with a place to stay (verse 4b).[3] If the avenger of blood did arrive on the scene, the elders would not allow him admittance to pursue the party in question. The initial, temporary sanctuary guaranteed

[1] For additional references, see Num. 35:19, 21, 24, 25, 27 (twice); Deut. 19:6, 12; 2 Sam. 14:11. The term translated *avenger* is in other contexts the *kinsman redeemer*. The Hebrew for this term is *go'el*. The *avenger of blood is go'el haddam*.
[2] Pitkänen makes the same point stating, 'In their present form, the towns have been set up roughly evenly across the Israelite territory ... This would grant people equally easy access to any city of refuge throughout the land.' Pitkänen, *Joshua*, 334.
[3] The crisp account of the procedure given in verse 4, stated in a series of *waw* perfect verbs, prescribe what shall happen every time the situation occurs.

protection. Until the case was fully heard, the facts known, and a decision rendered no punishment could be exacted.

At verse 6, however, the text backs up to give more details on how the full legal procedure worked. After seeking asylum in the city of refuge, the individual had to stand trial before the congregation. A person could not just say, 'It was an accident. I did not mean to kill him' and be granted an automatic pardon. He had to present the evidence of his innocence at a hearing (cf. Num. 35:24). The trial would be conducted in the town where the incident occurred and evidence and eyewitnesses were more readily available. If in the end the accused could prove that the death he caused happened accidentally, then the congregation (a jury of his peers) would declare his innocence and protect him from retaliation at the hand of the avenger of blood.

The remainder of verse 6 then assumes a not-guilty verdict. After the congregation determined that the manslayer accidentally killed his victim, he must then remain in the city of refuge until the death of the then current high priest. Only after the high priest's death may the manslayer return home.[1]

Life, justice, and mercy

The emphasis on these cities, first in the Pentateuch and again in the book of Joshua, demonstrates just how important they were, not only to the individuals who found themselves in such unfortunate circumstances, but also for the instruction of God's people as well. The regulations for these cities stress the importance of life. It is nothing less than tragic that someone accidentally (as we would say)

---

[1] This interpretation of the events is the result of a close reading of all the relevant texts and seems to make the most sense of the various steps involved. 'In ver. 6, the two regulations, '*until he stand before the congregation for judgment*,' and '*until the death of the high priest*,' are to be understood, in accordance with the clear explanation given in Num. xxv. 24, 25, as meaning that the manslayer was to live in the town till the congregation had pronounced judgment upon the matter, and either given him up to the avenger of blood as a wilful murderer, or taken him back to the city of refuge as an unintentional manslayer, in which case he was to remain there till the death of the existing high priest.' Keil and Delitzsch, *Comm. on the Old Testament*, 2:209.

lost his or her life. God, however, so values his sacred gift that he would not allow the avenger to spill yet more blood in an act of retribution. Perhaps the expression 'two wrongs do not make a right' best summarizes the point. Since the manslayer was not guilty of premeditated murder, it would have been wrong for him to lose his life for the incident. The Lord protected both the manslayer, from a penalty he did not deserve, and the avenger from wrongfully exacting punishment.

The Lord values life, and we should too. Modern films have brought so many scenes of gratuitous violence to the theatre and television that we have become insensitive to gruesome killings. School and workplace shootings have become all too common, providing demonstration after demonstration of a mindset that has no regard for the lives of others, the logical outgrowth of a worldview that teaches we are the products of blind chance. If we are not careful, we can easily become desensitized to violence and death. We can watch murder after murder, hear tragic stories on the news, and change the television channel to check the score of the game without a second thought.

As Christians we must be on our guard lest we begin to feel that way, not just about a shooting a thousand miles away but about abortions that occur in our own towns and neighbourhoods. Once we have been around a sin long enough, once it is talked about enough and practiced enough, we become insensitive to it. The edge gets taken off its horror. God values life, and we must keep that truth ever before us lest we grow callous to sin and end up implicitly endorsing what we explicitly say we reject.

These cities of refuge also teach us about the importance of justice. God wants the right thing to be done. Running throughout this passage and undergirding its basic procedures is a key principle of biblical justice—a person is innocent until proven guilty. The Israelite who fled to a city of refuge was protected by the elders until the congregation could hear his case and reach a conclusion regarding the evidence. Here the principle of innocent until proven guilty, a cornerstone of western law, is clearly reflected in the rules for these cities. Imagine the anxiety a manslayer must have felt. He had caused the death of another person. His actions, however unintentional they may have been, have forever changed his life and the lives of others. The deed could not be reversed. How gracious it was of God to provide an assumed innocence until the case could be adjudicated. This principle of justice that we hold so dear should be a cause of thanksgiving to God. Everyone should have the opportunity to proclaim and defend his innocence and be presumed innocent until proven otherwise. But we should also remember that many people do not live with the same freedoms. Many of our brothers and sisters in Christ live under the oppression of persecution and are deprived of justice. As we thank the Lord for what he has given to us, we must also pray for those in much less fortunate circumstances.

If you prize the principle of innocent until proven guilty, do you practice it in your heart? How often have you made assumptions, jumped to a conclusion, tried, condemned, and 'executed' someone in your thoughts before you really knew the facts of the matter? Have you assumed the worst about someone without stopping to investigate what really happened? The *Westminster Larger Catechism* warns us that 'receiving and countenancing evil reports ... stopping our ears against just defence; [and] evil suspicion' are all violations of the ninth commandment, the command not to bear false witness (Exod. 20:16).[1] When we reserve judgment and even ungodly and suspicious thoughts in our hearts until we know the truth of a matter, then we not only grant the assumption of innocence to the other person, we maintain a loving and truthful attitude. Observing the rules of the cities of refuge was a practical way to love your neighbour as yourself.

These cities also demonstrate the importance of mercy. God reached out in love and grace to the manslayer and spared his life because he is a merciful God (Deut. 4:31; James 5:11). Are you a merciful person? Can people approach you and know that you are gracious, or do they find you implacable? Do you exact punishment according to the letter of the law, or do you consider the circumstances? When Jesus taught us to love our enemies, he also called for us to be merciful as our Father is merciful (Luke 6:36).

---

[1] *Westminster Larger Catechism*, Question and Answer 145.

As 'mercied' people, believers are, in turn, to show mercy. If we are unwilling to extend compassion to others, then how can we expect to receive kindness from the Lord (Matt. 5:7; James 2:13; cf. Psa. 18:25)? God is a God of justice. If a person was guilty of premeditated murder, then he had to pay the penalty with his life (Num. 35:16-21; Deut. 19:11-13). God does not trifle with sin. But this just and holy God is also full of compassion and love.[1]

The cities

After the Lord set out the basic rules for the cities of refuge, verses 7 and 8 list the individual cities.[2] Three lay on each side of the Jordan River. West of the Jordan were Kedesh, Shechem, and Kiriath-arba or Hebron (verse 7). These cities were located in the hill country of Naphtali, Ephraim, and Judah respectively. To the east were Bezer from the tribe of Reuben, Ramoth from the tribe of Gad, and Golan from the tribe of Manasseh, (verse 8). Moses had already chosen these eastern cities in Deuteronomy 4:41-43. According to the regulations in Deuteronomy 19:8-10, three more cities could be added to these due, no doubt, to Israel's expected population growth and their increasing expansion to occupy more of the land.

Each of these cities was also a city of the Levites and will be labelled as such in chapter 21 (Kedesh, 21:32; Shechem, 21:21; Kiriath-arba [Hebron], 21:11-13; Bezer, 21:36; Ramoth, 21:38; Golan,

---

[1] 'By limiting the institution [of the avenger of blood], God the Creator exercises his ownership over all life and his absolute right to regulate it. In my view, this marks an act of divine grace on behalf of people I would regard as the victims of circumstances beyond their control. It extends divine mercy toward people accidentally caught in unfortunate, life-threatening situations.' Hubbard, *Joshua*, 462.

[2] This is not to imply that the exposition above contains all of the lessons that may be learned from the arrangement of these cities. Among the other lessons Calvin notes at least one reason the individual guilty of manslaughter was not allowed to return to his home town until after the death of the high priest, 'Meanwhile respect was so far paid to the feeling of the brethren and kindred of the deceased, that their sorrow was not increased by the constant presence of the persons who had caused their bereavement. Lastly, the people were accustomed to detest murder, since homicide, even when not culpable, was followed by exile from country and home, till the death of the high priest.' Calvin, *Comm. Joshua*, 240.

21:27). When an individual fled to one of the cities for safety, he would be living side-by-side with priests and others who served as staff for the tabernacle. The cities of refuge, therefore, were closely linked with Israel's worship.

The chapter concludes with a summary statement in verse 9: 'These were the cities designated for all the people of Israel and for the stranger sojourning among them, that anyone who killed a person without intent could flee there, so that he might not die by the hand of the avenger of blood, till he stood before the congregation.' This verse recaps most of what we have already learned: a manslayer could flee to a city of refuge in order to preserve his life from the avenger until he stood trial before the congregation. What is unique about verse 9 is its note that the cities were set apart for both Israelites and for strangers or 'resident aliens' who were living in the land.[1]

Anyone who accidently caused the death of another could flee to a city of refuge so that he might not die. No parochialism existed when it came to safety. God was just as concerned with justice for Gentiles in the land as he was for his own covenant people.[2] Our attitude, to seek justice and to show mercy, should be extended not only to believers but to those outside the church as well. Justice is not justice if it only exists for a select few. Paul wrote to the Galatians, 'So then, as we have opportunity, let us do good to everyone, and especially to those who are of the household of faith' (6:10). Yes, it is important for us to do good to our brothers and sisters in Christ. Especially among our fellow Christians we can show the love of the

---

[1] The term *ger*, *stranger*, means sojourner or alien and, in this context, would refer to Gentiles. The inclusion of strangers 'reflects a movement towards an inclusive, non-national concept of citizenship (cf. 8:33; Exod 12:48-49)'. McConville and Williams, *Joshua*, 81.

[2] It seems that this kind of concern was not exhibited elsewhere in the Ancient Near East. 'It appears that there are no known direct parallels to the system of cities of refuge from elsewhere in the Ancient Near East (see Barmash 2005: 203-204). Diplomatic asylum as such, however, is well known in the Ancient Near East (see e.g. BECKMAN, *passim*), and of course makes sense, just as diplomatic asylum is known in the modern world (e.g. Soviet defectors during the Cold War era, or North Korean defectors to the South even today). In this connection, it would also make sense that a killer might flee to another country (as did Moses, according to the Bible itself, in Exod. 2:11-15).' Pitkänen, *Joshua*, 334.

Lord Jesus in a context where it will be recognized and appreciated. We have a special responsibility to those in the church. But we are not to exclude others from acts of kindness, ministries of mercy, and especially justice. Before Paul mentions the household of faith he writes, 'let us do good to everyone'.

Flee for refuge

The cities of refuge not only teach us principles of justice and compassion, they also have a redemptive relevance as well. Though after Joshua 20 the Bible never mentions these cities again,[1] we may assume that the Israelites and sojourners availed themselves of the protection they offered. The stress on refuge after Joshua 20 focuses on the Lord as the real and lasting shelter of his people.

This truth is particularly clear in the psalms. All who take refuge in the Lord are blessed (2:12) and rejoice (5:11). Those who take refuge in the Lord do so to find safety from their adversaries (7:1; 17:7). The Lord is a shield for those who take refuge in him (18:30). It is better to take refuge in the Lord than to trust in man, even the most noble (118:8-9). The list could go on and on because the English word 'refuge' occurs a total of 47 times in the Psalter.[2]

Many of these same expressions of faith can also be found in the prophets. In Zion, the city of God, the afflicted may find refuge (Isa. 14:32). The Lord is the Rock, his people's refuge (Isa. 17:10; cf. Jer. 16:19; 17:17; Joel 3:16). Idols offer no shelter, but those who trust in the Lord will possess the land and inherit the Lord's holy mountain (Isa. 57:13). The Lord knows those who take refuge in him (Nah. 1:7). The living experience of all who trusted Israel's God was to find in him a sanctuary of safety and peace.

On at least a couple of occasions, however, the reference to God as a refuge points to the future and the coming Messianic age. Isaiah, the evangelical prophet, preached of a coming day when 'the branch of the LORD shall be beautiful and glorious' (4:2). When this Messiah, the branch or sprout of David, comes, 'Then the LORD will

---

[1] Howard, *Joshua*, 387.

[2] This statistic reflects the ESV which translates as *refuge* the Hebrew terms *chsah* (or a derivative thereof) and *ma'oz*.

create over the whole site of Mount Zion and over her assemblies a cloud by day, and smoke and the shining of a flaming fire by night; for over all the glory there will be a canopy. There will be a booth for shade by day from the heat, and for a refuge and a shelter from the storm and rain' (Isa. 4:5-6). Zephaniah prophesied the coming conversion of the nations in the Messianic age. What will happen in those days? The Lord will bring about a radical transformation, and 'a people humble and lowly ... shall seek refuge in the name of the LORD' (Zeph. 3:12).

If God is our refuge, then like the manslayer we must flee to him. The verb *flee* is the key term in Joshua 20 and occurs in verses 3, 4, 6, and 9. To flee is to seek safety and salvation. To flee is to trust. In fact, one of the key terms for faith in the Old Testament means *to seek refuge.*[1] When the Lord delivered David from his enemies he confessed, 'The LORD is my rock and my fortress and my deliverer, my God, my rock, in whom I take refuge, my saviour; you save me from violence. I call upon the LORD, who is worthy to be praised, and I am saved from my enemies' (2 Sam. 22:2-4). The Hebrew Scriptures are replete with references to God as our refuge, our sanctuary, the one who provides us with shelter, safety, and salvation.

As God's revelation progressively unfolds into the New Testament, it becomes clear that the true and lasting refuge of our souls is the Lord Jesus Christ. Amid warnings against apostasy and the assurance of God's covenant promises, Hebrews 6 describes Christians as those who have fled to Christ for refuge. Because God wanted to convince believers of the certainty of the hope that they have in the gospel, he not only gave his promise but he confirmed it with an oath, 'so that by two unchangeable things, in which it is impossible for God to lie, we who have fled for refuge might have strong encouragement to hold fast to the hope set before us' (verse 18). All those, therefore, who seek refuge in Jesus for salvation have a sure and steadfast hope because as our great high priest, he by his death and resurrection has entered into the holiest place of all and thereby secured our everlasting salvation (verses 19-20).

[1] The verb is *hasah*. It occurs 42 times in the Hebrew Bible and is often translated *trust* in the KJV.

When the innocent manslayer found refuge in one of the six Israelite sanctuaries, he had to live there until the death of the high priest (Josh. 20:6). Then, and only then, could he return home. That regulation provided a significant foreshadow of the New Testament parallel—only through the death of our high priest are we set free. We can go home, our eternal and heavenly home, because Jesus has died.[1] There is no more simple gospel message than this—through the death of another we are set at liberty. Have you been set free? Do you know the mercy of God in Christ so beautifully pictured in the cities of refuge? If not, then flee, flee to Christ. Cast yourself on him for the salvation he freely offers in the gospel, and you will be saved. No one ever sought refuge in Christ and was turned away. Jesus promised, 'All that the Father give me will come to me, and whoever comes to me I will never cast out' (John 6:37).

Charles Wesley, the great hymnwriter of the Evangelical Awakening, captured the essence of this chapter's theology in the hymn 'Jesus, Lover of My Soul':

> Jesus, lover of my soul,
>   let me to thy bosom fly,
> while the nearer waters roll,
>   while the tempest still is high.
> Hide me, O my Saviour, hide,
>   till the storm of life is past;
> safe into the haven guide;
>   O receive my soul at last.

[1] 'It is not specifically stated what removed the manslayer's guilt. He was sentenced to a period of exile in the city of refuge, away from his home, and he could not return home until the high priest died. Many have argued that the high priest's death marked a period of amnesty ushering in a new era. However, a more probable explanation is that since the high priest represented the sacrificial system, his death atoned for the sins of the manslayer. No ransom was to be accepted for a murderer or for a manslayer (Num. 35:30-31). Only on the occasion of a death— the high priest's—was the manslayer free to leave. As Greenberg states, "The sole personage whose religious-cultic importance might endow his death with expiatory value for the people at large is the high priest." In Numbers 35, the high priest is mentioned as having been anointed with "holy oil" (v. 25), which would tend to support his position as the acceptable "sacrifice." For Christians, the typological associations with the death of Jesus Christ—the great High Priest whose death atones for their sins—are certainly visible here.' Howard, *Joshua*, 385-86.

Other refuge have I none,
  hangs my helpless soul on thee;
leave, ah! leave me not alone,
  still support and comfort me.
All my trust on thee is stayed,
  all my help from thee I bring;
cover my defenceless head
  with the shadow of thy wing.

23

Special Cities—
Gospel Truths: The Lord Will Provide
Joshua 21:1-42

And they said to them at Shiloh in the land of Canaan, 'The LORD commanded through Moses that we be given cities to dwell in, along with their pasturelands for our livestock.' So by command of the LORD the people of Israel gave to the Levites ... (Josh. 21:2-3)

W hen I was a child and wanted something, I am told that my main line of argument was 'I need it!' I needed a new toy. I needed to play with my friends. I needed a piece of candy. Of course I did not really need any of those things, I simply wanted them and elevated my desires to needs. In my childish mind, wants were necessities. While neither children nor adults need everything they want, that does not negate the fact that we each have real needs.

We have physical needs for food, clothing, and shelter, and in our circumstances in the modern world, meeting those needs typically involves a substantial financial commitment. Those needs can raise some very anxious questions for us. Granted, it can be difficult to disentangle our needs from our desires, but thankfully that is not a problem for God. In fact, Jesus taught us not to ask anxious questions, 'What will we eat, or drink, or wear?' because our heavenly Father knows what we need (Matt. 6:31-32). Rather than worrying about our needs, we are to be engaged in the worship of God. We are to seek first his kingdom and his righteousness, and trust him to provide for our necessities (Matt. 6:33).

God knows and is concerned about his people's needs. Jesus taught that in the Sermon on the Mount, but we can also clearly see that truth in this chapter as well. In Joshua 20, God provided cities of refuge so that a person guilty of accidental manslaughter would not have to suffer the fate of capital punishment. In chapter 21 we find another set of special cities. These cities were set aside for the tribe of Levi. In this chapter we can see not only the heart God has for the needs his people, but we also see the power and grace of God to meet those needs. And that is not just a message for the long-ago days of Joshua. It is the message of Jesus as well. Your heavenly Father knows what you need. And God not only knows and is concerned about your needs, he provides for them as well. The cities of refuge were places of protection. The cities of the Levites were places of provision.

The Levites

Robert Hubbard has written, 'Genealogy and geography drive this chapter's catalog of Levitical cities.'[1] That being the case, it is important for us to understand who the Levites were. Levi was the third son born to Jacob and Leah (Gen. 29:34). The name *Levi* sounds similar to the Hebrew word for *attached*. Leah named him this with the hope that Jacob would finally become devoted to her. Levi himself had three sons. The directory of Jacob's family that Joseph brought to Egypt lists them as 'Gershon, Kohath, and Merari' (Gen. 46:11).

After Jacob's family had lived in Egypt for four hundred years, a member of the Kohathite clan named Moses rose to a place of prominence in the land. He became the leader to deliver God's people from their bondage. Moses' brother Aaron, his sons, and their descendants eventually became the priests of Israel. The other Kohathites who were not descendants of Aaron, along with the sons of Gershon and Merari, also served the Lord in various capacities

[1] Hubbard, *Joshua*, 453.

connected with the tabernacle. The non-Aaronic Kohathites were responsible for the ark of the covenant, the furniture of the holy place, and the vessels that were used there (Num. 4:1-15). The Gershonites took care of the curtains, coverings, and screens of the tabernacle (Num. 4:21-28). The sons of Merari had charge of the structure of the tabernacle: the frames, bars, pillars, bases, pegs, cords, and accessories (Num. 4:29-33). In the rest of the Old Testament, the sons of Levi figure primarily in the genealogical lists (see Num. 3; 1 Chron. 6) and appear only here in Joshua.

What made the tribe of Levi so special? Why were they singled out to live in certain cities throughout the land? Two answers or at least two parts to the answer can be given to this question.

First, the Levites were a strange mixture of cursing and blessing. They were cursed because Levi, along with Simeon, slaughtered the Shechemites (Gen. 34:30). As a punishment they were scattered throughout the twelve tribes (Gen. 49:5-7). But Levi became the tribe of priests and tabernacle servants because the men of the tribe were willing to stand for God in a time of apostasy. When Moses received the law on Mt Sinai, the Israelites camped on the plain below where they made a golden calf to worship. After Moses came down from the mountain and saw the idol and witnessed the rampant immorality that the people committed, he 'stood in the gate of the camp and said, "Who is on the LORD's side? Come to me." And all the sons of Levi gathered around him' (Exod. 32:26). Moses then commanded them to go throughout the camp and slay those who had turned from the Lord. It was a gruesome task that could only be accomplished by those who took seriously the holiness of God. The Levites proved to be the men for the task because immediately after the call from Moses they 'did according to the word of Moses. And that day about three thousand men of the people fell. And Moses said, "Today you have been ordained for the service of the LORD, each one at the cost of his son and of his brother, so that he might bestow a blessing upon you this day"' (Exod. 32:28-29). Levi slew the men of Shechem in his anger. His sons slew men out of zeal for God's holiness. The actions were identical, but the motives were vastly different. The blessing for Levi was that they became the priests and support staff for the tabernacle and later the temple.

They became the Lord's select tribe to lead Israel in the worship of God.

The second reason God set apart the tribe of Levi takes us back to the first Passover when the Lord consecrated all of the firstborn of Israel to be his. Later, in Numbers 3, instead of taking the firstborn son from all the families of Israel to serve as priests and attendants, God consecrated the tribe of Levi to stand in their place. We could say that God adopted the Levites as the firstborn of the nation (Num. 3:11-13, 40-41).

By their actions, position, and calling the Levites were unique among all the tribes of Israel, and as a result God provided for them in a unique way. He did not allow them to own land. They had no inheritance (see 14:3-4; 18:7), but they were given places to live and pastureland for their cattle. All of that is the background to the entreaty we find in this chapter.

Joshua 21 opens with the leaders of the Levites coming to Shiloh to present their request to the panel responsible for the land grants. What did they want? The places to live that God had promised them: "The LORD commanded through Moses that we be given cities to dwell in, along with their pasturelands for our livestock' (verse 2). Without hesitation or delay the tribes allotted them cities and pasturelands from their inheritance. The Levites' request exhibited a godly and bold confidence. We should see their appeal as an act of faith.[1] Like Caleb who confidently declared 'give me this hill country' (14:12), the Levites were eager to possess everything God had promised to them, and they did not hesitate to ask for it.

In this simple act lies a profound lesson for prayer: to get things from God, ask for what he has promised. The Bible is replete with gracious assurances of what the Lord will do for us and what he will undertake to give to us. He has pledged to never leave us (Heb. 13:5), to be our strength in weakness (cf. 2 Cor. 12:9), and to provide a way of escape from temptations (1 Cor. 10:13). To receive these many

---

[1] 'In their approach to *Eleazar, Joshua*, and *the heads of the families of the other tribes*, the Levites show the same initiative of faith as did Judah (and Caleb) in ch. 14. Some of the other tribes needed prompting (see 18:2-3).' Woudstra, *Book of Joshua*, 303-04.

blessings we should ask for them. We should bring God's promises to him and plead them in prayer.

The land distribution for the seven final tribal allotments had taken place at Shiloh (cf. 18:1ff.), so it only makes sense that this scene occur at the same location. What is significant, however, is that the text makes such a clear statement about it to emphasize the point, as if to say, 'Now do not forget. This took place at Shiloh where Israel set up the tent of meeting and established a central place of worship.' As the final distribution, the main events were coming to a conclusion and the reference to 'Shiloh in the land of Canaan' functions as an exclamation point (!). God had kept his promises.

The leaders of the Levites reminded the allotment commission that the Lord had commanded through Moses to give them cities in which to live and land to pasture their cattle (see Num. 35:1-8). So by the Lord's order Israel appointed forty-eight cities for the Levites. These cities were not forty-eight in addition to those the tribes had already received. They were cities owned by these tribes but set apart throughout the land so that the ministers at the tabernacle would have places to live. The sons of Israel gave them to the Levites 'from their inheritance'.[1] Rather than saying, 'This is our property and ours alone', the members of the tribes were willing to dedicate land from their possessions to be used by the priests and their colleagues.[2]

Divine commands and faithful obedience characterize the entire book of Joshua. From the outset phrases such as 'the word of the Lord' and 'as the LORD commanded Moses' repeatedly occur, and time and again the word of God is followed by the people's obedience. The phrase 'by the command of the LORD' or 'according

---

[1] This is the partitive use of the preposition *min*. Waltke and O'Connor, *Introduction to Biblical Hebrew Syntax*, 213-14. [11.2.11e] See also Paul Joüon and T. Muraoka, *A Grammar of Biblical Hebrew* (Rome: Editrice Pontificio Intituto Biblico, 2006), 460.

[2] As a result, 'the allocation of cities to Levi now comes as an integral part of the distribution of land to the tribes. It has the effect of limiting the possession of the eleven tribes, yet also of placing among them those who symbolized, by virtue of their vocation, the devotion of Israel to Yahweh.' McConville and Williams, *Joshua*, 82.

to the mouth of the LORD' occurs only two more times in the Old Testament. Both are in the book of Joshua, and both are in the land allotment section. Joshua gave Caleb Kiriath-arba or Hebron 'according to the commandment of the LORD' (15:13). The daughters of Zelophehad also received their inheritance 'according to the mouth of the LORD' (17:4). The land-allotment panel set the example of explicit obedience to the very words of the living God.

Location, location, location

After the initial request from the leaders of the Levitical clans, the bulk of chapter 21 is taken up with lists of the cities and which tribes contributed them.

Verses 4 through 8 offer a summary of the cities by clan: Aaronic Kohathites (verse 4), other Kohathites (verse 5), Gershonites (verse 6), Merarites (verse 7), with a concluding statement in verse 8, which again stresses the divine imperative and the people's response: 'These cities and their pasturelands the people of Israel gave by lot to the Levites, as the LORD had commanded through Moses.'

As we noted earlier, each of the families within the tribe of Levi served in different ways at the tabernacle and later at the temple. First, the Aaronic Kohathites were the priests proper. They took care of the sacrifices and offered prayers. Next, the non-Aaronic Kohathites were responsible for 'the most holy things' (Num. 4:4). These were the vessels used in the tabernacle (see Num. 4:4-20). Third, the Gershonites carried the heavy coverings and curtains for the tabernacle (see Num. 4:21-28). Finally, the sons of Merari carried the wooden framework that gave the tabernacle its shape (see Num. 4:29-33). Now that Israel was settled in the land and the tabernacle has been set up at Shiloh, the need for the 'burden-bearing' clans becomes almost non-existent. It seems that the only possible exception may have been David's assembly of a (the?) tabernacle in Jerusalem (2 Sam. 6:17). Later, when David was an old man, he realized that the original purpose of the service clans no longer existed: '"The LORD, the God of Israel, has given rest to his people, and he dwells in Jerusalem forever. And so the Levites no longer need to carry the tabernacle or any of the things for its service"' (1 Chron. 23:25-26). But he also knew that a lot of work needed to be done at the tabernacle and soon-to-be-built temple. So he organized the families of the Levites to take on other responsibilities. They were to assist the sons of Aaron with the care of the courtyards and chambers, with the showbread, to praise the Lord, and provide other acts of service and help (see 1 Chron. 23:28-32).

These are the people the Lord provides for, and the fact that he provides for them demonstrates the way he honors those who serve him. Whether it was their earlier tasks of carrying the structure and furniture of the tabernacle or later baking bread and singing praise, God treated their occupations as important. They did not have to be the priests sacrificing animals and burning incense for God to treat their responsibilities as significant. Though a definite distinction existed between the Aaronic and non-Aaronic Levites (see especially verses 9-19), they were all the Lord's servants whom he cared for and provided for out of his goodness.

In the church, some people are called to positions of leadership, ministries that are more visible and vocal, while others serve in less visible, quieter ways. But this difference in calling, position, and opportunity reflects God's sovereign providence. How has God called you to serve him? Your position may not be glamorous in the eyes of others, but your service is important to the Lord. Never denigrate your calling as insignificant. Each member of the body of Christ needs every other member in order to function properly for God's glory (see 1 Cor. 12:12-26).

Verses 9-19 cover the cities allocated to the descendants of Aaron, one of the Kohathite clans (verse 10)[1] and present us with a total of thirteen cities [Judah and Simeon donated nine cities and Benjamin donated four]. Most commentators point out that since the descendants of Aaron were the ones to serve as priests at the temple, the Lord strategically located them in the three tribes closest to Jerusalem in anticipation of the time during David's reign and thereafter when it would become Shiloh's replacement as the central sanctuary.

For the members of the tribe of Kohath who were not descendants of Aaron, the tribes of Ephraim, Dan, and West Manasseh set

---

[1] McConville notes that this points out the distinction between 'higher and lower priestly officials'. McConville and Williams, *Joshua*, 82.

aside ten cities (verses 20-26). The Gershonites received a total of thirteen cities donated by East Manasseh, Issachar, Asher, and Naphtali (verses 27-33). Zebulon, Reuben, and Gad contributed twelve cities to the Merarites (verses 34-40). This resulted in cities (cf. verse 41) scattered from north to south and from east to west throughout the land. The section concludes with verses 41 and 42 providing a summary: 'The cities of the Levites in the midst of the possession of the people of Israel were in all forty-eight cities with their pasturelands. These cities each had its pasturelands around it. So it was with all these cities.'

Earlier the text described the cities of the Levites as 'out of their [the other tribes'] inheritance' (verse 3). It is now described as 'in the midst of the possession of the people of Israel'. Though these two expressions may be judged conceptually equivalent, they stress two different aspects with regard to the relationship between the Levites and the rest of Israel. First, the expression in verse 3 'out of their inheritance' denotes the voluntary nature of the gift. The tribes gave the use of their cities to the Levites. Second, verse 41 stresses the fact that the Levites lived in the midst of the people. This one tribe, rather than being localized and centralized, was scattered throughout the entire land. With forty-eight Levitical cities dotting the landscape of Israel, one would not have to travel far to encounter a member of this band of God's servants.

The Lord will provide

Out of all of this detail of what must surely be one of the more obscure chapters of the Old Testament some very important lessons arise about God, his people, their needs, and his provision.

The first thing you should note is that *the Lord provides for the physical needs of his people*. The Levites had no inheritance in the land. There was no region they could mark out on the map and say, 'That belongs to us.' But they still had need for shelter. They had to live somewhere. Ancient Israel had an agricultural economy, so they had to pasture their livestock somewhere. These basic needs had to be met, and God knew it. That is why he set aside these cities and farmland for them. The Lord made us people with both bodies and souls, and we have physical as well as spiritual needs. God knew the Levites could not continue to exist in the land and serve at Shiloh and later in Jerusalem unless they were able to live in the land. The one was a necessary prerequisite to the other.

If God recognizes and provides for physical needs, we are foolish to ignore them. For example, have you ever tried to witness to a hungry person? One day I was distributing gospel tracts in centre city Philadelphia and gave one to a man on the street. He looked me in the eye and said, 'What I need is some food.' I could tell that he was serious, so I said, 'Okay, let us get you some food.' I had two dollars in my pocket. That was all the cash I had with me. I did not see a restaurant anywhere nearby, but I saw a pretzel vendor. I told the man that I had enough money to buy him a pretzel, and asked if he would he eat that. He said he would eat anything. I bought the pretzel, and he devoured it. My heart broke when I realized just how hungry he was. I then offered him the gospel tract I had attempted to give him earlier. He willingly took it and promised he would read it. Do not try to witness to a hungry person. Feed him, and then witness to him because he is not just a soul and he is not just a body. He is both.

The necessity of body and soul ministry is reflected in the very way God has arranged the government of his church. The church is to be led by both elders and deacons. The elders focus primarily on the spiritual oversight of the congregation and the deacons care for the physical wellbeing of the people. But the elders and deacons also work together. Ideally they should communicate about the various avenues of ministry each pursues and alert each other to needs that should be addressed. A church may find it helpful to pair up an elder and deacon for pastoral visits because as you try to help people who need food or clothing or money for the gas bill, you also realize that spiritual care needs to take place as well. The offices of elder and deacon are distinct, but one is just as important as the other because God has made us as whole people with both spiritual and physical needs.

The cities of the Levites should also encourage you because they are *a reminder that God knows what you need*. The church no longer has a caste of priests such as we find in the Old Testament. In the New Testament church, every Christian is a priest. Every believer can go directly to God (1 Tim. 2:5; 1 Pet. 2:9). In that sense, we are now the Levites, and God will provide for us. Our Father in heaven knows the needs that we have, and he will see to it that they are supplied (Matt. 6:31-33). In his letter to the Philippians, Paul thanked them for their generous gift that ministered to his needs, but he knew that it was difficult for them to give. They were not wealthy people. Yet he could assure them, 'And my God will supply every need of yours according to his riches in glory in Christ Jesus' (Phil. 4:19). God has riches in glory. All the wealth of the world is his. He can take care of you.

How does God most often care for his people? He uses us. *God uses his people to provide for his people.* Surely we cannot miss that aspect of this chapter. Verse 3 states, 'So by command of the LORD the people of Israel gave to the Levites the following cities and pasturelands out of their inheritance.' Caleb set the example: 'They gave them Kiriath-arba (Arba being the father of Anak), that is Hebron, in the hill country of Judah, along with the pasturelands around it. But the fields of the city and its villages had been given to Caleb the son of Jephunneh as his possession' (verse 11-12). God's faithful spy, claimed his land (14:6-15), fought for his land (15:13-19), and then donated it to the Levites!¹

God's method has not changed. Christians are to take care of their fellow believers. During the days of the early church, the saints in Jerusalem suffered greatly and needed support, so Paul raised money for them from the other assemblies. He commended the churches in Macedonia,

> for in a severe test of affliction, their abundance of joy and their extreme poverty have overflowed in a wealth of generosity on their part. For they gave according to their means, as I can testify, and beyond their means, of their own accord (2 Cor. 8:2-3).

¹ 'Hence appeared the rare, nay, the incomparable moderation of this aged saint, who readily gave up to others both the city and suburbs, which he had justly claimed as his right, the moment the lot shewed that this was pleasing to God.' Calvin, *Comm. Joshua,* 241.

He then challenged the Corinthians about their own attitude toward giving:

> The point is this: whoever sows sparingly will also reap sparingly, and whoever sows bountifully will also reap bountifully. Each one must give as he has decided in his heart, not reluctantly or under compulsion, for God loves a cheerful giver. And God is able to make all grace abound to you, so that having all sufficiency in all things at all times, you may abound in every good work (2 Cor. 9:6-8).

It is foolish for us to pray, 'Lord, feed the hungry, clothe the naked, and bless all the missionaries' if we are unwilling to give our money and resources to help make those things happen. How can we give? How should we give? The principles Paul laid out in 2 Corinthians 8 and 9 tell us that we should give as God enables us (8:12), we should give generously (9:6), willingly (9:7), and we should give from a cheerful heart (9:7). Giving with a cheerful heart does not happen if you give the money and all the time are thinking about the things that you could have bought with it. Giving with a cheerful heart happens when you fill your mind with the joy of Jesus and his gospel, when you say, 'He has given so much for me that this money is nothing in comparison. I gladly give it for him.'

That kind of joy-filled, gospel-filled giving leads to the final lesson we learn from these special cities. *God provides for the spiritual needs of his people.* By providing the Levites places to live from the various tribes, God scattered them throughout Israel (cf. verse 3 with verse 41). They lived among the people as salt and light to teach the law of God (see Lev. 10:11; Mal. 2:4-9).[1] The Lord knew that Israel needed

---

[1] 'In short, with their towns as home bases, the Levites served as Yahweh's local representatives throughout the land. In Howard's words [p. 387], "the Levites were to be 'salt and light' among their fellow Israelites, scattered as they were throughout the tribes." As it were, they gave the invisible Yahweh a local incarnational presence—a flesh-and-blood person with whom to deal—in the towns and villages where people lived. As part of the tribe set aside for his service, they symbolically constituted the people closest to him, the ones who presumably knew him best, the ones who understood his mysterious ways, the ones to consult with in order to make wise decisions. Through their instruction, Yahweh addressed local Israelites in his own words, challenging and calming them in his own voice.' Hubbard, *Joshua*, 464.

constant exposure to his word. That was the only way they could fulfil their covenant obligations, follow him, worship him, and continue to live in the land of promise. The curse of the Levites to be scattered throughout the nation (Gen. 49:5-7) became a blessing under the gracious hand of God. We need that constant exposure to Scripture as well. For that reason the Lord tells us not to forsake the gathering of his people (Heb. 10:25) because we need time together each week to listen to God speak through the preaching of his word. We need the fellowship of mutual encouragement to hear, believe, and obey the Scriptures. We have to know God if we are going to follow him.

Like the cities of refuge in chapter 20, the cities of the Levites are also a picture of Christ. The cities of refuge pointed to the safety anyone may have who flees to Jesus. In Christ you find the forgiveness of sins and the hope of heaven. The cities of the Levites demonstrate to us that everything we need for eternal life God will provide. Earlier we noted the promise Paul gave to the Philippians, 'And my God will supply every need of yours according to his riches in glory in Christ Jesus' (4:19). The Philippian believers needed to hear that message because they had financial needs. But do you think for a moment that God is willing to supply money but not forgiveness? The very promise of Philippians 4:19 is based on the inexhaustible resources of God, and that is more than his ownership of cattle on a thousand hills (Psa. 50:10). He is the author and giver of life in Christ Jesus!

Perhaps no text in the New Testament makes that more clear than 2 Peter 1:3-4:

His divine power has granted to us all things that pertain to life and godliness, through the knowledge of him who called us to his own glory and excellence, by which he has granted to us his precious and very great promises, so that through them you may become partakers of the divine nature, having escaped from the corruption that is in the world because of sinful desire.

No one else may know your needs, but God does. He is aware of what it will take to supply every necessity for you. Will you trust him to do that? Most of all, will you trust him to provide you with the salvation that comes only through his Son, Jesus Christ? If you are a Christian, you continue to have spiritual needs, needs for God's grace and power to face trials, to overcome temptations, to bring your life into obedience to Christ. Everything you need to walk with God, he will supply: 'His divine power has granted to us all things that pertain to life and godliness' (2 Pet. 1:3). Cast yourself on the Lord Jesus and discover the joy and peace of finding everything in him.

24

No Falling Words
Joshua 21:43-45

*Not one word of all the good promises that the LORD had made to the
house of Israel had failed; all came to pass.* (Josh. 21:45)

I n 1976, as America celebrated the 200th anniversary of its
war for independence, another battle was being fought across
the country. It was the battle for the Bible. That same year
Harold Lindsell published a book by that title. *The Battle for the
Bible*[1] chronicled some of the major, then current conflicts in
denominations and seminaries over the inerrancy of Scripture.
Those conflicts gave rise the very next year to the International
Council on Biblical Inerrancy. Over a nine-year period the Council
held three summits and produced three major statements the most
famous of which is the 'Chicago Statement on Biblical Inerrancy'.
Men such as Lindsell, James Montgomery Boice, J. I. Packer, and
John MacArthur fought valiantly for the truth of God's word, and
the 'Chicago Statement' became the benchmark for expressing and
defending the truthfulness of the Bible. For evangelicalism, the
question of the inerrancy of Scripture was a settled issue. God had
spoken and his word is without error. The battle for the Bible was
over. Or so we thought.

[1] Harold Lindsell, *The Battle for the Bible* (Grand Rapids: Zondervan, 1976).

315

About thirty years later, in 2005, Peter Enns published a book entitled *Inspiration and Incarnation: Evangelicals and the Problem of the Old Testament.*[1] In that work, Enns did not set out on a full frontal attack against inerrancy, but he raised enough questions and proposed enough dubious solutions to set off a clash, this time mainly in Reformed circles and at Westminster Theological Seminary, Philadelphia. Though not the full-scale battle of the 1970s, this skirmish for the Scriptures nonetheless cast doubt on the reliability of what God had spoken. While we may have thought that the battle for the Bible was over, it should come as no surprise that the church was once again engaged in a conflict over the reliability and inerrancy of the Scriptures. We should have learned from the history of Israel that the battle for the Bible is a recurring conflict.

The background to the events recorded in Joshua was a battle for the Bible. That battle did not play out in seminary classrooms or denominational assemblies but at Kadesh, in the wilderness of Paran, when the spies reported back to Moses (Num. 13:25-33). You can phrase it in many ways, but the spies report boils down to this, 'You cannot really rely upon what God has said. You cannot believe everything in the Bible.' That day Israel lost its battle for the Bible. With the exception of Joshua and Caleb, the nation failed to uphold and honour God's truth when it failed to take possession of the land.

Another generation would pass before Israel entered the land, but now as we reach the later chapters of Joshua, God has brought his people into Canaan, given them a series of victories, and they now possess the land of promise. Joshua 21:43-45 summarizes those victories and serves as the climactic text of the entire book. These three, brief verses reveal that Israel received all that God promised them, the conquest of the Canaanites and the possession of their land, because he swore his promise to the patriarchs and kept every word.

That was an important message for God's people 3,500 years ago, and it is still an important message for the church today because as this beam of light from the Old Testament shines into the New it

---

[1] Peter Enns, *Inspiration and Incarnation: Evangelicals and the Problem of the Old Testament* (Grand Rapids: Baker, 2005).

is refracted by the cross of Christ. It is magnified and intensified by the cross. Its essential theology does not change and its application reaches its new covenant fullness in Jesus. What is that full, new covenant message? As a believer, you have everything God has to offer in Christ because he is faithful to his word.

A place to call home

This biblical message ties together both Old Testament promise and New Testament fulfilment to reveal to everyone who has faith in Christ what the believing soul possesses in him. In Christ every believer has a place to call home. That is the emphasis of verse 43, 'Thus the LORD gave to Israel all the land that he swore to give to their fathers. And they took possession of it, and they settled there.' This verse is a précis of the entire book of Joshua and contains several of the key theological terms found in the book: *give*, *swore*, and *possess*. Here we find the land covenant expressed in the broadest possible terms. The Lord gave the land to Israel; this is the same land he swore to their fathers; Israel possessed this land and lived in it. As Matthew Henry so aptly stated,

> We have here the conclusion of this whole matter, the foregoing history summed up, and, to make it appear the more bright, compared with the promise of which it was the full accomplishment. God's word and his works mutually illustrate each other. The performance makes the promise appear very true and the promise makes the performance appear very kind.[1]

The promise to the fathers that God would give the land of Canaan to Abraham and his descendants, occurs a number of times in the Pentateuch. For example, when Abram and Lot's herdsmen could not get along, Abram suggested that the two go in separate directions in order to avoid further strife. Lot settled among the cities of the valley, while Abram camped in the land of Canaan, a stranger, a wanderer with no permanent home. Lot chose the well-watered Jordan Valley, yet he ended up losing everything when God destroyed Sodom and Gomorrah (see Gen. 19:23-29). Abram, however, received a promise:

[1] Henry, *Comm.*, 2:100.

The LORD said to Abram, after Lot had separated from him, 'Lift up your eyes and look from the place where you are, northward and southward and eastward and westward, for all the land that you see I will give to you and to your offspring forever. I will make your offspring as the dust of the earth, so that if one can count the dust of the earth, your offspring also can be counted. Arise, walk through the length and the breadth of the land, for I will give it to you.' So Abram moved his tent and came and settled by the oaks of Mamre, which are at Hebron, and there he built an altar to the LORD (Gen. 13:14-18).[1]

The promise given to Abraham and confirmed as a covenant in the most solemn terms was later repeated to his son Isaac and his grandson Jacob. Isaac fled to Gerar during a famine,

And the LORD appeared to him and said, 'Do not go down to Egypt; dwell in the land of which I shall tell you. Sojourn in this land, and I will be with you and will bless you, for to you and to your offspring I will give all these lands, and I will establish the oath that I swore to Abraham your father' (Gen. 26:2-3).

Later, when Isaac sent Jacob away from home to protect him from the revenge of his brother, Esau, Isaac blessed his son and said, '"May [the LORD] give the blessing of Abraham to you and to your offspring with you, that you may take possession of the land of your sojournings that God gave to Abraham"' (Gen. 28:4)!

After receiving this blessing, Jacob left his family in Beersheba and travelled towards Haran. He found a place out of doors to sleep that night, and as he slept God appeared to him in a dream. In his dream, Jacob saw a ladder extending from earth to heaven, 'And behold, the LORD stood above it and said, "I am the LORD, the God of Abraham your father and the God of Isaac. The land on which you lie I will give to you and to your offspring"' (Gen. 28:13).[2]

Israel took possession of and settled the land promised to their fathers. Those simple words from verse 43 capture all the major events of Joshua 6-21. The verb *to possess* occurs twenty-nine times in

[1] In Hebron, the very place that played a prominent role in Joshua as the inheritance of Caleb (14:13-15) and later a city of the Levites (21:11), Abram pitched his tent and worshipped God.

[2] For further references see Num. 11:12; 14:16, 23; Deut. 1:8, 35; 6:10.

the book. That statistic in and of itself is not particularly significant until you realize that averages over one occurrence per chapter. The concentration of these occurrences is, as we would expect, in chapters 13-17 where we find the record of Israel's inheritance. God gave the land to his people because it was his intention that they possess it. It was to be theirs and not belong to another. And they settled there. They lived in the land. At long last their wanderings were over. They no longer pulled up stakes and packed away tents as they trekked from one place to another. They now had permanent dwellings in houses they did not build but that God graciously provided (cf. Deut. 6:10-11).

God never intended the land of Canaan to be an end in-and-of itself. Abraham set out on a journey toward Canaan because he was looking, ultimately, for a heavenly city, an established and secure city whose architect and builder was God himself (Heb. 11:10). In the book of Revelation, the ultimate fulfilment of God's plan arrives in the new heavens and the new earth (Rev. 21:1-8), and into the midst of this paradise descends a city, the new Jerusalem, the church prepared for its Saviour (see 3:12; 21:2, 9-27). It is the new heavens and new earth that Abraham and his spiritual children inherit. God's promise extended far beyond land bounded by the Euphrates and the river of Egypt. The promise to Abraham and his offspring was 'that he would be heir of the world' (Rom. 4:13).

What Abraham searched for he and every believer has in Jesus—a home in heaven. But we do not have to wait until we die or Christ returns to enjoy our home. While the land of Israel points us to the new heavens and the new earth, it does so because it first points us to Jesus. He is the place we call home. Paul expressed that truth with the little phrase 'in Christ'. Christ is your dwelling place. You may not have grown up in a loving home. Your home now may be far from peaceful. But Christ is your true home where you are safe and secure.

A rest to enjoy
As we look further at the text you can see that you not only have a place to call home, you also have a rest to enjoy. 'And the LORD gave them rest on every side just as he had sworn to their fathers. Not one

of all their enemies had withstood them, for the LORD had given all their enemies into their hands' (verse 44).

Rest for Israel did not mean no more skirmishes. Judges 1 lists the Canaanites that still lived in the land, and the conquest of Canaan continued after the death of Joshua (see Judg. 1:1-26). Rest did mean, however, that the major hostilities, the major military campaigns and battles were over. The war had been won even though pockets of resistance continued to fight. There was rest in principle and rest largely in experience, though read in a larger context some tension continued to exist. Despite this tension,[1] the theme of rest encapsulates the message of the entire book.[2] When Joshua charged the eastern tribes to fight with their brothers in the land, he reminded them of Moses's words, 'The LORD your God is providing you a place of rest and will give you this land' (1:13). As the book draws to a close and Joshua addressed Israel's leaders, the author set the context as, 'A long time afterward, when the LORD had given rest to Israel from all their surrounding enemies, and Joshua was old and well advanced in years ...' (23:1).

From giving rest to the eastern tribes (1:15) to the priests resting their feet in the Jordan (3:13) and Israel setting up a memorial cairn where they first rested in the land (4:3, 8), to 'resting' Rahab and her family safely outside of Jericho (6:23),[3] the goal of the book has been

---

[1] McConville notes that with regard to this tension within the book, 'The discrepancy between the perspective of total conquest by virtue of God's gift and that of untidy, incomplete possession is such that it is most easily read as a feature intended to catch the reader's eye. It may be a device to convey the message that reality is far from ideal and that the call to live before Yahweh will have to be played out in a plural situation of conflicted loyalties.' McConville and Williams, *Joshua*, 83. Woudstra notes that, 'The book of Joshua views the conquest of Canaan as both complete and incomplete. In 23:4-5 these two lines run side by side, an indication that the author means them to be equally valid, although the emphasis on the completeness of the Conquest is predominant.' Woudstra, *Book of Joshua*, 314.

[2] 'The Old Testament understands "rest" as the gracious gift of God to his people. Against the background of a long journey and intense warfare (so ch. 21), it connotes a sense of relief from frightening threats, of safe, happy arrival, of realizing long-held dreams, of coming into unexpected wealth, of finally being "home." That is what Yahweh's faithfulness in settling Israel in its Promised Land means to Israel.' Hubbard, *Joshua*, 465.

[3] The verse reads, 'So the young men who had been spies went in and brought

to bring the Lord's people to the place where they can settle to live peacefully and obediently under the care of their merciful God. And this is what the Lord has done—just as he swore to their fathers.

Another way to express the fact that they had rest on every side is that 'not one of all their enemies had withstood them, for the LORD had given all their enemies into their hands' (verse 44). God had promised this all the way back in chapter 1 when he said, 'No man shall be able to stand before you all the days of your life. Just as I was with Moses, so I will be with you. I will not leave you or forsake you' (verse 5). None of Israel's enemies could stand. Note the way verse 44 stresses this truth. The expression 'all their enemies' occurs twice. Why could they not stand? Because the Lord *gave* them into Israel's hand.[1]

God had promised this through Moses: 'And he will give their kings into your hand, and you shall make their name perish from under heaven. No one shall be able to stand against you until you have destroyed them' (Deut. 7:24). This point was also the heart of the report the spies brought back from Jericho: 'And they said to Joshua, "Truly the LORD has given all the land into our hands. And also, all the inhabitants of the land melt away because of us"' (Josh. 2:24). The text underscores the truth that God fought for Israel.[2] From the first battle at Jericho to the full conquest of Canaan, the Lord destroyed the enemies of his people. He handed them over to his conquering band. This is yet another occurrence of the verb 'to give'. Israel deserved nothing, earned nothing, and stood as a debtor to grace alone.

As a result of God's grace, Israel settled peacefully into the promised rest. But this was not an uninterruptible peace. Rest existed in principle but not always in practice. The Lord allowed

---

out Rahab and her father and mother and brothers and all who belonged to her. And they brought all her relatives and put them outside the camp of Israel.' The key words 'put them' (ESV, NIV) are also translated as 'placed' (NASB) or 'set them' (RSV, NRSV) translate the hiphil of *nuah* which means 'to provide rest'.

[1] Note once again the use of the verb *nathan*, 'give'. This is, without doubt, one of the most significant terms in the entire book.

[2] This theme appears in a number of places but especially in chapter 10 (6:2; 8:1, 7; 10:10-11, 14, 19, 42; 11:8).

that for many reasons, but one of them was to demonstrate to us the nature of the Christian life. Since we have been justified by faith, we have peace with God through Christ (Rom. 5:1). By faith we have entered into the rest that there is in Jesus. The hostility and warfare between our souls and God has ceased. But do we always experience and enjoy that rest? Are we not often unsettled, even frantic in our hearts? Though you may paste a smile on your face, are there not times when your internal world is full of chaos? That experience is not so different from Israel's.

How do we get our standing in Christ, our objective rest, operating in the melee of our day-to-day world? By faith. Paul's counsel to the Colossians was, 'let the peace of Christ rule in your hearts, to which indeed you were called in one body. And be thankful' (Col. 3:15). We are justified by faith, and as we put on the new man, the new, resurrected self in Christ, we are to let the peace that comes from the gospel rule in our hearts. It all happens by faith. If the most important issue in your life has been settled, if your sins are forgiven through the Lord Jesus, then ask God to let the rest and peace of the gospel invade your daily life. Ask him for the faith to trust him in the midst of the chaos you often experience in life and feel in your heart.

A word to trust

The chapter concludes with what may well be identified as the theme text of the entire book: 'Not one word of all the good promises that the LORD had made to the house of Israel had failed; all came to pass' (verse 45). In Jesus you not only have a place to call home and a rest to enjoy, you have the Bible, a word you can trust.

You can rely upon everything that God says because he has sworn an oath as to its truthfulness and pledged himself to its fidelity. If you look back at verses 43 and 44, then you will see that the stress of those two verses forms the prelude to the conclusion of verse 45. The land that was given to Israel is the land that was *sworn* to the patriarchs (verse 43). The rest God gave Israel was the rest he had *sworn* to their forefathers (verse 44). To *swear* means to make a promise and invoke an oath with it, usually in the name of God.

When you swear a promise, you are calling upon God to judge you if it is not true or if you do not fulfil your obligations to which you have committed yourself.

You and I may say, 'Let us meet for coffee on Thursday at 2:00', and promise that we will see each other then. But one of us may have something come up so that we have to cancel or reschedule that meeting. To not meet may be disappointing, but one of us could not sue the other for breach of contract. We did not swear to each other or enter into a legally-binding agreement that we would keep the appointment. When you swear an oath in court, however, it is an altogether different matter. In that context, you promise to tell the truth and invoke upon yourself just penalties if you fail to do so. By swearing to the fathers of Israel that he would give them the land, God called a curse down upon himself if he failed to follow through with what he had promised.

We see this dramatically played out in Genesis 15 when God made his covenant with Abraham. The Lord commanded him to take a heifer, a female goat, a ram, a turtle-dove, and a young pigeon, to slaughter them, and to cut their carcasses in half (verses 9-10). Abraham then took the pieces and placed them in two piles. As darkness began to fall, he fell into a deep sleep, and God spoke to him. The Lord told Abraham that though his descendants would live as slaves in a foreign land for four centuries, he would judge the nation that oppressed them, deliver them, and bring them back to the promised land. This was the oath that God swore (see verses 13-16).

Then, when the sun went down, a smoking fire pot and a flaming torch passed between the two piles of carcasses (verse 17). That was the final step in the covenant-making process: 'On that day the LORD made a covenant with Abram, saying, "To your offspring I give this land, from the river of Egypt to the great river, the river Euphrates, the land of the Kenites, the Kenizzites, the Kadmonites, the Hittites, the Perizzites, the Rephaim, the Amorites, the Canaanites, the Girgashites and the Jebusites"' (verses 18-21).

What did these strange actions signify? In the Ancient Near East, passing between two piles of slain animals was an integral part of covenant making (cf. Jer. 34:18-20).[1] As an individual and the person with whom he made the covenant passed between the carcasses, both invoked upon themselves a curse if either broke his side of the agreement. By these actions each said, 'May it happen to me as it has happened to these animals if I do not fulfil my obligations.' Scholars typically refer to this as a self-maledictory oath.[2]

In the covenant-making ceremony of Genesis 15, who passed between the carcasses? Was it Abraham? No, he was fast asleep. A smoking fire pot and a flaming torch, physical depictions of the presence of God, passed between them.[3] In other words, the Lord took all the obligations of the covenant upon himself. He swore it with an oath and confirmed it in the ceremony.

With whom did God make his covenant that day? With Abraham, but also with all the children of Abraham, those who share the promise by faith. God took upon himself the full responsibility of the covenant and called down the curse upon himself should its stipulations be violated. That day God vowed that he would keep his word, but he also undertook to bear the penalty for any disobedience or unfaithfulness to the covenant. The Abrahamic covenant finds its ultimate fulfilment in the Lord Jesus Christ and his death on the cross. We are covenant breakers, but instead of bringing down the curse of death on us, it fell on Christ. He 'redeemed us from the curse of the law by becoming a curse for us' (Gal. 3:13; cf. Deut. 21:23). The Son of God bore our penalty so that we might be forgiven (1 Pet. 2:24).

God swore an oath to keep his promise, and he kept it (cf. Heb. 6:13-18). 'Not one word of all the good promises that the LORD had made to the house of Israel had failed; all came to pass' (verse 45). *Failed* is an accurate translation, but it does not quite convey the subtlety of the text. The phrase is *not a word fell*—not *fail* but *fell*.

---

[1] This is the first occurrence of the Hebrew expression 'to make [*carat*, to cut] a covenant'.

[2] For more information, see the helpful discussion in Robertson, *Christ of the Covenants*, 7-15 and Gentry and Wellum, *Kingdom Through Covenant*, 248-58.

[3] References to smoke/cloud and fire as emblematic of the divine presence occur earlier in the Pentateuch (Exod. 13:21-22; 14:24; 40:34-38; Num. 14:14; cf. Neh. 9:12, 19).

This distinction is essential to see the play on words between verses 44 and 45. None of Israel's enemies were able to stand; they *all fell*. But every one of God's promises stood the test of time and trial. Not one of them *fell*. Scripture never slips or stumbles. That truth is encapsulated in this brief paragraph in the word *all*. It occurs six times in these three verses. It begins with *all the land* and ends with *all coming to pass*—*all* the land given, *all* the enemies defeated, *all* the promises kept.

In the last phrase of the verse, all came to pass, Joshua 'speaks concretely about the word of the Lord'.[1] The author wrote 'it all entered' or 'it all came'. It was as though the good word of God marched into the heart of the nation's life, took charge, and fulfilled its purposes. Every promise of God came to Israel. A similar expression occurs in Jeremiah 17:15. The people mocked the prophet and said, 'Where is the word of the LORD? Let it come!' The word of God is something that *comes*. It not only comes to pass because it is true, but it comes—and will come again—in the person of Jesus Christ, the living Word of God (John 1:1).

God was completely faithful to his word and it echoed down through the ages in the praise of his people. When Solomon dedicated the temple, he kneeled, he prayed, then he rose to bless the people and said, 'Blessed be the LORD who has given rest to his people Israel, according to all that he promised. Not one word has failed of all his good promise, which he spoke by Moses his servant' (1 Kings 8:56).

In Nehemiah 9, the exiles who returned to Israel confessed their sins to God, but they prefaced their confession with the acknowledgement of God's faithfulness.

> You are the LORD, you alone. You have made heaven, the heaven of heavens, with all their host, the earth and all that is on it, the seas and all that is in them; and you preserve all of them; and the host of heaven worships you. You are the LORD, the God who chose Abram and brought him out of Ur of the Chaldeans and gave him the name Abraham. You found his heart faithful before you, and made with him the covenant to give to his offspring the land of

[1] Woudstra, *Book of Joshua*, 315, n.2.

the Canaanite, the Hittite, the Amorite, the Perizzite, the Jebusite, and the Girgashite. And you have kept your promise, for you are righteous (Neh. 9:6-8).[1]

The truthfulness and reliability of God's word applies to all of the Bible, not just the promises of the Abrahamic covenant. Jesus affirmed that the Scripture cannot be broken (John 10:35). Commenting on Jesus' assertion of the Bible's veracity Presbyterian theologian B. B. Warfield wrote,

> It is impossible for the Scripture to be annulled, its authority to be withstood, or denied ... What we have here, is therefore, the strongest possible assertion of the indefectible authority of Scripture; precisely what is true of Scripture is that it 'cannot be broken'.[2]

The inerrancy and authority of the Bible gives the believer the greatest source of confidence. What the Bible says, God says. The Scriptures bear his stamp of authenticity. They attest to themselves, and the Holy Spirit bears witness to what he has inspired to convince us that we can take our stand with God's word. In the battle for the Bible, the Bible itself is the greatest weapon because it is living, powerful, and sharper than any two-edged sword (Heb. 4:12).

In the closing words of his exposition of Joshua 21 Matthew Henry wrote,

> The inviolable truth of God's promise, and the performance of it to the utmost, are what all the saints have been ready to bear their testimony to; and, if in any thing the performance has seemed to come short, they have been as ready to own that they themselves must bear all the blame.[3]

We know that God keeps all of his promises because he sent the

---

[1] Like Israel, the faithfulness of God should fill our prayers and praise as well. That is why so much of our prayer should be praying the Scriptures. Christians often find themselves at a loss as to what to pray. You can ask God to heal the sick and bless the missionaries, but for your prayer life to go deeper, pray the Scriptures. Rehearse the promises, relish the psalms, plead with God to do what he has said he will do.

[2] Benjamin B. Warfield, *The Inspiration and Authority of the Bible* (Phillipsburg, NJ: P&R, 1948), 139, 140.

[3] Henry, *Comm.* 2:100-01.

Lord Jesus. 'All the promises of God find their Yes in him. That is why it is through him that we utter our Amen to God for his glory' (1 Cor. 1:20).

In every heart there rages a battle for the Bible. Will you believe God or not? Will you embrace the promises or not? Will you consider God to be true and deem every counter claim to be a lie? Will you embrace every promise in Christ as the 'Yes' of God and through Jesus say, 'Amen' to God for his glory?

25

We Are God's People
Joshua 22:1-34

---

*The people of Reuben and the people of Gad called the altar Witness,
'For,' they said, 'it is a witness between us that the LORD is God.' (Josh.
22:34)*

Nothing unites people like a common enemy. That unity
might arise from a light-hearted cause such as rallying
around one's favourite sports team, or against a rival of our
favourite team. Of course unity may have a more serious reason
behind it, such as that of the allied forces as they banded together
to combat the powers of fascism during World War II. It is also
true, as is evident in Joshua 22, that nothing can divide people like
natural barriers. Rivers, valleys, and mountain ranges, especially
in the ancient world, helped to create diverse cultures as different
regions and resources gave rise to varied industries, clothing styles,
sports, and cuisine. Israel had been united in their campaign against
the Canaanites, but now they would be physically divided by the
Jordan River.

The Jordan proved to be a culture-shaping barrier. The two and a
half tribes who had established their homes on its eastern bank were
already distinguished as having large herds. Their culture would,
no doubt, be dominated by their occupation as shepherds. Yet even
though Israel was divided by a natural, geographical marker, the

people believed in and lived under the same covenant promises. In spite of the differences that might develop in the future, the variations of diet, dress, cultural and professional pursuits, the transjordanian tribes were fundamentally one with their brothers who lived in the west. That truth lies at the heart of this very unusual chapter.

With the battles for conquest and the land distribution now behind them, the eastern tribes of Reuben, Gad, and half of Manasseh were allowed to return home. They had obeyed the Lord and fulfilled their obligation to fight with their brothers until the land of Canaan was under Israel's control (see Num. 32:20-22; Deut. 3:18-20; Josh. 1:12-18). The early events of chapter 22, therefore, come as no surprise. What is surprising, however, is the news that on their way home the eastern tribes built an altar.

When the rest of Israel first heard about this altar, they thought it was an act of disloyalty that threatened the unity of God's people. What many perceived to be an act of blatant apostasy, however, turned out to be an act of orthodox and whole-hearted devotion. How did that happen? The altar, instead of being an alternative place of worship, was a witness that pointed to the one true altar and reminded all Israel that they found their unity in the one place of sacrifice. What Israel demonstrated by their actions and expressed by their confession is an abiding reality for God's covenant people throughout the ages, whether they lived then on the east bank or west bank of the Jordan under the old covenant or now throughout the world under God's new covenant in Christ. The Lord's people find their true and lasting unity as brothers and sisters in the one place of sacrifice, the cross of our Lord Jesus.

Expressions of unity

Joshua chapter 22 begins with an emphasis on several expressions of unity found in verses 1-9. After summoning the tribes together, Joshua addressed them and commended their faithful obedience to both Moses and himself (verses 1-2). The opening words of the chapter contain a kind of 'farewell to arms' as Joshua praises the transjordanian troops for their faithful service to Israel. They had gone into the land of Canaan to help their brothers conquer the land of promise and now, in the first six verses, their leader acknowledges their loyalty. They had obeyed all that they were commanded to do. They did not allow their brothers to go over the Jordan River alone. They kept faith with them, accompanied them, and fought with them. Here was a band of brave men who had earned this commendation from their general. But more than merely following Moses and Joshua, these men have kept 'the charge of the LORD [their] God' (verse 3). Their loyalty bore the marks of being more than national fervour; it was an expression of their spirituality. When we support our brothers and sisters in Christ, we not only demonstrate our love for them but our love for God as well.

Obedience to Moses, to Joshua, and to the Lord are linked together in these verses because each act of submission entailed the others. The eastern tribes could not have obeyed Moses without also obeying Joshua and the Lord, nor could they have obeyed the Lord without also obeying Moses and Joshua. Like all armies, Israel had a chain of command, with God as the ultimate authority. If the president sends troops to war, he passes down orders to generals who pass them down to majors who pass them down to colonels and on down the chain of command they go. If a private refuses to march into battle, he disobeys more than his platoon leader. He disobeys the president himself. Obedience to God requires that we submit to those whom he has placed in authority over us in the home (Eph. 5:22-6:4), in the church (Heb. 13:17), and in society (Rom. 13:1-7).

Joshua then shifted topics from the tribes' past obedience to their future in the land across the Jordan (verse 4). With the conquest now over, the western tribes had achieved rest in the land just as God had promised, and the responsibility of the eastern tribes toward their brothers had been fulfilled. They should return home to their tents in the land Moses allotted to them on the other side of the river (verse 4).

The tribes must remember, however, that they have a continuing obligation to obey the Lord: 'Only be very careful to observe the commandment and the law that Moses the servant of the LORD commanded you, to love the LORD your God, and to walk in all his ways and to keep his commandments and to cling to him and to serve him with all your heart and with all your soul' (verse 5). *Only*, first and foremost be very careful to observe the commandment and the law that Moses gave you.[1] The emphasis of verse 5 draws attention to the duty that should be uppermost in the people's mind—careful obedience to God's word. Scripture requires this kind of diligent attention from everyone so that we might know what it is that God requires of us. Slipshod attention to the Bible will not result in an obedient and faithful life. For that reason the psalmist prayed, 'Teach me, O LORD, the way of your statutes; and I will keep it to the end. Give me understanding, that I may keep your law and observe it with my whole heart' (Psa. 119:33-34).

What does this kind of diligent obedience look like in practical terms? Joshua answered that question with five infinitives: (1) to love the Lord your God, (2) to walk in all his ways, (3) to keep his commandments, (4) to cling to him, and (5) to serve him with all your heart and with all your soul (verse 5). 'Joshua's words in v. 5 are passionate, and they capture the heart of the chapter's message about faithfulness and loyalty.'[2]

At the conclusion of his address, Joshua blessed the tribes, sent them away, and they went to their tents (verse 6). In this benediction, Joshua's final act recorded in Scripture, he pronounced all of the blessings and benefits God had for them. By his words he announced the power and goodness of God to them and bade them to receive and enjoy all that the Lord had for them. It was right for them to return to their homes and families, and they went with the blessing of God.

Verses 7 through 9 report another facet of Joshua's address. As the events played out at Shiloh, these verses fit somewhere between verses 5 and 6, but they are set apart to draw attention to another aspect of Israel's unity. The first half of verse 7 simply restates the fact that the tribe of Manasseh did not all live on the same side of the Jordan. Moses had given half of the tribe a possession in Bashan, the area known today as the Golan Heights, but the other half received their inheritance west of the river. They were, in the words of Robert

---

[1] The phrase 'only be very careful to observe' (*raq shimru meod la'sot*) summarizes the command Moses gave a number of times in Deuteronomy when he combined the verb *shamar* with the infinitive *la'sot*, 'to keep to do' or 'to observe to do' (Deut. 5:32; 6:3, 25; 8:1; 11:32; 12:1; 13:1; 15:5; 17:10; 24:8; 28:1, 15, 58; 31:12; 32:46).

[2] Howard, *Joshua*, 403-04.

Hubbard, 'a bridge people'.¹ Given this situation, when Joshua
blessed them and sent them away (verse 6), he instructed them to
take the spoils of war that they had obtained and divide them with
their brothers (verse 8). The livestock, silver, gold, bronze, iron, and
clothing that all of Manasseh had taken from plundering the cities
of Canaan were to be divided so that each half of the tribe was
allowed to keep its fair share. With these instructions, the eastern
tribes returned home. The text does not state but appears to assume
their obedience. After dividing the spoils of war, they departed from
Shiloh to return to their own land, the land of Gilead. The eastern
tribes had both stood with and shared with their brothers in the
east. The expressions of unity that we find in the first part of this
chapter are all very practical, tangible demonstrations rooted in a
personal relationship with the Lord himself. The primary factor in
Reuben, Gad, and East Manasseh's willingness to fight in Canaan
was their love for, and hence their obedience to, the Lord himself.

Obedience begins in the heart, and love is its motivator. Israel's
first obligation is also ours. Jesus said, 'If you love me, you will keep
my commandments' (John 14:15). The tribes were also to walk in all
of God's ways. To 'walk' is to conduct your life along a certain 'path',
a certain 'route', that reflects the character and revelation of God.
When you walk this path, you keep his commandments and obey
him.² That is the third infinitive Joshua listed. The emotional and
volitional come to the fore with the fourth requirement to cling to
God. When we cling to the Lord we do not merely adhere to a set
of ideas about God, as important as correct doctrine is. To cling to
him is a personal commitment of oneself to hold to him no matter
what may attempt to drive us away. To cling to God is an expression

¹ 'With one foot on each side of the Jordan, Manasseh comprises a "bridge
people," a tribe whose very geography symbolizes Israel's unity. They also embody
the chapter's central dilemma—the tension between geographical separation and
religious solidarity.' Hubbard, *Joshua*, 484.
² 'The figure of walking in *the way* of the Lord is widely used in Deuteronomy
and elsewhere (Deut. 5:33; Psa. 27:11). No mere externalities are expected, for
keeping the *commandments* must go hand in hand with holding *firmly* to the Lord
and with a service to him which involves the *whole heart and soul*.' Woudstra, *Book
of Joshua*, 317.

of trust. Finally, we are called to serve (verse 5). Service involves doing things for God, participating in his work, striving to further his cause, and to support and help his people. But service must also include worship. Our primary duty is to praise and honour God, and as his children it is our greatest privilege.

Joshua's five-point summation is an expression of what Jesus identified as the greatest commandment. A scholar of Old Testament law attempted to test Jesus and asked him, 'Teacher, which is the great commandment in the Law?' Jesus replied, 'You shall love the Lord your God with all your heart and with all your soul and with all your mind. This is the great and first commandment. And a second is like it: You shall love your neighbour as yourself' (Matt. 22:35-39).

The Bible never sets up a dichotomy between loving God and loving others. Jesus did not present his inquiring scholar with God *or* neighbour but with God *and* neighbour. This is the way unity works—it begins with love to God, and then it spreads. The transjordanian tribes loved the Lord and expressed love to their brothers in very tangible ways, and that is the way unity should manifest itself. When we start to talk about the unity of God's people, it is often tempting to begin to think in terms of organizational structures. 'Let us form an alliance of churches or a fellowship or an ecumenical council!' We think if we can rally people to join an association, then we can show the world that we are unified. But would it not be better if we just started loving each other? Of course visible unity is important. That is one reason I am a Presbyterian rather than a member of an independent church. But external organization is not the heart of unity. The best expressions of Christian unity are those in-the-trenches bonds that tell our brothers and sisters that no matter what they are going through, no matter how tough the going or hard the trial, we are there for them. We say to them, in essence, what the tribes said to each other: 'We will stand with you, fight for you, and serve you for your good and God's glory.'

If Jesus Christ has made us his children by suffering for our salvation, then we should count it all joy to be called to enter into his sufferings for the sake of the church, our family in Christ. The eastern tribes had done this very thing. They did not sit on the banks of the Jordan shouting, 'Have fun storming Canaan!' True Christian unity is not fully expressed by standing in church on Sunday morning and singing

> Blest be the tie that binds
> Our hearts in Christian love ...

It is seen in the dark, lonely hours of depression or in the emergency room or at a sick child's bedside when another believer is there to comfort, to pray, and to wait on God with you.

A perceived threat to unity

The eastern tribes had demonstrated their devotion in real and remarkable ways. But on their way home they built an altar, and it immediately became a perceived threat to unity. Reuben, Gad, and the half-tribe of Manasseh built their altar on the river's western bank before they crossed the Jordan. It was not just any altar but a large and imposing one. The text emphasizes how striking it was by saying, 'They built an altar, an altar of great appearance' (verse 10).

Word of this new, impressive altar soon reached the rest of Israel. The eastern tribes had built an altar 'at the frontier of the land of Canaan, in the region about the Jordan, on the side that belongs to the people of Israel' (verse 11).[1] As soon as the rest of Israel heard about the altar, they assembled their troops at Shiloh in order to pursue and fight with the eastern tribes (verse 12). Shiloh had become the centralized place of worship for Israel in Joshua 18:1. Another altar would be a rival altar and thus a sure sign of apostasy. It would have been a violation of the laws of Leviticus 17:8-9 and Deuteronomy 13:12-15. For all intents and purposes, it appeared that Reuben, Gad and East Manasseh had quickly turned away from

[1] The exact location of the altar is difficult to pinpoint. It may be, however, that the term translated *in the region about* in the ESV (*gelilot*) may be a proper noun (*Geliloth*). If so, it would appear to refer to Gilgal which was a very important place for Israel at the beginning of the conquest (4:19, 20; 5:1-12). Howard takes a definite position on the translation as a proper noun and comments, 'The tribes arrived at Geliloth, near the Jordan, which appears to have been the site of Gilgal, the place where they had first entered the land and set up a pillar of memorial stones and circumcised the nation (4:19-20; 5:9-10). At this place significant in the nations' history, the Transjordan tribes built a large altar.' *Joshua*, 406.

following the Lord. What could this new altar mean but that the eastern tribes were engaged in a competing version of worshipping the Lord, or worse yet, the worship of foreign gods.

In response to the news of this innovative altar, the western tribes, rather than barging in with swords gleaming, sent Phinehas, the son of Eleazar the priest, and ten leaders from the other tribes, identified as 'chiefs … every one of them the head of a family among the clans of Israel', to confront the eastern tribes about their apparent disloyalty to the Lord (verses 13-15).

As soon as the delegation arrived, they initiated their confrontation by asking a question (verse 16). It appears as a single question in our English Bibles, but it really contains a series of questions: What are you doing? Why are you turning away from the Lord by building this rival altar? Why are you in rebellion? The language is strong and direct. To commit a breach of faith or to be in rebellion against the Lord is to be an apostate, to turn away from the Lord and repudiate him as your hope. The letter to the Hebrews calls this kind of transgression a sin from which it is impossible to recover, a sin for which there is no repentance (Heb. 6:4-6).

Having raised this single-yet-multifaceted question, the delegation prosecuted its inquisition further with a forceful rhetorical question: 'Have we not had enough of the sin at Peor' (verse 17)? This question would take the eastern tribes back in their minds to the not-too-distant past when Israel committed heinous sins at a place called Shittim. The false prophet Balaam was unable to call a curse down on God's people, but what he could not accomplish by speech the Moabites achieved by seduction. Some of the men of Israel began to commit immorality with the women of Moab and also began to worship Baal, just like the Moabites. God sent a plague to judge them, and 24,000 died (see Num. 25:1-9).

'Have we not had enough of that sin?' they asked. 'Even now we have not cleansed ourselves from it.' The effects of the sin at Peor were so devastating that they continued to trouble Israel to that very day. Why would that be? Because no sin is ever a matter of the moment. While a sin may be committed at a certain point in time, the effects of sin are never confined to that instant. Sin has residual effects. Its impact lingers. Had Israel not sinned enough that they had to go and add to their transgressions by establishing a competing sanctuary? If the eastern tribes played the rebel today, then tomorrow God would be angry with the entire nation (verse 18b). Just as you can never sin for the moment without any consequences, so too you can never sin alone without affecting others.

This point is further stressed in verse 19: 'If your land is unclean', they say, 'then live with us in the west.' God's tabernacle was in the west, and the ten western tribes were willing to give up part of their possessions in order to keep the eastern tribes from sinning. 'Only do not rebel against the LORD or make us as rebels by building for yourselves an altar other than the altar of the LORD our God' (verse 19). It was better for Reuben, Gad, and East Manasseh to give up their broad and fertile grazing lands than to turn against the Lord. Their spiritual well-being was more important than their financial prosperity. But note again the emphasis on the unity of God's people. If the eastern tribes rebel, what effect will it have on their brothers in the rest of Israel? In the words of the delegation, it will 'make us as rebels' as well.

That is also the point of verse 20 with its reference to Achan's sin. The delegation raised a second rhetorical question: 'Did not Achan break faith and wrath fall upon all the congregation?' Achan took the devoted things (see Josh. 7:1), but God's anger fell on the whole nation and resulted in the only defeat Israel suffered, the defeat at Ai (7:2-5). In case any doubt existed about this point, the end of verse 20 states it clearly: 'he did not perish alone for his iniquity'. You cannot confine sin to one moment or to one place. Sin has consequences. It shapes attitudes, deforms thought processes, and disrupts relationships. No one is ever left unscarred by sin. Even sins that we may commit only in our minds, sins such as lust, covetousness, or anger, leave their marks on our souls and harm others in the way we think about, act toward, or react to them.

Many years ago my uncle was on a camping trip in the mountains when he was bitten on his arm by a rattlesnake. He and his friends quickly used a belt to make a tourniquet. They tightened it around his arm and headed for town. If my uncle had said, 'No worries! It is just my arm. The rest of me is fine', he would have been a fool. He and everyone with him knew the seriousness of the situation. They knew that poison spreads quickly through the body and unless it is stopped it will kill you. Sin is like that. It gets into the circulatory system of a family or a church and spreads its deadly venom. If a tourniquet of repentance and confession before the Lord of mercy and grace is not applied quickly, the results can be fatal.

The preservation of unity

Sin has the full potential to disrupt and destroy the unity of believers, and that is exactly what appeared to be happening. The perceived threat turned out, however, to be an attempt to preserve the unity of Israel. That becomes clear in verses 21 and following. Once confronted with the seriousness of the situation, the eastern tribes responded to the delegation by saying, 'If it was in rebellion or in breach of faith against the LORD, do not spare us today for building an altar to turn away from following the LORD' (verses 22-23). To the seriousness of the situation, they respond with an equal seriousness: "The Mighty One, God, the LORD! The Mighty One, God, the LORD! He knows' (verse 22)! They use three names for the Lord and repeat them twice, not to take his name in vain, but to stress the sincerity and earnestness of their reply. The essence of their response is this: God knows what we were up to, and we want you to know as well. We did not build this altar as an act of rebellion. We did not build it for burnt offerings or grain offerings or peace offerings. If we had, then may the Lord himself deal with us in judgment.

The explanation continues in verses 24-29. Reuben, Gad, and East Manasseh did not stop with a mere denial of wrong doing. They went on to clarify the purpose of the altar—they built it for their children and the generations to come. They were concerned that a time may come when the Israelites on the western side of the Jordan may say to their descendants, 'What have you to do with the LORD, the God of Israel? For the LORD has made the Jordan a boundary between us and you, you people of Reuben and people of Gad. You have no portion in the LORD' (verses 24-25). Their concern was that in the future those kinds of statements would keep their children and their descendants from fearing God.

Once we read their explanation, we begin to see the motives that lay behind the altar's construction. They did not build it for burnt offerings or for sacrifices but as a witness between the current and the coming generations that the eastern tribes also worship the Lord. Should those in the west ever say, 'You have no portion in the LORD' (verse 27), those east of the Jordan could point to this altar. The altar that the tribes built was a copy of the one that stood at Shiloh, but its physical similarity served only as a reminder, not as a substitute, for the one place of sacrifice. These tribes understood that the altar outside the tabernacle was the only place to worship the Lord by offering blood, and it was that altar, the one that bound the tribes together, that ultimately mattered.

Believers still find their unity in the one place of sacrifice, a hill called Calvary. By dying for his people, Jesus unites all of them through his atoning work and glorious resurrection. True Christian unity is rooted in the gospel because the finished work of Christ is the basis and criteria for all Christian fellowship. When we look at other Christians, we love them and embrace them, not because they wear our denominational label or rally behind our pet causes, but because they were bought with the same price! When Jesus stretched out his arms on the cross, he not only reached out to bring God and man together, he also enfolded in those arms everyone for whom he was dying. We must not, therefore, push away or reject other Christians because they do not bear the same denominational label we do. The gospel—who Jesus Christ is and what he has done for our salvation—provides the foundation for us to embrace our fellow believers in him.

Christians have differences that keep us from all joining the same church, denomination, or association. No self-respecting Baptist church would ever call me to be its pastor because I sprinkle babies. But that does not mean I cut myself off from my Baptist friends. We may disagree among ourselves about the mode and subjects of baptism, the proper form of church government, or events surrounding the second coming of Christ. But if we are united in the Christ, the eternal Son of God who became man, and if we rely upon what he accomplished on the cross for our salvation, then we are truly one in the Saviour.

How do we preserve this unity within the body of Christ? We must keep building altars of witness. That does not mean that we go out into the churchyard and start piling up stones, but it does mean that we need to remind each other that the Lord is God and that Jesus' sacrifice is more valuable and more joyful and more hope-filled than anything in this world. Baptism and the Lord's Supper also serve as these means of witness. When someone is baptized, we have the opportunity to 'improve' our own baptism, to remember what our baptism symbolized and the way in which it united us to the visible body of Christ.[1] The same should be true when we sit at the Lord's table. As we take the bread, our thoughts should turn to the reality of the church which is one body because of its relationship to the Lord Jesus the head (see 1 Cor. 10:17).

The peace of unity

When Phinehas the priest and the other members of the delegation heard Reuben, Gad, and Manasseh's explanation, they were pleased. Phinehas said to them, 'Today we know that the LORD is in our midst, because you have not committed this breach of faith against the LORD. Now you have delivered the people of Israel from the hand of the LORD' (verse 31). The eastern tribes were not guilty of infidelity, and the other tribes were kept from unjustly punishing them. On both accounts, spiritually and physically, the people were

---

[1] *Westminster Larger Catechism*, Question 167: 'How is our baptism to be improved by us? Answer. The needful but much neglected duty of improving our baptism, is to be performed by us all our life long, especially in the time of temptation, and when we are present at the administration of it to others; by serious and thankful consideration of the nature of it, and of the ends for which Christ instituted it, the privileges and benefits conferred and sealed thereby, and our solemn vow made therein; by being humbled for our sinful defilement, our falling short of, and walking contrary to, the grace of baptism, and our engagements; by growing up to assurance of pardon of sin, and of all other blessings sealed to us in that sacrament; by drawing strength from the death and resurrection of Christ, into whom we are baptized, for the mortifying of sin, and quickening of grace; and by endeavouring to live by faith, to have our conversation in holiness and righteousness, as those that have therein given up their names to Christ; *and to walk in brotherly love, as being baptized by the same Spirit into one body* [emphasis added].'

preserved and their unity maintained so that it became evident that God was with them. Unity brings peace.

Phinehas and the chiefs of the tribes returned to Canaan (presumably Shiloh) and reported their findings. The western tribes rejoiced at the news. The message was good in their eyes. They worshipped the Lord, and they did not go ahead with their plans to attack their brothers (verses 32-33). The unity of believers is the evidence of the Lord's presence, and it brings with it great blessing. David described the unity of God's people as both good and pleasant. It was like the fragrant anointing oil that ran down Aaron's beard and robes and the refreshing dew that soaked the slopes of Mount Hermon. Where brothers dwell in unity there God commands his blessing in abundance (see Psa. 133:1-3).

The chapter concludes with an etiology: 'The people of Reuben and the people of Gad called the altar Witness, "For," they said, "it is a witness between us that the LORD is God"' (verse 34). The eastern tribes named their altar *Witness* because it stood as a testimony to all of Israel, no matter on which side of the Jordan they may happen to live, that the Lord, and he alone, is God.

Christian unity is not always easy to maintain. Believers can find themselves at odds, especially if they misunderstand each other's motives and actions. To the credit of the western tribes, they did not jump to conclusions. Their concern led to an investigation, but as soon as the truth became apparent no breach occurred in their fellowship. Misunderstanding need not lead to division if we are willing to let patience and love prevail.

26

Faithful Living in an Unfaithful World
Joshua 23:1-16

<hr>

'Therefore, be very strong to keep and to do all that is written in the Book of the Law of Moses, turning aside from it neither to the right hand nor to the left, that you may not mix with these nations remaining among you or make mention of the names of their gods or swear by them or serve them or bow down to them, but you shall cling to the LORD your God just as you have done to this day.' (Josh. 23:6-8)

J oshua stood before Israel as an old man (verse 2), soon to meet his Maker (verse 14; cf. 1 Kings 2:1-2). Many years had passed—perhaps as many as twenty-five[1]—since the major battles for Canaan ceased and the land allotment began. God's great general now summoned Israel's leaders, 'the elders and heads, its judges and officers' (verse 2) to hear his final instructions.

As Joshua looked to the future—a future Israel would have to face without his leadership—he knew the spiritual challenges that would confront them. Ever since their time in Egypt, when they worshipped the Egyptians' gods, Israel had battled the temptation to turn aside to the idols of the surrounding nations. The golden calf at the foot of Mount Sinai (Exod. 32) and the massive immorality and apostasy at Peor (Num. 25) were two glaring examples. With pagan Canaanites remaining in the land, the draw of false religion

<hr>

[1] Madvig, *Joshua*, 361.

would continue. How could Israel resist these temptations? How could they maintain their unique identity as the Lord's covenant people? Joshua's burden in this address was to remind the nation of what God had done for them, to exhort them to remain faithful to him, and to warn them of the dire consequences of turning away.

We stand 3,500 years this side of Joshua's address to Israel's leaders. In relation to when Joshua first preached this sermon, it is now certainly 'a long time afterwards' (cf. verse 1). While Woody Guthrie may have crooned 'The times, they are a' changin'', the human heart has not. The dangers Israel faced, the threats to their life and liberty in the land of promise, are the same dangers believers continue to face today. We are at risk of being influenced by the culture around us and of being drawn away from our faithfulness to the Lord Jesus Christ.

This hazard comes in many shapes and sizes. Sometimes it is as blatant as being duped by the moral relativism that suffuses the air we breathe. Ethical absolutes that were once firmly held are now up for grabs. 'Perhaps homosexuality is not so bad after all.' This threat may raise its head through the pervasiveness of religious pluralism: 'Maybe Allah is the same as Jehovah' or 'Mormons are evangelical Christians too.' The danger may not be as obvious as these two scenarios but can be just as hazardous as so many of us are drawn into the materialism and hedonism of western culture. There is no more fitting time than the present for us to reissue Joshua's call, a call to faithful living in an unfaithful world.

We all face the dilemma of following God's word and being loyal to his Son in a culture that is becoming more and more hostile to Christianity. We are daily misrepresented as a religion of hate and homophobia, of coercion and radical right-wing politics. When we are tempted and shamed at the same time, the pressures to compromise increase. The awareness of what we face should lead us to ask some serious questions. How do we remain loyal in a licentious world? How do we remain faithful when we are surrounded by faithlessness? How do we live for Christ when everything around us is trying to pull us away?

A close look at Joshua 23 will help us to answer these questions. This chapter contains four discernible divisions. After an introduction in verses 1-2, it seems to break into three more sections: verses 3-8, verses 9-13, and verses 14-16. It is difficult to outline these segments sequentially because each contains the same or similar themes woven together to create a theological tapestry. When you stand back to look at this tapestry, however, three scenes appear or three answers to our questions emerge.

The faithfulness of God

How do you live faithfully in an unfaithful world? First, you *ground yourself in the faithfulness of God*. A full quarter of this chapter is taken up with rehearsing what God had done (verses 3-4) and will do (verse 5) for his people. By now in our studies in Joshua these are well-rehearsed themes, but a reason exists for treading these well-worn paths. The record of God's saving acts forms the fundamental theology upon which all practical living is built. Just as the exodus provided the rationale for obedience to the ten commandments (Exod. 20:1-2), the faithfulness of God in the conquest provided the impetus for godly living in the land. Both of those Old Testament events form the backdrop for the finished work of Christ which laid the foundation for holy living (cf. e.g. 1 Cor. 6:18-20).

Joshua began his address by an appeal to Israel's personal experience of God's faithfulness. 'You, you yourselves have seen' all that the Lord did. What had he done? God had destroyed 'all these nations for your sake' because as the warrior of the covenant he had fought for Israel (verse 3). Whether miraculously, like at Jericho, when the walls came tumbling down (6:15-21) and in the Valley of Aijalon when the sun stood still (10:1-15), or whether through granting wisdom for keen military strategy, as in the second assault on Ai (8:1-9), the Lord was the power behind every one of Israel's victories.

Verses 9 and 10 clearly highlight this point: 'For the LORD has driven out before you great and strong nations. And as for you, no man has been able to stand before you to this day. One man of you puts to flight a thousand, since it is the Lord your God who fights for you, just as he promised you.' Once again the text focuses on the work of God in driving out the nations. No one was able to stand before Israel because of God's great power. The Lord dispossessed them, though they were great and mighty nations. As for Israel, no enemy could stand before them (verse 9). We have seen this point emphasized several times already in the book. For example, in 1:5 God said, 'No man shall be able to stand before you all the days of your life. Just as I was with Moses, so I will be with you. I will not leave you or forsake you.' The promise was repeated in chapter 10: 'And the LORD said to Joshua, "Do not fear them, for I have given them into your hands. Not a man of them shall stand before you"' (verse 8). In the victory report of 21:44 we read, 'And the LORD gave them rest on every side just as he had sworn to their fathers. Not one of all their enemies had withstood them, for the LORD had given all their enemies into their hands.'

The Lord's promise was that one man could put to flight a thousand (verse 10). Those are incredible odds. Talk about an army of one! But it was not really an army of one; it was an army of two—an Israelite soldier backed by the power of God! The reason one soldier could chase away a thousand was that the Lord fought for Israel just as he had promised. This is the same descriptive phrase found in verse 3 (cf. Deut. 3:22). Joshua repeated it to emphasize the source of Israel's victories so that all of the credit, and therefore all of the glory, would go to God.

Not only had the Lord fought for his people, but Joshua also played a key role by portioning out the land among the tribes for their inheritance. This involved even allotting land that had yet to be possessed. God had given Israel the land, and even though full occupation was to be a slow process, the sweeping military campaign conducted earlier in the book had brought Canaan under Israel's control. Verses 4 and 5 are very important for the doctrine of the land. In verse 4 Joshua recognized two groups: (1) nations that remain, and (2) nations that were already cut off. He allotted the lands of both to Israel as their inheritance. Joshua saw no inconsistency in apportioning the inheritance in this way. He still considered all of God's promises to have been fulfilled (cf. 21:43-45; 23:14). God had given Israel the land. It was legally and covenantally their possession in spite of the fact that Canaanites continued to live there. Their presence posed an ongoing threat to God's people because the grave danger existed of associating with the Canaanites and inter-marrying with them. Such actions would prove spiritually devastating, but the land still belonged to Israel.

There is a strong emphasis in these verses on what the Lord *will do* for his people. The verbs in verse 5 are future tense. The Lord will 'shove out' and 'dispossess' the people of their land. Israel will then possess it. The Lord had told Israel that their full possession of the land would be gradual: 'Little by little I will drive them out from before you, until you have increased and possess the land' (Exod. 23:30).

Possessing the land of Canaan was the end result of the promises made to Abraham and enacted through God's redemption of Israel from Egypt. Every one of those acts of faithfulness displayed the goodness and reliability of God who saves his people. By rehearsing this salvation history (something he will do again in more detail in chapter 24), Joshua gave the nation a firm basis upon which to build a life of faithfulness. When he later calls the people to obedience and devotion, his summons will not appear out of thin air but will arise from a redemptive foundation. God's sovereign grace set the tone and atmosphere for everything he called upon his people to do.

This same pattern appears in the New Testament. It is common parlance to talk about the *indicative* and the *imperative* in Paul's writings.[1] What do we mean by that? We mean that Paul was careful in his letters not just to set out a list of things to do (imperatives) without first grounding them in the reality (indicatives) of the gospel. In other words, Paul never told people to live for Jesus without first telling them that Jesus died for them.

Look at this from a different angle. In one of the classic warning passages in the book of Hebrews the author wrote, 'Therefore let us leave the elementary doctrine of Christ and go on to maturity' (6:1). The writer then identified these elementary doctrines as repentance and faith, and even the future resurrection. Are we to leave these behind so that we can move on to the more practical stuff of Christian living? Are these unimportant, merely the husk that can be cast off once you get down to the kernel? That is certainly not

[1] For an excellent explanation of this theological pattern in Paul's letters, see Herman Ridderbos, *Paul: An Outline of His Theology*. Translated by John Richard de Witt (Grand Rapids: Eerdmans, 1975), 253-58.

what the author means. It is true that Christians need to mature, to get beyond A-B-C and 1-2-3 in their theology, but they never abandon the basics. What, then, can it mean to *leave* them?

There are several ways to use the word *leave*. I could say, 'I am leaving Hudson, Ohio (the town where I live). I am moving to Philadelphia and never coming back!' In that sense, of course, the word *leave* means to abandon. On the other hand, I could say, 'I am leaving Hudson to drive to Philadelphia. I think I will take historic Route 30.' In that case, I am not abandoning Hudson in any kind of absolute sense. Rather, Hudson is my starting point. I orient myself in Hudson, find Philadelphia on a map, and choose my route. As the origin of my trip, the place where I begin keeps me oriented for the journey ahead. That is the way the gospel works in our lives. We leave the elementary principles of Christ not because we abandon them. We use them as the point of origin which maps out the rest of our journey. If I could put it another way, godly living must grow out of gospel faith.

Our real danger is that we tend to get bored with the gospel. This will happen if we become enamoured with the world. Children often open a present only to become more fascinated with the packaging than the content. They focus on the relatively worthless cardboard and plastic and ignore the valuable gift inside. When the pursuit of our desires in the pleasures the world offers takes precedence in our life, we exchange the valuable for the worthless, and our hearts grow cold towards God and weary with his word as a result. This world is passing away, along with all of its pleasures. Why would you invest so heavily in it when you should lay up treasure in heaven where it cannot be corrupted or stolen (see Matt. 6:19-21)?

We can become bored with the gospel because our focus is too narrow. We fail to see the implications of the good news for every area and facet of life. If we only think of the gospel in terms of 'getting saved', then once we are saved what use does it have for us? The gospel is certainly about our salvation (see, e.g., Acts 4:12 and 1 Cor. 15:3-4), but it is so much more. The gospel is the revelation of God's character and the life-shaping power of sanctification, to name but two implications. No matter what issue you face, ask yourself how the person and work of Jesus Christ should shape the

way you think about and react to the issue. Ask the Lord to shape
your thinking through his word so that you can see the beauty and
power of the gospel in all of life.

Preachers can make the gospel boring. That can happen in a
number of ways. The use of hackneyed phrases, endless repetition,
and the failure to stay spiritually fresh and vibrant in a close walk
with God are some of the reasons that often lie behind the tedious
handling of texts. Whatever the cause, boring preaching is an awful
thing. Not only is it awful because of the drudgery of sitting through
a dull or ill-prepared message, but it is awful because it belies the
glory of the truths it claims to present. Dr Martyn Lloyd-Jones said,
'there is something radically wrong with dull and boring preachers.
How can a man be dull when he is handling such themes? I would
say that a "dull preacher" is a contradiction in terms; if he is dull he
is not a preacher.'[1]

Pray for your pastor that he will not preach glorious truths in
boring ways, that the message of Scripture and the glory of the
gospel will always come from the pulpit with freshness. Keeping that
freshness alive also depends to a great extent on your own prayer life,
on using prayer as the means of personal, daily renewal as you ask
God to teach you more and more of what Christ has done for you.
Pray the gospel into your soul as a means of inoculating yourself
against the disease of unbelief and ingratitude. Then live out of the
gospel as a motivation for holiness.

Faithful devotion

Ground yourself in the faithfulness of God. That's the first point of
emphasis in Joshua's address. Joshua then gave the leaders a second
piece of counsel. Not only had God been faithful to them, but they
were to *cling to God with faithful devotion*. The kind of dedication
God calls for may be summarized in four terms: obedience,
separation, faith, and love.

First, in light of what God has done, walk a straight path that
follows the dictates of the law of Moses: 'Therefore, be very strong to
keep and to do all that is written in the Book of the Law of Moses,

[1] D. Martyn Lloyd-Jones, *Preaching and Preachers* (Grand Rapids: Zondervan,
2011), 100-01.

turning aside from it neither to the right hand nor to the left' (verse 6). What Moses had written was Israel's authoritative guide to life because he was the mouthpiece and penman of God. As in so many other passages, the law is pictured here as a path for one to walk (cf. Psa. 25:4-5; 119:35). Temptations abound to veer from that straight path, to deviate either to the left or to the right. Obedience, however, requires one to walk within the confines of Scripture. Neither adding to it nor taking away from it are acceptable alternatives (Deut. 12:32; Rev. 22:19).

What is needed to walk this path? Strength. 'Therefore, be very strong ...' This is the exact same command that God gave Joshua in 1:7. To obey you must have a strength of resolve, a strength of character, a strength of spirit. That strength, however, is not an internal fortitude that we have naturally. The command to be strong drives us away from ourselves to the only source of our strength, the Lord himself. The command to be strong drives us to our knees to pray for strength. It drives us to Scripture to find the encouragement for strength. It draws us together to encourage each other to 'be strong in the Lord and the power of his might' (Eph. 6:10 KJV).

Second, why must Israel be so careful to adhere to God's word? So that they would not fall into the idolatry that surrounded them. Do not turn aside from the law so that (1) you may not mix with these nations, (2) make mention of the names of their gods, (3) swear by them, (4) serve them, or (5) bow down to them (verse 7). Of the five actions forbidden in verse 7, four of them are acts of worship. To mention the name of a god does not mean that you utter his name, as though it were a sin to say the words 'Baal' or 'Moloch' or 'Ashtaroth'. To *mention* is to *cause to remember*. It involves acknowledging and praising the name of a foreign god. To mention such a name is to invoke that name for power, as in an incantation. Also forbidden to Israel are the acts of swearing or taking oaths in the name of another god, offering service to a foreign deity, or bowing down in reverence and obeisance.

Third, the opposite of idolatry ('but', verse 8) is to cling to the Lord. Israel had clung to him, and they were to keep clinging (cf. 22:5). Clinging to the Lord involves faith, loyalty, and devotion. It is the same word used for a husband's devotion to his wife. He is to leave his father and mother and cleave to or cling to his wife (Gen. 2:24; see also Deut. 4:4; 10:20; 11:22; 13:4). The tragic tale of Israel's history is that they did not maintain their faithful dedication to the Lord. After the roller coaster ride of the Judges era, the reigns of David and Solomon were a spiritual zenith for the nation (2 Sam. 5:10-12; 7:8-16; 1 Kings 10:6-9). Then came the divided kingdom (1 Kings 12:16-24), the introduction of Jeroboam's cult in the northern kingdom (1 Kings 12:25-33), and a general spiritual defection in the south. One bright spot in the kingdom of Judah was the reign of King Hezekiah. His monarchy saw some spiritual progress because he was a man who had been devoted to the Lord:

> He trusted in the LORD, the God of Israel, so that there was none like him among all the kings of Judah after him, nor among those who were before him. For he *held fast* to the LORD. He did not depart from following him, but kept the commandments that the LORD commanded Moses (2 Kings 18:5-6).

The verb *to cling* in the Old Testament is at the root of the modern Hebrew word for glue. It is generally unwise, linguistically speaking, to try to draw too many parallels between the ancient and modern meanings for similar words. In this case, however, the modern term provides a good illustration of the Old Testament's meaning.[1] When you glue two pieces of wood together, you join them with the intent that they will stay together and nothing will get between them. That is a good picture of marriage. A man is to leave his parents and be 'glued' to his wife. Stick together and do not let anyone else in-between. That is also the kind of devotion the Lord wants from us. He wants us to be 'glued' to himself. Are you clinging to the Lord or are you letting other people and other things intrude into the relationship and divert your devotion?

Fourth, the final aspect of faithful piety is love. 'Be very careful', Joshua urges, 'to love the LORD your God' (verse 11). He had given this same exhortation to the eastern tribes before they returned home. In fact, his exhortation to that group included essentially the same counsel given here: 'Only be very careful to observe the commandment and the law that Moses the servant of the LORD

---

[1] Howard, *Joshua*, 422, n.46.

commanded you, to love the LORD your God, and to walk in all his ways and to keep his commandments and to cling to him and to serve him with all your heart and with all your soul' (22:5).

The eastern and the western tribes were united as brothers, heirs of the same promises, and devotees at the same altar. It is little wonder that their reverence was to express itself in the same way. God is love (1 John 4:8) and those who believe in him must express that faith through love (Gal. 5:6). When we love God and others, we reflect from our hearts the very nature of God and testify that we have been born of him (cf. 1 John 4:7, 16).

Warning

How do you remain faithful in a faithless world? You must begin by grounding yourself in the faithfulness of God. Next, you must express your trust by clinging to God with faithful devotion. Finally, *you must heed the warning of unfaithful rebellion.* As Joshua concluded his address, he gave two solemn warnings about what would happen if Israel failed to maintain their devotion to God.

The first warning focused on intermarriage. The text draws a deliberate contrast between clinging to the Lord (verse 8) and turning aside to cling to the nations that remain in Canaan. The wording is specific. Both verse 8 and verse 12 begin with 'but', translated in verse 12 as 'For if …', but the underlying text is the same.[1] Both verses also use the second person plural verb, 'you cling'. The author intends for us to see this contrast. To turn back and cling to these nations will result in intermarriage. This mutual association of the most intimate kind would in time obliterate the distinct covenant line of Abraham. If Israel intermarried with the Canaanites, they would become a Semitic-Hamitic amalgam with no distinct worship and no distinct law, and the testimony to God's saving grace would be lost.

If Israel followed the pagan ways of the land's remaining inhabitants, they would experience untold hardship and eventually perish from the good land. This they could know for certain.[2] There

---

[1] The Hebrew in both instances is *ki 'im*.

[2] The text uses the infinitive absolute plus the imperfect to stress the point being made (*yadoa' ted'u*). See Waltke and O'Connor, *Introduction to Biblical Hebrew Syntax*, 588 [35.3.1i].

was to be no doubt that rather than becoming close friends and allies, rather than becoming beloved husbands and wives, these Canaanites would become 'a snare and a trap for you, a whip on your sides and thorns in your eyes' (verse 13).

Snares and traps catch the unsuspecting. A bit of bait lies in plain sight and looks alluring. But when the trap is sprung, the thing desired becomes our ruin. Likewise, whips beat the unwilling into subservience, into an ungodly form of submission that is coerced by fear rather than led by love. Thorns in the eyes inflict severe pain and result in blindness. You have probably heard the old saying 'Love is blind, but marriage is an eye-opener.' That would hardly be the case for Israel. Marriage to an unbeliever would lead to blindness.

Faithfulness boils down to this: To whom will you cling? The Bible, as this passage illustrates, often expresses this point through the relationship of a husband and wife. Are you going to marry someone and cling to that person because he or she will help you to cling closer to God? The biblical standard for marriage has not changed. A believer must only marry 'in the Lord' (cf. 1 Cor. 7:9). What Joshua forbade in this passage was not interracial marriage. The Bible never forbids interracial marriage and to use a text like this to argue for such is to abuse the word of God. The point here is to not marry an unbeliever. Do not marry someone outside the covenant. A person who does not believe the same promises and embrace the same hope will lead you away from God and cause you untold suffering.

One simple practice can help to safeguard against disobeying this biblical principle. If you never date an unbeliever, then you will never marry one. If you want to see just how serious this issue is, look at the life of Solomon. Did anyone ever embark on his career in a better situation than he? He was God's anointed king. His father provided for him to build the temple. The Lord himself appeared to him and granted his plea for wisdom (1 Kings 3:1-15). He became fabled for his insight and wealth (1 Kings 3:16-28; 4:20-34). Then he turned from God. Why, after all the Lord had done for him and after all he had done in service to God, would he turn to idols? We find the answer in 1 Kings 11:1-2:

Now King Solomon loved many foreign women, along with the daughter of Pharaoh: Moabite, Ammonite, Edomite, Sidonian, and Hittite women, from the nations concerning which the LORD had said to the people of Israel, 'You shall not enter into marriage with them, neither shall they with you, for surely they will turn away your heart after their gods.' Solomon clung to these in love.

Do you see the contrast? He clung to these forbidden women rather than his faithful God.

Yet there is more involved here than marriage. As Christians we must be careful of the associations we make and the attachments we form. Of course we cannot go out of the world and still fulfil the will of God (cf. 1 Cor. 5:9-10), nor should we refuse to have unbelievers as friends. Jesus himself was the friend of sinners (Matt. 11:19). Note, however, the way Jesus handled those friendships. He went into them with the explicit goal of turning his friends from their sin. He went into the friendship with the goal of shining the light of his truth into the relationship.

The second warning sounds in verses 14-16. This last paragraph of the chapter begins with an abrupt 'and now' or 'and behold'. The verse then goes on to stress God's faithfulness to every one of his promises. Not one word has failed! Israel knew this. They had first-hand, experiential knowledge. They had seen all that the Lord did for their sakes (cf. verse 3). Israel knew that not one of God's promises had been broken.

As we near the end of this great book, the theme of God's faithfulness occurs several times. We saw it in 21:45 where the text uses the same terminology: not one word of God fell to the ground. God's faithfulness to his promises is a comfort, but it is also a warning. Just as every good word will come to pass, so too will every evil word or word of threat and judgment. You can rely upon the Lord to do exactly as he says, whether that means bringing blessing or inflicting punishment (verse 15). If the people turn their backs on God, then they will perish at the hand of the pagan nations (verse 13). Such ill treatment will ultimately be, however, the judgment of God: 'But just as all the good things that the LORD your God promised concerning you have been fulfilled for you, so the LORD will bring upon you all the evil things, until he has destroyed you from off this good land that the LORD your God has given you.' '"The bad" (*hara'*) describes the 'disasters' Yahweh will send over time (e.g., the covenant curses in Deut. 28:16-68) until he achieves his purpose for Israel.'[1]

If you transgress the covenant and pursue and serve other gods, then the Lord's anger will be kindled against you. If that happens, you will perish quickly from off the good land (verse 16). In verses 13-16, we find a repeated emphasis on the good land and repeated threats that disobedience will result in the forfeiture of Israel's place in that land. They will be driven from it. This depicts for us a 'back-to-Eden' kind of scene. The good land was a kind of Eden. It was a land of blessing, a land that flowed with milk and honey (Exod. 3:8; Josh. 5:6). Sin, however, would drive them from that land just as it caused Adam and Eve to be expelled from the garden. Sin drove Adam from the good land of Eden. Idolatry eventually drove Israel from the good land of Canaan. It would take a second Adam and the true Israel, Jesus Christ himself, to exercise absolute faithfulness and secure for us an everlasting inheritance. Sin entered the world through Adam's transgression (Gen. 3:6; Rom. 5:12, 18). His one act of disobedience brought condemnation to all mankind. The Lord Jesus Christ, however, obeyed God's law and also died for our transgressions. By his 'obedience the many will be made righteous' (Rom. 5:19). Sin reigned in death, but in Christ grace reigns and leads to everlasting life (verse 20). While we strive for faithfulness and obedience, our ultimate hope and security lies in the Son of God.

In the end, the question of faithfulness comes down to this—to whom will you cling? Will you look to Christ? Will you trust in him and love him with all of your heart? Will you heed his warnings and turn from any alliance that will pull you away from absolute loyalty to him? Or will you cling to something or someone else?

[1] Hubbard, *Joshua*, 522.

27

Today's Choice
Joshua 24:1-33

'Now therefore fear the LORD *and serve him in sincerity and in faithfulness. Put away the gods that your fathers served beyond the River and in Egypt, and serve the* LORD. *And if it is evil in your eyes to serve the* LORD, *choose this day whom you will serve, whether the gods your fathers served in the region beyond the River, or the gods of the Amorites in whose land you dwell. But as for me and my house, we will serve the* LORD.' *(Josh. 24:14-15)*

Jacob was a man on the run. He fled from his brother, Esau, after he had stolen his birthright and blessing. He then fled from Laban, his father-in-law, to return to the land of his birth. Jacob's return to Canaan proved to be both problematic and providential. He was pursued by Laban who approached him with anger and accusations. He feared seeing Esau again. What would his brother do after all those years of pent-up anger? What he discovered, however, was a warm welcome, even if the mistrust between the two brothers was difficult to overcome.[1]

Jacob's return home also proved to be a spiritual turning point in his life. At the ford of the Jabbok River he wrestled with a man who both injured him and blessed him, and Jacob never walked the same again. Jacob also returned to Bethel, the place where God had

---

[1] The record of these events occurs in Genesis 27 through 35.

357

met him and given him a vision when he first fled from his brother, Esau. Bethel was the place Jacob saw a ladder that spanned from heaven to earth. It was, as its name signifies, the house of God, and it was to Bethel Jacob retreated to meet with God again, to renew his devotion, and deepen his commitment to worship and follow the LORD. As he halted toward that sacred spot, his thoughts could no doubt be summed up in the words of B. B. McKinney's gospel song,

> Back to Bethel I must go,
> Back where the rivers of sweet waters flow.
> Back to the true life my soul longs to know,
> Bethel is calling and I must go.

To signify his consecration and commitment, Jacob took the idols his family had kept, buried them under the terebinth tree at Shechem, and pursued a closer walk with God.[1]

Some four hundred years later, after Israel had begun their conquest of Canaan and God had given them two initial and decisive victories, first at Jericho and then at Ai, they too gathered near Shechem. The tribes positioned themselves on Mounts Ebal and Gerizim to renew the covenant God had given through Moses (8:30-35). There they recommitted themselves to holiness and covenant fidelity.

As the book of Joshua comes to an end, Israel once again assembled at Shechem to hear Joshua rehearse their covenant history and, in light of that history, to call the nation to rededication and whole-hearted devotion to God. Israel had a choice to make. Now that they had settled in the land, would they continue to serve the Lord who had done so much for them, or would they follow and serve other gods? Would they deepen their commitment to the Lord or turn away? That is the choice that lies before each of us. In light of all that God has done for us in Jesus Christ, the question we must answer is 'Will we serve him or someone else?' Will you deepen your commitment to Christ, or will you turn away? If you say, 'Yes, I want to go on with God. I want to follow him with renewed zeal', then how do you deepen your commitment to him? Joshua 24 has the answer.

[1] For the full account of these events, see Genesis 27-35.

Reconnect with covenant history

The chapter begins with Joshua gathering all the tribes to Shechem. We have already seen something of the significance of Shechem in the life of Jacob, but if we reach back even further in Israel's history we discover that it was the first place Abraham pitched his tent when he entered the land of Canaan (Gen. 12:6). The very mention of the place should evoke strong memories and emotions in God's people.

But verse 1 also raises a question: What relationship does chapter 24 have to chapter 23? In both passages, Joshua assembled the people, but were these two separate meetings or only one? Calvin believed that chapter 24 recorded the same event as chapter 23 only with more detail.[1] That may indeed have been the case. Certainly the expression 'all Israel' (23:2) and 'all the tribes of Israel' (24:1) are semantically equivalent, and in any case this would indicate representatives from all of the tribes and not every single Israelite. Both of these assemblies may also have taken place at Shechem, though chapter 23 does not specify the location. It is very likely that they took place near the same time because Joshua was approaching his death (cf. 23:14). Whether these chapters represent one assembly or two, the significance of the gathering was the fact that once they were summoned the nation's leaders presented themselves before the Lord (24:1). Joshua brought the nation together to do business with God.

The significance of what follows in verses 2-13 lies in the survey of Israel's history. Joshua summarized God's great acts to provide them with a redemptive basis upon which to make his appeal in verses 14 and following. This recap of redemptive history does not reach back to the Fall and the first promise of a redeemer (Gen. 3:15) but rather begins with Israel's origins when God called Abraham to leave Ur and follow him. It then proceeds in three stages: first, from Abraham's call to the exodus (verses 2-7); second, Israel's time in the wilderness (verses 8-10); and third, their experience in the land of Canaan (verses 11-13).

Abraham, along with his father Terah and his brother Nahor, had served other gods (verse 2). The key term in this verse is *served*.

[1] Calvin, *Comm. Joshua*, 271.

This verb is going to play a major role in the chapter. Service to God includes obedience to his commands, a willingness to work for him and to worship him, honouring him with all of our actions, and loving him with all of our heart, mind, soul, and strength (see Deut. 6:5; Josh. 22:5; 23:11; Matt. 22:37). Their ancestors, however, had served other gods beyond the Euphrates. Israel's origins were in a pagan land filled with pagan practices. The text implicates Abraham, along with the rest of his family, as an idolater. For Israel, their ancient past was one of spiritual darkness in a place beyond the borders of the land of promise. As the Lord's people, Israel did not owe their origins to the particular spiritual genius of Abraham that led him to develop a monotheistic religion. Abraham would have remained a pagan worshipper of idols except for the fact that God took him from the land of darkness, led him to Canaan, and gave him the promised son, Isaac (verse 3). God sovereignly intervened in the patriarch's life, gave him faith (Gen. 15:6), and made him his servant.

Abraham's son, Isaac, had two sons, Jacob and Esau. Esau lived in the hill country of Seir. Jacob, on the other hand, went down to Egypt (verse 4). And it was in Egypt, once again a place outside the land of promise, that God raised up his servants, Moses and Aaron. Through a series of plagues, culminating in the Passover and death of the firstborn males throughout the land, God brought his people out of slavery (verse 5). These verses cover a span of approximately 500 years of Israel's history (Genesis 11 through Exodus 12). Throughout his address Joshua linked the present generation with the past. Note the reference to *your fathers* in verses 2 and 6. Their fathers had lived in foreign lands, but the Lord called them out of both. When called out of Egypt, Pharaoh's army pursued Israel to the Red Sea, but once again God intervened in answer to their prayers. He protected his chosen ones, and drowned Egypt's elite troops (verses 6-7). Joshua made it clear in these few verses that Israel owed their existence to the gracious and saving interventions of God in history.

David Howard points out that verses 5 through 7 also present 'a dramatic shift in perspective'. Joshua had spoken about Israel's ancestors as *he* and *they*, but in verse 5 he addressed the current generation: 'I brought *you* out.' Then, in verses 6 and 7, the pronouns alternate between *you* and *they*. After verse 7 the focus is exclusively on those present and *you* becomes the exclusive pronoun. The alternation 'puts the focus on the present generation in a dramatic way… [it] also shows the unity of this generation with the fathers'. Howard goes on to write, 'God did not just make himself known in ages past; he also worked mightily and graciously for the people being addressed. The impact of God's words were greater because of this focus on them. Christians today are still part of that great spiritual heritage (see, e.g., Rom 11:11-24; Hebrews 11).'[1]

From the end of verse 7 through verse 10 we have a brief overview of the period in the wilderness. These verses roughly cover the events recorded in Exodus 16 through Numbers 24. During Israel's wanderings in the Sinai peninsula, they were attacked by the Amorites, but God gave his people the victory over the Amorite armies as well as possession of the Amorites' land (verse 8; cf. verse 12 and Num. 21:21-35). Balak, the king of Moab, also wanted to destroy Israel. He attempted a different tactic, a more 'spiritual' approach by having the prophet Balaam come to curse them. His curses, however, turned out to be blessings as God compelled the prophet to speak better than he wanted to or even understood (verses 9-10; cf. Num. 23:11, 20; 24:1, 10).

Finally, verses 11 through 13 recount Israel's most recent history in the land. They went over the Jordan and defeated Jericho and the seven nations (verse 11). God gave them victory after victory, driving out their enemies by his sovereign power that struck terror in their hearts (verse 12). What Israel now possessed was God's good gift, not something they earned. For they now lived in cities that they did not build and ate the produce of vineyards and orchards that they did not plant (verse 13; cf. Deut. 6:10-11).

The sons of Korah, reflecting on the Lord's gracious and dramatic interventions sang,

> for not by their own sword did they win the land,
>   nor did their own arm save them,
> but your right hand and your arm,
>   and the light of your face,
>   for you delighted in them.

[1] Howard, *Joshua*, 431.

> You are my King, O God;
>   ordain salvation for Jacob!
> Through you we push down our foes;
>   through your name we tread down those who rise up against
>   us. (Psa. 44:3-5)

In Joshua's overview of Israel's covenant history, two points become crystal clear.

First, covenant history is the story of God's sovereign grace. Abraham was taken from Ur. God chose Abraham and not his brother Nahor. God spoke to Abraham and led him to the land of Canaan. The only explanation for this is God's electing love. This same predestinating choice becomes clear in the story of Isaac's sons, Jacob and Esau (verse 4). God chose Jacob and rejected Esau according to his sovereign purpose (Mal. 1:2-3; Rom. 9:13). God's sovereign grace is especially stressed by the verb 'to give'. This verb has dominated the narrative of Joshua as we are told again and again that God gave the land to Israel. It occurs six more times in these twelve verses (verses 3, 4, 8, 11, 13).

Covenant history is also the story of God's saving grace. Verses 2 through 13 are dominated by first person verbs that have the Lord as their subject: I took (verse 3), I gave (verse 4), I sent, I plagued, and I brought you out (verse 5). God redeemed his people from the bondage of Egyptian slavery, gave them protection and victory in the wilderness, and brought them safely home. Each of these events were acts of *his* deliverance.

Though these events happened a long time ago in a far away place, they mirror our history as well. As believers, we share the heritage and faith of Abraham (cf. Rom. 9:4ff.; Gal. 3:15-22). The story of God's sovereign and saving grace is the testimony of everyone who is a Christian. Our salvation does not depend upon our abilities and religious achievements. We are Christians, not because we are better than our neighbours or unsaved family members, nor because God saw great potential in us and thought it would be nice to have us on his side, but because God in his grace chose to love us (Eph. 1:4; 2 Thess. 2:13). He reached out to us in sovereign grace because sovereign grace is the only grace there is. And the Lord saved us the same way he saved Israel—by the blood of the Lamb (Exod. 12:7, 13; 1 Pet. 1:19).

If you and I would deepen our commitment to Christ, if we would seek God to deepen his work of grace in our lives, then it is this history with which we must reconnect. But you have to keep in mind that what we are talking about is not like your experience in a history class where reconnecting with the past involves remembering dates, people, and places. Our links with covenant history involve the facts of people, places, and events culminating in the cross and resurrection of Jesus, but reconnecting with those past events involves more than memory or recitation. Reconnecting with redemptive history means an encounter with the living God, and encounter that brings the events of the past and the hope of the future into the present as we embrace the person and work of Christ on our behalf. By the Holy Spirit we reach back in our minds, through the words of Scripture, to what Jesus did long ago, and we reach forward with eschatological hope, again by the use of Scripture, to all that he has promised for our inheritance, and draw the past and future together to inform the present reality in which we live. By the Holy Spirit we are connected to Jesus Christ to live in the reality and power of his endless life.

This is what lies behind the means that God uses to bring grace to us. The Bible, prayer, and the sacraments are the tools the Holy Spirit employs to unite us with the power of the living Christ. We do not promote these facets of worship as things to do to keep our 'religious club' going but as the God-ordained methods of enmeshing our life in the power of the gospel. Do you look at the word, prayer, and the sacraments in this way? Do you come to each expecting to meet Christ? Do you see the church at worship as the context where this most often happens? Each Lord's Day the church meets to reconnect with its covenant history, to reconnect with Christ and his work. This is the reason we must not neglect to assemble with God's people (Heb. 10:25). You need to let the importance of that sink in and shape the way you view the church and its worship.

Recommit to covenant loyalty

Once we have reconnected with our covenant history, the second thing we need to do is recommit to our covenant loyalty. The tone of Joshua's address makes a definite turn at verse 14 with the words 'Now therefore'. Israel stood at Shechem with a decision to make. Would they put away the gods that their fathers served beyond the river and the gods of Egypt from which they were delivered and serve the Lord? Which would they choose?

God's sovereign, saving grace calls for single-hearted service. That was the challenge the nation faced. Would they serve the Lord? Verses 14-28 comprise a dialogue between Joshua and Israel's representatives as he challenges them and they respond. First, Joshua challenged the people to devote themselves whole-heartedly to the worship, obedience, and service of God. He set out his challenge in a series of imperatives: fear the Lord, serve him, put away foreign gods, and, in case we missed it, he repeats the command to serve (verse 14).[1] If this kind of devotion seemed wrong to them, then they have another choice to make. They can either serve the ancient gods of their fathers or the gods of the Egyptians. If they do not choose to follow the Lord, the only thing left for them is two bad choices, both of which are damning. Joshua then asserted his own determination to serve the Lord. He pledged devotion and loyalty for himself and for his family. The closing words of verse 15 are the most well-known in the book: 'But as for me and my house, we will serve the LORD.'

Second, how do the Israelites respond? With a robust determination to follow the Lord. They confirm their resolution in verse 16: 'Far be it from us that we should forsake the LORD to serve other gods.' Furthermore, they affirm that the Lord is their God, and they acknowledge that he is the one who redeemed them (verses 17-18). He brought them from the house of slavery to the new-found freedom of service, and the Lord was the one who had done it all. The clear implication is that the gods of the fathers and the gods of Egypt had done nothing for them. The people determined that they would serve the God of Israel because he had done so much

---

[1] On Israel's idolatry in Egypt, see Lev. 17:7; Deut. 32:16-17; Ezek. 20:7-8; 23:3, 8.

for them. They had experienced his saving grace, and whole-hearted service was the only response they could make.

Service does not sound very liberating, but it is if you serve the right person. You will serve either the Lord or an idol that you have made, but you have to serve someone. When pop singer and songwriter Bob Dylan went through his 'born again' phase, he wrote a quasi-Christian song 'Gotta Serve Somebody'. He was right. John Lennon of Beatles fame did not like Dylan's song and its implications so he wrote 'Serve Yourself'. But Lennon only proved Dylan's point. You have to serve someone, and if that someone is yourself, then you are a slave to your own self-seeking pleasure, and that is the worst bondage of all.

Third, in response to Israel's affirmation, 'We will serve the LORD' Joshua replied with a shocking retort, 'You are not able!' (verse 19). What? Not able? Why not? Because the Lord is a holy and jealous God. He is unlike any other. He is zealous for his own glory and name. He will not share his worship or fame with any other god. He will not forgive Israel if they abandon him to serve another god. He demands whole-hearted loyalty, and Israel had better know that when they vow to serve him. They must serve him and him alone. The Lord demands exclusive worship. He is not jealous of other gods and their glory because he knows that they are nothing. But he is zealous for his own glory and for the good of his children. He knows that if they turn from him they cannot enjoy his benefits. Joshua's emphatic rejoinder was not an absolute statement. The Lord had, after all, called the people to serve him. It was, however, a stern warning to the Israelites of just how serious the promise was that they made.[1]

It is a serious matter to be a believer. Faith, in the biblical sense of the word, is not a mere add-on to life. When the Lord Jesus Christ calls us to follow him, he calls for complete devotion, for death to self, for our lives to be dedicated and consecrated to him alone. In

---

[1] '*You cannot serve the Lord*: it is evident from other parts of the book (e.g., 23:8) as well as from this chapter (v. 31) that these words, although their seriousness should not be minimized, should nevertheless not be taken in an absolute sense. Joshua simply wants to confront Israel with the seriousness of the solemn promise it has just uttered.' Woudstra, *Book of Joshua*, 353.

light of all that he has done for us, is that too much for him to ask? Joshua's argument in this chapter is not at all unlike that of the apostle Paul in Romans. After spending eleven chapters delineating the need for and the blessings of the gospel (the rehearsal of God's covenantal and saving acts), he then calls for a decision: 'I appeal to you therefore, brothers, by the mercies of God, to present your bodies as a living sacrifice, holy and acceptable to God, which is your spiritual worship' (Rom. 12:1). Have you responded to that appeal and laid down your life, your dreams and ambitions, in order to take up the cross and serve the Son of God?

Joshua spells out the implications of what God demands in verse 20. If Israel fails to live up to their covenant obligations, the Lord is going to do three things: first, he will turn, second, he will do them harm, and third, he will consume or exterminate them. Later, when the nation turned from God to the idolatry of Canaan and the surrounding nations, he brought this judgment upon them. In the end, the three expressions in verse 20 describe both the Assyrian and Babylonian captivities. They also summarize the curses of Deuteronomy 28. Joshua's 'dramatic words here emphasize the solemnity of the requirements, to purge from the Israelites any false notions of "cheap grace." Theirs was not to be a nominal, superficial faith.'[1] Joshua's words are a cautionary tale. Beware what you take upon yourself. Count the cost. Do not put your hand to the plough and look back (cf. Luke 9:62).

Fourth, the dialogue concludes with the people insisting that they will serve the Lord in spite of the dire warning (verse 21), agreeing that by their decision they will serve as their own witnesses against themselves should they fail to follow the Lord (verse 22). In light of this commitment, Israel now had a two-fold responsibility: to put away any foreign gods and to stretch out their heart to the true God (verse 23). To this responsibility they responded with a further affirmation of their resolve: 'The LORD our God we will serve, and his voice we will obey' (verse 24).

Immediately following this exchange, Joshua ratified the covenant by doing three things. First, he made a covenant and coupled it with statutes and judgments (verse 25). The verb translated *made* in the

[1] Howard, *Joshua*, 438.

ESV is the Hebrew word that means 'to cut'. To 'cut' a covenant
signified that animals were sacrificed to seal the bond between the
two parties in the agreement, and at the same time a self-maledictorty
oath was taken. In other words, by cutting the animals in two, the
sacrifice graphically depicted the promises the covenant makers were
pledging. They said, in essence, 'May what has happened to these
animals happen to me if I fail to live up to our agreement.' By 'cutting'
this covenant, Joshua was renewing the covenantal commitment
made forty years earlier at Sinai. This renewal ceremony was a means
to renew and deepen their commitment to the Lord.[1]

Second, he wrote all the words in the book of the law (verse
26a). A covenant never occurs without statutes and rules (verse
25). They were the guidelines for covenant living. What were these
statutes and rules? Very likely they were the words from the Book
of the Covenant in Exodus 21-23, though they may have included
the challenge and response between Joshua and Israel that had just
taken place.

Third, Joshua erected a large stone under the terebinth tree to
serve as a witness (verses 26b-27). The stone served as a testimony
against Israel because it 'heard' all the words that the Lord spoke.
This stone was a witness to God's words and a witness against God's
people if they dealt falsely with the Lord. It testified to what God
had spoken, and it will testify against the people if they fail to follow
the Lord's commands.

The three elements of a sacrifice, a book, and a witness continue
to point the way for believers to engage in covenant renewal today.
When the church experiences renewal on a large scale, we call it
revival. The first and second Great Awakenings as well as the 1859
Revival are some of the outstanding examples in more recent church
history when God visited his people with fresh power. Believers have
a responsibility to pray for such times and to seek God for renewal in
the church, but revival must first begin in our own walk with God.
Like Israel, we need to go back to the basics of redemption, back
to the cross and sacrifice of our Lord Jesus, back to the authority of
God's holy law, and back to the witness-bearing work of the Holy

[1] Gentry and Wellum, *Kingdom Through Covenant*, 389-90.

Spirit and ask that these realities burn brightly in our hearts and shine brightly through our testimonies.

Three graves in Canaan

The book of Joshua ends in a most unexpected and unusual way with the story of three graves in Canaan. The first grave is that of Joshua (verses 29-31). Israel's great general died at the age of 110. The text calls him 'the son of Nun, the servant of the LORD'. He was truly the successor of Moses, taking on the honorific title 'servant of the LORD', a man who faithfully followed the Lord. His burial took place at Timnath-serah, the very place he had received as his inheritance (cf. 19:50).

As for the people of Israel, they served the Lord during Joshua's lifetime and during the leadership of the elders who survived Joshua, described here as the men who 'had known all the work that the LORD did for Israel' (verse 31). This implication, however, is that after those days, when those with first-hand experience of the conquest passed off the scene, the people of God turned from the Lord and served idols. The period of the Judges testifies that this is exactly what took place. After the elders who followed Joshua and their generation passed away, 'there arose another generation after them who did not know the LORD or the work that he had done for Israel' (Judg. 2:10). It was this generation that did what was right in their own eyes (cf. Judg. 17:6; 18:1; 19:1; 21:25).

Next, we have the record of Joseph's burial (verse 32). Joseph had died many years before in Egypt, but he died full of faith and hope in the promises of God. His last words to his brothers were, "'I am about to die, but God will visit you and bring you up out of this land to the land that he swore to Abraham, to Isaac, and to Jacob." Then Joseph made the sons of Israel swear, saying, "God will surely visit you, and you shall carry up my bones from here"' (Gen. 50:24-25).

In obedience to his instructions, the Israelites buried his bones in Shechem (cf. verse 1). The author wants you to know two important things about Shechem. First, this was the land that Jacob bought from the sons of Hamor, the father of Shechem. After he returned from serving Laban, Jacob purchased this property, pitched his tent,

and built an altar which he called *El-Elohe-Israel*, God, the God of
Israel (Gen. 33:19-20). But if we reach back further into Hebrew
history we discover that Shechem was also the first placed in Canaan
mentioned in connection with Abraham (Gen. 12:6). In Shechem,
at 'the oak of Moreh', he built an altar. The parallels to these final
events in Joshua are striking. When Joshua made the covenant for
Israel, it was by the sanctuary so there was an altar (verse 26). The
stone of witness was set up under 'the terebinth that was by the
sanctuary' (verse 26). The place, the oak or terebinth, and the altar
tie this passage to Genesis 12 and the promise given to Abraham
when he first entered Canaan. Now, hundreds of years later, the
pledge is fulfilled because God keeps every promise of his word.
This truth is further confirmed by the second thing the author wants
you to know—that Shechem became an inheritance for the sons
of Joseph. Joshua was buried in his inheritance, and Joseph was as
well.[1]

The book ends with the record of Eleazar's death and burial (verse
33). Eleazar was the son of Aaron and father of Phinehas (cf. 22:13,
31, 32). He served as the high priest during Joshua's era of leadership
(Num. 20:25-28; Josh. 14:1; 17:4; 19:51; 21:1). As a Levite, he did not
have an inheritance in the land, but Gibeah, in the hill country of
Ephraim, was given to him as a place to live, and he was buried
there.

The documentation of these three deaths seem like an unusual
tack-on at the end of the book, a few historical notes that are
important for record-keeping but oddly placed for lack of a better
location. But nothing in God's word is superfluous. It is the odd
thing, the surprise in the text that should make us dig a little deeper
to discover its purpose.

Put the pieces together. The concluding words of Joshua present us
with the record of Israel's leader (Joshua), their saviour (Joseph), and
their high priest (Eleazar) all dead and buried in the land of promise.
They were buried in the land because God fulfilled his word, just as

[1] It is a curious fact that both Joshua and Joseph were 110 years old when they
died (Josh. 24:29; Gen. 50:22, 26), though there appears to be no other significance
to the number other than coincidence.

Joseph said he would (Gen. 50:24-25). But they all died. And after the era of the elders, the people turned away from the Lord (cf. verse 31). The book of Joshua ends, therefore, with assurance and hope but also with a sense of longing and incompleteness. It leaves us with the desire for a leader, a Saviour, and a high priest who, though crucified and buried in the land of promise, rose again to everlasting life to give us an eternal inheritance, one that is pure and undefiled, reserved in heaven for all those who put their hope in him.

The book of Joshua leaves us longing for and looking for a greater Joshua, the Saviour Jesus Christ. Each of the studies in this book has attempted to lead you to him. He is the sum and substance of the Christian faith. He is the heart of the Scriptures, the focus of redemptive history, the brightness of heaven's glory, and his praise is the final goal of the Father's wise and eternal plan (Eph. 1:3-10). If, through this book you have been led to see more of him and to love him more, then the time I have spent writing and the time you have spent reading will not have been in vain.

ABOUT THE PUBLISHER

THE Banner of Truth Trust originated in 1957 in London. The founders believed that much of the best literature of historic Christianity had been allowed to fall into oblivion and that, under God, its recovery could well lead not only to a strengthening of the church, but to true revival.

Inter-denominational in vision, this publishing work is now international, and our lists include a number of contemporary authors along with classics from the past. The translation of these books into many languages is encouraged.

A monthly magazine, *The Banner of Truth,* is also published. More information about this and all our publications can be found on our website or supplied by either of the offices below.

THE BANNER OF TRUTH TRUST

<table>
<tr><td>3 Murrayfield Road
Edinburgh, EH12 6EL
UK</td><td></td><td>PO Box 621, Carlisle,
Pennsylvania 17013,
USA</td></tr>
</table>

www.banneroftruth.org